# Mongolia

### Paul Greenway
### Robert Storey
### Gabriel Lafitte

**Mongolia**

**2nd edition**

**Published by**
**Lonely Planet Publications**
Head Office:   PO Box 617, Hawthorn, Vic 3122, Australia
Branches:      150 Linden Street, Oakland CA 94607, USA
               10a Spring Place, London NW5 3BH, UK
               1 rue du Dahomey, 75011 Paris, France

**Printed by**
Craft Print Pte Ltd, Singapore

**Photographs by**
Michael Buckley          Ron Gluckman
Paul Greenway            André de Smet
Robert Storey

Front cover: Young jockey on horse at Naadam Festival, Ulaan Baatar (Paul Greenway)

**First Published**
May 1993

**This Edition**
June 1997

**Although the authors and publisher have tried to make the information as accurate as possible, they accept no responsibility for any loss, injury or inconvenience sustained by any person using this book.**

National Library of Australia Cataloguing in Publication Data

Greenway, Paul 1960–
Mongolia

2nd ed.
Includes index.
ISBN 0 86442 500 7.

1. Mongolia – Guidebooks. I. Title. (Series : Lonely Planet travel survival kit).

915.173

text & maps © Lonely Planet 1997
photos © photographers as indicated 1997

### Paul Greenway

When Paul told Lonely Planet that he 'would go anywhere', he should have realised he would end up in Mongolia – and was certainly glad he did. During three months of research, and over 15,000km of overland travel in this magnificent country, Paul lived on fatty mutton, was chased by a yak, nearly drowned while sitting in the back of a jeep, was lost for days in the Gobi Desert and was arrested near the Chinese border.

During the rare times Paul is not travelling, or thinking, reading or writing about it, he watches every minute of every possible Australian Rules football match, has regressed to his teens and wants to play in a heavy rock band again, and will do anything to avoid settling down. He is now based in his mother's spare bedroom in Adelaide, South Australia.

Paul has contributed to the Maluku and Irian Jaya chapters of Lonely Planet's *Indonesia*, co-wrote *Indian Himalaya* and has just returned from researching exotic Madagascar.

### Robert Storey

Experienced budget traveller and renowned cheapskate, Robert has spent much of his time trekking around the world on a shoestring. During his travels, he survived a number of near-death experiences, including marriage and riding the subway in New York City. Robert now lives in Taiwan, where he has devoted himself to safe and serious pursuits such as writing books, studying Chinese, computer hacking and motorcycle stunt-driving.

### Gabriel Lafitte

Gabriel first went to Mongolia in 1990 to attend an international Buddhist conference for peace and has been leading tours there ever since. He established the Australia-Mongolia Society and is research officer for the Australia Tibet Council, where he works with the Dalai Lama's staff formulating plans for the future of Tibet.

---

### From Paul Greenway

I was overwhelmed by the number of people – Mongolian and foreign – who wanted to help me. There are just so many people to thank; I apologise if I have omitted anyone.

In Mongolia: the indefatigable Tsogtbaatar from the Mongolian Ministry of External Relations; Kate Glastonbury from Nomads; Eliot Bikales (USA); Dr D Shombodon from Tacis, Mongolia; Kim Sunjung at the Gandan Buddhist University, Ulaan Baatar; Jenni Storey from the *Mongol Messenger*; 'Saraa' Saranbayar at the UK embassy, Ulaan Baatar; KC Dedinas (USA); Robin Grayson (UK) from Tacis, Mongolia; Mike and Jan Connor from the US embassy, Ulaan Baatar, now in Dar es Salaam; and Giacometti Manu & Philipona Claude (Switzerland).

Lisa York (USA), Mark Ahern (NZ), Marie-Josée Desjardins (Canada) and Nicky Worth (Australia), for keeping me entertained on the Trans-Mongolian train from Beijing; and, for sharing a memorable four-day trip in an East German ambulance to western Mongolia, Sean Burke (UK), Nick Winter (UK), Helge Reitz (Germany) and A Batchuluun (Mongolia) – and, particularly, Jennifer Smith (UK) and Carrie Engelbrecht (Canada), who both shared their linguistic and culinary skills.

Back home in Adelaide, South Australia: Jane Hamilton; Margaret Rohde from One World Travel; Richard Allen for keeping me informed about what really matters – the football scores; Richard and Janet for putting up with me on most weekends; and to my family for worrying about me.

Elsewhere: Kent Madin from Boojum

Expeditions; Alma De Bisschop and Seonaid Alma (USA); Alan Sanders, who co-wrote Lonely Planet's *Mongolian phrasebook*; and Gabriel Lafitte from the Australia-Mongolia Society for his help with the introductory chapters.

At Lonely Planet: thanks to Greg Alford, the senior editor who sent me to this wonderful country; and the poor editorial and cartographic staff who have coped with my manuscript and maps.

Lonely Planet always greatly appreciates the letters it receives. We received several stupendous letters, some of which were reprinted in the book, from: Krystyna Chabros (USA), Piotr Gaszynski (Poland), Heidi Heinzerling (USA), James Huang (Singapore), John Kupec (USA), Robb LaKritz (USA), Patrick McDonnell (USA) and Mark Rossiter (UK).

## This Book

The first edition of this guide was researched and written by Robert Storey. Paul Greenway researched and thoroughly updated the book for this second edition, with assistance from Gabriel Lafitte on the introductory chapters.

## From the Publisher

This second edition of *Mongolia* was edited in LP's Melbourne office by Diana Saad and taken through layout and proofread by Linda Suttie. Adam McCrow designed and laid out the book. Sally Gerdan and Louise Klep drew the maps, with assistance from Anna Judd and Adam. Anna and Adam provided the illustrations, Paul Piaia drew the climate chart, and Anne Mulvaney and Sharon Wertheim did the indexing. Dan Levin created the fonts for the Cyrillic script, and Lou Callan edited the language section. Simon Bracken and Adam designed the cover. Thanks to the art department of the Buddhist University, Gandan monastery, Ulaan Baatar, for additional illustrations.

## Warning & Request

Things change – prices go up, schedules change, good places go bad and bad places go bankrupt – nothing stays the same. So, if you find things better or worse, recently opened or long since closed, please tell us and help make the next edition even more accurate and useful.

We value all of the feedback we receive from travellers. Julie Young coordinates a small team who read and acknowledge every letter, postcard and email, and ensure that every morsel of information finds its way to the appropriate authors, editors and publishers.

Everyone who writes to us will find their name in the next edition of the appropriate guide and will also receive a free subscription to our quarterly newsletter, *Planet Talk*. The very best contributions will be rewarded with a free Lonely Planet guide.

Excerpts from your correspondence may appear in updates (which we add to the end pages of reprints); new editions of this guide; in our newsletter, *Planet Talk*; or in the Postcards section of our Web site – so please let us know if you don't want your letter published or your name acknowledged.

## Thanks

Many thanks to the travellers who used the last edition and wrote to us with helpful hints, useful advice and interesting anecdotes.

Linda Ball, B Batbuyan, John Andrew Bennett, Natalie Bennett, Karl Bernhardt, Jessica Bernstein, Eliot Bikales, R Blau, Patrick Boman, Betsy Bowden, Krystyna Chabros, Carol Evans, Tom Fell, Tatiana Flade, Giovanni Gaspari, Piotr Gaszynski, Karl Gorczynski, Samantha Grabham, D & N Sierens Gysen, Heidi Heinzerling, K Heydorn, Patricia Hoffman, James Huang, Gordon Johnson, Lee Jones, M Kaplan, David Kessell, Diana Kincaid, Cheeky Krubeck, Piotr Krylov, John Kupec, Rolf-Peter Lacher, Arco Lagerwerf, Robb LaKritz, Pietro Lucchini, Patrick McDonnell, Craig Mehra, Feye Meyer, Mark Myers, Luciana Nicoli, Gioergio Palmieri, Kurt Piemonte, Christian Pyper, Josep Ribas, Ian Robinson, Mark Rossiter, Anil Sain, Marie-Helene Schmitt, Robert Schofield, Andrew Seid, Barb & Larry Strong, Salis Thierry, Mr & Ms Tuvshinjargal, V Wickramaratne, Nick Winter

# Contents

# Map Legend

## BOUNDARIES

International Boundary

Regional Boundary

## ROUTES

Freeway

Highway

Major Road

Unsealed Road or Track

City Road

City Street

Railway

Underground Railway

Tram

Walking Track

Walking Tour

Ferry Route

Cable Car or Chairlift

## AREA FEATURES

Parks

Built-Up Area

Pedestrian Mall

Market

Cemetery

Non-Christian Cemetery

Mountain Range

Rocks

## HYDROGRAPHIC FEATURES

Coastline

River, Creek

Intermittent River or Creek

Rapids, Waterfalls

Lake, Intermittent Lake

Canal

Swamp

## SYMBOLS

| | | |
|---|---|---|
| ✪ CAPITAL | National Capital | |
| ◉ Capital | Regional Capital | |
| CITY | Major City | |
| ● City | City | |
| ● Town | Town | |
| ● Village | Village | |
| ■ ▼ | Place to Stay, Place to Eat | |
| ☕ ♟ | Cafe, Pub or Bar | |
| ✉ ☎ | Post Office, Telephone | |
| ❶ ❸ | Tourist Information, Bank | |
| ◔ ▣ | Transport, Parking | |
| ⛪ ⛺ | Museum, Youth Hostel | |
| ⚏ ⛏ | Caravan Park, Camping Ground | |
| ❏ ✚ | Church, Cathedral | |
| ☪ ✡ | Mosque, Synagogue | |
| 卍 卐 | Buddhist Temple, Hindu Temple | |
| ▦ ☬ | Temple, Sikh Temple | |

| | | |
|---|---|---|
| ◔ ⛽ | Embassy, Petrol Station | |
| ✈ ✝ | Airport, Airfield | |
| ▭ ✿ | Swimming Pool, Gardens | |
| ❖ 🐘 | Shopping Centre, Zoo | |
| ✛ ★ | Hospital, Police Station | |
| ← A25 | One Way Street, Route Number | |
| 🏛 ⚑ | Palace, Monument | |
| ▥ ▣ | Castle, Tomb | |
| ⌒ ⌂ | Cave, Hut or Chalet | |
| ▲ ☀ | Mountain or Hill, Lookout | |
| ⛩ ⚐ | Lighthouse, Golf Course | |
| )( ◎ | Pass, Spring | |
| ⚑ ⚒ | Beach, Surf Beach | |
| ∴ | Archaeological Site or Ruins | |
| | Ancient or City Wall | |
| | Cliff or Escarpment, Tunnel | |
| | Railway Station | |

Note: not all symbols displayed above appear in this book

# Introduction

The name 'Mongolia' has always stirred up visions of the exotic – Chinggis (Genghis) Khaan, camels wandering in the Gobi Desert and wild horses galloping across the steppes. Even today, Mongolia seems like the end of the earth – outside the few major cities you begin to wonder if you haven't stepped into another century, rather than another country.

Mongolia's survival as an independent nation is miraculous. For the first time in centuries the Mongolians, once rulers of the vast Eurasian steppe, are no longer colonial subjects of the Russian and Chinese empires. Only a century ago, so few Mongolians were left it seemed that their ancient, nomadic civilisation might disappear altogether.

Today Mongolia is free, democratic and energetically rediscovering its many pasts, but it's broke. In the postwar years, the Soviet big brother transformed Mongolia from a nomadic society into an industrialised and urbanised country with its own astronauts, physicists and nationwide health and education systems. By the 1980s, even nomadic camel herders in the Gobi Desert knew the state would supply them with a pension in their old age. All that stopped suddenly and dramatically when the Soviet Union fell apart in the early 1990s.

Survival of the nomadic people, and the country, still depends enormously on domestic animals – camels, cattle (including yaks), horses, sheep and goats (plus reindeer in the far north). An intimate knowledge of animals, both wild and domestic, and the environment is a major feature of Mongolian life.

Although travel in the countryside can be hard and facilities poor, a warm welcome

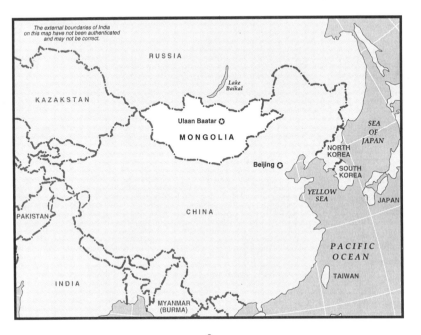

awaits the adventurous traveller at every traditional *ger* (tent). The capital, Ulaan Baatar (UB to travellers), is full of surprises and offers far better places to stay and eat than the countryside. It is home to the largest Naadam Festival, Mongolia's famous three-day sports event, and has fascinating monasteries and many museums and art galleries.

It's also the best place to see a performance of traditional music and dance, which should not be missed.

Mongolia, the 'Land of Blue Sky', is a wide country of mountains, stunning lakes, vast deserts, rolling grasslands, dense forests and unique wildlife. It remains one of the last unspoiled travel destinations in Asia.

# Facts about the Country

## HISTORY

The Mongolians, or Mongols as they were previously known, recorded their history for centuries in oral epics, sung by bards, until writing was introduced nearly 800 years ago. Because of their substantial – and mostly unhappy – contacts with neighbouring countries, much has also been written about them. Chinese dynastic histories, stretching back 5000 years, tell of the Mongols and their predecessors, describing them as ravenous barbarians greedy for Chinese produce and likening them to wolves. However, much of the history has now been rewritten from a more objective point of view.

### In the Beginning

Little is known about Mongolia's earliest inhabitants, but archaeological digs have uncovered human remains in the Gobi and other regions dating back nearly 500,000 years. Agriculture seems to have preceded nomadic herding of animals, and despite Mongolia's short summers, wheat growing has co-existed with nomadic life for thousands of years. It was only after the Mongols tamed horses, yaks and camels that they took to a nomadic herding lifestyle.

Early Chinese manuscripts refer to 'Turkic-speaking peoples' living in what we now call Mongolia as early as the 4th or 5th century BC. The Chinese – who had numerous military clashes with these nomadic tribes – referred to them as the Xiongnu.

The Chinese fought their first major war with the Xiongnu – a taste of things to come – in the 3rd century BC. Xiongnu military tactics were fierce and effective – warriors charged on horseback while wielding lances and swords and firing arrows. The Xiongnu advanced far into China before being repelled.

In about 200 BC, the Xiongnu launched a major invasion and again reached the Yellow River. It wasn't until the middle of the 1st century AD that the Chinese succeeded in expelling them. Although some Xiongnu continued to harass the Chinese, it wasn't long before the Chinese found themselves fighting other nomadic tribes from the north. Among these northern enemies were the Xianbeis, Tobas, Ruruans and Turks.

Some remnants of the Xiongnu moved west, and their descendants, the Huns, united under Attila and terrorised central Europe in the last days of the Roman empire. Ruins of Xiongnu cities have been excavated in several Mongolian provinces, one site being close to Ulaan Baatar at Gua Dob.

### The Mongols

The name 'Mongol' was first recorded by the Chinese during the Tang dynasty (618-907 AD). At that time, Mongolia was dominated by the Uighurs, a Turkic people who built several cities. The Uighurs followed the teachings of a Persian saint, Mani, who was much influenced by Christianity. An inscription found in the ruins of their city, Kharbalgasun, tells how Manicheism transformed 'this country of barbarous customs, full of the fumes of blood, into a land where people live on vegetables; from a land of killing to a land where good deeds are fostered'. The Uighurs, after taking control of Mongolia, went on to help out the ailing Tang rulers of China, saving them from an internal revolt.

The Uighurs continued to control most of Mongolia until 840 AD, when they were defeated by the Kyrgyz, who now live in the Chinese province of Xinjiang. The Kyrgyz' lasting legacy in Mongolia is the downward flowing script – the *Secret History* epic and all subsequent Mongolian texts were written in this script until Stalin intervened in the 1940s.

The defeat of the Uighurs created a vacuum, which was filled by the Kitans, a Mongol tribe from what is now north-east China. By the 10th century, the Kitans had control of most of Manchuria, eastern Mongolia and much of

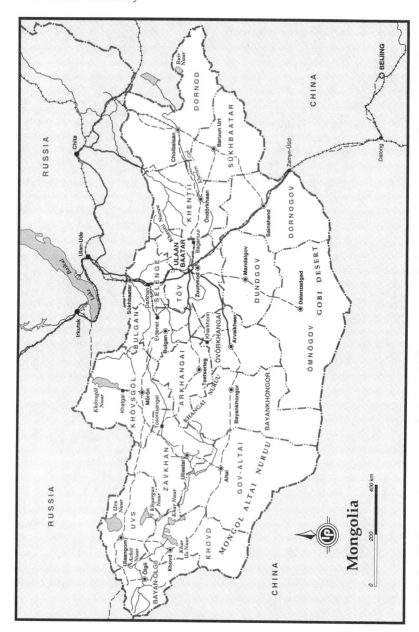

China north of the Yellow River. The Kitans continued warring with other Mongol tribes, most significantly the Western Xia during the 11th and 12th centuries. The Kitan empire was finally defeated in 1122 AD by the Chinese and their allies, the Jurchen (predecessors of the Manchus).

The Mongols and other nomadic peoples of northern Asia seldom united and had little inclination to do so; they preferred to be nomadic, widely scattered over great areas, frequently on the move with their animals in search of pasture. They wanted to live as separate clans, united only in the face of a common threat. Chinese penetration of the pastures of the Xiongnu (1300 years before Chinggis Khaan) prompted the nomads to eventually regroup and create a federation of nomadic tribes strong enough to challenge China.

### Chinggis Khaan

The Genghis Khan imprinted in the memory of the west bears little relation to the Chinggis Khaan revered by Mongolians. Not only is the spelling different: to Europeans, his name lives on as the epitome of merci-lessness and ravaging war; to the Mongolians, he embodies strength, unity, law and order. He is the young king who united the warring clans, stamped out feuds and gave Mongolians a sense of direction. This is what post-communist Mongolia looks for today, and Chinggis epitomises the historic ability to rise above confusion and uncertainty.

Until the end of the 12th century, the Mongols were little more than a loose confederation of rival clans. A Mongol named Temujin was born in 1162. At the age of 20, he emerged from a power struggle to become the leader of the Borjigin Mongol clan, and later managed to unite most of the Mongol tribes. In 1189 he was given the honorary name of Chinggis Khaan, meaning 'universal (or oceanic) king'. No Mongolian leader before or since has held the Mongolians together.

Chinggis set up his capital in Karakorum, in present-day Kharkhorin (Avarga, in Delgerkhaan district of the Khentii province, also claims to be Chinggis' capital), and launched his cavalry against China and Russia. By the time of his death in 1227, the Mongol empire extended from Beijing to the Caspian Sea.

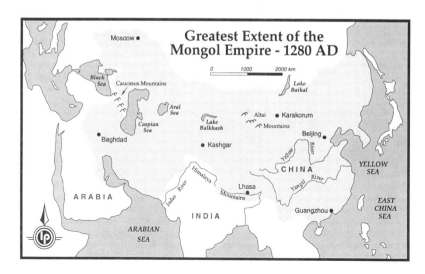

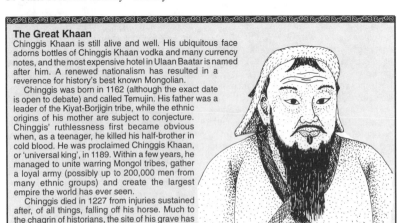

## The Great Khaan

Chinggis Khaan is still alive and well. His ubiquitous face adorns bottles of Chinggis Khaan vodka and many currency notes, and the most expensive hotel in Ulaan Baatar is named after him. A renewed nationalism has resulted in a reverence for history's best known Mongolian.

Chinggis was born in 1162 (although the exact date is open to debate) and called Temujin. His father was a leader of the Kiyat-Borjigin tribe, while the ethnic origins of his mother are subject to conjecture. Chinggis' ruthlessness first became obvious when, as a teenager, he killed his half-brother in cold blood. He was proclaimed Chinggis Khaan, or 'universal king', in 1189. Within a few years, he managed to unite warring Mongol tribes, gather a loyal army (possibly up to 200,000 men from many ethnic groups) and create the largest empire the world has ever seen.

Chinggis died in 1227 from injuries sustained after, of all things, falling off his horse. Much to the chagrin of historians, the site of his grave has still not been found, although it is believed to be somewhere in the Khentii mountains. ■

### The Great Khaans

Power passed into the hands of Chinggis' favourite son, Ogedei, who continued the programme of military conquest. His generals pushed as far west as Hungary and were all set to invade Western Europe when Ogedei died. Mongol custom dictated that all noble descendants of Chinggis had to return to Mongolia to democratically elect a new *khaan* (king). This forced the abandonment of the European campaign.

Chinggis' grandson, Kublai Khaan (circa 1216-94), completed the subjugation of China, effectively ending the Song dynasty (960-1279). He became the emperor of China's Yuan dynasty (1271-1368). Kublai established his winter capital in Tatu ('great capital'), today's Beijing. (So thoroughly have the Chinese erased the traces of the Mongol conquest that only two major monuments in Beijing remain: the Lama Temple and the giant white stupa in Beihai Park.)

Kublai soon realised that the Mongol empire had reached the limits of its expansion. In 1260 the Mongols lost a major battle to the Egyptian Mamluks. An attack on Java briefly succeeded, but the Mongol troops were finally expelled. Two attempts to invade Japan (in 1274 and 1281) ended in failure; the second was thwarted when a typhoon destroyed the Mongol fleet. The Japanese claimed this was divine intervention – the Mongols said it was bad weather.

Instead of looking for more wars to fight, Kublai concentrated his efforts on keeping the vast empire together. This was the height of the Mongols' glory: the empire stretched from Korea to Hungary and as far south as Vietnam, making it the largest empire the world has ever known. The Mongols improved the road system linking China with Russia and promoted trade throughout the empire and with Europe. Tens of thousands of horses were on standby to enable pony express riders to cross the empire with important messages at great speed.

In China, the Mongol Yuan dynasty instituted a famine relief scheme and expanded the canal system, which brought food from the countryside to the cities. It was the first to enforce paper money as the sole form of currency. This was the China that Marco Polo and other travellers visited and described in their journals to an amazed Europe.

The grandeur of the Mongol empire in China lasted over a century. After Kublai

Khaan died in 1294, the Mongols became increasingly dependent on the people they ruled. They were deeply resented as an elite, privileged class exempt from taxation, and the empire became ridden with factions vying for power. By the 1350s, Mongol rule began to disintegrate. They were expelled from Beijing by the first emperor of the Ming dynasty (1368-1644), Zhu Yuanzhang, who took the title of Hongwu.

## The Decline

The collapse of the Yuan dynasty caused over 60,000 Mongols to return to Mongolia. Their unity dissolved and they resumed their traditional lifestyle of frequent clan warfare. A major civil war was fought from 1400 to 1454 between two main groups, the Khalkha in the east and the Oirad in the west. A long period of stagnation and decline followed.

A revival of sorts occurred under Altan Khaan (1507-83), who united the Khalkha, defeated the Oirad and brought most of Mongolia under his control. The war with Ming China was renewed in an attempt to recapture the lost empire of the Yuan dynasty, but this effort proved fruitless. China's Great Wall was built at this time in an effort to find a technological solution against Altan Khaan and the resurgent Mongols. Altan signed a peace treaty with China in 1571 and turned his troops south-west against Tibet.

At the height of his power, Altan was seduced by Buddhism (ironically, the religion of Tibet). He became a devout believer and Buddhism – the religion of the Mongol nobility for 200 years – became the state religion. The monks tried desperately to reunite the quarrelling clans, but Mongolia's tendency to fragment persisted.

After the death of Altan Khaan, Mongolia reverted to a collection of tiny tribal domains. Meanwhile, the Manchus (whose predecessors were the Jurchen), ancient enemies of the Mongols, established the Qing dynasty (1644-1911). Despite their military prowess, the Manchus at first made no aggressive moves against Mongolia; they didn't need to – the Mongols were doing a great job of defeating themselves. The Zungar Mongols of the west were locked into a fierce military struggle with the Khalkha Mongols of the east.

The Zungar seemed to be gaining the upper hand, and it was at this time that the Khalkha made what was probably a fatal mistake – they invited the Manchu Qing emperor, Kangxi, to send troops to fight their Zungar enemy. Like most Mongols, the Zungar warriors were highly skilled horseback archers. However, the Manchus possessed new technology which the Mongols couldn't combat – muskets and cannon. By 1732 the Zungar were resoundingly defeated and Mongolia came under the control of Manchu China.

Some of the Manchu emperors were devout Tibetan Buddhists, so the Manchus built temples throughout Mongolia. Manchu rule over China was competent and reasonably benign up until around 1800; thereafter, the Qing emperors became increasingly corrupt and despotic. In both China and Mongolia, peasants suffered ruthless exploitation, ruinous taxes and brutal punishment (including torture) for the slightest offence or resistance to authority. (The brutality of the Manchu era has never been forgiven or forgotten, and to this day Mongolians despise the Chinese.) Mongolia was ripe for rebellion, and so was China.

## Revolutions

In 1911 China's last dynasty, the Qing, crumbled. The Mongol princes quickly saw their opportunity: Mongolian independence from China was declared on 1 December 1911, with a theocratic government under the leadership of the eighth Jebtzun Damba (Living Buddha), who was declared the Bogd Khaan (Holy King). The Chinese government did not recognise Mongolian independence, but it was fully preoccupied with its own domestic chaos. On 25 May 1915, the Treaty of Kyakhta – which granted Mongolia limited autonomy – was signed by Mongolia, China and Russia.

The Russian Revolution of October 1917 came as a great shock to Mongolia's aristocracy. Taking advantage of Russia's weakness, a

Chinese warlord sent his troops into Mongolia in 1919 and occupied the capital. In February 1921, retreating White Russian (anticommunist) troops entered Mongolia and expelled the Chinese. At first the Bogd Khaan seemed to welcome the Russians as saviours of his regime, but it soon became apparent that the Russians were just a ruthless army of occupation. The brutality of both the Chinese and Russian forces inflamed the Mongolians' desire for independence.

As the Russian Bolsheviks were steadily advancing against the White Russian forces in Siberia, Mongolian nationalists believed their best hope for military assistance was to ask the Bolsheviks for help. In July 1921, Mongolian and Bolshevik fighters recaptured Ulaan Baatar, and on 11 July of that year the People's Government of Mongolia was declared. The Bogd Khaan was retained as a ceremonial figurehead with no real power. The newly formed Mongolian People's Party (the first political party in the country's history, and the only one for the next 69 years) took over government. Mongolia's first leader was Damdin Sükhbaatar, the former commander of Mongolia's troops.

The military campaign continued for a few more months. Thousands of Bolshevik forces poured into Mongolia from Russia. The White Russian forces were finally defeated in January 1922. Almost from the first moment of victory, there was rivalry between the Bogd Khaan and the communists – the latter clearly intended to eliminate the monarchy entirely and seemed to be moving in on the newly 'independent' Mongolia.

### Soviet Control

On 26 November 1924, the Mongolian People's Republic (MPR) was declared and Mongolia became the world's second communist country. The Mongolian People's Party was renamed the Mongolian People's Revolutionary Party (MPRP). Soviet and Mongolian communists worked secretly to eliminate all noncommunist contenders for power.

After Lenin's death in Russia in 1924, Mongolian communism remained much independent of Moscow until Lenin's successor, Stalin, gained absolute power in the late 1920s. Then the purges began in Mongolia. Once former MPRP leaders Lana Bodoo, Danzan Khorloo and Sükhbaatar were dead (one or two in suspicious circumstances), and Party Chairman Tseren-Ochiryn Dambadorj was exiled to Moscow in 1928, Stalin's stooge, Khorloogiyn Choibalsan, was selected as leader of the standing legislature, the Little Khural.

Following Stalin's lead, Choibalsan ordered the seizure of land and herds which were then redistributed to peasants. In 1932 more than 700 people – mostly monks – were imprisoned or murdered, their property seized and collectivised. Farmers were forced to join cooperatives and private business was banned, Chinese and other foreign traders were expelled and all transport was nationalised. The destruction of private enterprise without sufficient time to build up a working state sector had the same result in Mongolia as it did in the Soviet Union – famine.

While the government moderated its economic policy during the 1930s, its campaign against religion was ruthless. In 1937 Choibalsan launched a reign of terror against the monasteries in which thousands of monks were arrested and executed (see the Religion section later in this chapter). The antireligion campaign coincided with a bloody purge to eliminate 'rightist elements'. It is believed that by 1939 some 27,000 people had been executed (3% of Mongolia's population at that time), of whom 17,000 were monks.

### The Wars

By 1931 the Japanese had seized north-east China (Manchuria), renamed it Manchukuo and returned the last Manchu (Qing) emperor to the throne to serve as a Japanese puppet. Japan planned a similar takeover of Mongolia, creating a state called Mengukuo – the kingdom of the Mongols. Stalin correctly feared Japanese military moves against both the USSR and Mongolia, so the Soviet army started moving back into Mongolia during the early 1930s and built up the Mongolian military as well; eventually, nearly 10% of Mongolia's population was in the military.

In 1939 the Japanese decided to invade eastern Mongolia, but were resoundingly defeated by a joint Mongolian-Soviet force (see the Eastern Mongolia chapter for details). Largely as a result of this battle, Japan signed a neutrality pact with the USSR in 1941 and the Japanese turned their war machine south instead.

The Soviet Union and Mongolia declared war on Japan in 1945 during the very last days of WWII. After the war, Stalin extracted grudging recognition of the independence of Outer Mongolia from Chinese Kuomintang (Nationalist Party) leader Chiang Kaishek when the two signed an anti-Japanese Sino-Soviet alliance. (The Kuomintang, which was defeated by the Chinese communists, subsequently withdrew recognition of Outer Mongolia's independence and – still claiming to be the legitimate government of all China – continues to press its territorial claim. Maps produced in Taiwan today still show Mongolia as a province of China.)

## Progress & Conflict

Choibalsan died in January 1952 and was replaced by Yumjaagiyn Tsedenbal – no liberal, but not a mass murderer. Stalin died the following year. From that time until the mid-1960s, Mongolia enjoyed, in relative terms, a period of peace. Relations between the Soviet and Chinese governments warmed during the 1950s and this had beneficial effects on Mongolia. The Soviets felt confident enough about Chinese intentions to withdraw all Soviet troops from Mongolia in 1956. Taiwan and the USA continued to oppose Mongolia's membership in the United Nations, but this was finally achieved in 1961.

With the Sino-Soviet split in the early 1960s, the Mongolians chose the lesser of evils and sided with the Soviet Union. Chinese aid to Mongolia ceased; the Mongo-

lian government expelled thousands of ethnic Chinese and all trade with China came to a halt. More than 100,000 Soviet troops poured in and Mongolia was once again a potential battlefield.

Throughout the 1970s, Soviet influence gathered strength. Young Mongolians were sent to the USSR for technical training and brought back Russian habits (including the overconsumption of vodka). Many aspects of Russian culture – food, music, opera, dance – were adopted by the Mongolians and Russian became the country's second language. Mongolia swarmed with Polish archaeologists, Czech tractor-makers, Hungarian technicians and East German propaganda film makers.

## Reform

As the Soviet regime stagnated and faltered, Party Secretary-General Tsedenbal was forcibly retired in 1984 and moved to Moscow. He was replaced by Jambyn Batmonkh, a reformer heartened by the Soviet reforms under Mikhail Gorbachev. In 1986 Gorbachev announced that the withdrawal of Soviet troops from Mongolia was being considered.

Batmonkh instigated a cautious attempt at perestroika and glasnost (known as *il tod* in Mongolian) in 1986. Decentralisation was the key word in the economic reform package – enterprises were given more freedom to operate without central officials making all the decisions. Government departments were reorganised and high-ranking officials were reshuffled.

By the late 1980s, relations with China gradually thawed. Air services between Beijing and Ulaan Baatar – suspended since the 1960s – were resumed in 1986. In 1989 full diplomatic relations with China were established.

The unravelling of the Soviet Union resulted in decolonisation by default. Few in Mongolia were ready for the speed of the collapse, or the possibilities of seizing the moment. In March 1990, large pro-democracy protests erupted in the square in front of the parliament building in Ulaan Baatar and hunger strikes were held. It was only a few months after the Tiananmen Square massacre in Beijing, and many in the MPRP wanted to deal with the protests with tanks and troops. Batmonkh, however, did not sign the order, and a young man by the name of Zorig exposed the plan to the Mongolian press.

Things then happened quickly: Batmonkh lost power; new political parties with a bewildering variety of names sprang up; and hunger strikes and protests continued. In May the MPRP government amended the constitution to permit multiparty elections in July 1990.

### Elections

Ironically, the communists won the elections, taking 85% of the seats in the Great Khural and 62% of the seats in the Little Khural (see Government & Politics). Although Ulaan Baatar residents gave much support to the opposition parties, rural areas voted overwhelmingly for the communists. The MPRP, now calling itself 'ex-communist', announced it would share power with several young democrats – some were even given

ministries. Freedom of speech, religion and assembly were all granted. The era of totalitarianism had ended.

The Mongolian constitution was revised again and elections were held in June 1992. The MPRP again came out on top, winning 57% of the popular vote and an astounding 71 parliamentary seats out of 76. The 'ex-communists' ran on a platform promising ill-defined reforms and blaming the country's economic problems on the democratic opposition. The government was soon under pressure from big lenders, including Japan and the World Bank, to privatise ownership of the big state enterprises, but this only resulted in ownership by the same men who had been the managers.

Four years later, on 30 June 1996, the Mongolian Democratic Coalition unexpectedly trounced the ruling MPRP, ending 75 years of unbroken communist rule. Despite the sparse population and vast distances, the majority of the 1.2 million eligible voters chose the Coalition, which secured 50 seats. The MPRP only managed to keep 25 seats;

| Chronology | |
| --- | --- |
| 200 BC | Xiongnu Mongolian empire reaches Yellow River in China |
| 1st century AD | Xiongnu expelled from China |
| 840 | The Kyrgyz defeat ruling Uighurs |
| 1122 | The ruling Kitans defeated by the Chinese |
| 1162 | Chinggis Khaan is born as Temujin |
| 1189 | Temujin takes the title of Chinggis Khaan |
| 1211 | Chinggis Khaan launches attacks on China |
| 1227 | Chinggis Khaan dies |
| 1229 | Ogedei Khaan, Chinggis' third son, proclaimed the second Khaan |
| 1279 | Kublai Khaan completes conquest of China |
| 1294 | Kublai Khaan dies |
| 1400-1454 | Civil war in Mongolia |
| 1578 | Altan Khan converts to Buddhism |
| 1586 | Erdene Zuu, Mongolia's first monastery, is started |
| 1641 | Zanabazar proclaimed leader of Buddhists in Mongolia |
| 1911 | Independence from China |
| 1915 | Russia, China and Mongolia sign agreement to grant limited autonomy to Mongolia |
| 1919 | Chinese invade Mongolia again |
| 1921 | Chinese defeated; Mongolia's independence proclaimed by Sükhbaatar |
| 1924 | The Bogd Khaan dies; the Mongolian People's Republic declared by the communists |
| 1939 | Russian and Mongolian troops fight Japan in eastern Mongolia |
| 1990 | Pro-democracy protests held; communists win multiparty elections |
| 1992 | New constitution announced; communists win another election |
| 1996 | Mongolian Democratic Coalition unexpectedly thrashes communists in June election. |

the sole independent is from the Mongolian Traditional United Party. Mendsaikhanu Enkhsaikhan, the 41-year-old leader of the Coalition, was named prime minister.

## GEOGRAPHY

Mongolia is a huge, landlocked country: 1,566,000 sq km in area – about three times the size of France; over twice the size of Texas, USA; and almost as large as Queensland, Australia. Apart from the period of Mongol conquest under Chinggis Khaan and Kublai Khaan, Mongolia was until the 20th century about twice its present size. A large chunk of Siberia was once part of Mongolia but is now securely controlled by Russia, and Inner Mongolia is now firmly part of China.

Conservationists divide Mongolia into six zones:

Desert
Spread out over the most southern sliver of the Gobi Desert and stretching into China, this zone has very little vegetation, livestock, wildlife, population or rain.

Desert Steppe
This includes the lower-lying areas of western Mongolia and most of the Gobi (except for the far southern section). Covering about 20% of the country, this dry and sparsely populated zone has salt lakes and sand dunes.

Mountain
This zone covers the Khangai and Mongol Altai mountains in Arkhangai, Khovd and Bayan-Ölgii provinces. It is very cold and wet all year and sparsely populated, but home to some of the country's most endangered animals.

Mountain Forest Steppe
These grasslands are found in the central and northern provinces (dominated by the Orkhon and Selenge rivers), and in the western provinces of Khovd and Bayan-Ölgii. The zone covers about 25% of Mongolia, is home to gazelles and antelopes, and has a relatively high number of people and livestock.

Steppe
This is spread over the southern part of Töv province and most of eastern Mongolia. Covering about 20% of the country, it is home to vast numbers of gazelles, birdlife and livestock, but is sparsely populated.

Taiga
This area of larch and pine forests is found in Khentii province, around Khövsgöl Nuur lake, and stretches into Siberia. It is also wet and cold.

The southern third of Mongolia is dominated by the Gobi Desert. Although barren-looking, it has sufficient grass to support scattered herds of sheep, goats and camels. Most of the Gobi is not sandy, nor full of sand dunes. Much of the rest of Mongolia is covered by grassland, home to Mongolia's famed horses which Chinggis Khaan used so successfully in his wars of conquest.

Mongolia is also one of the highest countries in the world, with an average elevation of 1580m. In the far west are Mongolia's highest mountains, the Mongol Altai Nuruu, which are permanently snowcapped. The highest peak, Tavanbogd Uul (4374m), has a magnificent glacier towering over Mongolia, Russia and China. Between the peaks are stark deserts where rain almost never falls. It's an incredibly beautiful, rocky landscape with a few scattered forests in some of the better-watered valleys.

Near the centre of Mongolia is the Khangai Nuruu range, with its highest peak (Otgon Tenger Uul) reaching 3905m. On the north slope of these mountains is the source of the Selenge Gol, Mongolia's largest river, which flows northward into Lake Baikal in Siberia. While the Selenge Gol is the largest in terms of water volume, the longest river is the Kherlen Gol in eastern Mongolia.

Just to the north-east of Ulaan Baatar is the Khentii Nuruu, the highest mountain range in eastern Mongolia and by far the most accessible to hikers. It's a heavily forested region with raging rivers and impressive peaks, the highest being Asralt Khairkhan Uul (2800m).

Mongolia has numerous saltwater and freshwater lakes which are great for camping, watching birdlife, hiking, swimming and fishing. The most popular is the magnificent Khövsgöl Nuur, which contains up to 2% of the world's fresh water. The largest is the low-lying, saltwater Uvs Nuur. Also worth exploring are Achit, Üüreg, Khar Us and Terkhiin Tsagaan lakes.

Other geological and geographical features include underwater and above-ground caves, some with ancient rock paintings; dormant volcanoes; hot and cold mineral

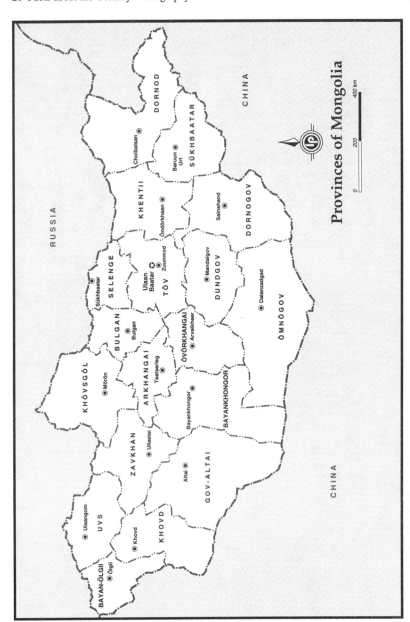

Provinces of Mongolia

springs; the Great Lakes depression in western Mongolia and the Darkhadyn Khotgor depression west of Khövsgöl Nuur; and the Orkhon Khürkhree waterfalls.

Mongolia is divided into 18 provinces *(aimag)* – plus four independent municipalities, which are also sometimes called aimags. These are Ulaan Baatar, Darkhan-Uul (which contains Darkhan city), Orkhon (with Erdenet city) and Gov-Sumber (with the Free Trade Zone town of Choir). The aimags are further divided into a total of 298 districts *(sum)*.

In this book, the provinces have been grouped under the following chapters:

Central Mongolia
    Arkhangai, Övörkhangai and Töv
Northern Mongolia
    Bulgan, Khövsgöl, Selenge and Zavkhan
Eastern Mongolia
    Dornod, Khentii and Sükhbaatar
Western Mongolia
    Bayan-Ölgii, Khovd and Uvs
Gobi
    Bayankhongor, Dornogov, Dundgov, Gov-Altai and Ömnögov

## CLIMATE

Mongolia is a land of extremes. It is so far inland that no sea moderates the climate. Only in summer does cloud cover shield the sky. Humidity is zilch and sunshine is intense. With over 260 sunny days a year, Mongolia is justifiably known as the 'Land of Blue Sky'.

Long subarctic winters are the norm, however, and you can see snow in the Gobi Desert as late as April, and some lakes remain frozen until June. There is a short rainy season from mid-July to September, but the showers tend to be brief and gentle. Because of the high altitude, evenings are cool even in summer. Mongolia is a windy place, especially in spring.

When the wind blows from the north, temperatures drop sharply, but when the wind drops, the weather warms up just as rapidly. One day you're walking around in a T-shirt and sandals, the next day you need an overcoat and boots, then the following day

it's back to T-shirts. This is especially the case during the brief autumn and spring.

In the Gobi, summer temperatures hit 40°C but winter winds often send the mercury plummeting to minus 30°C or lower. Even in summer, the evenings can be astoundingly cold. The steppe is always chilly – the July average is only 10°C and even spring and autumn are frosty. Winter is no joke – minus 50°C is not unknown. Mountainous areas are always cold and windy; many peaks are permanently snow-capped. Low-lying areas, such as Uvs Nuur lake in the west, also suffer from extreme temperatures.

In Ulaan Baatar, the winter (October to April) is long and cold – with temperatures often dropping down to minus 30°C in January and February. You can expect some horrific dust storms during the short spring (May to June). The summer (July to September) is pleasant without being hot. It can still suddenly turn cold and, unfortunately, most of the city's rain falls in this period.

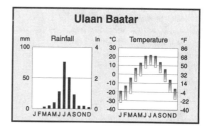

## ECOLOGY & ENVIRONMENT

Mongolia's natural environment remains in good shape compared with that of many western countries. The country's small population and nomadic subsistence economy have been its environmental salvation. The great open pastures of its northern half are kept open and ideal for grazing by retaining just enough forest, usually on the upper slopes of the rounded hills, to shelter the abundant wildlife.

However, it does have its share of problems. Communist production quotas put pressure on grasslands to yield more than was sustainable, so soil erosion and desertification resulted. In addition, forest fires are common during the windy spring season. In early 1996, an unusually dry winter fuelled widespread and intense fires over tracts of steppe and forest in most parts of Mongolia. The human toll was not excessively large – nearly 30 dead and 700 homeless – but tens of thousands of sq km (an area larger than Belgium) of pastures, and up to 600,000 livestock (and unknown numbers of wildlife) were destroyed. Damage to the Mongolian local economy was officially estimated at a staggering US$1.9 billion.

Other threats to the land include mining (there are some 300 mines) and deforestation. Urban sprawl, coupled with a demand for wood to build homes and use as heating and cooking fuel, is slowly reducing the forests. (Where there are no trees, animal dung is widely used for fuel.)

Pollution is also becoming a serious problem. At the top of Zaisan Memorial, just south of Ulaan Baatar, a depressing layer of dust and smoke from the city's power stations regularly hovers over the city – this is often appalling in winter, when all homes are continuously burning fuel and the power stations are working overtime. Ulaan Baatar has suffered from acid rain, and pollution is killing fish in the nearby Tuul Gol. Oil leaks from trucks crossing the frozen lakes in winter continue to pollute the pristine Khövsgöl Nuur and Uvs Nuur, despite an official ban on these crossings.

Mongolia's first hydroelectric dam is being built on the Egiin Gol with the financial assistance of the Asian Development Bank. Despite its arguable usefulness, it will damage pristine wilderness and numerous unexplored archaeological sites. Another dam is being planned along the Zavkhan Gol, with Chinese assistance and finance.

### Environmental Organisations

If you want information on Mongolia's environment and the problems it faces, contact the following organisations:

Green Movement
   PO Box 38/117, Ulaan Baatar (☎ 325 485)
Mongolian Association for the Conservation of Nature & Environment (MACNE)
   PO Box 1160, Ulaan Baatar (☎ 328 002; fax 321 331) This is a nongovernment and nonprofit organisation with substantial foreign assistance. It has successfully helped to re-introduce the wild horse *takhi* to Mongolia, raised awareness of the potential threat to the environment among Mongolians and foreigners, and established national parks throughout the country.
Mongolian Gazelle Society
   Institute of General and Experimental Biology, Academy of Sciences, Ulaan Baatar 51 (☎ 53 347; fax 364 616)

## FLORA & FAUNA
### Flora
Mongolia can be roughly divided into three zones: grassland and shrubs (52% of the country), forests (15%) and desert vegetation (32%). Less than 1% of the country is used for human settlements and crop cultivation. Grasslands are used extensively for grazing, and despite the vast expanses, overgrazing is not uncommon.

Forests of Siberian larch (sometimes up to 45m high), Siberian and Scotch pine, and white and ground birch are regularly cut down for fuel and building, and are affected by mining and agriculture. In the Gobi, the saxaul shrub covers millions of hectares. Although it has virtually no leaves, the saxaul is highly adaptable and protects the environment from degradation and erosion, while providing protection and shade for animals.

Khentii province and some other parts of central Mongolia are famous for the effusion of red, yellow and purple wildflowers, mainly rhododendrons and edelweiss. Extensive grazing is the major threat to Mongolia's flowers, trees and shrubs: over 200 species are endangered.

### Fauna
In Mongolia, the distinction between the domestic and wild (untamed) animal is often blurry. Wild and domesticated horses and camels mingle on the steppes with wild asses and herds of wild gazelles. In the mountains

The wild ass roams the steppes.

there are enormous, horned wild argali sheep and domesticated yaks along with wild moose, musk deer and roe deer. Reindeer herds are basically untamed, even if they come back to the same tent each night for a lick of salt and can be ridden.

**Wildlife** Wildlife flourishes in Mongolia despite an extreme climate, the nomadic fondness for hunting, the communist persecution of Buddhists who had set aside areas as animal sanctuaries, and a penniless government which lacks resources to police nature protection laws. However, your chances of seeing any wildlife are pretty slim, and the closest you will get to a wild ass, argali sheep or moose is the stuffed animals section of a museum.

Despite the lack of water in the Gobi, some species (many of which are endangered) somehow survive: the wild camel,

Pesky marmots are often encountered by travellers.

Gobi argali sheep, Gobi bear, ibex and Black-tailed gazelle. In the wide open steppe, you may see the rare Saiga antelope, Mongolian gazelle, wild ass, small jerboa, wolf and millions of furry marmots busy waking up after the last hibernation, or preparing for their next.

Further north in the forests live the wild boar, brown bear, antelope, reindeer, elk, musk deer and moose, as well as plenty of sable and lynx whose furs, unfortunately, are in high demand. Most of the mountains are extremely remote, thus providing an ideal habitat for argali sheep, very rare snow leopards and smaller mammals such as the fox, ermine and hare.

The two-humped Bactrian camel is indigenous to Mongolia.

**Livestock** Mongolians define themselves as the 'people of five animals': horses, cattle (including yaks), sheep, goats and camels. The odd one out is the reindeer, which is herded in small numbers near the Siberian border.

You will see much more livestock than wildlife. Half of Mongolia's population lives on the land and primarily raises animals, which is why you see so many in the countryside. They are vital to the nomadic way of life, providing milk, meat and skins for clothing, housing and transport, and are a statement of wealth.

Camels (of which there are 367,000) are good for long-distance, though slow, transport, but they're valuable for their adaptability, especially in the desert. The horse is the pride of Mongolia and there are few nomads, if any, who haven't learned to ride as soon as they can walk. Mongolian horses (2.6 million), which are shorter than those in other countries (don't call them ponies – Mongolians will get offended) provide perfect transport, can endure harsh winters and, importantly, produce that much-loved Mongolian drink: fermented mare's milk, known as *airag*.

Cows and yaks (together, 3.3 million) are best for milk and meat (especially *borts*, dried and salted meat) and provide hides. Yaks are excellent for transport uphill. Sheep (13.7 million) are easy to herd and provide wool (for housing, clothes and carpets) and meat (the ubiquitous mutton) – every nomadic family wants at least a few sheep. Goats (8.5 million) are often difficult to please, but they are still popular for the meat and, especially, for cashmere wool.

The yak is a common form of transport in Mongolia.

**Birds** Mongolia is home to over 400 species of birds. In the desert you may see the Desert Warbler, Houbara Bustard and Saxaul Sparrow, as well as sandgrouse, finch and the Cinerous Vulture.

On the steppes, you will certainly see many grey Demoiselle Cranes – the most common bird in Mongolia. Other steppe species include the Upland Buzzard, Steppe Eagle, Black Kite and some assorted owls and hawks.

These magnificent creatures, perched majestically on a rock by the side of the road, will rarely be disturbed by your jeep or the screams of your guide: 'Look. Eagle!! We stop?' Following the almost inaudible click of your lens cap, however, these birds will move and almost be in China before you have even thought about apertures. Here again, your best bet at seeing them is the stuffed birds section of a museum.

In the mountains, you may be lucky to spot species of ptarmigan, finch, woodpecker and owl. The best places to get out your binoculars and telephoto lens are the following lakes: Sangiin Dalai Nuur (where you will see the Mongolian Lark, eagles, geese and swans), Khar Us Nuur (geese, wood grouse and the Relict Gull), Khar Nuur and Airag Nuur (migratory pelicans), Uvs Nuur (spoonbills, cranes and gulls) and Ganga Nuur (migratory swans).

**Fish** Rivers such as the Selenge, Orkhon, Zavkhan, Balj, Onon and Egiin, as well as dozens of lakes including Khövsgöl Nuur, are home to about 380 species of fish. They include trout, grayling, lennok, sturgeon, pike and perch. Fish even survive in several saltwater lakes in the Gobi, though many have died recently after extreme heat caused evaporation and increased the lakes' saltiness.

If you are an enthusiast, one book to look out for is the newly released *Fishing in Mongolia* published by the US-based Avery Press.

**Cruelty to Animals**
Poaching and hunting are common practice in the countryside, despite efforts by conservationists and some government officials. As long as there is demand in countries like China and Japan for 'delicacies' such as powdered argali sheep horns, boiled Gobi bear gall bladders and potions from glands of musk deer, precious – and often highly endangered – wildlife will be killed.

The very occasional fence or vehicle, as well as mining, overgrazing, deforestation and pollution, are responsible for the deaths of many domesticated and wild animals. An estimated three million are killed every year by nomadic people for food and skins, plus many more by poachers. Animal lovers may not be impressed with the way some domesticated animals are neglected and maltreated.

**Endangered Species**
Organised hunting of endangered animals such as the ibex, snow leopard and elk is officially condoned and quietly promoted. It's a hard-currency earner for the Mongolian government, as foreign hunters pay exorbitant prices for hunting licenses. Lonely Planet does not encourage such activities.

According to conservationists, 28 species of mammals are endangered. The more commonly known species are the wild ass *(khulan)*, wild camel *(khavtgai)*, Gobi argali sheep *(argal)*, Gobi bear *(mazalai)*, ibex *(yangir)* and the Black-tailed gazelle *(oono)*; others include otters, wolves, antelopes and jerboas.

There are 59 species of endangered birds, including many species of hawk, falcon, buzzard, crane and owl. Despite Mongolian beliefs that it's bad luck to kill a crane, the White-naped Crane is threatened with extinction.

Two very successful attempts at conserving endangered species are MACNE's preservation of the takhi wild horse. The takhi – also known as Przewalski's horse – was actually extinct in the 1960s. It was successfully reintroduced into national parks and, later, the wild after an extensive breeding programme overseas.

In preserved areas of the mountains, about 1000 snow leopards remain. They are hunted for their pelts (which are also part of some Shamanist and Buddhist traditional practises), as are the snow leopards' major source of food, the marmot.

**National Parks**
For centuries, Mongolians have been aware of the need for conservation. The area around Bogdkhan Uul mountain, near Ulaan Baatar, was protected from hunting and logging as early as the 12th century, and was officially designated as a national park over 200 years ago.

The various Mongolian governments have always accepted the need for conservation. Thankfully, in 1996 the new government retained the Ministry of Nature & Environment (MNE) – one of only nine ministries – but the annual budget for the upkeep of the country's national parks is unlikely to increase from the current pitiful US$70,000 per annum. This is clearly not enough, but through substantial financial assistance and guidance from international governments and nongovernmental organisations, the animals, flora and environment in some parts of the country are being preserved.

The MNE classifies the national parks into four categories which, in order of importance, are:

Strictly Protected Areas
  Very fragile areas of great importance; hunting, logging and development is strictly prohibited.
National Parks
  Places of historical and educational interest; fishing and grazing by nomadic people is allowed.
Natural Reserves
  Less important regions protecting rare species of flora and fauna and archaeological sites; some development is allowed within certain guidelines.
Natural & Historical Monuments
  Important places of historical and cultural interest; development is allowed within guidelines.

The 26 national parks – which represent an impressive 8% of the total land – are dealt with individually and in more detail throughout the book. The most important and popular parks are:

Bogdkhan Mountain Strictly Protected Area
  Very close to Ulaan Baatar, this area of 42,000 hectares protects the sacred mountain and the local environment from urban sprawl; in Töv.
Gorkhi-Terelj National Park
  Easily the most visited park in the country, the 286,000 hectares primarily help to protect the environment from tourism; in Töv.
Great Gobi Strictly Protected Areas
  Two regions, totalling 5.3 million hectares, were established to protect the wild camel, takhi, saxaul forests, wild ass and Gobi bear; in Bayankhongor, Gov-Altai and Khovd.

Gurvansaikhan National Park
    Covering two million hectares of the Gobi, the park includes sand dunes, valleys and mountains; in Ömnögov.
Khan Khentii Strictly Protected Area
    Bordering the Gorkhi-Terelj National Park, this 1.2 million hectare park preserves the unique environment, fauna, flora and forests, as well as ancient burial sites; in Töv, Khentii and Selenge.
Khövsgöl Lake National Park
    One of the most popular attractions in Mongolia, this park (840,000 hectares) was established to preserve the lake, forests and fish; in Khövsgöl.
Uvs Lake Strictly Protected Area
    This 771,000 hectare area was created to conserve the lake, its birdlife, the extraordinarily diverse local ecology and the source of Uvs Nuur, and other lakes, in the region; in Uvs.

**Permits** To visit these parks – especially a strictly protected area or national park – you will need a permit. They are easy to get (or forget) but are little more than an entrance fee – they are an important source of revenue for the maintenance of the parks, however. You rarely actually receive a permit on paper.

At the main gates to the most popular and accessible parks – ie Khövsgöl Lake, Great Gobi, Gorkhi-Terelj and Bogdkhan Mountain – the entrance fee is from T1000 to T1650 per (foreign) person per day, plus an extra T300 to T3000 for a vehicle, depending on whether it is driven by a Mongolian or foreigner. If you are not entering these parks from the main road, or if you are visiting other parks, try to find a local park ranger and give him your fee. In fact, very few rangers work in the remote parks, and finding one in a two-million-hectare area without fences or gates may be just a little difficult.

Alternatively, pay your entrance fee at the National Service for Protected Area and Ecotourism (NSPAE), which is part of the Ministry of Nature & Environment, before you visit the park. The NSPAE (☎ 322 011, 320 233; fax 321 401) is at Baga Toiruu 44, just behind the Ulaan Baatar Hotel. If you are not able to get a permit and are found in a park without one, the worst penalty you're likely to suffer is being asked to leave or pay a fine to the park ranger.

## GOVERNMENT & POLITICS

In 1992, after much debate, a radically new constitution was enacted. The new parliament is known as the Great *(Ikh)* Khural and has a total of 76 seats (down from 430 seats after the constitution was amended). Representatives are elected for four-year terms. The smaller standing legislature, the Little *(Baga)* Khural, was abolished in 1992. The president serves a four-year term, is elected by direct popular vote and can be re-elected only once. The president must be at least 45 years of age (a rule which would have excluded national hero Sükhbaatar, among others).

Local governments are not directly elected. Rather, the voters in every sum elect a number of deputies who meet in the aimag capital to select the governor and local mayors. Ulaan Baatar, Darkhan, Choir (in Gov-Sumber district) and Erdenet are autonomous municipalities: they don't officially belong to any province and have mayors with as much power as aimag governors.

For over 65 years, power was monopolised by the Mongolian People's Revolutionary Party (MPRP). The elections of 1990 and 1992 still left the MPRP in control, with a renewed mandate to navigate Mongolia's entry into modernity with a Mongolian face. The MPRP, while promising reform, often looked after its mates, resisted the prescriptions of the international bankers, and took more and more loans to patch up existing unproductive enterprises.

By the time of the June 1996 elections, voters had had enough: they handed the new Democratic Coalition a stunning and unexpected victory. The Coalition – made up of the Mongolian Social Democratic Party, the Mongolian National Democratic Party, the Mongolian Democratic Party of Believers and the Mongolian Party of Greens – was clearly given a mandate to speed up economic reform.

The inexperienced government, full of educated young men (only seven of the 76 seats are held by women), must urgently revive the economy, encourage foreign investment and preserve independence from the omnipotent neighbours, China and Russia. Unfortunately, the new government won only 50 of the 76 seats in the Ikh Khural, which is marginally less than the two-thirds majority required by the constitution to pass any new legislation. The one independent member, from the Traditional United Party, is expected to side with the opposition party, the MPRP.

One of the first decisions made by the new government was to reduce the number of ministries from 13 to nine: External Relations (foreign affairs), Agriculture & Industry, Development of Infrastructure (which includes the latent tourism department), Education, Finance, Justice, Nature & Environment (which shows how important this is to the current government) and Health and Social Welfare.

## ECONOMY

Long before the days of Chinggis Khaan, Mongolia's economy rode on the backs of sheep, goats, cattle, horses, yaks and camels. Nowadays, sheep are the most important stock, constituting half of all animals raised. For each Mongolian, there is almost exactly one horse, 1.4 cattle (including yaks), nearly four goats and six sheep; there's also one camel for every six Mongolians. In 1995 there were 28.5 million head of livestock in Mongolia, an increase of nearly two million from the previous year – but this is an increase of less than 2% since 1930, while the population more than trebled. Agriculture, including livestock, makes up more than a third of the country's Gross Domestic Product (GDP).

Wheat has been grown on the steppes for thousands of years, but the Mongolian way of life took off when animals were first tamed. Livestock raising is practical because of the extensive grasslands – the harsh, dry climate makes most forms of agriculture impossible. Less than 1% of the land is under cultivation, and this is mostly used to grow wheat. Potatoes, vegetables, hay and other fodder crops are also grown. Small-scale timber production along the Russian border provides wood for building material.

**Some Economic Statistics (1995)**
**Inflation Rate:** 53.1%
**GDP per Capita:** US$309 pa (underestimated because of cashless society)
**Official Unemployment:** 2% (bound to be much higher)
**Major Exports:** molybdenum & copper concentrate, sheepskins, intestine rolls, cashmere
**Major Imports:** vehicles, oil, glass, sugar, industrial equipment
**National Income Growth:** 2.1% (in 1994)
**Monthly Wage:** in Ulaan Baatar, US$94; in the countryside, US$65 ∎

The country has over 300 mines producing coal (17 mines produced seven million tons in 1995), copper and molybdenum (the mine in Erdenet earns the country US$900 million pa), gold (75 mines produced 4500kg in 1995), fluorspar (15% of the world's output), uranium, tungsten and zinc. These minerals make up nearly one-third of Mongolia's GDP and earn half of all foreign currency.

Cashmere wool is also a vital industry. Mongolia has no active oil fields, but recent explorations show that oil can be a potential export if regional transport improves.

### Central Planning & Subsidies
The model of economic development adopted earlier this century by both the USSR and Mongolia became known as the 'planned economy'. The communist Mongolian government instituted a series of five-year plans to decide how much should be invested and where, what the production quotas should be, and so on. The state owned all means of production and private enterprise was forbidden. When profits were made, they were given to the government. To keep the massive plan on course, the state created an enormous bureaucracy of economists, planners and supervisors. This required widespread literacy, and statistics on everything were collected. To this day, massive data on everything from herd size to cloud cover to geology is available.

Herders and urban workers weren't taxed, but they were paid very little for their labour.

However, the state heavily subsidised all goods and services. Thus, medical care and education were free, though basic. Even herders in remote nomadic camps had access to boarding schools in nearby towns, pensions for the old, veterinary services for their flocks and basic health care, including state-run mineral spring spas. The subsidies from the Soviet Union amounted to hundreds of dollars per Mongolian each year.

State planning had relatively little impact in the countryside. Although the government organised farmers and herders into cooperatives, supervision in rural areas was slack and herders earned much the same wage whether they were under or over their production quotas. The government did manage to create a few large, mechanised farms on the Soviet model.

In the cities, the Russian elite could not understand why an independent, self-sufficient, proud, nomadic people might be reluctant to work in factories. Factory workers were assigned to jobs in which they had little interest, and there were no financial rewards for working hard. The government tried to encourage people to work hard by giving medals and recognition to 'labour heroes', but this wasn't very successful.

Wages were low, but no-one starved. The state provided all that was needed to survive, and though the standard of living was basic, there were no great differences between rich and poor.

## Economic Collapse

The Mongolians paid a heavy price for their dependency on the USSR. The bubble burst in 1991 when subsidies from the Soviet Union ended. Barter trade was halted and the Russians started demanding hard currency – not wool and mutton – for their petrol and machinery. The Mongolians, however, had no hard foreign currency – all they had were debts. As a result, trade with Russia dropped so fast that cross-border trade all along Mongolia's long northern border has virtually disappeared.

With petrol supplies drying up and spare parts for Soviet-built machinery not arriving, the Mongolians watched in dismay as trucks, buses, power stations and agricultural equipment stood idle. During the early 1990s, shop shelves were bare, people lost their jobs, and a severe lack of building materials brought the construction industry to a halt.

The failure of the Russians to deliver fuel crippled the Mongolian economy. Getting food to the urban masses required benzene, the Mongolian term for petrol (gasoline). In a country heavily reliant on agriculture, farmers were unable to get products to market. Not that they really wanted to, as price controls remained on their produce and the state paid the farmers absurdly low prices in an effort to hold down prices of basic survival foods for panicky city folk.

## Privatisation & Reform

In the 1990s, Mongolia chose a unique path to privatisation. All state-owned enterprises, with a few notable exceptions, were nominally given away. Blue vouchers worth T10,000 were issued to every Mongolian citizen. In reality no-one had money to buy up the vouchers, so enterprises issued shares in exchange for vouchers, and suddenly former managers became owners. The same communist bureaucrats continue to run these 'privatised' companies with the same inefficiency as before. For a while no-one was fired, and workers continued to get paid even though they didn't work, but eventually the biggest of enterprises collapsed.

The government has retained at least 50% ownership of crucial industries, such as the telephone company, railways, MIAT airlines, mines, the carpet factory in Erdenet, power stations, cashmere exports, dollar shops and so on. Most of these industries earn lots of hard currency; the government is keeping the plums for itself.

## Foreign Assistance

The possibility of total economic collapse has been largely averted. From 1990 to 1994, Mongolia was granted more than a total of US$765 million in aid from Western Europe, South Korea, Japan and the USA; plus soft loans from the International Monetary Fund,

World Bank and Asian Development Bank, among others; and technical assistance.

The Mongolians hoped western aid would simply replace the Soviet subsidies; western powers initially hoped the aid would be a temporary measure to help Mongolia through a difficult stage on the road to a market economy. So far, the market economy hasn't fully emerged and requests for foreign aid have increased.

In 1995 Mongolia received loans of US$210 million, which one day will have to be repaid. The major investors from 1990 to 1996 were the USA (39%), Japan (12%), Russia (12%) and China (10%).

The government has overcome its reluctance to approve joint ventures that allow foreigners to own anything in Mongolia, but few of the 400 ventures on paper have materialised. Mongolia's law on foreign investment, starting from 1993, explicitly encourages foreign investment and protects the right of investors to repatriate their profits, set up joint ventures, buy shares in Mongolian enterprises or create a wholly foreign-owned business. The law awards tax holidays to mining companies for five years, with halved tax payments for a further five years.

### Tourism

The collapse of the Soviet-subsidised economy has forced Mongolians to take a second look at tourism. The country desperately needs the hard currency which foreign tourism could bring but, unfortunately, some of the old communist attitudes still prevail – such as the Draconian visa regulations which continue to actively discourage tourism. Prices asked by foreign and Mongolian-based travel agencies for organised tours are getting higher and becoming prohibitive.

In addition, because of its isolation, transport difficulties and short summers, Mongolia managed to attract only 34,000 foreigners (excluding Chinese and Russians) in 1995. Half of these were tourists, mainly on organised tours from Japan, South Korea, the USA and Germany.

Mongolian tourist authorities are yet to work out the financial importance of inde-pendent travellers. Most people on organised tours stay a short time and buy an all-inclusive tour in their home country; they contribute very little to the Mongolian economy but plenty to the coffers of a handful of influential Mongolian travel companies. Independent travellers, who invariably stay longer than those on organised tours, may spend less per day, but *everything* they spend stays in the local economy.

**Responsible Tourism** To ensure that independent travellers are encouraged by Mongolian authorities and accepted by the nomadic people, two vital factors should be taken into account.

Firstly, hospitality is an old custom on the steppes, where distances are great; visitors are always taken in without question on arrival at a distant *ger* (nomadic tent). While you should enjoy Mongolia's unique hospitality, please do not take advantage of it. We continue to hear disturbing reports about travellers staying for weeks or months in gers around the country and not contributing to their upkeep or paying (in money or kind) for their accommodation or food.

Secondly, as explained elsewhere in this chapter, Mongolia's environment, flora and fauna are precious. Decades of Soviet exploitation, urban sprawl and development have greatly affected the ecology; Mongolia does not need the detriments of tourism to exacerbate the problems. If you are travelling independently in the countryside, please bear in mind the considerable impact that the thoughtless deeds of one person can have on a forest, grassland, water supply, fossils site, mountain or desert.

### POPULATION

In 1918, when the population was 648,100 and the density was 0.41 person per sq km, Mongolia faced a precarious future. The population has increased to about 2.3 million, but this still only represents 1.4 persons per sq km.

Inspired by classic Mongolian nationalism, the government actively promoted population growth, which now stands at 2.58%

Some Population Statistics (1995)
Population Growth: 2.58%
Percentage under 14 Years: 40%
Percentage over 65 Years: 4%
Birth Rate: 3.26%
Death Rate: 0.6%
Infant Death Rate: 4.18% (in 1992)
Life Expectancy: males, 64 years; females, 69 years
Fertility Rate: 4.5 children per woman ■

annually – the highest in North-East Asia and one of the highest in the world. Until recently, Mongolians were offered all sorts of incentives and subsidies to reproduce. Women who produced five children were awarded the Order of Glorious Motherhood Second Class, and those with eight got the Order of Glorious Motherhood First Class. Couples with many children received cash awards, whereas those who remained childless were penalised with higher taxes. The distribution of contraceptives and abortion were made illegal.

The pastoral economy could not sustain a large population increase without greater competition for grazing land and damage to the environment. Some of Mongolia's rapidly growing workforce was exported to Siberia, where labourers were badly needed, but the majority wound up in the cities. The government actively encouraged migration to urban areas in the belief that this would increase industrialisation and productivity. However, these days there is a severe labour shortage in agriculture. (Half the population still lives in a handful of urban centres.)

In the early 1990s the government was unable to meet the needs of urban Mongolians, and many returned to relatives in the countryside. Nutrition dropped to bare survival level, even for soldiers, and child deaths rose sharply.

Families are now being encouraged to take up farming again. The punitive taxes for remaining childless have been removed, and there are no longer any prizes for prolific reproduction. The international aid agencies promote family planning, but Mongolians, aware of how outnumbered they are on all sides, are reluctant to curb family size.

Couples can now have as many or as few children as they wish. The only means of birth control available to some Mongolians today (but very rarely in the countryside) are condoms and abortion, both of which were prohibited under communism.

PEOPLE
More Mongolians live outside of Mongolia than in it – about 3½ million in China and nearly a million in Russia. Even along the Caspian Sea, thousands of km from Mongolia, there are descendants of Mongolian armies. Those armies impressed Europe with Mongol unity, but throughout history nomads have usually preferred to go their own way, scattered across a huge land, with their primary loyalty being to their tribe.

The great majority (about 86%) of Mongolians are Khalkh Mongols. The other major ethnic group, the Kazaks, make up about 6% (130,000) of the population. Most Kazaks live in western Mongolia, mainly in Bayan-Ölgii aimag, but their numbers are decreasing as more and more return to Kazakstan.

The other major ethnic groups are:

Barga – originally from the Lake Baikal region of Siberia, they number about 2000 and live in remote pockets of Dornod and Töv.
Bayad – once a powerful race; about 40,000 live in Uvs.
Buryat – also found in Siberia, they number about 47,500 and congregate in the northern provinces of Bulgan, Dornod, Khentii and Selenge.
Dariganga – about 32,300 live in southern Sükhbaatar.
Darkhad – descended from Turks; there are about 15,000 in Khövsgöl.
Khoton – of Turkish descent; about 6000 live in Uvs.
Myangad – also of Turkish descent; about 5000 live in Khovd.
Oold – about 11,400 live in Khovd and Arkhangai.
Torguud – about 10,500 live in Khovd.
Tsaatan – also known as the 'reindeer people', they are perhaps the smallest ethic group; only about 200 live in northern Khövsgöl.
Uriankhai – about 21,000 live in the Mongol Altai Nuruu mountains in Khovd and Bayan-Ölgii.
Uzemchin – only about 2000 live in Dornod and Sükhbaatar.
Zakhchin – about 24,700 live in Khovd.

## Nomads

Ethnographers divide Mongolia's population according to their ethnicity, but all Mongolians have one thing in common: they are nomads, or nomads at heart, even if they are urbanised. About half of the 2.3 million people live in gers, and 390,000 herdsmen look after nearly 30 million livestock. They are truly nomadic, moving their gers and animals several times a year, constantly searching for better feed, water and weather.

The life of a nomad, and therefore Mongolia, is inextricably linked to the environment and animals. Nomads learn to ride as soon as they can walk; they spend about half their time looking for stray animals (there are almost no fences in Mongolia), carrying a type of lasso pole called an *uurga*. Mongolia's paintings, music and literature are dominated by the beauty of the landscape and animals, and the isolation of the countryside. Urban Mongolians love to go to the countryside during their holidays and often dream of retiring to a ger on the steppes.

While you are travelling around the countryside for a week or two in summer, you may think the simple nomadic lifestyle is ideal, but the long winters are desperately harsh, the food is unchanging, and looking after animals, preparing food and finding water is very hard work.

The communists failed to conquer the nomads with collectivism but, ironically, capitalism may threaten the nomadic lifestyle through strict regulations, consumerism (26,000 nomadic families own motorbikes and 16,000 have TVs), private ownership of land, urbanisation and unequal distribution of wealth (69% of nomads own less than 100 livestock head). ■

Before 1990, Russians constituted about 1.5% of Mongolia's population. Very few remain, as the rouble has sunk even faster than the Mongolian currency, the *tögrög*, and trade has withered. Except for some Mongolians who'd been educated in the USSR at Soviet expense, most Mongolians resented the Russians' colonial arrogance. Mongolian drunks have beaten and stoned Russians in the streets.

## EDUCATION

Until the start of communism, education was entirely provided by the hundreds of monasteries which once dotted the landscape. Since 1921, modern Mongolian education has been a reflection of its Russian roots.

On the one hand, elementary education is universal and free, with the result that Mongolia boasts a literacy rate of between 80% and 90%. Mongolians receive 11 years of education, from ages seven to 18. In remote rural areas where there are no schools, children are often brought to the aimag capitals to stay in boarding schools, returning home only for a two week rest during winter and a three month holiday in summer.

On the other hand, educational standards are low and technical skills poor. Under the centrally planned economic system, the goal of most young Mongolians was to get a diploma and, therefore, a job as an office worker or bureaucrat – everyone received about the same pay regardless of merit, whereas bureaucrats often gained extra privileges without doing extra work. The new, noncommunist government has not had time yet to concentrate too much on the reorganisation of the education system.

The Mongolian State University (originally named Choibalsan University in honour of Mongolia's most bloodstained ruler) was opened in 1942. Since then, private universities, teaching everything from computing to traditional medicine, have sprung up: the country currently has 29 state and 40 private universities, mostly in Ulaan Baatar.

Sadly, the high number of institutions does not result in quality education: tertiary students realise they will have to study abroad to gain a worthwhile, internationally accepted qualification. Corruption among low-paid teachers is reportedly rife; students can virtually 'buy' good marks at some universities.

Monastic schools have reopened, but 70 odd years of repression has left Mongolia without qualified Buddhist teachers. The priority, with some quiet help from the Dalai Lama, is to train teachers.

## ARTS

From prehistoric oral epics to the latest movie from MongolKino, the many arts of Mongolia convey the flavour of nomadic life. Watching dancers in a ger or a professional ensemble on the stage of a theatre in Ulaan Baatar is a reminder that Mongolia has evolved traditional and unique songs, music, dances, costumes, painting styles, sculptures, plays, films, crafts, carpets and textiles.

One surprise about Ulaan Baatar is the number, and quality, of cultural shows in the various theatres. The buildings themselves – from the salmon-pink walls with Greek columns of the opera and dance theatres to the bold copper Mongolian roof of the Palace of Culture – express the hybrid culture Mongolia has forged from all sides.

Most Mongolians may be unable to afford to see their own circus and dance and opera troupes, but a major cultural renaissance is under way, as Mongolians rediscover what the Soviets had repressed.

If you want more information about the arts in Mongolia, contact the Mongolian Green Horse Society (☎ 320 054; PO Box 128, Central Post Office, Ulaan Baatar), which is linked to other Green Horse Societies in Europe.

### Music

**Modern** Young Mongolians in Ulaan Baatar can now watch videos of western music on satellite TV, but they also enjoy listening to local groups, which sing in the Mongolian language but have definite western influences. These include the soul vocal group, Camerton; the heavy metal rockers, Niciton; and the sweet sounds of the popular female vocalist, Saraa. In summer, especially around Naadam, they often perform at the Palace of Culture. Most souvenir stores sell cassettes and compact discs of these, and other, Mongolian musicians.

**Traditional** Get an urbanised Mongolian into the countryside, and he or she will probably

---

### Tsam Dances

Like other Buddhist countries, religion dominates a lot of Mongolia's traditional dances. Except during the communist reign, the most common dance was the *tsam* mask dance. Performed to exorcise evil spirits, tsam dances in Mongolia are theatrical and influenced by Mongolian nomadic folklore and Shamanism.

Tsam was introduced into Mongolia in the 8th century from India, via Tibet. It was first performed at the Erdene Zuu monastery (where many tsam masks are on display). A few hundred years ago, an estimated 500 of the 700 monasteries in the country had their own versions of masks and dances. The biggest tsam dances – mainly the *Mil Bogdo* and *Geser* – were usually held on the ninth day of the last month of summer.

The masks are usually made from papier-mâché and often implanted with precious stones. Some of the more common masks represent the terrifying Begdze-Darmapala, a defender of Buddhism; Lash-Khan, the patron of art (they're round and jolly); and the White Old Man.

Tsam dances, which were suppressed during communism, are very rarely held but will probably make a comeback. You can see some of the tsam masks which survived the Stalinist purges at the Monastery-Museum of Choijin Lama in Ulaan Baatar and at Erdene Zuu. ■

A Begdze-Darmapala mask

PAUL GREENWAY

PAUL GREENWAY

PAUL GREENWAY

PAUL GREENWAY

Top: Children at a roadside ger in Övörkhangai.
Middle Left: Archery judges raise their arms and utter a traditional cry evaluating the shot.
Bottom Left: Spectators at Naadam wearing *loovuzes*, traditional Mongolian hats.
Bottom Right: A musician at Naadam playing the *morin khuur*, a horse-head fiddle.

PAUL GREENWAY

PAUL GREENWAY

PAUL GREENWAY

PAUL GREENWAY

Top: Some of the 367,000 camels in Mongolia.
Middle Left: Yaks are especially useful for uphill transport, though these aren't going far.
Middle Right: Goats and sheep provide wool as well as meat.
Bottom: Mongolian horses provide perfect transport and can endure harsh winters.

sing and tell you it is the beauty of the countryside which created the song on their lips. Mongolians sing to their animals: lullabies to coax sheep to suckle their lambs and songs to order a horse forward, make it stop or come close, control a goat, milk a cow or imitate a camel's cry. Often the beauty and isolation of the land, yearning for the beloved nomadic lifestyles and pride in the nation are all exquisitely expressed in one image.

Traditional music involves a wide range of instruments and uses for the human voice found almost nowhere else. The *khoomi* singing of Mongolia, in which carefully trained male voices produce a whole harmonic from deep in the throat, gives the impression of several notes coming at once from one mouth. It is often sung solo, but when combined with fiddles, lutes, zithers, drums and other python-skin, bamboo, metal, stone and clay instruments, one begins to understand the centrality of music in Mongolian life.

Another unique traditional singing style is called *urtyn-duu*. Sometimes referred to as 'long songs' because, well, they are long (some famous singers have memorised epics with up to 20,000 verses), they are also called 'drawling songs'. With possible ancient Chinese influences, urtyn-duu involves extraordinarily complicated, drawn-out vocal sounds which relate traditional stories about love and the countryside. As the legend goes, urtyn-duu sounds best while galloping on a horse along the steppe.

In some traditional Mongolian music, the small drum *(zo)* and large drum *(damar)* are used; percussion and brass instruments are rarely used. The main instruments, played alone or accompanying singers, are the horse-head violin or fiddle *(morin khuur)* and the lute *(tovshuur)*.

Music is often played at weddings and other traditional and religious gatherings. If you cannot attend any traditional ceremonies, make sure not to miss a performance of Mongolia's traditional music while in Ulaan Baatar. Several souvenir shops in UB, including the State Department Store, sell recordings of traditional music.

## Morin Khuur

The instrument most identified with Mongolia is arguably the horse-head fiddle, known as the *morin khuur*. It has two strings, made from horse hair, with the distinctive and decorative carving of a horse's head on top. According to legends, the sound of the morin khuur is similar to that of the animals reared by nomads – the cow, sheep, camel and horse.

Traditionally, the morin khuur often accompanies the unique long songs which regale the beauty of the countryside and relive tales of nomadism. You can hear the morin khuur at ceremonies during the Naadam Festival in Ulaan Baatar, or at a performance of traditional music and dance in the capital city. ■

## Literature

The heroic epics of the Mongols – historic texts of war and feuding, myths of origin, administrative manuals of empire, diplomatic histories of hordes and dynasties and biographies of great khaans – were all first committed to writing over 750 years ago. Later, Mongolia developed an enormous Buddhist literature, with thousands of subtle treatises on meditation, philosophy and the meaning of life, including the 108 volume *Kanjur*, and *Sandui Djud*, a 10 volume collection of sutras (Buddhist sayings) decorated with an estimated 50kg of gold and 400kg of silver. These are now on display at the State Central Library in Ulaan Baatar.

Despite a variety of scripts, Mongolia has produced a huge literature, almost none of

## 'My Native Land'

Mongolia's most respected poet, playwright and author is D Natsagdorj (1906-1937). His most famous poem, 'My Native Land', perfectly sums up the beauty of the Mongolian countryside. Here are three of the 12 verses.

The crystal rivers of sacred Kherlen, Onon and Tuul,
Brooks, streams and springs that bring health to all my people,
The blue lakes of Khövsgöl, Uvs and Buir – deep and wide,
Rivers and lakes where people and cattle quench their thirst;
This, this is my native land,
The lovely country – my Mongolia.

The land of pure grasses waving in the breeze,
The land of open planning full of fantastic mirages,
Firm rocks and out-of-reach places where good men used to meet,
And the ancient ovoos – the standing stones to gods and ancestors;
This, this is my native land,
The lovely country – my Mongolia.

Land where in winter all is covered with snow and ice,
And the grasses twinkle like glass and crystal,
Land where in summer all is carpet of flowers,
And full of songbirds from the distant lands to the south;
This, this is my native land,
The lovely country – my Mongolia.

which is known to speakers of European languages. Only recently have scholars translated into English the most important text of all – *Mongol-un Nigucha Tobchiyan*, or 'The Secret History of the Mongols' – which celebrates Mongolia's days of greatness on the world stage. The date of the work is known (1240), but so far the author remains a mystery.

### Painting & Sculpture

In Ulaan Baatar, and the very occasional aimag museum, you can see some excellent displays of modern and traditional art, though, tragically, many earlier examples were destroyed during the communist regime. The Mongolian Art Gallery mostly contains 20th century paintings, with a strong leaning towards social realism and heroic poses. The Museum of Fine Arts features the deities who first subdued the warrior khaans, and the sublime bronzes of Mongolia's most famous Buddhist and sculptor, Zanabazar.

**Traditional** Mongolia's most renown painter was Balduugiyn Sharav (1869-1920s). He spent his childhood in a monastery and later travelled all around the country. His most famous painting is *One Day in Mongolia*, which you can see in the Museum of Fine Arts. It is classic *zurag* (landscape storytelling), crowded with intricate sketches depicting just about every aspect of the Mongolian life. Mongolians can stand in front of it and spin yarns for hours.

Zanabazar was a revered sculptor, politician, teacher of meditation and diplomat. Many Mongolians refer to the time of Zanabazar's life as Mongolia's Renaissance period. His most enduring legacy is the sensuous statues of the incarnation of compassion, the deity Tara. Some of his bronze sculptures and paintings can be seen today in Ulaan Baatar's Gandan monastery, the Museum of Fine Arts and the Winter Palace.

**Scroll Painting** Religious scroll paintings (*thangka*), many by Zanabazar, can be viewed in museums. These once graced the inner sanctuaries and chanting halls of monasteries all over the country, and some survived communist persecution and have been recovered from the sands of the Gobi and other hiding places. They are tools of meditation, used by practitioners to visualise themselves developing the enlightened qualities of the deities depicted.

Thangkas can be found once again in many homes, now that there are no more bans on family altars. The most popular deity is White Tara, the incarnation of compassion; paintings of her are readily available in art shops and on the streets. If you do buy Mongolian art of any sort, make sure it's not old. Customs authorities are zealous in preventing the export of an artistic heritage which has already lost so much.

The Mongol-Korean Buddhist Institute of Culture at the Gandan monastery in Ulaan Baatar plans to start Buddhist and thangka-painting classes, which foreigners are welcome to attend. At the time of research, no further details were available, but if you are interested, contact the Buddhist University (☎ & fax 363 831) at the Gandan monastery.

## SOCIETY & CONDUCT
### Traditional Culture

The Mongolian way of life is laid-back, patient, tolerant of hardship and intimately connected with the ways of animals. Despite urbanisation, the traditions of the steppes live on. In the cities, many Mongolians continue to live, by preference, in a ger, snug inside their canvas and felt tent against the bitter winds from Siberia. In summer, city folk head for the hills to gather wild berries and pine cones, enjoying the open spaces. Whenever possible, apartment dwellers arrange with relatives in the country to get a big churn of airag sent to town. Mongolians can drink a dozen or more litres of the sour, fizzy, mildly alcoholic liquid in a day.

On the steppes, the population is scattered more or less evenly over the available pasture, depending on the season, so neighbours are few but always present in the distance. There's always a rider on the horizon, and in the event of trouble – eg a bogged jeep – there's usually someone who can get a tractor to tow you out; though it would take some time.

### Gers

The large, white felt tent, known as a ger (pronounced 'gair') and seen all over Mongolia, is probably the most identifiable symbol of Mongolia. (The word *yurt* was introduced by the Russians. If you don't want to offend the nationalistic sensibilities of the Mongolians, use the word 'ger'.)

The outer and innermost material of the ger is usually canvas, with an insulating layer of felt sandwiched in between, all supported by a collapsible wooden frame. They appear flimsy, but gers hold up amazingly well to Mongolia's fierce winds. Ancient gers were more solidly built: when it was necessary to move them, they had to be placed on carts and pulled by horses. This proved very cumbersome, so the invention of collapsible models was a great advance in Mongolian technology.

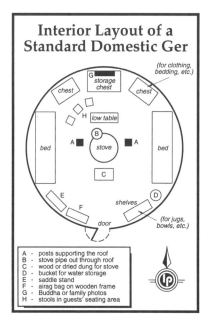

# Interior Layout of a Standard Domestic Ger

A - posts supporting the roof
B - stove pipe out through roof
C - wood or dried dung for stove
D - bucket for water storage
E - saddle stand
F - airag bag on wooden frame
G - Buddha or family photos
H - stools in guests' seating area

Most Mongolians still live in gers, even in the suburbs of Ulaan Baatar. It's not hard to understand why. Wood and bricks are scarce and expensive while out on the steppes, animal hides are cheap and readily available (canvas, imported from Russia, is now expensive). Mongolians remain nomadic: gers can be moved easily – depending on the size, a ger can be assembled in one to three hours.

Gers can be surprisingly comfortable. In urban areas, they may have electricity, but in rural regions candles or lamps supply the only artificial light. There is normally a stove in the centre of the ger which provides both heat and cooking facilities. In forested areas, firewood can be burned in the stove, but out on the steppes, the main fuel is dried dung. Without exception, toilets will be outside. If showers are available at all, which is very rare, they will normally be in some sort of public bathhouse (khaluun us – 'hot water') serving a whole group of gers. Lakes and rivers are the normal place to bathe.

**Ger Etiquette** It is bad manners to knock on the brightly decorated or painted doors of the ger. Instead, you should call out 'Nokhoi khor', which roughly translates as 'Can I come in?', but literally means as 'Hold the dog!'. To avoid being eaten alive by a vicious and highly protective (and, possibly, rabid) mongrel, learn how to say this properly.

The layout of a ger is universal throughout Mongolia. The door always faces south. Once across the threshold, men move left (to the west, under the protection of the great sky god, Tengger); women to the right (east, under the protection of the Sun). Towards the back, and a little to the west, is the place of honour set aside for guests, to which you will be politely ushered. There you will be seated, with the man of the ger beside you.

The back of the ger is the khoimor, the place for the elders, where the most honoured people are seated and treasured possessions are kept. On the back wall is the family altar, with Buddhist images once again publicly displayed, family photos

---

### Making a Ger

Nomadic people obviously have to be flexible and mobile. A ger is ideal: it is cheap to make or buy, collapsible, environmentally friendly, stable and adaptable. During winter, more felt layers are added. The small opening at the top, called a toono, which allows smoke to go out and air to come in, is covered with an örkh during rain.

The wooden poles are orange (the colour of the sun) and called uni; the walls are known as khana. Each ger has four to 12 khanas, each with about 10 to 15 unis. Depending on the mobility and wealth of the family, the ger is placed on a wooden, felt or bare earth floor. In western Mongolia, gers owned by Kazaks are often browner and larger, and almost always decorated inside with bright carpets and rugs.

The first part of the ger to be assembled is the floor. Next, the stove (zuukh) is placed in the centre of the ger. The khanas and doors (khaalga) – always brightly painted, and facing south – are erected; two columns (bagana) are connected to the toono; the unis are attached to the khanas; and then the ger is covered with felt (esgi) and weighed down against strong winds.

The average weight of a ger is about 250kg, without furniture. It can be placed on a cart and pulled by yaks, camels or horses. In early summer, you may see many nomadic families taking their gers, all their worldly goods and animals for several hundred km in search of better water, fodder or weather. ■

## Customs & Gers

Whenever you approach a nomadic family or enter a ger, you will, without knowing, break one or several of the many traditional, religious and superstitious customs. If you get confused, don't worry: many Mongolians (especially those in the cities) often forget or get confused, and minor indiscretions will be forgiven and tolerated.

One of the most important things to remember when you enter a ger is to be confident: don't smile sheepishly or look nervous. Feel at home, relax and don't worry if people come and go. Here are some of the more important rules to observe:

### Don't:
- lean against a support column.
- whistle inside a ger.
- stand on or lean over the threshold.
- stamp out a fire or put water or any rubbish on it; fire is sacred.
- walk in front of an older person.
- turn your back to the altar and religious objects at the back of the room (except when leaving).
- take food from a communal plate with your left hand.
- touch other people's hats.
- have a long conversation in your own language in front of hosts who do not understand it.

### Do:
- take at least a sip, or a nibble, of the delicacies offered.
- keep your sleeves rolled down, if you have any, or pretend to, if you have short sleeves; try not to expose your wrists.
- accept food and drink with your right hand (or with both if the dish or cup is heavy), with the left hand supporting the right elbow.
- pick up anything with an open hand, with your palm facing upwards.
- leave any weapons outside.

### Superstitions
- Don't write anything in a red pen.
- Don't point a knife in any way at anyone.
- Don't spill any milk (and don't cry about it).
- When offered some vodka, dip the ring finger of your right hand into the glass, and lightly flick a drop (not too much – vodka is also sacred!) once towards the sky, once in the air 'to the wind', and once to the ground. If you don't want any vodka, go through the customs anyway, put the same finger to your forehead, say thanks, and return the glass to the table.
- Don't point your feet at the hearth.
- Don't walk over an uurga (lasso pole).
- If you have stepped on anyone or kicked their feet, immediately shake their hand.

(mostly taken during very occasional visits to Ulaan Baatar) and some suitcases. Near the door, on the male side, are saddles and the big leather milk bag and churn to stir the brew of milky tea and airag. On the other (female) side of the door are the cooking implements and water buckets. Around the walls there are two or three low beds and cabinets; in the centre, a small table with several tiny chairs; and hanging in any vacant spot, toothbrushes, clothes, children's toys and plenty of tasty slabs of uncooked mutton.

Most gers will have a hospitality plate, usually an aluminium bowl, piled with offerings, ready for any passer-by who drops in. You will almost certainly be offered some dairy products, especially in summer, such as dried cheese, as well as a bowl of milky and salty Mongolian tea, or sometimes a vodka. You should always take what is offered – try not to refuse anything. If you don't like what you have been given, take a small sip or bite – or pretend to if it greatly upsets you – and leave the rest on the table. If you finish anything, the plate or bowl will be filled up. In a Kazak ger, placing a hand over the plate or bowl simply indicates that you do not want a refill.

An older man may offer his snuffbox to a male visitor, even if you don't have one to exchange. If you want some snuff (powdered tobacco), empty a tiny portion on your hand, between your (downward-facing) first finger and thumb. Raise your hand to a nostril, take a long, deep inhalation and smile widely. If you don't want any snuff, just go through the motions anyway, but don't inhale. If the snuffbox is empty, don't make any comment (he has run out of snuff, or can't afford any) – pretend there is some.

### Traditional Dress

Many young Mongolians in Ulaan Baatar wear western-style clothes, but at traditional gatherings, and for just about anyone who lives in the countryside, there is a distinct, simple and common type of traditional clothing. The main garment is the *del*, a long, one-piece gown made from wool. The del has a high collar, is often brightly coloured, comes with a multipurpose sash, and is worn

A woman in traditional Mongolian dress

by men and women all year. Many Mongolians, but not untrained westerners, can differentiate ethnic groups from the colour and shape of their del.

The *gutul* is the high boot made from thick leather. They are easy to fit on – both the left and right boot are the same shape. The reasons for the curled, upturned toe are varied, but are more likely to be religious – possibly to avoid disturbing the loose earth in accordance with Tibetan Buddhist teachings. Many Mongolian men prefer, however, to wear the almost-indestructible Russian army boots.

To top this off, men often wear the Mongolian hat known as a *loovuz*. Usually made from wolf or fox skins, they are particularly useful for protection against the howling winter winds. Other traditional hats such as the decorative *toortsog* and the *khilen malgai* are rarely worn.

Most museums in Ulaan Baatar and the aimag capitals have displays of traditional clothing. The best collection is on the 2nd floor of the National Museum of Mongolian History in Ulaan Baatar.

A Mongolian man in a *del*, *loovuz* and *gutuls*

## Traditional Medicine

Based on Indian, Tibetan and Chinese teachings, and heavily influenced by Buddhism, traditional medicine was first introduced into Mongolia by the revered (and unpronounceable) Luvsandanzanjantsan in the late 17th century – but was suppressed during communist domination from 1921 to 1990.

Diagnosis and treatment are based on the five vital elements of earth, water, fire, wind and wood. Medicines are often made from herbs, plants, mineral water and organs from unfortunate animals, and administered according to the weather, season and individual's metabolism. Acupuncture, massage and blood-letting, as well as prayers, are also important factors.

With the lifting of prohibitions against religion, and several highly publicised and successful treatments of Mongolians whose illnesses could not be cured by western medicine, traditional practices are popular once more. Forty-five hospitals and monasteries, including the Geser temple and Gandan monastery in Ulaan Baatar, contain trained, registered doctors of traditional medicine.

For more information, a consultation, medicine or courses, contact the Manba Datsan (☎ 23 658) at the Otochmaaramba Khiid monastery, PO Box 918, Ulaan Baatar 23. The training courses are strictly for the serious student: there is a long waiting list, and courses last five years and are taught in the Tibetan and Mongolian languages.

## Traditions & Symbols

**Zolgokh** *Zolgokh* is a traditional greeting, rather like shaking hands in the west, usually reserved for *Tsagaan Sar* (lunar new year). The younger person places his or her forearms under those of the elder to gently support the arms of the elder person. It is always important to show respect to anyone who is elderly and if you're under 20 years old, to anyone older.

### Mongolian Calendar

Mongolians use a lunar calendar to celebrate traditional holidays like the new year and have adopted the Chinese zodiac with its 12 animal signs.

If you want to know your sign in the zodiac, look up your year of birth in the chart below. The new year usually falls in late January or early February, so if you were born during this time your zodiac sign would be in the preceding year.

| Snake | 1917 | 1929 | 1941 | 1953 | 1965 | 1977 | 1989 |
|---|---|---|---|---|---|---|---|
| Horse | 1918 | 1930 | 1942 | 1954 | 1966 | 1978 | 1990 |
| Sheep | 1919 | 1931 | 1943 | 1955 | 1967 | 1979 | 1991 |
| Monkey | 1920 | 1932 | 1944 | 1956 | 1968 | 1980 | 1992 |
| Rooster | 1921 | 1933 | 1945 | 1957 | 1969 | 1981 | 1993 |
| Dog | 1922 | 1934 | 1946 | 1958 | 1970 | 1982 | 1994 |
| Pig | 1923 | 1935 | 1947 | 1959 | 1971 | 1983 | 1995 |
| Rat | 1924 | 1936 | 1948 | 1960 | 1972 | 1984 | 1996 |
| Ox/Cow | 1925 | 1937 | 1949 | 1961 | 1973 | 1985 | 1997 |
| Tiger | 1926 | 1938 | 1950 | 1962 | 1974 | 1986 | 1998 |
| Rabbit | 1927 | 1939 | 1951 | 1963 | 1975 | 1987 | 1999 |
| Dragon | 1928 | 1940 | 1952 | 1964 | 1976 | 1988 | 2000 |

Nomads divide winter into periods of time in multiples of nine – the lucky number for Buddhists. The winter is 81 days long (nine lots of nine). At the start of winter, the first nine days are named the 'Lambs Must Be Covered'; the weather starts to improve when it is 'Not Cold Enough to Freeze Soup'; and the oncoming spring 'Brings Back Life to Normal'.

At the end of the 81 days the Tsagaan Sar, or 'White Month', is widely celebrated at the start of the lunar new year. Names of some of the other seasons are 'Dairy Goods Are Plentiful' and 'The Animals Cast Off Their Hair'. ■

**Family Book** Traditionally, every Mongolian family kept a book – a record of births, deaths and important events. For early historians, these family books must have been a gold mine of information. Sadly, after the 1921 revolution, the communists denounced this practice as a link with the feudal past and most of the family books were destroyed or hidden.

One of the reasons for these books was to prevent inbreeding– relatives had to be separated by at least seven generations before it was possible to marry within the family.

**Soyombo** The Soyombo, the national symbol of Mongolia which dates back at least to the 14th century, signifies freedom and independence. It is found on the covers of Mongolian passports and on the flag.

Explanations of the complicated symbolism have changed and become lost over time. From top to bottom, the shapes are most likely to represent the following: the flame symbolises the past, present and future of the country; the sun and moon are obvious; the upside-down triangles are spears indicating victory; the two horizontal, small rectangles symbolise honesty and integrity; the interlocking symbols in the middle represent fire, water, earth and sky; and the two large, vertical rectangles stand for friendship. The communist star at the top has virtually disappeared.

### Dos & Don'ts

Besides the complicated set of dos and don'ts to observe when entering a ger and interacting with a nomadic family (see the Customs & Gers boxed aside), there are several others to remember. Hats are crucial to your survival, but it's rude to wear them indoors, especially in a temple, a ger or somebody's office. When visiting people, you should also take your coat off, particularly when sitting, eating or drinking tea.

When mounting a horse or camel, never do so from the right side. The animals have been trained to accept human approach from the left, and may rear if approached the wrong way. (It seems that when you get into a car, it's the opposite – you enter from the right-hand side. Usually you won't have much choice: the left-hand doors will probably be locked and the handles removed.)

Mongolians are normally disturbed by any talk or suggestion of death, divorce, accidents and the like. Any such talk is considered an ill omen and will be taken seriously, even if it was meant as a joke. For example, when flying MIAT, don't say something like 'I hope the wings don't fall off'. Even if the aircraft does have bald tyres and an overloaded cargo hold, Mongolian passengers will not appreciate the suggestion. As the Mongolians say: 'If you are afraid, don't do it. If you do it, don't be afraid'.

### Gifts

If it's late, you may be invited to stay the night. Some travellers feel they should pay for this, but unless money is asked for, it

The Soyombo is an old ideogram symbolising the Mongols' freedom and independence.

would be insulting to offer your host a cash payment. Hospitality is the rule of the steppes.

However, small gifts are always appreciated, especially items in short supply, in return for food and accommodation. It's far better to provide worthwhile gifts for the whole family, including the women (who look after the guests), rather than just for the men. Cigarettes and vodka are appreciated by men, but are harmful and rarely enjoyed by women. Similarly, sweets for young children aren't going to do their teeth any good.

Some useful gifts are small packets of soap and shampoo, needles (with large eyes) and thread for women; riding, hunting and fishing equipment for men; stickers, postcards, ribbons, pens and paper for children; pictures of the Dalai Lama, batteries, candles, scissors, biscuits, fruit, rice and pasta for the whole family. Don't offer any tinned goods, because they may not have a tin opener, and they certainly won't have any suitable means of disposing of the can. Make sure the gifts are small, otherwise there are greater expectations from future visitors. To show respect, and to avoid any arguments, you should give all gifts to the oldest man; he will distribute them accordingly.

If you've got nothing to spare, at least offer to photograph your host's family and send the photos to them later. Be sure to get their address and, please, keep your promise. Even if your host is dirt poor, you may be offered a small sum of cash when you get ready to depart. Rather than refuse, which would be insulting, accept the money. Then a few minutes later, offer a gift of money to the children. Hand this directly to the children, not to the adults. This saves face, since you are not acknowledging that the adults need the money.

## RELIGION
### Buddhism

Mongolians have always taken Buddhism of the Tibetan (Lamaist) variety wholeheartedly. Their minds were tamed by Tibetan lamas (monks) when the Mongolian empire was at its height and warriors were coming to grips with the complexities of controlling a multicultural empire.

Kublai Khaan found himself with a court in which all philosophies of his empire were represented. Teachers of Islam, Taoism, Nestorian Christianity, Manicheism, Confucianism and Buddhism all congregated at court, offering advice in managing state affairs. It was a Tibetan, Phagpa, who turned the mind of the great khaan. Only two generations after Chinggis Khaan, the imperial court took to Buddhism and was persuaded that the energies at the command of the lamas were greater than those of the warriors and their gods.

It took centuries before Buddhism really took hold. In the late 16th century Altan Khaan, a descendant of Chinggis Khaan, met the Dalai Lama Sonam Gyatso and converted. The Dalai Lama issued new laws forbidding the sacrificial slaughter of women, slaves and animals as funeral offerings. He ordered that an image of Gombo (Mahakala) be worshipped in every ger.

Reincarnate lamas were also born in Mongolia, the most prominent being the Jebtzun Damba of the Khalkh Mongols, who usually lived at Da Khüree, the monastic ger encampment which grew to become Ulaan Baatar. The first Jebtzun Damba reincarnation was the great Zanabazar, sculptor and energetic diplomat. He had to yield ultimate secular authority to the emperor of China in 1691 as the power of the Manchu Qing dynasty reached its zenith. Many of the Manchu emperors were themselves devout Tibetan Buddhists, and their patronage ensured Buddhism flourished throughout Mongolia, with many Mongolian reincarnate lamas regularly visiting Beijing to bless the emperor.

As Buddhism became the heartfelt faith of the masses, the Jebtzun Damba reincarnations never lost their dream of Mongolian independence, and as soon as Qing China collapsed in 1911, the eighth Jebtzun Damba declared Mongolia's independence. He wielded sacred and secular power, as did the Dalai Lama in Tibet.

## Important Figures of Tibetan Buddhism

The following is a brief guide to some of the gods and goddesses of the Tibetan Buddhist pantheon. It is neither exhaustive nor scholarly, but it may help you to recognise a few of the statues you encounter in the monasteries of Mongolia.

Avalokitesvara

Sakyamuni

Tara

**Padmasambhava** – the 'lotus-born' Buddha – assisted in establishing Buddhism in Tibet in the 8th century. He is regarded by followers of Nyingmapa Buddhism as the second Buddha. He is also known as Guru Rinpoche.

**Avalokitesvara** – 'glorious gentle one' – one of the three great saviours or Bodhisattvas. He is the Bodhisattva of compassion and is often pictured with 11 heads and several pairs of arms. His Tibetan name is Chenresig. The Dalai Lama is considered an incarnation of Avalokitesvara.

**Manjushri** – the 'princely lord of wisdom' – is regarded as the first divine teacher of Buddhist doctrine. He is also known as Jampel.

**Vajrapani** – 'thunderbolt in hand' – is one of the three great saviours or Bodhisattvas. He is also known as Channadorje. The thunderbolt represents indestructibility and is a fundamental symbol of Tantric faith.

**Sakyamuni** – the 'historical Buddha' – born in Lumbini in the 6th century BC in what is now southern Nepal, he attained enlightenment under a pipal (Bo) tree and his teachings set in motion the Buddhist faith. In Tibetan-style representations he is always pictured sitting cross-legged on a lotus flower throne.

**Maitreya** – the 'Buddha of the future'. He is passing the life of a Bodhisattva and will return to earth in human form 4000 years after the disappearance of Sakyamuni Buddha.

**Milarepa** – a great Tibetan magician and poet who is believed to have attained the supreme enlightenment of buddhahood in the course of one life. He lived in the 11th century and travelled extensively throughout the Himalayan border lands. Most images of Milarepa picture him smiling, holding his hand to his ear as he sings.

**Tara** – 'the saviouress' – has 21 different manifestations. She symbolises fertility and is believed to be able to fulfil wishes. Statues of Tara usually represent Green Tara, who is associated with night, or White Tara, who is associated with day.

**Gombo** – the wrathful-looking god wields the flaming sword which severs all attachment. He is a common sight in the inner sanctums of temples. The oldest monastery in Mongolia, Erdene Zuu, is dedicated to Gombo. ■

**The Purge** When the revolution of 1921 brought the communists to power, an uneasy peace existed between Mongolia's monasteries and the government. The communists realised that they were not strong enough to take on the revered religious establishment, which in 1921 numbered 110,000 lamas (including young boys), or one-third of the male population, who lived in about 700 monasteries. (Currently, there are about 1000 lamas in 30 monasteries.)

In 1924, when the eighth Jebtzun Damba died, the communist government prevented a successor from being found. (Mongolians believe that a ninth Jebtzun Damba reincarnated at a later date and is today a middle-aged lama living among exiled Tibetans, including the Dalai Lama, in Dharamsala, India. Refer to the Ulaan Baatar chapter for more details about the ninth Jebtzun Damba.) In 1929 some of the property and herds belonging to the monasteries were seized and redistributed. Arrests and executions came in 1932, but the government quickly backed off as rebellions broke out. However, harassment continued – young lamas were conscripted into the army and it was forbidden to build new monasteries.

Arrests of high-ranking lamas resumed in 1935. In 1937 the bloody purge began in earnest. Choibalsan's secret police descended on the monasteries. Young students were spared, but it is estimated that over 17,000 monks of middle and high rank were arrested, and virtually none was ever heard from again. Presumably they were either executed or died in Siberian labour camps. The monasteries were closed, ransacked and burned. Only four monasteries (out of more than 700) were preserved as museums of the 'feudal period' – but even these were damaged.

Besides ideology, the government had other reasons for wanting to eliminate the lamas. First of all, they didn't work, and the Russians were anxious to send Mongolian labourers to Siberia. Secondly, lamas were celibate and Mongolia's population was either stable or declining, which ran counter to the Marxist goals of 'more people, more

> **Mongolia & Tibet**
> The links between Mongolia and Tibet are old and deep. Once in a lifetime, every devout Buddhist Mongolian tries to reach the holy city of Lhasa on a pilgrimage, despite the hardship and distance. Mongolian Buddhists have translated hundreds of texts into Mongolian, and most of the Jebtzun Dambas were born in Tibet. The Tibetans in turn relied on various Mongolian tribes to sustain their power: when the British invaded Tibet in 1903, the Dalai Lama fled to Mongolia for safety and stayed there a few years. ■

production'. Thirdly, the communists believed – with some justification – that the monasteries were backward and opposed to modernisation. Finally, the monasteries were the centre of political and economic power in the country, and the government didn't appreciate the competition.

Except at Gandan monastery in Ulaan Baatar – which was kept as a showcase temple to impress foreigners – all religious worship and ceremonies remained outlawed until 1990. It was then that the democracy movement took hold and freedom of religion was restored. In the past few years, there has been a phenomenal revival of Buddhism (and other religions). This is most evident during the Dalai Lama's visits, when hundreds of thousands of people flock to be blessed. Monasteries have reopened, and even some ex-Communist Party officials have become lamas.

**Monasteries** Every visitor must try to visit at least one of the 'big three' monasteries *(khiid)*: the busy and popular Gandan-tegchinlen (or Gandan) Khiid in Ulaan Baatar, which also contains a Buddhist university; the magnificent Erdene Zuu Khiid, built on the ruins of the ancient capital of Karakorum at Kharkhorin in Övörkhangai aimag; and the remote Amarbayasgalant Khiid, near Darkhan, which is still being extensively renovated.

The best time to visit a monastery is in the morning (from about 9 to 11 am), when chanting and prayers are usually in progress.

You may enter a temple during chanting but must not step in front of the monks. Instead, go clockwise around the back. You can even go up to the altar, make a small cash offering, and then bow before the altar. You can also bow before the monks, and they will touch your head with their prayer books.

You should never take photos of anything or anyone inside a temple, but you can photograph the outside of temples and anything in the monastery grounds. Ask before snapping any lama. Most temples open at about 9 am and close around 3 pm, although the Gandan Khiid is open during daylight hours.

Monasteries and temples *(süm)* always have Tibetan names. After the communist purges, many religious artefacts were returned to the monasteries from their hiding places – though over time, many hiding places have been forgotten and artefacts lost for ever. Thangkas, statues, butter lamp candles, altar cloths and prayer wheels (which must be spun in a clockwise direction) decorate the monasteries and temples, but they are rarely as old as the ones in India, for example.

## Islam

In Mongolia today, there is a significant minority of Sunni Muslims, constituting as much as 5% of the total population. Most of them are ethnic Kazaks who live primarily in the far western aimag of Bayan-Ölgii (there is also a small Kazak community in and around Nalaikh, near Ulaan Baatar).

## Christianity

Nestorian Christianity was part of the Mongolian empire long before western missionaries arrived. These days, with poverty, unemployment, alcoholism, domestic violence and confusion in abundance, Christian missionaries, often from obscure fundamentalist sects, have been keenly seeking converts.

Mongolian authorities are wary of these missionaries, who sometimes come to the country under the pretext of teaching English. In Ulaan Baatar, there are now more than 30 non-Buddhist places of worship,

including a new US$1 million Catholic Mission Centre.

## Shamanism

Whether shamanism is actually a religion is open to debate (there is no divine being or book of teachings), but it is practiced by some Mongolians, mainly the Tsaatan, Darkhad, Uriankhai and Buryat in northern Mongolia.

Shamanism centres on the shaman, a 'doctor' and priest – known as a *boo* if male and *udgan* if female. People become shamans through heredity, or following a sudden and prolonged period of sickness and apparitions.

### Ovoos

A few minutes in the countryside is all that it takes to see your first *ovoo*. An ovoo is a pyramid-shaped collection of stones, wood and other rubbish, like vodka bottles and silk scarves, placed on top of a hill or mountain pass in a shamanistic traditional offering to the gods. They are often just a handful of rocks, but sometimes spectacular arrangements are made with the head of a moose or yak or wooden poles thrown in. Ovoos are sacred and all digging, hunting and logging nearby is strictly prohibited.

If travelling in a jeep, the driver will probably drive to the left of the ovoo, and often stop at important ones. Mongolians argue about what to do exactly when you come to an ovoo, but it normally involves walking around it clockwise up to three times, making an offering of anything (a rock, a broken vodka bottle, small amounts of money) and making a wish.

You may be lucky and see an ovoo worship ceremony. ■

The main purposes of a shaman is to cure illness caused by the soul straying from the body, accompany the soul of a dead person to the other world, and protect the clan and livestock from evil spirits. The major shamanist ceremony is the Great Sacrifice, often held on the third day of the lunar new year, when many animals are sacrificed to the gods.

Shamanism has coexisted comfortably with Buddhism. The most obvious example of its endurance is the abundance of *ovoos*, the piles of stone or wood which you see on top of most hills and mountain passes in the countryside. Museums contain examples of clothes and implements used in shamanism.

## LANGUAGE

The official national language is Mongolian, a member of the Ural-Altaic family of languages, which includes Finnish, Turkish, Kazak, Uzbek and Korean. Since 1944, the Russian Cyrillic alphabet has been used to write Mongolian. The only difference between Mongolian and Russian Cyrillic is that the Mongolian version has two additional characters, for a total of 35.

Mongolian can also be written in Romanised form, though the 35 Cyrillic characters give a better representation of Mongolian sounds than the paltry 26 of the Roman alphabet. Partly a result of Russian influence, different Romanisation schemes have been used, causing widespread confusion. A loose standard was adopted in 1987, so the capital city, previous written as Ulan Bator (Russian spelling), is now Ulaan Baatar.

One thing that confuses foreigners is the appearance of 'double vowels', such as the 'aa' in the word 'baatar'. This only indicates that the vowel is stressed. A tricky sound is the 'kh' in Romanised Mongolian. In the Cyrillic alphabet this character is written as x. This sound does not exist in modern English, though it survived in Old English and in Scottish English ('loch'). The Mongolian characters ө and ү are not found in Russian Cyrillic. Two Cyrillic characters, ъ and ь, are not pronounced by themselves but affect the pronunciation of the previous character – ъ makes the previous sound hard and ь makes the previous sound soft.

See Lonely Planet's *Mongolian phrasebook* for more information.

### Basics

Yes.
   *tiim*           Тийм.
No.
   *ügüi*          Үгүй.

Thanks.
   *bayarlaa/gyalailaa*
   Баярлалаа/Гялайлаа.
I'm sorry/Excuse me!
   *uuchlaarai!*
   Уучлаарай!

| | | | | | | | |
|---|---|---|---|---|---|---|---|
| Аа | *a* | | | Бб | *b* | Вв | *v* |
| Гг | *g* | | | Дд | *d* | Ее | *ye* |
| Ёё | *yo* | | | Жж | *j* | Зз | *z* |
| Ии | *i* | | | Йй | *i* | Кк | *k* |
| Лл | *l* | | | Мм | *m* | Нн | *n* |
| Оо | *o* | | | Өө | *ö* | Пп | *p* |
| Рр | *r* | | | Сс | *s* | Тт | *t* |
| Уу | *u* | | | Үү | *ü* | Фф | *f* |
| Хх | *kh* | | | Цц | *ts* | Чч | *ch* |
| Шш | *sh* | | | Щщ | *shch* | Ъъ | *(no sound)* |
| Ыы | *y* | | | Ьь | *i* | Зз | *e* |
| Юю | *yu* | | | Яя | *ya* | | |

Sorry? What (did you say)?
*yuu genee?*
Юу гэнээ?
Excuse me, sir/madam!
*khün guai!*
Хүн гуай!

### Greetings & Civilities
Hello.
*sain bainuu*
Сайн байна уу?
(literally, 'how are you?')
Fine. How are you?
*sain ta sain bainuu?*
Сайн. Та сайн байна уу?
Fine.
*sain bainaa*
Сайн байна аа.
What's new?
*sonin saikhan yuu bain?*
Сонин сайхан юу байна?
Nothing really.
*taivan bain*
Тайван байна.
(literally, 'It's peaceful.')
Goodbye.
*bayartai*
Баяртай.

If you are visiting a family, especially in the country, having agreed that everybody's fine, you should proceed to asking about family members and livestock and only then to more general matters:

How is your family?
*tanaikhan sainuu?*
Танайхан сайн уу?

I hope your animals are fattening up nicely?
*mal süreg targan tavtaiyuu?*
Мал сүрэг тарган тавтай юу?
Are you very busy?
*ta ikh zavgüi bainuu?*
Та их завгүй байна уу?
I'm very busy.
*ikh zavgüi bain*
Их завгүй байна.

### Small Talk
What's your name?
*tany ner khen be?*
Таны нэр хэн бэ?
My name is Bold.
*minii ner Bold*
Миний нэр Болд.
What country are you from?
*ta yamar ulsaas irsen be?*
Та ямар улсаас ирсэн бэ?
I'm from ...
*bi ... ulsaas irsen*
Би ... улсаас ирсэн.
How old are you?
*ta kheden nastai ve?*
Та хэдэн настай вэ?
I am ... years old.
*bi ... nastai*
Би ... настай.
Are you married?
*ta urgalsanuu?*
Та урагласан уу?
No, I'm not.
*ügüi, bi urgalaagüi*
Үгүй, би ураглаагүй.
Yes, I'm married.
*tiimee, bi urgalsan*
Тиймээ, би ураглсан.
Do you have any children?
*ta khüükhedteiyüü?*
Та хүүхэдтэй юу?

### Language Difficulties
Do you speak English?
*ta angilar yairdaguu?*
Та англиар ярьдаг уу?
Could you speak more slowly?
*ta jaal udaan yarinuu?*
Та жаал удаан ярина уу?
Please point to the phrase in the book.
*yariany nom deer zaaj ögööch*
Ярианы ном дээр зааж өгөөч.
I understand.
*bi oilgoj bain*
Би ойлгож байна.
I don't understand.
*bi oilgokhgüi bain*
Би ойлгохгүй байна.

## Getting Around

How can I get to ...?
*bi ... yaaj yavakh ve?*
Би ... яаж явах вэ?

How much is it to go to ...?
*... yavakhad yamar üntei ve?*
... явахад ямар үнэтэй вэ?

Where is the ... ?
*... khaan bain ve?*
... хаана байна вэ?

train station
*galt tergenii buudal*
Галт тэрэгний буудал

bus station
*avtobusny buudal*
Автобусны буудал

bus stop
*avtobusny zogsool*
Автобусны зогсоол

trolley-bus stop
*trolleibusny zogsool*
троллейбусны зогсоол

ticket office
*biletiin kass*
Билетийн касс

Is it far?
*kholuu?*
Хол уу?

Can I walk there?
*bi tiishee yavgan yavj bolokhuu?*
Би тийшээ явган явж болох уу?

What times does ... leave/arrive?
*kheden tsagt ... yavakh/irekh ve?*
Хэдэн цагт ... явах/ирэх вэ?

the bus
*avtobus*               автобус

the trolley-bus
*trolleibus*            троллейбус

the train
*galt tereg*            галт тэрэг

the plane
*nisekh ongots*         нисэх онгоц

Does this bus go to ...?
*en avtobus ... ruu yavdaguu?*
Энэ автобус ... руу явдагуу?

Which bus goes to ...?
*... ruu yamar avtobus yavdag ve?*
... руу ямар автобус явдаг вэ?

Can you tell me when we get to ...?
*ta nadad bid khezee ... deer
ochikhyg khelj ögööch?*
Та надад бид хэзээ ... дээр
очихыг хэлж өгөөч?

I want to get off!
*bi buumaar bain!*
Би буумаар байна!

Is this seat taken?
*en suudal khüntei yüü?*
Энэ суудал хүнтэй юү?

What is this station called?
*en buudlyg yuu gedeg ve?*
Энэ буудлыг юу гэдэг вэ?

What is the next station?
*daraagiin buudal yamar buudal ve?*
Дараагийн буудал ямар буудал вэ?

## Directions

What ... is this?
*en yamar ... ve?*
Энэ ямар ... вэ?

square
*talbai*                талбай

street
*gudamj*                гудамж

suburb
*düüreg*                дүүрэг

north
*khoid/umard*           хойд/умард

south
*urd/ömön*              урд/өмнө

east
*züün/doron*            зүүн/дорно

west
*baruun/örnöd*          баруун/өрнөд

behind/after
*khoin/ard*             хойно/ард

in front/before
*ömön*                  өмнө

to the left
*baruun tiish*          баруун тийш

to the right
*züün tiish*            зүүн тийш

straight ahead
*chigeeree*             чигээрээ

## Accommodation

Can you recommend a good hotel?
*saikhan neg zochid buudal zaaj
ögökhgüi yüü?*
Сайхан нэг зочид буудал зааж
өгөхгүй юу?

Can you show me on the map?
*ta nadad gazryn zurag deer
üzüülekhgüi yüü?*
Та надад газрын зураг дээр
үзүүлэхгүй юу?

Do you have any rooms available?
*tanaid sul öröö bainuu?*
Танайд сул өрөө байна уу?

I'd like a single room.
*bi neg khünii öröö avi*
Би нэг хүний өрөө авъя.

I'd like a double room.
*bi khoyor khünii öröö avi*
Би хоёр хүний өрөө авъя.

What's the price per night/week?
*khonogt/doloo khonogt yamar
üntei ve?*
Хоногт/долоо хоногт ямар
үнэтэй вэ?

Can I see the room?
*bi öröögöö üzej bolokhuu?*
Би өрөөгөө үзэж болох уу?

Are there any others?
*öör öröö bainuu?*
Өөр өрөө байна уу?

## Around Town

Where is the nearest ...?
*oirkhon ... khaan bain ve?*
ойрхон ... хаана байна вэ?

bank
*bank* банк

post office
*shuudangiin salbar* шуудангийн салбар

department store
*ikh delgüür* их дэлгүүр

hotel
*zochid buudal* зочид буудал

market
*zakh* зах

When will it open?
*khezee ongoikh ve?*
Хэзээ онгойх вэ?

When will it close?
*khezee khaakh ve?*
Хэзээ хаах вэ?

Where is the toilet?
*jorlong khaan baidag ve?*
Жорлон хаана байдаг вэ?

I'd like to change some money.
*bi möng solimoor bain*
Би мөнгө солимоор байна.

I would like to change some
travellers' cheques.
*bi juulchny chek solimoor bain*
Би жуулчны чек солимоор байна.

What is the exchange rate?
*solikh jansh yamar bain?*
Солих ханш ямар байна?

Do you have a map/town map?
*tanaid gazryn/khotyn zurag
bainuu?*
Танайд газрын/хотын зураг
байна уу?

Can I take photographs?
*bi zurag avch bolokhuu?*
Би зураг авч болох уу?

Can I take your photograph?
*bi tany zurgiig avch bolokhuu?*
Би таны зургийг авч болох уу?

## Signs

| | |
|---|---|
| ОРЦ | ENTRANCE |
| ГАРЦ | EXIT |
| ОРЖ БОЛОХГҮЙ | NO ENTRANCE |
| ГАРЧ БОЛОХГҮЙ | NO EXIT |
| ЭМЭГТЭЙН | LADIES |
| ЭРЭГТЭЙН | GENTLEMEN |
| ХАДГАЛСАН | RESERVED/ENGAGED |
| ХООСОН | VACANT |
| КАСС | CASHIER |
| ЛАВЛАГАА | INFORMATION |
| ШУУДАН | POST |
| ТАКСИ | TAXI |
| ХААСАН | CLOSED |
| БОЛГООМЖИЛ | CAUTION |
| ЗАСВАРТАЙ | UNDER REPAIR |
| ТАМХИ ТАТАЖ БОЛОХГҮЙ | NO SMOKING |
| ЗУРАГ АВЧ БОЛОХГҮЙ | NO PHOTOGRAPHY |

## The Herder's Home

We would like to see inside a
herder's yurt (felt tent).
*bid malchny gert orj üzmeer bain*
Бид малчны гэрт орж үзмээр
байна.

How long will it take to get there?
*tend khürekhed ailkher udakh ve?*
Тэнд хүрэхэд аль хэр удах вэ?

Can we walk?
*bid yavgan yavj bolokhuu?*
Бид явган явж болох уу?

Call off the dogs!
*nokhoigoo!*
Нохойгоо!

We'd like to drink some koumiss.
*bid airag umaar bain*
Бид айраг умаар байна.

| | |
|---|---|
| cooking pot | |
| *togoo* | тогоо |
| cowdung box | |
| *argalyn dörvölj* | аргалын дөрвөлж |
| felt material | |
| *esgii* | эсгий |
| felt roof cover | |
| *deever* | дээвэр |
| koumiss bag | |
| *khökhüür* | хөхүүр |
| skylight cover | |
| *örkh* | өрх |
| stove | |
| *zuukh* | зуух |
| wall section | |
| *khan* | хана |
| yurt | |
| *ger* | гэр |

## Livestock

| | |
|---|---|
| camel | |
| *temee* | тэмээ |
| chicken | |
| *takhia* | тахиа |
| cow | |
| *ünee* | үнээ |
| goat | |
| *yamaa* | ямаа |
| herding | |
| *mal aj akhui* | мал аж ахуй |
| horse | |
| *moir* | морь |
| pig | |
| *gakhai* | гахай |
| sheep | |
| *khoin* | хонь |
| yak | |
| *sarlag* | сарлаг |

## Health & Emergencies

| | |
|---|---|
| Help! | |
| *tuslaarai!* | Туслаарай! |
| Stop! | |
| *zogs!* | Зогс! |

Call a doctor!
*emch duudaarai!*
Эмч дуудаарай!

Call an ambulance!
*türgen tuslamj duudaarai!*
Түргэн тусламж дуудаарай!

Call the police!
*tsagdaa duudaarai!*
Цагдаа дуудаарай!

I am ill.
*bi övchtei bain*
Би өвчтэй байна.

Please take me to hospital.
*namaig emnelegt khürgej ögnüü?*
Намайг эмнэлэгт хүргэж өгнө үү?

Could you help me please?
*ta nadad neg tus bolooch?*
Та надад нэг тус болооч?

I'm sorry.
*uuchlaarai!*
Уучлаарай!

I didn't realise I was doing
something wrong.
*bi sanaandgüi muukhai yum khiilee*
Би санаандгүй муухай юм хийлээ.

# Facts for the Visitor

## PLANNING
### When to Go
The travel season is from May to early October, though Ulaan Baatar can be visited any time of year if you can tolerate the cold. From mid-October to mid-May, sudden snowstorms and extreme cold can ground flights, block roads and cause the transport system to break down completely.

June and September are both very pleasant times to visit. Early July gives you the best weather for the northern part of the country, though it will be hot in the Gobi – the best time to see the Gobi is September and October. July and August are the rainiest months, which can make jeep travel on dirt roads difficult. July is also the time to see the Naadam Festival. Unfortunately, this is the peak tourist season, when Ulaan Baatar's inadequate accommodation and creaky transport is stretched to breaking point

### What Kind of Trip?
This depends on your flexibility and intrepidity, available time and money. An organised tour gives you more comfort and less hassle, but it is inflexible, and you may not see what you really want. Travelling by public transport will limit your travel unless you are prepared to do some hitching also – but you will still need to hire a jeep to see most attractions.

Easily the best way is to arrive independently, in a group of three or more (to share costs), and stay for at least one month. Bring a tent, sleeping bag and petrol stove from home, hire a jeep with a driver and/or guide in a major city, and bring food from Ulaan Baatar. With this combination, you'll make the most of your trip.

### Maps
In 1978 President Tsedenbal decided to double the number of Mongolian place names overnight by giving the district *(sum)* capitals different names to the districts themselves. Most available maps are post-1978 and confusing. Slowly, the capitals and districts are reverting to the same name on some maps and in the minds of locals, but until that happens completely, we have used the name of the district capitals, and indicated the name of the district as well.

If you are on an organised tour (especially if it's combined with a trip to China), the following maps provide some details but are not good enough for independent travel: *China & Far East* (1:6,000,000) by Hallway, *China* (1:5,000,000) by Kümmerly & Frey and *China* (1:6,000,000) by Cartographia – the latter probably the best of the lot.

If you are travelling independently, the best country maps are available along the streets and at the main tourist spots in Ulaan Baatar (but nowhere in the countryside). To travel independently in the countryside, you will probably need to master some Mongolian Cyrillic. If you do, there are several good maps, but you may need one or more to get the whole picture. The best map for place names (ie district names) is the 1985 unnamed, pale map (1:3,000,000), identifiable by the two smaller, brightly coloured maps of Mongolia on the bottom.

The 1984 map (1:2,500,000) is helpful because the *aimags* (provinces) are coloured in pink, green, brown and yellow, and it includes a list of district capitals *and* districts (in Cyrillic). It is large and cumbersome, however, and roads are not detailed. The best overall (Cyrillic) road map is the one printed in 1984, identifiable by the table in the corner listing distances. This map includes district, rather than capital, names and, surprisingly, does not show aimag borders – but it's about the best for showing the roads.

If you are doing some serious independent travel in the countryside, the series of 1992 maps (1:1,000,000) of each aimag is very good. You may be lucky and find one in English, but generally they are in Cyrillic. Identifiable by their blue cover and the silhouette of the aimag on the front, they are the best maps for topographical features, roads and place names – but they also list the names of districts, not their capitals.

In many western countries, you can buy the ONC and TPC series of topographical maps published by the Defense Mapping Agency Aerospace Center in the USA. The maps are detailed, but dated, and do not include a lot of place names, and what looks like main roads are nothing more than jeep trails. ONC, and the more detailed TPC, maps are covered by map Nos E-7, E-8, F-7 and F-8.

In Ulaan Baatar, you can buy maps of the capital city, but you will need little, if anything, more than the map included in this guidebook. Refer to the Ulaan Baatar chapter for more details about maps of Ulaan Baatar, and where you can buy maps.

## What to Bring

Before deciding what to bring, think what you are going to carry it in. If you decide to base yourself in Ulaan Baatar and use buses or planes radiating from the capital to get to the provinces, then you can leave a lot of gear securely in the luggage room of your hotel or at the train station and take only what you need.

A backpack is still popular as it is convenient and the only choice if you have to do any walking. However, a backpack is awkward to load on and off buses and trains, and doesn't offer much protection against theft. Rather than the 'open top' design, a backpack with zipped compartments is best. You can close the zips with some small padlocks to make the bag more thief-proof.

The next big decision is whether to bring a sleeping bag. If you are on an organised tour during the summer, it is not necessary. A sleeping bag is vital, however, if you are travelling independently in the countryside on any form of transport (breakdowns are inevitable) or if you are in Mongolia between October and May (when heating in hotels often fails). So is a tent: camping in the countryside gives you far more flexibility

and is a worthy alternative to the lousy choice of hotels in the provinces.

A portable stove to cook your own food, rather than rely on the bland and tasteless stuff served in restaurants in the countryside, is definitely worth considering. Take a petrol stove because petrol is the only fuel widely available. For any other type of stove, you will have to bring your own fuel, which is often dangerous and illegal to carry on planes.

Basic toiletries are available in Ulaan Baatar and at most markets in provincial capitals, but the quality and choice will be inferior to what you may be used to. You may want to bring personal items from home, or buy up in Russia or China. Refer to the Food section later in this chapter to decide whether to bring along anything to supplement your meals. Warm clothes will be needed for any time of year: even summer evenings can be chilly. Most Mongolians dress informally but you should avoid wearing revealing clothes, even on hot summer days.

Refer to the Society & Conduct section in the Facts about the Country chapter for ideas about gifts to bring. In the city, some Mongolians are trying to learn English and appreciate foreign magazines, books or newspapers, especially if written simply.

The following is a comprehensive checklist of things to consider packing when travelling:

Passport, US dollars cash, money belt, address book, sleeping bag, space blanket, daypack, writing paper and envelopes, pens, sticky tape, business cards, spare passport photos, Swiss army knife, coffee, tea, sweetener, padlock, camera, camera batteries, film, alarm clock, leakproof water bottle, torch (flashlight) with extra bulbs and batteries, cigarette lighter, comb, pocket mirror, compass, long pants, long-sleeved shirt, T-shirt, nylon jacket, down overcoat, jumper (sweater), woollen stocking cap, ski mask, mittens, boots, wet weather gear, razor, razor blades, shaving cream, sewing kit, spoon, sunhat, sunscreen (UV) lotion, sunglasses, Chapstick, Vaseline, mosquito repellent, tampons, dental floss, deodorant, soap container, underwear, long underwear, socks, thongs, nail clipper, vitamins, painkillers, laxatives, medical kit (see the Health section later in this chapter), contraceptives, contact lens solution, books, plastic bags and twist ties.

Other things you may want to bring specifically for Mongolia include:

- plastic bags to protect your gear against the elements
- a grater to shred rock-hard cheeses
- songbooks, or any musical instrument, because you'll often be asked to sing or play something
- photos of your family (but not including displays of wealth, such as expensive homes, cars or furniture)
- pocket calculator, as an easy way to indicate, and calculate, prices
- binoculars for the distant wildlife
- ear plugs and eyeshades, because nights are short in summer
- a one- or two-litre water bottle
- an electrical immersion coil for caffeine addicts, assuming you have the correct plug adaptor (see the Electricity section later in this chapter)
- a gluestick to ensure that your postage stamps remain stuck to the envelope or postcard
- sticky tape to hold your maps together (and even to repair your jeep!)
- candles for blackouts
- a short-wave radio to find out what is happening in the rest of the world, and in Mongolia (for instance, in 1996 there were huge forest fires and a cholera outbreak, and it was very difficult to get proper news)

## SUGGESTED ITINERARIES
### Hitching & Public Transport
To travel independently in the countryside you will also probably have to hitch, which is generally safe and a recognised form of transport.

From Ulaan Baatar, it is relatively easy to get to Kharkhorin (for the Erdene Zuu monastery) and Khujirt, to Delgerkhaan via Baganuur, to Mörön and Khatgal – but not around Khövsgöl lake, to Dalanzadgad – but you will need a jeep to get around the south Gobi, and to the big cities of Erdenet and Darkhan.

It is also easy to travel this way around western Mongolia, but you must fly there first.

### Jeep
If you have a private jeep, and a good driver (driving a jeep yourself around the countryside is not a good idea), four trips are recommended:

(1) From Ulaan Baatar go to Darkhan, Amarbayasgalant monastery, Erdenet (via Bugant) and then to Mörön, and around the area of Khövsgöl lake. From the lake, head south to Terkhiin Tsagaan lake and back to Ulaan Baatar via Tsetserleg, Kharkhorin and Khujirt. The total distance is about 2000km, and will take a minimum of eight days, but 12 is more realistic.

(2) If you fly to Khovd (or to Ulaangom, and do it in reverse), you can visit Khovd city, Kazak communities, Tsast Uul, Ölgii, Achit lake, Üüreg lake, Ulaangom, Uvs lake, Kharkhiraa Valley and Khar Us lake. This is about 1200km; allow at least a week to see it all.

(3) From Ulaan Baatar, Baganuur or Öndörkhaan, travel around the Dariganga district via Baruun Urt, and visit Shiliin Bogd, numerous lakes, volcanoes and sand dunes. This will only take a few days.

(4) From Ulaan Baatar or Dalanzadgad, travel around and see the natural beauty of the south Gobi. Allow at least four days from Dalanzadgad to see it all.

### Horse
Of the dozens of possible horse treks, several are popular and not difficult to arrange: between Tsetserleg and Khujirt, via Kharkhorin; from Khatgal to Khövsgöl lake and the region around it, and onto Tsagaannuur to visit the Tsaatan people; around Khentii province, and possibly as far as Dadal, near the Siberian border; and, from Ulaan Baatar, a shorter trek between Terelj, Gachuurt, Manzshir monastery and Bogdkhan mountain.

### Mountain Bike
Mongolian roads are made for strong mountain bikes and masochist riders: the weather is unpredictable, villages and people are few and far between, and the terrain is tough. Getting your bike to a starting point by plane (which has luggage limits) or on very crowded public transport is the main problem.

The best places to try are: the trails from Ulaan Baatar to Terelj, Khandgait and/or Manzshir monastery; from Mörön or Khatgal along either side of Khövsgöl lake; from Darkhan to Amarbayasgalant monastery and on to Erdenet via Bugant; or from Kharkhorin to Khujirt and onto the Orkhon waterfall.

## Around Ulaan Baatar

If you have limited time and want to base yourself in Ulaan Baatar, you can go on day trips (or stay overnight) by private jeep, or possibly public transport, to such wonderful places as Gachuurt, Khustain Nuruu natural reserve, Nairamdal Zuslan International Children's Centre, Terelj, Manzshir monastery, Bogdkhan national park, Darkhan (by train), and Amarbayasgalant monastery.

## HIGHLIGHTS
### Lakes

For outstanding natural beauty, you would be hard-pressed to find anywhere lovelier than Khövsgöl Nuur. Also impressive are Khar Us Nuur and Uvs Nuur for birdlife, and Achit Nuur, Terkhiin Tsagaan Nuur and Üüreg Nuur for hiking and camping.

### Mountains

For camping and general hiking around the mountains, head out to Sutai Uul, Tsast Uul, Monkh Khairkhan Uul, Tsambagarav Uul, Türgen Uul and, closer to Ulaan Baatar, Bogdkhan Uul and Tsetseegun Uul.

### National Parks

Of the many national parks the better, and more accessible, are the Gurvansaikhan National Park, the divided Uvs Lake Strictly Protected Area which covers the lake and nearby area, the Khan Khentii Strictly Protected Area and, near Ulaan Baatar, the Bogdkhan Mountain Strictly Protected Area and Gorkhi-Terelj National Park.

### Landscapes

The Kharkhiraa Valley and Dadal, with its pine forests and streams, the Orkhon waterfall, and the lakes, sand dunes and animals at Dariganga are all spectacular, and a far cry from the popular and barren Gobi desert. The best of the rest are the sand dunes at Mongol Els and Khongoryn Els, the springs at Khujirt and Shargaljuut, and the lovely scenery near Ulaan Baatar at Gachuurt, Terelj and the Bogdkhan Mountain Strictly Protected Area.

### Monasteries

The communists did not leave much. The Erdene Zuu Khiid is superb, and the Amarbayasgalant Khiid is architecturally special, but remote. Nearer to Ulaan Baatar, the Manzshir Khiid is in a delightful location. In Ulaan Baatar, the Winter Palace of Bogd Khaan and the Monastery-Museum of Choijin Lama have great exhibits, but the Gandantegchinlen Khiid is the best in the capital city.

Gandantegchinlen Khiid is the largest and most important monastery in Mongolia.

### Museums & Art Galleries

In Ulaan Baatar, the Museum of Natural History has dinosaur exhibits; the Zanabazar Museum of Fine Arts contains sculptures by the great Zanabazar and the intriguing *One Day in Mongolia* painting; the National

Museum of Mongolian History has an excellent collection of ethnic costumes and ornaments; and the Mongolian Art Gallery is well worth a look.

## Ger Camps

If you want a taste of some 'traditional' accommodation, the most accessible ger camps are at Terelj; the most useful are in the remote south Gobi, near Dalanzadgad; the most luxurious and expensive (but worth a splurge) is at Bogdkhan national park; and the prettiest are at Terelj, the Chandmam camp near Kharkhorin, and the Manzshir monastery.

# TOURIST OFFICES
## Local Tourist Offices

Juulchin, once the sole agency responsible for the entire tourist industry, has now been privatised. It is just another travel agency, but still the biggest. Despite a recent change of government and shake-up of ministries, there is still no dedicated government tourist department.

The Tourism Policy Department (refer to the Ulaan Baatar chapter for details) is desperately trying to implement a policy and sort out the messy tourist industry; it is not available for advice and information. In Mongolia, you will have to rely on subjective travel agencies and guides and not very knowledgeable hotel staff.

## Tourist Offices Abroad

Mongolia also has no official tourist offices abroad. For information about the country, contact a local embassy, consulate or honorary consulate; write to one of the various friendship organisations (see Useful Organisations later in this chapter); get on the Internet (see Online Services); or ring one of the specialised travel agents (listed in the Getting There & Away chapter).

# VISAS & DOCUMENTS
## Passport

A passport is essential, and if yours is within a few months of expiry get a new one now, as many countries will not issue a visa if your passport has less than six months of validity. Also, be sure that it has at least a few blank pages for visas and entry and exit stamps. Losing your passport in Mongolia is very bad news indeed, so try not to do it. If your country has an embassy in Ulaan Baatar, it's a good idea to register there in case of an accident or lost passport.

## Visas

One grievance for independent travellers is the current Draconian visa regulations, a throwback to the old Soviet days when only rich, packaged tourists were welcome.

To get a visa, you must be invited or sponsored by a Mongolian, a foreign resident or a Mongolian company, or be part of an organised tour from a Mongolian or foreign travel agency. Your sponsor will need to know your full name; date and place of birth; country of citizenship; passport number, date and place of issue and expiry date; your date of arrival and departure; and a general itinerary. They must send your invitation to the Ministry of External Relations in Ulaan Baatar. If accepted, a copy will be sent from the ministry to your designated embassy or consulate, where you fill out a visa application form and hand over your cash. Try to get a copy of your invitation if possible.

However, there are ways to bypass the above provisions. Some determined travellers have contacted hotels in Ulaan Baatar and asked them to arrange an invitation in exchange for staying a few days at the hotel. Some consulates and embassies interpret the regulations more liberally – if you're in Moscow, Beijing, Ulan-Ude or Irkutsk (the latter two in Russia), you should have less difficulty getting a visa. In China, entrepreneurs have started to hang around the Mongolian embassy in Beijing and, for a negotiable fee, will arrange a 'friend' in Mongolia to 'sponsor' you. Another excellent place to arrange a Mongolian visa is the information office (☎ (10) 6722 2211, ext 359) at the popular Jinghua Hotel youth hostel, Nansanhuan Xilu, Yongdingmen Wai, Beijing, which can somehow bypass normal regulations and get a three-week visa in four days for US$80, or in two days for US$90.

**Types of Visa** There are transit visas that last 48 hours (sometimes 72 hours) from the date of entry, only allowing you get off the Trans-Mongolian train for a very short while before catching another train to Russia or China. A single entry/exit transit visa costs US$15 (US$30 for double), but cannot be extended.

Tourist visas generally last 30 days from the date of entry, though it is not uncommon to get 90 days, and definitely worth asking for – you must enter Mongolia within three months of issue. Tourist visas cost US$25 for a single entry/exit (US$50 for a double), and 30-day (but not 90-day) visas can be extended. Visas normally take several days, and even up to two weeks, to issue. If you want your visas quicker, possibly within 24 hours, you will have to pay an 'express fee', which is double the normal cost.

Multiple entry/exit tourist visas (which cost US$65 and are valid for six months after the date of issue) are usually only issued to foreign residents who do a lot of travel.

Mongolian honorary consulates can issue transit visas and non-extendable tourist visas but only for 14 days from the date of entry. Importantly, they often issue visas without requiring a sponsor or invitation. However, these visas are for entry only; they cannot issue normal entry/exit visas, so you will have to spend some of your precious time in Ulaan Baatar arranging an exit visa from the ministry.

**Visa Extensions** If you have a 30 day tourist visa you can extend it by another 30 days – but only once, which is just as well because it can be a real hassle.

For extensions, go to the Ministry of External Relations, on Enkh Taivny Örgön Chölöö; it is the grey building just south of Sükhbaatar Square. The consular department, where you will have to wrestle with the visa people, is at the back (enter from the southern door). The contact numbers (☎ 324 435; fax 322 127) may change after the recent re-arrangement of the department following the change of government. The department is currently open from 2.30 to 5.30 pm on Monday, and from 9.30 am to noon on Wednesday, Friday and Saturday.

You should apply for an extension about a week before your visa expires. It officially costs US$15 for the first seven days and a further US$2 per day for a maximum of 30 days, and you will need a passport-sized photo. It should take two or three days to process, and a bottle of vodka will probably help.

If getting an extension seems too hard, it may be worth flying, or taking the train, to Beijing, Hohhot (Inner Mongolia, China), Ulan-Ude or Irkutsk and reapplying for a visa there (after organising your 'invitation' before you leave Mongolia).

**Exit Visas** Transit and tourist visas are good for one entry and one exit (unless you have a double or multiple entry/exit visa). If you are working in Mongolia, or if you obtained your visa at an honorary consulate, you are usually issued a single-entry visa – ie it is valid for one entry only. In this case, another visa is required to leave the country. These visas are available from the Ministry of External Relations, involve the same procedures as an extension (see above) and cost US$20.

**Chinese Transit Visas** This is a special note to remind travellers that if you are transiting Beijing on the way to/from Ulaan Baatar by plane, you currently still need a Chinese transit visa. In Ulaan Baatar, check with the Chinese embassy; other Chinese embassies have given wrong information to some travellers.

### Registration

Registration is required but rarely enforced. Technically, you must register with the police in Ulaan Baatar within 10 days of arriving in Mongolia, but only if you are staying in Mongolia for more than three weeks. You are not issued any permit, but the page in your passport with the Mongolian visa will probably be marked in some way.

Registration is not difficult, and until regulations change, it's best to do it. You must go to the 3rd floor of the unsigned, striped Police Registration Office (☎ 327 182), about 1km north of the corner of Ikh Toiruu and Erkhuugiin Gudamj, on the right-hand side of the road. Outside the building is a small sign in English which reads 'Office for Foreigners'. The registration form is in Mongolian, but some of the staff speak enough English to help you. If you have any difficulties, take the form, find someone else to help you and bring it back later. You will need T30 to pay for the registration form, a copy of your invitation (if possible), one passport-size photo and your passport. Registration can be processed in a few minutes.

Technically you should de-register each time you leave the country (and then re-register when you come back in), but this is not enforced. If you forget to de-register, don't worry unless you intend to come in and out of the country several times in one year.

### Travel Permits
In 1995 a new rule stipulated that all foreigners had to obtain special permits to travel around the countryside. This caused such an outcry, particularly from influential embassies and development agencies in Mongolia, that the regulations were quickly rescinded. Thankfully, no such permits have been required since then, and they're unlikely to be reintroduced.

**Shiliin Bogd** We were arrested because we did not have a permit to visit the sacred mountain of Shiliin Bogd, near the Chinese border in Sükhbaatar province. If you are going there independently, check the current situation at the police station at Baruun Urt, Chonogol or Ovoot. Refer to the relevant chapter for more details.

**National Parks** According to the Ministry of Nature & Environment, all foreigners need permits to visit the various national parks

around the country. Details are in the National Parks section in the Facts about the Country chapter.

**Mountain Climbing** Despite what some agencies may tell you, permits are not required to climb any mountain unless it is in a designated national park. Refer to the Activities section later in this chapter for more details.

### Travel Insurance
If ever there was a country where you needed travel insurance, Mongolia is it. Virtually no travel agency, hotel or ger camp in the whole country has any insurance, including public liability, so you will be liable for all costs incurred from any accident. Make sure your insurance covers you for flights to Beijing, Hong Kong or your home if you get ill: staying in a Mongolian hospital will probably only make you get worse. With the outdoor lifestyle, unpredictable weather and bad roads, accidents are not uncommon. If that is not enough, Air China or MIAT airlines may lose your luggage.

### Other Documents
It's a good idea to carry a driver's licence or any ID card with your photo on it – some embassies want this before issuing a replacement passport. Any document with your photo on it is a very useful alternative to giving your passport to the hotel receptionist when you check in. If you are game enough to drive your own vehicle in the country, an international driving licence is required.

If you're thinking about working in Mongolia, or anywhere else along the way, photocopies of university diplomas, transcripts and letters of recommendation could prove helpful – especially if translated into Mongolian. If you're travelling with your spouse, a photocopy of your marriage licence just might come in handy should you become involved with the law, hospitals or other bureaucratic authorities. Also useful, though not essential, is an International Health Certificate to record your vaccinations.

## EMBASSIES
## Mongolian Diplomatic Missions Abroad

Mongolia has a few embassies which can issue entry/exit visas and provide some limited tourist information. Remember that honorary consulates can only issue entry visas.

Austria
    Honorary Consulate: Auhofstrasse 65-67, A-113, Vienna (☎ (1) 877 373 336; fax 877 335 333)
Belgium
    Embassy: 18 ave Besme, 1190 Brussels (☎ (2) 344 6974; fax 344 3215)
China
    Embassy: 2 Xiushui Beilu, Jianguomenwai, Beijing (☎ (10) 532 1203; fax 532 5045)
    The embassy is open all day but the visa section (enter from the back of the embassy) keeps short hours – Monday, Tuesday, Thursday and Friday from 8.30 to 11.30 am. It closes for all Mongolian public holidays and shuts down completely for a few days before, during and after the Naadam Festival, which is from 11 to 13 July.
    Single entry/exit transit visas (for two or three days) costs US$15 if you are prepared to wait five days for issue; or US$30 if you want it 'urgently'. Single entry/exit tourist visas are usually issued for 14 days, so ask for longer – you may get one for up to three months. They cost US$25/50 for normal/urgent issue. Two photos are needed for a tourist visa, but none for a transit visa. This embassy is particularly fussy about an invitation, but they don't care who it is from, just as long as they have a fax from the Ministry of External Relations in Ulaan Baatar.
    If you are planning to enter Mongolia from China and then return to China, get a double-entry Chinese visa. Otherwise, you will need to obtain another Chinese visa in Ulaan Baatar, and these are pricey.
    Consulate: Xincheng gu Wulanxiagu, 5 hac lou Menggu Lingshiguau, Hohhot (☎ (471) 495 3254; fax 495 3250)
Czech Republic
    Embassy: Na Marne 5, 16 000, Prague 6 (☎ (2) 312 1501; fax 2431 1198)
Denmark
    Honorary Consulate: UNISCRAP A/S, Genvindings Industri, Fiskerihavnsgade 6, DK-2450, Copenhagen (☎ 3312 8373)
France
    Embassy: 5 ave Robert Schumann, 92100 Boulogne, Billancourt (☎ 01 46 05 23 18; fax 01 46 05 30 16)
    Independent travellers, with invitations, have received 90-day visas at this embassy without problems.
Germany
    Embassy: 4 Siebengebirgsblick, Siegler 53844, Troisdorf, Bonn (☎ (22) 4140 2727; fax 414 7781)
    Consulate: Gotlandstrasse 12, 10439, Berlin (☎ (30) 446 9320; fax 446 9321)
Hong Kong
    Honorary Consulate: 4 Somerset Rd, Kowloon (☎ 2338 9034; fax 2338 0633)
Hungary
    Embassy: 1022 Budapest II-K, Bogar Utca 14/C, Budapest (☎ (1) 212 4579; fax 212 5731)
India
    Embassy: 34 Archbishop Makarious Marg, New Delhi, 110003 (☎ (11) 463 1728; fax 463 3240)
Italy
    Honorary Consulate: Viale XX Settembre, 37-24126, Trieste (☎ (40) 362 241; fax 363 494)
Japan
    Embassy: Shoto Pinecrest Mansion, 21-4 Kamiyamacho Shibuya-ku, Tokyo 150 (☎ 3469 2088; fax 3469 2216)
Kazakstan
    Consulate: Kazybek Bi (☎ (3272) 536 1372)
Poland
    Embassy: 00478 Warsawa ul Rejtana, 15 m16 (☎ (22) 487 920; fax  484 264)
Russia
    Embassy: Ul Borisoglebskaya 11, RF-121069, Moscow (☎ (95) 241 1049; fax 241 4060)
    The embassy is close to the Smolenskaya metro station. It is open on weekdays from 9 am to 1 pm. Single entry/exit transit visas for 48 hours cost US$15, and can be collected the same day (between 4.30 and 5.30 pm) if you pay double. Single entry/exit tourist visas cost US$25, or US$50 for the 'express' service.
    Consulate: ulitsa Lapina 11, Irkutsk (☎ (3952) 342 447)
    Consulate: Hotel Baikal, ploshchad Sovietov, Ulan-Ude (☎ (30122) 20507)
South Korea
    300-24 Dongbuichon-Dong, Yong San-Ku, Seoul 1-104 (☎ (2) 792 8860; fax 794 7605)
Sweden
    Honorary Consulate: Gotabergsgatan 34, S-411 34, Goteborg (☎ & fax (31) 160 770)
Switzerland
    Consulate & UN Representative, 4 chemin des Mollies, 1293 Bellevue, Geneva (☎ (22) 774 1974; fax 774 3201)
    Independent travellers have reported real difficulties with getting a visa here.
    Honorary Consulate: Secretariat, Beraterkreis JBK, CH-8006, Zurich (☎ (1) 272 40045; fax 361 7144)

Thailand
    Honorary Consulate: 16/3 Sukumvit Soi 33,
    Bangkok, 10110 (☎ (2) 585 3853; fax 259 0359)
UK
    Embassy: 7 Kensington Court, London W8 5DL
    (☎ (0171) 937 0150; fax 937 1117)
        This is one of the better embassies for indepen-
    dent travellers. An invitation from a hotel is all
    that is required if you are not 'sponsored' and,
    therefore, staying with anyone.
Ukraine
    Embassy: Ul M Kotsyubinskogo 3, Kiev
    (☎ (44) 216 8891; fax 216 8751)
USA
    Embassy: 2833 Main St NW, Washington, DC
    20007 (☎ (202) 298-7137; fax 298-9227)
        This embassy will issue 90-day visas if you
    have an invitation.
    Consulate & UN Representative: 6 East 77th St,
    New York, NY 10021
    (☎ (212) 472-6517; fax 861-9464)

### Foreign Embassies in Mongolia

Although a few countries are represented in
Ulaan Baatar, most use their embassies in
Beijing and/or Moscow to cover Mongolia.
For a list of foreign embassies in Mongolia,
see the Ulaan Baatar chapter.

### CUSTOMS

Customs officials want to keep out pornog-
raphy, drugs and expensive imports which
might be sold to Mongolians; and want to
keep in old paintings, statues, works of art
and mineral samples. Baggage searches of
foreigners exiting Mongolia by air are sometimes rigorous, but rarely so at border crossings by train to China or Russia, when most
passengers are asleep.

If you are legally exporting any antiques,
you must have a receipt from the place you
bought them and from the relevant ministry
(the name of which was not clear after the
recent shuffle of the ministries). Even if you
have anything which *looks* old, it is a good
idea to get a document from the ministry to
indicate that it is not an antique. That goes
for Buddha images and statues as well.

During your trip you will probably be
offered furs of rare animals, antique items
like snuffboxes, bits and pieces from the
Erdene Zuu monastery, and even fossilised
dinosaur bones and eggs. Locals will only

sell these things as long as foreigners buy
them, so please do not buy anything rare, old
or precious to Mongolia's history.

When you enter Mongolia, you must fill
out a Customs Declaration form (written in
English) to declare any prohibited items
(which aren't listed, but include drugs and
guns), all precious stones and all 'dutiable
goods' (again, these are not listed). You are
then meant to personally 'calculate the duties
and taxes' (the rates are not listed) on these
items – there is no need to list any of these.
You are also asked to list all 'money
instruments' – ie currencies – which you
bring into the country. There is no need to be
too accurate; this form is not checked on your
way out. You should, nevertheless, keep all
receipts when you change money at banks,
though changing money with licensed moneychangers (who will not issue receipts) is legal.

The Customs Declaration is checked by the
customs official and then returned to you. When
you leave Mongolia, you will be asked to hand
in the form – so keep it safe during your trip.

### MONEY

Take US dollar travellers' cheques for security; have some US dollars to change anywhere in Mongolia, or major Asian and
European currencies to change in Ulaan
Baatar; use tögrögs in the country almost
exclusively; and use credit cards for upmarket
hotels, all flights *from* Ulaan Baatar and for
emergency advances in Ulaan Baatar.

---

**Mongolian Currencies**

Mongolia's various rulers have ensured a constant change of currencies. During Chinggis
Khaan's time, coins, called *sükh*, made from
gold and silver, were used as currency. During
the Manchurian rule, Chinese currency was
used, but Mongolian traders preferred to use
Russian gold, British notes and goods such as
tea, silk and furs.

In 1925, fours years after independence from
China, the tögrög was first introduced. At that time,
one tögrög was worth US$0.88 cents; by 1928 one
tögrög was up to US$52! Currently, about 600
tögrögs are worth just one US dollar. ■

## Costs

If you are travelling on an organised tour you will probably pay around US$100 per day (more for extra luxuries), plus transport fare to Mongolia. You can travel independently and see the same sights and stay in the same places as an organised tour for about US$80 per day – a lot less if you share the cost of a private jeep and camp rather than stay in expensive ger camps.

Accommodation and food will cost at least US$10 per day in Ulaan Baatar, but allow up to US$20 per day for half-decent accommodation, some tastier, western meals and trips to the theatre and museums. If you are hitching and using public transport around the countryside, allow about US$15 per day. The main component of this is the 'foreigners' price' often charged by some provincial hotels; if you take a tent and camp, and especially if you have a portable petrol stove, you will be hard-pressed to spend more than about US$7 per day.

## Cash

At several banks in Ulaan Baatar, you can change most major European and Asian currencies – but only into the local currency, the *tögrög*. The US greenback is still the easiest to change in Ulaan Baatar, and the only currency (besides the Chinese yuan and Russian rouble) which you can change with moneychangers, some banks and individuals in the countryside.

You can change US dollar travellers' cheques into US cash in Ulaan Baatar for 2% commission. When carrying US dollars, keep a lot of small denominations; anything more than US$20 will be hard to change at smaller stores or banks. It is important to note that US dollars dated before 1988 are, for some unknown reason, virtually unacceptable anywhere in Mongolia.

## Travellers' Cheques

Most major banks and upmarket hotels in Ulaan Baatar will change travellers' cheques – but only those in US dollars and from major companies – into tögrögs, usually with no commission. Uncashed travellers' cheques

are useless for any transactions in Mongolia and cannot be changed anywhere outside the capital city.

If you lose your American Express travellers' cheques or credit card, or Thomas Cook travellers' cheques, contact the Trade & Development Bank in Ulaan Baatar. Although it's not the representative of these companies (the nearest office for both is in Beijing), it will start the ball rolling for replacements. If you have another brand of travellers' cheques, don't lose them.

## Credit Cards

You can use Visa, MasterCard, American Express and sometimes Diners' Club cards in Ulaan Baatar at upmarket hotels, expensive souvenir shops, all airline offices and most travel agencies. With the exception of the souvenir shop at Erdene Zuu, you won't be able to buy anything on credit anywhere outside the capital.

The Trade & Development Bank in Ulaan Baatar can arrange US dollars cash advances on your Visa, MasterCard and American Express cards for a 4% commission. Allow a few days for the authorisation to come through from overseas.

## International Transfers

These days Mongolia is awash with aid workers, missionaries, petty traders, consultants and big corporations, all sending money in and out, so currency transactions are no longer a mystery to bank clerks. But don't be too surprised if things go awry. Whatever you do, have the money sent in US dollars.

The Trade & Development Bank in Ulaan Baatar (3rd floor) can efficiently arrange transfers of money to/from Mongolia through the Midland Bank (UK), Bank of Tokyo, Bank of China, BFEC (France), Deutsche Bank (Germany) and Chase Manhattan (USA). However, it charges US$50 for the transaction.

## Currency

The currency of Mongolia is called the tögrög (normally written as T, but may in the future change to MNT). There used to be 100 *mongo* to the tögrög, but years of hyperinflation put the mongo out of circulation. Banknotes are issued in denominations of 1, 3 (which is rare), 5, 10, 20, 50, 100, 500 and 1000 (also rare) – all with the faces of the ubiquitous Chinggis Khaan or Sükhbaatar on them. Most denominations have two types of notes, and many look similar to each other, so be careful.

On 1 July 1996, the Mongolian government announced that all transactions must be made in tögrögs and not in US dollars. Excepted are companies and individuals with special permits, such as airlines and major travel agencies. All hotels have to accept tögrögs, but most tourist ger camps continue to accept US dollars, albeit illegally.

Prices in this book are quoted in tögrögs, unless US dollars are required.

## Currency Exchange
The following currencies (cash only, except for US dollar travellers' cheques) are convertible in Ulaan Baatar. The exchange rates in October 1996 were:

| Canada | C$1 | = | T446 |
|---|---|---|---|
| China | Y1 | = | T73 |
| France | FFr1 | = | T116 |
| Germany | DM1 | = | T394 |
| Italy | 1 Lira | = | T0.40 |
| Japan | ¥1 | = | T5.4 |
| Russia | R1 | = | T0.111 |
| Switzerland | SwFr1 | = | T481 |
| UK | UK£1 | = | T951 |
| USA | US$1 | = | T604 |

## Changing Money
**Banks** In Ulaan Baatar, several banks and most upmarket hotels change major currencies and, usually, US dollar travellers' cheques. Refer to the Ulaan Baatar chapter for details about where to change money.

Most aimag capitals and major cities have at least one bank but very few change money. If they do, it is certain to be only US dollars cash.

**Moneychangers** Licensed moneychangers in Ulaan Baatar will often give you about a 2% better exchange rate than banks. You can only change US dollars, Russian roubles and Chinese yuan. The chances of being ripped off by licensed moneychangers are slim.

At some shops and most markets in aimag capitals, and at Darkhan and Erdenet (and possibly at tourist ger camps), you can find someone to change US dollars, as well as Chinese yuan and Russian roubles in areas close to the respective borders. However, take all the tögrög you need from Ulaan Baatar as you cannot rely on always finding moneychangers in the countryside. In addition, they would not be licensed and more likely to rip you off with very poor rates.

## Black Market
Recent legislation outlawing the use of US dollars (except with a permit) may result in an emergent black market, but at the time of research any dealings with the black market were illegal, dangerous and not recommended.

## Tipping & Bargaining
In upmarket restaurants and hotels in Ulaan Baatar, there is often a mandatory 10%, 'government' tax, but most places don't bother adding it onto the bill or haven't heard of this tax. Tipping is often expected in upmarket places, but is still definitely optional. (We have seen waiters run out of restaurants wanting to return the T50 tip we left.) Don't calculate the tip as a percentage of the meal cost, rather chose a figure between T50 to T100 depending on how satisfied you were with the service. Give the tip at the time you pay the bill, because if you leave money lying on the table someone besides the staff may take it. It is not customary to tip taxi drivers.

Nobody bargains in government shops, but in the budding private sector bargaining is definitely catching on. In the markets, a fair price is very much a matter of negotiation, whether it's a carpet, a Mongolian costume or a pair of jeans. It's also possible to barter in the market; for example, a bottle of scarce foreign-made vodka or an old

Walkman may be swapped for a high-quality Mongolian-made overcoat or a set of boots.

### Dual-Pricing

Thirty per cent of Mongolians earn less than a few dollars a month, so try to understand why westerners are expected to pay more than Mongolians for some things. In any case, travelling independently around Mongolia is still far cheaper than doing it in your own country, and in most other countries in the region.

Be prepared to pay about four times more than a Mongolian for theatre tickets and about five to seven times more for internal airline tickets. At the Naadam Festival, you are often charged whatever you are willing to pay. The most extreme example of dual-pricing is at hotels and ger camps, where you may be forced to pay up to 10 times more than a local. On some internal road and rail transport and at restaurants, you may be charged a little more than locals, but you probably won't know.

### POST & COMMUNICATIONS
### Postal Rates

Postal rates are often relatively expensive, especially for parcels, for which there is only an 'air mail' rate – yet they often arrive months later (probably by sea). To Australia/New Zealand, Europe and North America, normal-sized letters cost T264 and postcards cost T220. Leave enough room on your postcard for the five T44 stamps.

### Sending Mail

The postal service is reliable but can often be *very* slow. Allow plenty of time for letters and postcards to arrive from Mongolia. To Australia, mail goes via Beijing and can take three months to reach its destination; to Europe, mail goes via Moscow and often takes less than a week. Foreign residents of Ulaan Baatar find it much faster to give letters (and cash to buy stamps) to other foreigners who are departing.

You won't find letter boxes on the streets. In most cases, you will have to post your letters from the post office. You can buy stamps in post offices (and upmarket hotels) in Ulaan Baatar and aimag capitals; elsewhere, stamps are in short supply.

### Poste Restante

The poste restante at the Central Post Office in Ulaan Baatar seems to work quite well; don't even think about using a poste restante anywhere else in the country. Locals prefer to receive mail at post office boxes because residential deliveries are uncertain in a city without clear addresses.

### Telephone

The best word to describe Mongolia's telecommunications system is 'primitive'. You'll often have to dial many times before you get connected, the lines are dim and noisy, and poor insulation on the underground wires causes interference from other people's conversations (crosstalk). Most Mongolians don't have telephones in their homes.

Outside of Ulaan Baatar, making calls is difficult: no-one will understand you unless you speak reasonable Mongolian or Russian, and the telephones may not work anyway. In the countryside, the telltale satellite dish indicates a telephone office. Try to make all your calls from Ulaan Baatar, however.

**Domestic Calls** In Ulaan Baatar, most telephones have six numbers (older ones have five); Erdenet has six digits; and elsewhere in the country, where there are very few telephones, numbers often have just three or four digits. If you are given a five-digit number in Ulaan Baatar, and it doesn't work, try adding a 3 in front.

For domestic calls, try to use the telephone at your hotel, or at a friend's house or business, rather than battle with the local post or telephone office. Domestic calls can also be made by dialling the domestic operator (☎ 107) first, if you are able to speak Mongolian or have a friend who can help.

**International Calls** If you have access to a telephone, you can make direct long-distance calls by dialling the international operator (☎ 106), who may know enough English to make the right connection (but don't count on it). Otherwise, you will have to book a call from your local post office. You pay in advance for the number of minutes (minimum of three), and when the time is up you'll be automatically cut off. To Australia/New Zealand, Europe and North America, it costs about T2750 per minute; less to Russia and China.

If you want to save the hassle, but not the money, you can easily make international calls from any of the business centres or reception desks at the top-range hotels, namely the Chinggis Khaan, Bayangol, Ulaan Baatar and Flower hotels.

Making a call *to* Mongolia is a lot easier. From most countries, there is international direct dialling to Mongolia. The country code is 976. Only Ulaan Baatar (1) and Darkhan (37) have telephone codes. You only use these numbers if you are ringing from overseas; there are no internal telephone codes within Mongolia.

### Fax & Email
In Ulaan Baatar, the Central Post Office, the business centres at the Bayangol, Flower, Ulaan Baatar and Chinggis Khaan hotels, and a few private operators charge about T4000 to fax one page to Europe, North America and Australia/New Zealand – but ask about any extra 'transmission fees'. These business centres, and some private operators, charge about T500 per page to receive a fax.

Email has now reached Mongolia and is easily the quickest and cheapest form of communication – assuming, of course, that the other person has the required technology. Business centres will charge a reasonable T1100 per email page to anywhere – far cheaper than a fax, and less hassle than a telephone call. The only service provider in the country is Datacom (☎ 326 259; email support@magicnet.mn).

A daily email news service from Ulaan Baatar in English provides useful information about Mongolian issues and entertainment, and costs T5000 per month (☎ & fax 372 925; email ganbold@magicnet.mn).

### Old Postal System
Mongolia can pride itself on developing one of the world's first long-distance internal postal systems. During the time of Chinggis Khaan, a 'pony express' postal service, known as *urton*, would cover over 100km per day. Bells were attached to the saddle to warn locals of an approaching rider. The rider was quickly fed and the horses changed before he went on his way. All male herdsmen were required to work for several weeks a year to ensure the continuing success of urton. The postal system was steadily improved over the centuries, and continued until 1949. ■

### BOOKS
Over the centuries, thousands of works about Mongolia and the Mongolians have been written, in a wider range of languages than even the most erudite of scholars could manage. You can pick up a few souvenir-type books in Ulaan Baatar, but bookshops and libraries in your own country are the best places to start searching for most books about Mongolia.

Four companies which specialise in books about Mongolia are:

Avery Press
    600 Kalmia Ave, Boulder, CO 80304, USA
    (☎ (303) 443-1592; email kalmiale@aol.com)
Eastern Books of London
    125a Astonville St, Southfields, London SW18
    5AQ (☎ & fax (0181) 871 0880)
The Mongolia Society Inc
    322 Goodbody Hall, Indiana University, Bloomington, IN 47405, USA (☎ (812) 855-4078; fax 855-7500; email monsoc@indiana.edu)
    A major source for anything regarding Mongolia, they also sell an extraordinary range of maps, dictionaries, language and music tapes and T-shirts.
University of Washington Press
    PO Box 50096, Seattle, WA 98145-5096, USA
    (☎ (206) 543-8870; fax 543-3932)

### Lonely Planet
Lonely Planet publishes the pocket-size *Mongolian phrasebook*, which is indispensable for travelling around Mongolia, especially in the countryside. If you are travelling to other nearby countries, Lonely Planet

publishes books on *Central Asia, Russia, Ukraine & Belarus, China* and *Beijing.*

## Travel

Becker, Jasper, *The Lost Country: Mongolia Revealed* (1993).This book is insightful, well written and recommended reading for anyone going to Mongolia.

Lattimore, Owen, *Nomads and Commissars: Mongolia Revisited* (1962). Arguably the greatest scholar on Mongolia this century; Lattimore's many books are analytical and wise.

Middleton, Nick, *The Last Disco in Outer Mongolia* (1992). An easy-to-read, but dated, journal of his limited travels in the late 1980s.

Severin, Tim, *In Search of Genghis Khan* (1991). Well written and with great photos, this book provides an in-depth and fascinating look at nomadic lifestyles.

## History & Politics

Kahn, Paul, *The Secret History of the Mongols: the Origin of Chinggis Khan* (1984). This is regarded as the best study of the *Secret History.*

Langlois, John D, *China under Mongolian Rule* (1981). Details the impact of the Mongols during their century of rule over all of China.

Morgan, David, *The Mongols* (1986). A comprehensive account of Mongolia's history.

Rossabi, Morris, *Khublai Khan* (1988). A biography of the less-revered invader.

Sanders, Alan, *Encyclopaedia of Asian History*. This new, 19-volume opus includes a separate book by renowned Mongolist, Alan Sanders. It details ancient and recent history and politics, and includes a vital bibliography.

*The Secret History of the Mongols.* Mongolia's most famous book has no known author. This epic history of the life and deeds of Chinggis Khaan has been translated into English by Igor de Rachewiltz (1996), Francis Cleaves (1982) and Urgunge Onon (1990).

## Culture

Art Museum of San Francisco, *Mongolia: The Legacy of Chinggis Khan.* Available in Ulaan Baatar, and expensive (US$60), it contains extraordinary photographs.

Avery, Martha, *Women of Mongolia* (1996). This new book contains a fascinating look at the changes affecting nomadic women.

Balhaazav, TS, *My Mongolia* (1993) and *Contributions of Mongols to World Civilization* (1995). These cheap booklets, available in Ulaan Baatar, provide a brief, interesting but subjective overview of the country and its people and culture.

Ipsiroglu, MS, *Painting and Culture of Mongols* (1967). The Persian-influenced art of the Mongols who came with Chinggis, converted to Islam and settled in the Middle East is reproduced in colour.

*This Is Mongolia* (1991). Available in Ulaan Baatar, this pocket-sized, colourful and easy-to-read booklet provides interesting explanations of culture, history and traditions – recommended reading, and a good souvenir.

## Religion

Bowde, Charles, *The Jebtsundampa Khutukhtus of Urga* (1961). This is a renowned Buddhist history of the greatest Mongolian lamas.

Eliade, Mircea, *Shamanism: Archaic Techniques of Ecstasy* (1972). A lyrical study of shamanism worldwide, including Mongolia.

Heissig, Walther, *Religions of Mongolia* (1980). This is one of Heissig's best works about religion.

Hyer, Paul & Jagchid, Sechin, *A Mongolian Living Buddha* (1983). One of the great lamas, the Kanjurwa Khutukhtu, collaborated with these scholars to produce a biography before he died in 1980.

## Nature & Environment

Andrews, Roy Chapman, *On the Trail of Ancient Man* (1926). An autobiography about his exploits seeking dinosaur fossils in the Gobi and around the world. One of the many books written by, and about, Andrews.

Etchecopar, RD, *Les Oiseaux de Chine, de Mongolie at de Corée* (1978). This is the most thorough work about birdlife in Mongolia and the region. It is written in French.

Finch, Christopher, *Mongolia's Wild Heritage* (1995). Written in collaboration with the Mongolian Ministry of Nature & Environment, this is an outstanding book about Mongolia's fragile ecology and contains excellent photos. It is a great souvenir, and available in Ulaan Baatar for US$15.

## Today's Mongolia

Enkhbat, R, *Mongolia: Country of Contrasts.* On sale in Ulaan Baatar for about US$20, this is a startling collection of contemporary photos by one of the country's top photographers.

Goldstein, Melvyn & Beall, Cynthia, *The Changing World of Mongolia's Nomads* (1994). This book, which has great photos (if the captions are a little odd), is an interesting account of the changes affecting the nomads.

## Dictionaries

Besides the Lonely Planet phrasebook, which includes a concise vocabulary list, a few dictionaries have been published:

English-Mongolian

Hangin, John G, *A Concise English-Mongolian Dictionary* (1970) and *A Modern Mongolian-English Dictionary* (1986)

Itangerel, D, *A New English-Mongolian Dictionary* (1993), available in Ulaan Baatar for about T3000 and excellent value

Rozycki, William, *A Concise Mongol-English and English-Mongol Dictionary* (1996), a handy, pocket-sized book which translates both ways, but there aren't enough words to justify the price tag (US$12.95)

German-Mongolian

Vietze, Hans-Peter *Worterbuch Mongolisch-Deutsch* (1988)

Mostaert, Antoine, *Dictionnaire Ordos* (circa 1940s), the definitive dictionary; in three volumes

Japanese-Mongolian

*Nihongo Mongorugo Joyo Goishu* (1977).

Korean-Mongolian

*Mongol Oros Angli Tol* (1971).

## FILMS

Movies made in Mongolia bring to life the steppes and nomadic way. Mongolian directors seldom get a screening outside Mongolia, but video stores may well have the 1991 art house hit, *Close to Eden*, also released as *Urga*, by the Russian director Mikhalkov.

Epic documentaries and feminist fantasies of the German director Ulrike Ottinger are the most intimate immersion in the life of Mongolian reindeer herders. And, of course, Hollywood did its fantasies too, with Richard Widmark in the war epic *Destination Gobi* (1953) and Orson Welles, Tyrone Power and Herbert Lom in *The Black Rose* (1950) as Saxon warriors off to meet the great *khaans*.

## NEWSPAPERS & MAGAZINES

The media used to be little more than state-controlled propaganda vehicles, but liberalisation has certainly changed the atmosphere. Literally hundreds of newspaper have sprung up, with controversies and scandals forming popular topics; but some are little more than soft porn rags. A shortage of newsprint, all imported from Russia and paid for in hard currency, and the subsequent increase in prices have closed many and reduced others to little more than pamphlets.

The major daily paper is still the government's official mouthpiece, *Ardiin Erkh* (People's Right). Major private dailies include *Ulaanbaatar* and *Önöödör* (Today). Three English-language weekly newspapers are available in upmarket hotels and around Sükhbaatar Square in Ulaan Baatar. They are the *Business Times* (which is mostly in Mongolian Cyrillic), *The Mongol Messenger* and *The UB Post*. For around T150 an issue, they are well worth picking up for local news and information about entertainment.

## Online Services

| Online Service | Information | Address |
| --- | --- | --- |
| Avery Press | publishing & general information | http://www.halcyon.com/mongolia |
| Infosystem Mongolei | gopher system dedicated to Mongolia | http://userpage.fu-berlin.de/corff/mf.html |
| Italia Mongolia | information in Italian | http://www.arpnet.it/mongolia |
| Lonely Planet | current information about Mongolia for, and by, travellers | http://www.lonelyplanet.com/letters/nea/mon_pc.htm |
| Mongolia FAQ | covers a lot of interesting questions | http://fub46.zedat.fu-berlin |
| Mongolia WWW Virtual Library | outstanding source of general information | http://www.bluemarble.net/mitch/monglinks.html |
| Mongolia Society (USA) | excellent source about books and other information | http://www.bluemarble.net/mitch/monsoc.html |

ROBERT STOREY

RON GLUCKMAN

ANDRÉ DE SMET

Top: A few of Mongolia's 2.6 million horses enjoying springtime on the steppes.
Middle: An old Russian car, a relic of Soviet influence.
Bottom: Passengers squeeze into a 2nd class train on one of Mongolia's few railways.

PAUL GREENWAY

PAUL GREENWAY

Top: The horse is the pride of Mongolia and there are few nomads who haven't learned to ride as soon as they can walk.

Bottom: The Russian-made Planeta motorcycle is a popular form of transport.

## RADIO & TV

Mongolian state-run radio is strong on rhetoric, keeps alive traditional folk music and oral epics, and often contains good-quality classical music, as well as weird Russian disco. Three stations are worth tuning into while you are in Ulaan Baatar:

A1 and Jag (107FM) broadcasts a lot of modern western music, sometimes with English-speaking deejays. It is popular with trendy Mongolian youth.

Blue Sky Radio (100.9FM) broadcasts Mongolian and western music, as well as English language courses.

Radio Ulaanbaatar (102.5FM), the first privately owned and independent station, broadcasts a lot of western music, and interviews and readings in English.

The reception of short-wave services, such as Voice of America, the BBC and Radio Australia, are usually good, and often excellent in the steppes. Outside of Ulaan Baatar it can sometimes feel like you're in another world; a short-wave radio is useful in linking you back to the 'real' world.

Except where satellite TV is available, Mongolian TV is nothing to get excited about. Ulaanbaatar TV and Mongol TB (not a disease), and stations beamed from Russia, provide a poor diet of badly dubbed Russian films and Mongolian news and sports (including hours and hours of wrestling), as well as interesting documentaries about nomads (even if you don't understand them, the scenery is great).

The new privately owned station, Eagle TV, regularly shows US NBA basketball and CNN news on most days. Sansar TV is the cable network in Ulaan Baatar which serves better-off locals and foreigners with western music, sports and movies.

## PHOTOGRAPHY & VIDEO

Mongolia is probably the most photogenic country in the world. Take loads of film with you and be constantly on the lookout for gems, such as a yak sipping by a lake at twilight, a herd of horses stampeding in front of snowcapped mountains or nomadic children herding their camels.

In summer, days are long, so the best time to take photos is before 10 am and after 5 pm. As bright, glaring sunshine is the norm, a polarising filter is essential. If you do a jeep trip on an unsurfaced road, you can expect plenty of dust, so keep the camera well sealed in a plastic bag.

### Film & Equipment

Major brands of print and Polaroid film are available in upmarket hotels and souvenir shops in Ulaan Baatar (but nowhere in the countryside), but prices tend to be high, and you should always check the expiry date. Several places around Sükhbaatar Square will process print film cheaply, but the quality may not be great; it's best to wait until you get home. Slide film is rare, so bring what you need and get it developed elsewhere. Mongolia is definitely *not* the place to buy camera accessories, though you never know what sort of ancient relic you might find in the department stores. Bring spare batteries.

### Restrictions

Photography is prohibited in monasteries and temples, but you can sometimes obtain special permission to take photographs in exchange for an extra fee. Remember that monks are not photographic models, so if they say 'No photos', their wishes should be respected. A few foreigners have done some pretty offensive things like climbing up onto the lap of a Buddha statue to get a photo.

In some museums in Ulaan Baatar, you may need to pay an extra fee to use your still or video camera. It is best to have a look around first before you decide whether to fork out the extra tögrögs for photographs. Officially, you need a video permit to use a video camera at Khövsgöl Nuur lake, but no-one will care if you forget to pay the ridiculous fee.

In 1996 a French journalist was fined and had his film confiscated for taking a photo of the State Parliament House at Sükhbaatar Square – in accordance with an anachronistic regulation about taking photographs within

50m of a Special State Protected Area. Apparently, information about these specially protected areas can be obtained from a special department (☎ 322 456), but no-one speaks English there, nor could they tell us which buildings are 'special'. Hopefully, this rule will become obsolete with the change of government, but in the meantime, always be careful about photographing potentially sensitive areas, especially border crossings and military establishments.

## Photographing People

Mongolians are not especially enthusiastic about having their photos taken. The days of state surveillance are a recent memory, and some Mongolians are ashamed of the shabbiness they and the whole country have been reduced to. Many westerners don't seem to care what the locals think, and poke camera lenses into the face of whoever looks interesting. This has led to arguments and even fist fights. Markets are often a place where snap-happy foreigners are not welcome. Some visitors have even been stoned after taking photos at the Central (Black) Market in Ulaan Baatar.

On the other hand, people in the countryside are often happy to pose for photographs if you ask first. If you have promised to send them a copy, *please* do it, but explain that it may take several months to reach them – some nomads believe that all cameras are (instant) Polaroids. Several nomads also told us how devastated they were because they had not received photos as promised by foreigners. Ask them to write their address in Mongolian on a piece of paper. You can then glue the address on an envelope, and add the word 'Mongolia' in the roman alphabet to ensure that it gets to the right place.

## TIME

Mongolia is divided into two time zones: the three western aimags of Bayan-Ölgii, Uvs and Khovd are one hour earlier than Ulaan Baatar, while the rest of the country follows Ulaan Baatar's time.

The standard time in Ulaan Baatar is UTC/GMT plus eight hours. When it is noon in Ulaan Baatar, it is also noon in Beijing, Hong Kong, Singapore and Perth; 2 pm in Sydney; 8 pm the previous day in Los Angeles; 11 pm the previous day in New York; and 4 am in London. Mongolia observes one hour's daylight-saving time between the last Sunday in March and the last Sunday in September.

There is another form of 'Mongolian time' – add two hours to any appointments you make. Mongolians are notorious for being late, and this includes nearly everyone likely to be important to you, such as jeep drivers, your guide or the staff at a museum you want to visit. You could almost adjust your watch to compensate for the difference.

It is interesting to note that dates are usually written with the years first, followed by the month in roman numerals, and then the day in normal numbers. For example, 16 August 1996 is often written as 1996-VIII-16.

## ELECTRICITY

Lenin defined communism as socialism plus electricity. Mongolia's abundant coal has meant widespread electrification; however, the power stations are in the middle of the towns, belch black smoke, and use technology on the brink of breakdown. In western Mongolia, power (electricity and hot water) supplies were heavily restricted during the summer of 1996.

Power surges, blackouts and hot water shortages, including in Ulaan Baatar, are common. Expats will tell you horrendous stories about electricity and hot water 'blackouts' lasting weeks during winters of -20°C. The surges can also damage sensitive electrical equipment. Electrical wiring in old hotels can be dangerous. Where water meets electricity, be doubly careful.

Electric power is 220V, 50Hz. Thanks to Russian influence, the sockets are designed to accommodate two round prongs in the European style.

## WEIGHTS & MEASURES

Mongolia follows the international metric system. As in the USA, the ground floor is called the 1st floor – as opposed to the UK system, where the next floor above ground level is the 1st floor.

## LAUNDRY

Most hotels in Mongolia, especially in Ulaan Baatar, will do your laundry for a negotiable price. There is a dry-cleaner in the capital. Brand-name detergent, and even bleach, is available in Ulaan Baatar, and in most larger aimag capitals, so with the (normally-available) hot water and very dry climate, you'll probably end up washing your own clothes.

## HEALTH

Except for getting frostbite in winter, Mongolia is generally a healthy country to travel in. The dry, cold climate and sparse human habitation means few problems with infectious diseases like malaria and dysentery which plague tropical countries. However, illness and accidents can still occur, so it pays to take certain precautions.

Mongolia is a terrible place to get ill. The number of people per doctor is 2700 and the standard of medical training is patchy at best, and often very bad. When the communists shot the Buddhist lamas they shot the doctors too, because healing was one of the many arts of the Buddhist clergy. The Soviets had to start from scratch to build scientific medicine, and they neglected preventative medicine and primary health care for a scattered nomadic population. There are now about 850 poorly trained and under-equipped Mongolian medical graduates struggling to maintain the health of a country gone broke.

### Medical Treatment

Medical facilities in Mongolia are quite poor. Once I had an asthma attack, probably due to the sands and gusty winds. The hotel doctor was unable to speak English. We got hold of a Russian to act as a translator. However, the hotel clinic was locked and the person holding the key was 'unavailable'. It is quite apparent that Mongolian doctors are quite afraid of treating foreigners. They probably fear that if the patient dies, the patient's country's authorities will come pounding on Mongolia's neck. So, always come medically prepared.

**James Huang, Singapore**

If you get seriously ill in Mongolia, contact a reputable travel agent, your local embassy (or any embassy which speaks your language), a foreign resident or your hotel (or any upmarket hotel) for current advice about which hospital or doctor to visit. A couple of hospitals in Ulaan Baatar cater for foreigners, but suffer from a shortage of medicines and reliable medical staff. In the countryside, head for the nearest aimag capital or, if you can, rush back to Ulaan Baatar.

Blood-letting (removal of blood) is part of traditional practices, and Mongolian doctors just love to inject things like vitamins. Except in dire emergencies, avoid injections like the plague – the syringe may not be clean (so bring your own), and you will have little idea what they are pumping into you.

If you are unlucky enough to stay for a while in a Mongolian hospital, you will definitely need a good friend to look after you – the nurses won't have the time, resources or motivation to do it themselves. This means someone to get your own food, change your sheets, find medicines and things like syringes, and cheer you up. Blackouts are common in Ulaan Baatar (more so in the countryside), and hospital generators don't exist, or, if they do, they often fail. Each year, several Mongolians die in the middle of simple operations after power failures.

If you are suffering from any illness or injury that you feel could be very serious, but not immediately life-threatening, make a beeline for Beijing. In a real life-threatening emergency, international medical evacuation services claim they can send a private plane from Beijing to fly you out of Mongolia, but we haven't heard of it happening. (By the time the Mongolian and Chinese authorities decide where to hold the first round of negotiations to discuss air space etc, it will probably be too late.) This service does not come cheaply, unless you know your travel insurance company will bear the cost, which can be tens of thousands of dollars.

### Predeparture Preparations

Get your teeth checked and any necessary dental work done before you leave home.

Always carry a spare pair of glasses. If you wear contact lenses, bring an ample supply of lens-cleaning solution, and a pair of glasses to fall back on if the weather turns dusty. Good-quality sunglasses are essential at any time of the year; amber-coloured lenses give the best UV protection, followed by grey and green.

Visitors should bring their own health products, including lip balms, lotions, tampons and contraceptives – none are available in Mongolia. You can get some aspirins in Ulaan Baatar and at some major aimag capitals, but this is the extent of available, and reliable, medicines. The stuff sold in the pharmacies may have incomprehensible instructions and will often be out of date. Take everything you may need with you, including syringes.

No specific vaccinations are required for Mongolia, though there are a few that could prove useful. Some vaccinations which have been recommended by western health authorities include rabies, hepatitis A, hepatitis B, polio, typhoid and tetanus. Whatever vaccinations you get should be recorded in an International Health Certificate. If you bring children to Mongolia, it's especially important to make sure that their vaccinations are up to date.

**Health Insurance** Although you may have medical insurance in your own country, it is probably not valid in Mongolia or neighbouring countries like China. A travel insurance policy is a very good idea – to protect you against cancellation penalties on advance purchase flights, against medical costs through illness or injury, against theft or loss of possessions, and against the cost of additional air tickets if you get really sick and have to fly home. Read the small print carefully since it's easy to be caught out by exclusions.

If you are ill enough to cancel a tour which has been paid in advance, you'll be lodging a claim to recover the cost of that part of the tour you never took. Insurance companies like to have your circumstances documented and certified by doctors they recognise.

**Medical Kit** Because of the shortage of western medicines in Mongolia, you should carry everything that you might possibly need. Some of the items which could be included are: Band-aids; a sterilised gauze bandage; plaster (adhesive tape); a thermometer; tweezers; pins; scissors; antibiotic ointment; an antiseptic (Dettol or Betadine); water purification tablets; diarrhoea medication (Lomotil or Imodium, plus an oral rehydration solution); laxative; acetaminophen (Panadol), aspirin or Ibuprofen for pain and fever; contraceptives (including condoms); a couple of syringes; and any special medication you're already taking plus a copy of your prescription.

**Antibiotics** Antibiotics are difficult to come by in Mongolia, and it would be a very good idea to bring your own supply. This does *not* mean that you should dose yourself with antibiotics without medical supervision.

There are numerous kinds of antibiotics and you can hardly be expected to carry your own travelling pharmacy, but tetracycline in 250mg capsules taken four times daily for seven days (a total of 28 capsules) is a fairly standard course for most general infections. However, tetracycline is contraindicated in women who are pregnant or breastfeeding and must not be given to children.

In western countries, antibiotics are prescription drugs so you'll need to see a doctor. In many Asian countries (China, Thailand, Taiwan and Indonesia) antibiotics are sold over the counter. In Mongolia, medicine is not yet privatised, but sometimes the only place to find the drugs you need is in the open air market.

If you're contemplating bringing a child to Mongolia, see a qualified doctor for advice about how to treat childhood illnesses.

### Basic Rules
**Food & Water** Mongolian food may not taste very good but it's usually safe to eat. The biggest problem is likely to be unboiled milk (see the following section on brucellosis).

Mongolians insist that the tap water is safe to drink in Ulaan Baatar and most other places – indeed, we never had any problems drinking tap water in the larger cities. However, there can be occasions in late summer when the water table in the city rises as a result of heavy storms and the water becomes unsafe to drink – in this case, public health alerts are issued.

If you think the water could be contaminated and you don't have any way to boil or purify the water, locals may brew some tea for you to drink. Before filling your cup with water from the tap, let it run for about 30 seconds to get the rust out of the pipes. Bottles of mineral water are available in Ulaan Baatar (not in the countryside), but try alternatives because the plastic bottles are not biodegradable.

Underground well water is almost always safe to drink, though in the Gobi it's high in mineral content and not too good for the liver if you drink it continuously for several years. However, the big problem is drinking surface water from rivers and lakes, especially in areas where it may be contaminated by livestock. If you do any camping and hiking, you will occasionally find it necessary to drink unboiled surface water. It's always better to drink water moving rather than stagnant water, and away from livestock. See the section on giardia for information on using water purification tablets.

It's essential to carry a water bottle with you, regardless of where you are going or how you are travelling. Even in cold weather, the bone-dry climate demands that you increase your water intake. If you find you are urinating infrequently or if your urine turns a deep yellow or orange, you may be dehydrating – you may also find yourself getting headaches.

## Medical Problems & Treatment

**Brucellosis** The UN Food & Agricultural Organisation (FAO) reports that Mongolia is a high-risk area for brucellosis. This is a disease of cattle, yaks, camels and sheep, but it can also infect humans. The most likely way for humans to contract this disease is by drinking unboiled milk or eating homemade cheese. Another way is for humans with open cuts on their hands to handle freshly killed meat. Cow dung (which the Mongolians use for building fires) is another possible source of infection.

In livestock, the main symptom is spontaneous abortion. In humans, brucellosis causes severe headaches, joint and muscle pains, fever and fatigue. There may be diarrhoea and, later, constipation. The onset of the symptoms may be rapid or slow, and can occur from five days to several months after exposure, with the average time being two weeks.

One of the sinister aspects of this disease is that the fever may come and go. Most patients recover in two or three weeks, but some people get chronic brucellosis which recurs sporadically for months and years and can cause long-term health problems. Fatalities are rare but possible.

Brucellosis is a serious disease which requires blood tests to make the diagnosis. If you think you may have contracted the disease, you need medical attention, preferably outside Mongolia. The disease often presents as an intermittent fever and the many other causes of such a fever should be excluded. Returning travellers should mention the possibility of the disease to their doctor if they remain unwell after their return from Mongolia.

**Travellers' Diarrhoea** All travellers get diarrhoea eventually – even Chinggis Khaan had it. Diarrhoea is often due simply to a change of diet. A lot depends on what you're used to eating and whether or not you've got an iron gut. In some parts of Mongolia, the high mineral content of the water can trigger diarrhoea, but your body should soon adjust. If you do get diarrhoea, the first thing to do is wait, since it rarely lasts more than a few days.

Diarrhoea will cause you to dehydrate, which will make you feel much worse. The solution is not simply to drink water, since it will run right through you. You'll get much better results by mixing your water with oral rehydration salts, which are almost impossible to find in Mongolia. If you didn't bring any, Mongolian salty tea could be your salvation.

If the diarrhoea persists, then the usual treatment is Lomotil or Imodium tablets. The maximum dose for Lomotil is two tablets three times a day. Antidiarrhoeal drugs don't cure anything, but slow down the digestive system so that the cramps go away and you don't have to go to the toilet all the time. Excessive use of these drugs is not advised, as they can cause dependency and other side effects.

It will help if you eat a light, fibre-free diet. It's hard to keep your diet 'light' in Mongolia, but fibre-free should be no problem given the lack of fruit and vegetables. Yoghurt, cheese or boiled eggs with salt are basic staples for diarrhoea patients, assuming you can find these. Later you may be able to tolerate plain white rice.

If the diarrhoea persists for a week or more and you feel particularly rotten, it's probably giardia (see below).

**Constipation** Most travellers worry about diarrhoea, but Mongolia's standard diet of mutton, fat and flour lacks fibre and can cause the opposite problem, constipation. Eating fruit and vegetables is the best solution, but these are not readily available. Although constipation is usually nothing to get worried about, it is uncomfortable. Some travellers throw a bottle of laxatives into their first-aid kit. Laxatives are OK for occasional use, but their overuse is harmful and can even lead to illnesses like irritable bowel syndrome. The best solution for constipation might be to bring some bran flakes or chewable high-fibre pills or fibre bars.

**Giardia** Giardia is a type of amoeba which inhabits the intestine and is spread by drinking contaminated water. This amoeba causes severe diarrhoea, nausea, cramping and weakness. Without treatment, the symptoms tend to go away, come back, go away again, then return, ad infinitum, ad nauseam. Some

people manage to live with it for years, but others find it unbearable.

The simplest treatment for giardia is Fasigyn (tinidazole) 2gm as a single dose. If this doesn't work, repeat the dose or go onto Flagyl (metronidazole) 250mg three times a day for five to 10 days.

Never drink alcohol with these tablets – the combination produces severe nausea and vomiting, an effect described by some as a feeling of 'imminent death'. Even with treatment, it can sometimes be difficult to rid yourself of giardia, so you might need laboratory tests after you return home to be certain that you're cured.

Bringing water to the boil is sufficient to kill most bacteria, but 20 minutes of boiling is required to kill the amoebic cysts that cause giardia.

Water purification tablets are available in two varieties: chlorine-based and iodine-based. The chlorine tablets are sufficient to kill most bacteria, but they may not kill the amoebic cysts that cause giardia. Only iodine-based tablets are certain to kill amoeba, but iodine has a wretched taste and is unsafe for prolonged use.

**Cholera** In the summer of 1996, Mongolia reported its first outbreak of cholera. It started in the northern provinces, possibly from infected meat imported from Russia, and killed several people. Health authorities swiftly reacted (if not overreacted) by placing a cordon sanitaire around about one-quarter of the country, closing stalls and markets in Ulaan Baatar, and stopping all travel to infected areas. The cause of the disease was soon discovered, and the problem solved.

Cholera is a disease of insanitation, so if you've heard reports of cholera be especially careful about what you eat, drink and brush your teeth with. Symptoms include a sudden onset of acute diarrhoea with 'rice water' stools, vomiting, muscular cramps and extreme weakness. You need medical help – but meanwhile treat for dehydration, which can be extreme. If there is an appreciable delay in getting to hospital then begin taking tetracycline – 250mg four times daily for adults – but this is not recommended for pregnant women or for children aged eight or less. An alternative drug is Ampicillin.

The cholera vaccine is not very effective and is not recommended. Fluid replacement is by far the most important aspect of treatment. With cholera, up to 20 litres of fluid may be excreted in one day. Thus, large volumes of fluid, sometimes up to 20 litres, may be required to ensure adequate hydration.

**Tetanus** This serious illness is due to a bacillus which usually enters the blood system through a cut or as the result of a skin puncture by a rusty nail, wire etc. A vaccination against tetanus is cheap, readily available and worth getting even if you don't go travelling. A tetanus booster shot should be given every five years.

**Hepatitis A** Hepatitis is a disease which affects the liver. There are several varieties, most commonly hepatitis A and B. See the section on sexually transmitted diseases for information about hepatitis B.

Hepatitis A occurs in countries with poor sanitation. It's spread from person to person via infected food or water, or contaminated cooking and eating utensils. Salads which have been washed in infected water, or fruit which has been handled by an infected person might carry the disease. Hepatitis is not caused by alcohol consumption, but booze makes it more difficult to recover. Given the low level of sanitation and high level of vodka addiction, it's not surprising so many people suffer from hepatitis in Mongolia.

Symptoms consist of fever, loss of appetite, nausea, depression, complete lack of energy and pains around the bottom of your rib cage (the location of the liver). Your skin turns progressively yellow and the whites of your eyes change from white to yellow to orange.

The best way to detect hepatitis is to watch the colour of your urine, which will turn a deep orange no matter how much liquid you drink. If you haven't drunk much liquid or you're sweating a lot, you may just be dehydrated, so don't jump to conclusions.

The severity of hepatitis A varies; it may last less than two weeks and give you only a few bad days, or it may last for several months and give you a few bad weeks. You could feel depleted of energy for several months afterwards. If you get hepatitis, there's not much you can do apart from resting, eating good food to assist recovery and drinking lots of fluids. Don't use alcohol or tobacco since that only gives your liver more work to do.

Taking care with what you eat and drink can go a long way towards preventing this disease. As this is a very infectious virus, additional cover is recommended. This comes in two forms: gamma globulin and Havrix.

Havrix 1440 provides long-term immunity, possibly more than 10 years, and has many advantages over gamma globulin, which provides immunity from the virus for only a limited time.

**Sexually Transmitted Diseases** Even if you don't expect to have sex on your travels, make sure you're well informed about safe sexual practices before you go, and take some condoms just in case. Condoms are not 100% effective against sexually transmitted diseases (STDs), but are better than nothing.

Gonorrhoea and syphilis are two of the more common STDs. The symptoms include sores, blisters or rashes around the genitals and discharges or pain when urinating. However, symptoms may be less marked or not observed at all in women. Syphilis is insidious in that the symptoms eventually disappear completely, but the disease continues and can strike back years later with devastating consequences. Fortunately, both gonorrhoea and syphilis can be cured with antibiotics, but don't delay treatment.

Prostitutes now hang out at the bars in some of the big tourist hotels in Ulaan Baatar, and not surprisingly there have been reports that venereal disease is on the increase. This is no doubt worsened by the current scarcity of antibiotics.

Of course, antibiotics are no use at all against AIDS, which is currently believed to be incurable. The Mongolian government announced its discovery of the first known case of AIDS in 1993, but given the low standard of medical care and medical testing facilities, it's likely many other cases will remain undetected for some time. It's also possible that Mongolian 'national pride' will keep cases from being reported. With the increase in trading throughout Asia and eastern Europe and tourism (and associated prostitution), it's likely that others have been infected.

Quite apart from unsafe sexual practices, AIDS can be spread through infected blood transfusions; most developing countries – and this includes Mongolia – cannot afford to screen blood for transfusions. It can also be spread by dirty needles, so vaccinations, acupuncture and tattooing can be as dangerous as intravenous drug use if the equipment is not clean. Bring your own acupuncture needles if you're interested in this form of medicine. It's worth taking a couple of new syringes with you, but you may need a letter from your GP to wave at customs, in case they start jumping to the wrong conclusions. Try not to need a blood transfusion; if you do, and you happen to have an HIV-negative friend with the same blood group nearby, ask them to donate blood for you. In many cases, a drip may be all you need.

Hepatitis B is transmitted in the same ways as AIDS. However, it's been around longer and is far more infectious, and the Mongolian authorities estimate that 16% of the population are carriers. There is an expensive and elaborate vaccine (three jabs, over a minimum of three weeks), but it must be given before you've been exposed. The symptoms of the disease are similar to those of hepatitis A, but there's a possibility of serious long-term liver damage, and between five and 10% of sufferers become carriers after they recover.

The message is the same as for AIDS: safe sex, and no dirty needles of any kind.

**Rabies** In the Mongolian countryside, virtually every family has a dog. Country dogs are often vicious, deliberately bred and trained to protect flocks of sheep from all intruders, including humans and wolves. Their occasional battles with wolves and other dogs can spread rabies. This is another disease worth guarding against. A vaccination is available, but few people get it. The vaccine must be given three times over three weeks and is good for about two years. However, if you're bitten, the vaccine by itself is *not* sufficient to prevent rabies; it will only increase the time you have to get treatment, and you will require fewer injections if you've been vaccinated.

If you are bitten or licked by any animal, you should wash the wound thoroughly with soap (but without scrubbing since this may push the infected saliva deeper into the your body) and then start on a series of injections which will prevent the disease from developing. Once it reaches the brain, rabies has a 100% fatality rate. New rabies vaccines have been developed which have fewer side effects than the older, animal-derived serums and vaccines.

The incubation period for rabies depends on where you're bitten. If on the head, face or neck then it's as little as 10 days, whereas on the arms it's 40 days and on the legs it's 60 days. This allows plenty of time to be given the vaccine and for it to have a beneficial effect. Try to get proper medical treatment outside Mongolia. If proper treatment is given quickly after having been bitten, rabies will not develop.

**Bubonic (Black) Plague** For the past 10 years this disease, which wiped out one-third of Europe's population during the Middle Ages, has made an appearance in remote parts of Mongolia in late summer (from August to October), when the ban on hunting marmots stops, and their meat is eaten.

The disease is normally carried by marmots, squirrels and rats and can be transmitted to humans by bites from fleas which make their home on the infected animals. It can also be passed from human to human by coughing. The symptoms are fever and enlarged lymph nodes. The untreated disease has a 60% death rate, but if you get a doctor it can be quickly treated. The best drug is the antibiotic streptomycin, which must be injected intramuscularly, but it is not available in Mongolia. Tetracycline is another drug which may be used.

During an outbreak, travel to affected areas is prohibited, which can greatly affect overland travel. All trains, buses and cars travelling into Ulaan Baatar from infected areas are also thoroughly checked when an outbreak of the plague has been reported.

**Eye Infections** Although Mongolia doesn't have a particularly severe problem with eye disease, it's almost impossible to keep dust and dirt out of your eyes during a Gobi jeep trip. Wearing goggles helps – just forget about how you look. Be careful about wiping your face with the towels supplied by hotels, as this is an easy way to transmit eye infections. Try to keep your hands away from your eyes.

There are several types of eye infections, a simple one usually being conjunctivitis, and the most serious being trachoma. Pain in the eyes, headaches, burning, itching, redness, swelling and a white discharge are some of the symptoms of eye disease.

If you have an eye infection, it's not wise to attempt to treat yourself – at least try to get a medical opinion first. In many cases, burning and itching eyes are not the result of infection at all, but simply the effects of dust, petrol fumes and bright sunshine. Treating simple eye irritation with antibiotics is worse than useless. After a day in the jeep, using eyewash can help to rid your eyes of dust, but don't overdo it, since excessive use of eyewash and eye drops can also make your eyes burn. If you don't have any commercial eyewash, just use water, but make sure it's clean.

Considering the lack of medicines, those who are preparing for a long stay may want to bring eye drops for conjunctivitis, and antibiotic eye ointments (tetracycline or erythromycin) for trachoma. Bring plenty of antibiotic eye ointment, as trachoma may require up to six weeks of treatment.

**Hypothermia & Frostbite** In a country where temperatures can plummet to minus 40°C, cold is something you should take seriously.

Hypothermia is the lowering of the whole body temperature and can lead to death. It is surprisingly easy to progress from very cold to dangerously cold through a combination of wind, wet clothing, fatigue and hunger, even if the air temperature is above freezing. Sudden thunderstorms in the mountains can have just this effect – you can die of cold during the summer at high altitude. Even in the lowlands, sudden winds from the north can send the temperature plummeting, and people have indeed frozen to death during 'balmy' May weather.

The solution is to be properly equipped. Besides warm clothing, carry basic supplies, including food that contains simple sugars to generate heat quickly and lots of fluid to drink (if you're lucky, it won't freeze into a block of ice).

Symptoms of hypothermia are exhaustion, numb skin (particularly of the toes and fingers), shivering, slurred speech, irrational or violent behaviour, lethargy, stumbling, dizzy spells, muscle cramps and violent bursts of energy. Irrationality may take the form of sufferers claiming they are warm and trying to take off their clothes.

To treat hypothermia, first get the patient out of the wind, rain or cold. If possible, remove wet clothing and replace it with dry, warm clothing. Give them hot sweet liquids – not alcohol – and some high-energy, easily digestible food. This should be enough for the early stages of hypothermia, but if it has gone further it may be necessary to place the victim in a warm sleeping bag and get in with them since their body will not be able to generate enough heat by itself. Hypothermia victims cannot feel much pain, so be careful about putting them too near a stove – burn injuries only complicate the problem. A warm bath is best of all, but make sure it's not too hot.

Frostbite is a cold injury of the limbs, most commonly occurring on the toes, fingers and sometimes the nose and ears. Like hypothermia, frostbite is insidious; the victim feels nothing but a little numbness during the time the injury occurs, but severe pain follows when the tissue is thawed out. Ironically, the result looks and feels much like a severe burn, and can be just as traumatic. Prevention is the best medicine, but if you do get frostbitten, don't delay in seeking medical attention. It is possible that the dead tissue will need to be removed surgically and antibiotics given to prevent infection. Scarring and permanent injury are possible.

**Bites & Stings** Mongolia has four species of poisonous snakes: Halys viper *(agkistrodon halys)*, common European viper or adder *(vipera berus)*, Orsini's viper *(vipera ursini)* and the small *taphrometaphon lineolatum*.

Despite what you see in the movies, most snakes are not aggressive, at least not when it comes to creatures larger than themselves. At the sight of a human, most snakes will flee. If a snakes crosses your path, don't grab a stick and attack it – that's the most likely way to get bitten. Just keep a respectful distance, make a bit of a noise or stamp your feet, and the chances are good that it will quickly move on its way.

Most snakes bite when humans accidentally step on them. High boots, or trousers and long socks, are better protection than tennis shoes, but it's still advisable to watch where you put your feet. When hiking around in the countryside, keep your hands out of holes and crevices.

Being cold-blooded animals, snakes don't come out during freezing temperatures, but when the mercury gets just above 0°C, snakes may emerge to sun themselves on a warm rock, so watch where you sit!

Snake bites do not cause instantaneous death. Indeed, most victims survive, and the majority of people who are bitten are not poisoned, or receive only a small dose. If there's no more than a little swelling around the wound, the patient is unlikely to be in serious danger.

If one of your party has been unlucky enough to be badly bitten, the best thing to do is to get to a hospital and get a prescribed antivenin. You will need to identify the snake: some people do this by killing it and showing it to the doctor, but it's better not to take risks, and don't handle the snake even once it's dead. However, the chances of finding antivenin in Mongolia are fairly remote, though a hospital can still do the patient much good with oxygen, intravenous solutions and various life-support systems. Some of the first-aid techniques commonly used in the past, such as tourniquets (which can lead to gangrene), cutting open the bite and sucking out the poison, or immersion in cold water – are now comprehensively discredited.

So, what should you do when there is no medical help available and you are far from civilisation? Keep the patient still and as calm as possible – encourage them to breathe deeply and remind them that they may not have been poisoned at all. Tie a cloth band between the wound and the heart to slow the absorption of the poison, or wind an elastic bandage around the whole limb. If the limb begins to turn blue, the band is too tight and you should loosen it a little. The idea is to slow down the body's absorption of the poison. Victims will become quite ill if they have been bitten, but they will most likely survive. Having the patient lie down with the feet slightly raised helps to supply blood to the brain and control shock. Try to get the patient to hospital by car or jeep.

The situation is much the same with scorpions. Scorpion stings are rarely fatal, but are usually very painful and can cause severe illness. There is no specific antivenin, but hospital treatment can do a lot of good. If you are far from a hospital, the victim should remain calm (which sounds easier than it is), rest and allow the poison to be slowly absorbed and then excreted through urine and sweat.

Scorpions hide under rocks and in brush – poking around in those places with bare hands is asking for trouble. Don't be impressed by size, as the smallest scorpions are the most venomous! Scorpions do sometimes come into buildings and gers at night and crawl into shoes left on the ground, so shake your shoes out in the morning before putting them on.

Tarantulas are large, poisonous spiders which are also found in Mongolia. However, their venom is not very strong, and unless you pick one up and play with it, you aren't likely to be bitten.

Bees, wasps and red ants are no worse in Mongolia than elsewhere, but if you are allergic to their venom, bring a 'bee sting kit' consisting of the drug adrenalin (epinephrine) and the paraphernalia to inject it. Adrenalin is also available in pill form but is less effective if administered that way. Don't expect to find this drug in Mongolia.

While there are no deadly plants (unless you eat them), you can often find stinging nettles along the river banks during summer. Touching these will be painful but hardly fatal. Once you've had an encounter with a stinging nettle, you won't forget what the plant looks like!

### Women's Health

**Gynaecological Problems** Vaginal yeast infections, characterised by a rash, itch and discharge, can be treated with a vinegar or even lemon-juice douche, or with yoghurt. Nystatin suppositories are the usual medical prescription. You'll have a hard enough time finding lemon juice in Mongolia, let alone nystatin suppositories, so come prepared.

Trichomonas is a more serious infection; symptoms are a discharge and a burning sensation when urinating. Male sexual partners must also be treated, and if a vinegar-water douche is not effective, medical attention should be sought. Flagyl is the prescribed drug.

**Pregnancy** Most miscarriages occur during the first three months of pregnancy, so this is the riskiest time to travel as far as your own health is concerned. Miscarriage is common and occasionally leads to severe bleeding, in which case you may need medical help quickly.

The last three months should also be spent within reasonable distance of good medical care, as a baby born as early as 24 weeks stands a chance of survival in a good, modern hospital – that is, not in Mongolia.

Pregnant women should avoid alcohol, nicotine and all unnecessary medication, but vaccinations should still be taken where possible. Additional care should be taken to prevent illness and particular attention should be paid to nutrition, so keep those vitamin pills handy. Your Mongolian diet may not be adequate for the developing foetus, which is thought to be at its most vulnerable between eight and 16 weeks' gestation.

### TOILETS

In most hotels in Ulaan Baatar and aimag capitals (except in the Muslim-influenced Bayan-Ölgii province), and in most ger camps, toilets are the sit-down, European variety. In other hotels, and some more remote ger camps, you will have to use pit toilets. These are generally abominable – often you cannot breathe through your nose because of the smell or your mouth because of the swarms of flies.

In the countryside, where there may not be a bush or tree for hundreds of km, modesty is not something to worry about – just do it where you want to, but away from gers. Also, try to avoid such places as an *ovoo* (a sacred pile of stones), rivers and lakes (water sources for nomads) and marmot holes.

The plumbing is decrepit in many of the older hotels, and toilet paper can easily jam up the works. If there is a rubbish basket next to the toilet, this is where the paper should go. The hotel management will get quite upset if you plug things up.

### WOMEN TRAVELLERS

Mongolia doesn't present too many problems for foreign women travelling independently. The majority of Mongolian men behave in a friendly and respectful manner, without ulterior motives. However, you may come across an annoying drunk or the occasional macho idiot, and you should be more circumspect in the mostly Muslim Bayan-Ölgii province. Those who have travelled in Central Asia can breathe easier while in Mongolia.

## USEFUL ORGANISATIONS

If you need some information about Mongolia before you come, or want to meet some people once you arrive, there are several organisations to contact. Professionals working in Mongolia are not, however, a travel advice service for distressed backpackers who don't discover until it's too late how hard it can be getting around Mongolia alone; nor are they interested in providing invitations to help with your visa.

### Aid & Development

International Federation of Red Cross and Red Crescent Societies
   PO Box 537, Central Post Office, Ulaan Baatar (☎ 321 684)
Save the Children Fund
   PO Box 678, Central Post Office, Ulaan Baatar (☎ 321 590)
United Nations Development Program
   UNDP publishes reports on Mongolia and has volunteer programmes; PO Box 49/207, Ulaan Baatar; 7 Erkhuugiin Gudamj (☎ 327 585; fax 326 221; email mon01%mon01.undp-mon@nylan.undp.org)
World Health Organisation
   PO Box 663, Ulaan Baatar (☎ & fax 327 870)

### Mongolian Friendship Societies & Information Services

Australia
   Australia-Mongolia Society, PO Box 1091, Collingwood, Victoria 3066 (☎ (3) 417 5953)
France
   Association Culturelle Franco-Mongolie, 94 rue Broca, F-75013, Paris
Germany
   Mongolische Notizen, Waldfriedenstr 31, D-53639, Königswinter (☎ (2244) 6081)
Italy
   Associazone Italia-Mongolia, PO Box 979, Viale XX, Settembre 37, Trieste (☎ (40) 362 241; fax 363 494)
UK
   Anglo-Mongolian Society, Dept of Far Eastern Studies, University of Great Britain, Leeds LS2 9JT (☎ (0113) 233 3460; fax 233 6741)
   Tibet-Mongolian Enterprise, 167 West End Lane, West Hampstead, London NW6 2LG (☎ (0171) 624 7534; fax 379 0465)
USA
   Mongolia Society Inc, 322 Goodbody Hall, Indiana University, Bloomington, IN 47405, USA (☎ (812) 855-4078; fax 855-7500; email monsoc@indiana.edu)

Mongol-American Cultural Association, 50 Louis St, New Brunswick, NJ 08901 (☎ & fax (908) 297 1140)

### General

Hash House Harriers, the internationally known running group, has even made it to Mongolia. They currently meet for a jog (and a few cleansing ales afterwards) at the Bayangol Hotel, in Ulaan Baatar, on Tuesdays at 6.30 pm.
International Ladies Association of Mongolia (☎ 326 579)
Mongolian Women's Federation (☎ 328 060)
Rotary is active in Mongolia. Contact details changed and were unknown at the time of research. If you are in Mongolia, ask at a local embassy.

## DANGERS & ANNOYANCES

Before you get angry and complain about why things just don't work as well as they could or should, take a second to think about what Mongolia has experienced and is still enduring: years of Chinese domination and Soviet communism; a perverse climate; a terrible road and transport system; a lifestyle based on nomadism which rarely complements western thinking and economics; a young, sparse population which suffers from poverty and bad health; and unrestrained capitalism and development since 1990.

### Theft

Most Mongolians are very poor and foreign goodies are a real temptation. Theft is seldom violent against foreigners, just opportunistic. Pickpocketing and bag slitting with razor blades are increasingly common in crowded buses and trains in Ulaan Baatar, but is not nearly as rife as in China. At the Gandan monastery, unsuspecting tourists, mesmerised by enchanting ceremonies, have been relieved of their money and passports. If you camp at Yarmag during the Naadam Festival, be especially careful.

Valuables should be kept in a money belt and buried under your clothes. Some people find this arrangement uncomfortable, so another alternative is to keep these valuables in pockets sewn on the *inside* of a vest (waistcoat).

## After Dark

It is not a good idea to walk around ger suburbs in Ulaan Baatar, and in the countryside, after dark, especially if you are travelling alone and don't speak Mongolian. In Ulaan Baatar, street lights often cease at 2 am, so be home by then, or take a taxi. Foreigners, especially women, should use a proper taxi – as opposed to a private vehicle – for lifts around town late at night.

Be careful when coming out alone from nightclubs in Ulaan Baatar, where alcohol and comparatively rich foreigners are a potentially vulnerable mixture. Virtually no stairways in the whole country have lights, so a torch (flashlight) is a good idea, but using one along the streets in the dark will clearly indicate that you are a foreigner (locals never use a torch).

## Dogs

Stray dogs in the cities and domestic dogs around gers in the countryside can be vicious, and possibly rabid. In the countryside, some dogs are so damn lazy that you are unlikely to get a whimper if a hundred lame cats hobbled past; others may almost head-butt your vehicle and chase it for 2 or 3km while drooling heavily. Before approaching any ger, especially in the countryside, make sure the dogs are friendly or under control.

If you need to walk in the dark in the countryside – eg you need a midnight trip to the toilet – swing a torch in front of you. We have been told that dogs don't attack any light.

## Alcoholism

Alcoholism is a real problem and is far worse in the cities than in the countryside. Drinking often starts early in the morning, and the problem becomes progressively worse in the evenings. Drunks are more annoying than dangerous, except when they are driving your bus or taxi – so avoid any vehicle which you know or suspect is driven by a drunk.

On the streets, drunks are easy to avoid because they are usually unable to walk or function properly, and they rarely walk around in groups. Be sensible in bars: don't get into arguments about the virtues or otherwise of Chinggis Khaan, or flash around a lot of money. If camping, always make sure that you have pitched your tent somewhere secluded, and that no drunks have seen you set up camp – otherwise, they will invariably visit you during the night.

## The Mongolian Scramble

It could be the warrior-like bloodlines from Chinggis Khaan, a penchant for wrestling or habits from the communist days where demand always exceeded supply, but Mongolians rarely queue – they bustle, huddle and scramble. You will often need to sharpen your elbows, learn some appropriately argumentative phrases in Mongolian, and plough head first through the throng. Some places in Ulaan Baatar where the Mongolian Scramble is imperative if you want to get what you want are the Central Market, the train and bus stations and ticket offices, and the Russian embassy. In the countryside, where the population is sparse, you will only have to do the Scramble when boarding or getting off trains and buses.

## Corruption & Greed

Corruption is getting worse. Mongolians complain loudly because they suffer the consequences daily – aid money doesn't reach its intended beneficiaries, the old elite still controls everything and no-one believes the prime minister survives just on his official salary. Anyone trying to do business in Mongolia will soon discover that corruption is rampant and growing.

Most tourists probably won't have to deal with corrupt officials, except to extend a visa, register a vehicle or buy an airline or train ticket in peak season. Bribery is best negotiated with the assistance of a Mongolian friend who knows the going rate and won't overpay. If you don't have someone to help, just ask to see someone higher up.

## Other Annoyances

Electricity, heating and hot water shortages and blackouts are common all year, and permanent restrictions are endemic in the countryside. Although official policies have relaxed considerably since the arrival of democracy, some of the old KGB-inspired thinking still occurs among the police, especially in rural backwaters. A few aimags still have checkpoints where jeep drivers must stop and register their passengers.

Most offices have security guards in the lobby checking the ID cards of everyone who enters and leaves the buildings – it can sometimes be a nightmare getting past them. Beggars, near the major hotels in Ulaan Baatar, are an increasing annoyance, and will only get worse. Pollution in Ulaan Baatar and the major cities is often appalling and gets worse in winter when much more fuel is used.

## BUSINESS HOURS

Opening hours are often at the whim of staff. You can order a meal and then be told an hour later that it won't be ready because the cook is 'out to lunch'; the caretaker of the local museum might be in the local bar getting drunk; hotels can sometimes close, even in summer, if there are no guests. There are official business hours, however, and things are slowly improving.

Government offices are usually open from 9 am to 5 pm on weekdays, and from 9 am to noon on Saturday. Banks are supposed to open from 10 am to 3 pm weekdays, and from 9 am to noon on Saturday. Most offices are closed on Sunday. Most private and state-run businesses open at about 10 am and close sometime between 5 and 8 pm. Most restaurants open at noon, but the few that serve breakfast open around 7.30 am.

Most shops and businesses will close for an hour at lunch, sometime between noon and 2 pm. In Ulaan Baatar, many restaurants – especially the good ones – will be busy, and often full, between about 1 and 2 pm. It pays to get a table before 12.30 pm to beat the rush.

## PUBLIC HOLIDAYS & SPECIAL EVENTS

The following public holidays are celebrated in Mongolia, but not necessarily with a day off work: 1 January, New Year's Day *(Shin*

*Jil)*; 13 January, the adoption of the 1992 constitution (normally not a day off); Lunar New Year *(Tsagaan Sar)*, a three-day holiday in January/February; 1 June, Mother & Children's Day; 8 March, Women's Day (not normally a day off); 11 to 13 July, National Day, mainly celebrated as the Naadam Festival; and 26 November, Mongolian Republic Day (not normally a day off work).

## Naadam Festival

The Naadam Festival showcases Mongolia's finest in the three 'manly sports' of horse racing, archery and wrestling (though females participate in the first two). The festival is the biggest event of the year for foreigners and locals alike and is held all over the country, normally between 11 and 13 July (the anniversary of the 1921 Mongolian Revolution). The first two days are when most of the major events take place, and the third day tends to be a day of conviviality.

In country centres close to Ulaan Baatar, Naadam festivities may be held the week before, or the week after, the major festival in Ulaan Baatar because some people like to attend both the local and national celebrations. The quality and number of sports and activities at Naadam festivals in the countryside will be lower than in Ulaan Baatar, but at a country Naadam you are more likely to get better seats, witness genuine (non-touristy) festivals and, possibly, make up the numbers during a wrestling tournament!

Naadam is now the prime tourist spectacle, with tour companies jostling for ringside seats for their clients, and some upmarket hotel rooms booked a year in advance. Unless you are fanatical about these three sports, the festival itself can be a little disappointing and may not be worth coming especially to Mongolia for. But the opening and closing ceremonies, many associated activities and shows, and the general *joie de vivre* around the country, are reasons enough to base a visit to Mongolia around the Naadam Festival.

On or about 9 August, another, tourist-oriented, Naadam festival called a Small *(Baga)* Naadam is held. Some travel agents may sell you a programme including this

## Naadam Festival in Ulaan Baatar

The highlight of the tourist season and the main draw card on most tour programmes is the Naadam Festival in Ulaan Baatar, known as the *eriyn gurvan naadam*, after the three 'manly' sports of wrestling, archery and horse racing.

Wrestling, archery and horse racing are held during the first and second days. Very little happens on the third day, so get drunk the day before and use it to recover from a hangover like everyone else. During the three days, few restaurants and shops are open and virtually no-one works. Accommodation can be scarce and prices often higher than normal.

Day one starts at about 9 am with a fantastic, colourful ceremony outside the State Parliament House, at Sükhbaatar Square. Hundreds of soldiers in bright uniforms play stirring warlike music on brass instruments, and Mongolians dressed in Chinggis-style warrior outfits parade around the Square, then circle Parliament House before marching to the stadium.

The opening ceremony, which starts at about 11 am at the Naadam Stadium, includes a show of Mongolia's military might as well as impressive marches of monks and athletes, and plenty of music. The closing ceremony, with more marches and dancing, is held at about 7 pm on day two. (In 1996 the closing ceremony was cancelled because the final round of the wrestling took over four hours to finish!)

The first round of wrestling, which starts at about noon on day one in the main stadium, is the more interesting and photogenic. Later rounds can get boring – most Mongolians don't bother returning to the stadium until the final rounds on the second day. If the wrestling gets too much, you can start whistling like the locals do, walk around the outside of the stadium and watch the Mongolians (which is far more interesting than a lot of what is happening in the stadium), and watch the changing of the guards.

Archery is held in an open stadium next to the main stadium. The judges, who raise their arms and utter a traditional cry to indicate the quality of the shot, are often more entertaining than the archery itself. But watch out for stray arrows!

The horse racing can attract well over 1000 horses (so watch your step, because this is a lot of dung!). (During the festival, you may see dozens of horses being herded down the main streets of Ulaan Baatar, as if they were on the steppes.) The horse racing is held at the village of Yarmag (Ярмаг), about 10km along the main road to the airport – it is very easy to spot. The atmosphere is electric, and there is always plenty to watch. You can even pitch your tent at the 'tent city' at Yarmag, but don't expect any privacy whatsoever, and watch out for drunks.

To get to Yarmag, will need to catch one of the very regular buses (T50) to Buyant-Ukhaa (Буянт-Ухаа), or a minibus (T100), from along the road to the Naadam Stadium. A taxi there will cost about T1800.

The best and busiest time to watch the horse racing is the final race, late on the second day, but you will be hard-pressed to see what is going on or take any good photos because of the crowds. Get there really early for the final, go to other races on both days, or walk up a few hundred metres along the track where the crowds thin out.

Tickets to the stadium and to the archery and horse racing are free, but foreigners pay US$12 for the opening ceremony and US$8 for the closing ceremony. A ticket does not usually give you a seat number, so get there in plenty of time for a good position, especially for the closing ceremony, when good seats may have been taken during the afternoon.

If on a packaged tour, your travel agency will arrange tickets. If travelling independently, getting a ticket to the opening and closing ceremonies is difficult. From 4 to 10 July, you can buy tickets from the Central Stadium Company (☎ 343 123; fax 343 320). You may be able to buy tickets at the stadium before the two ceremonies, but don't count on it. Coming to Ulaan Baatar a week early is a good idea to ensure accommodation and find tickets.

To find out what is going on during the festival, look for a detailed programme in the English-language newspapers.

You can find plenty of warm drinks and cold *khuurshuur* (meat pancakes), as well as ice cream, bread and some of the best fruits you will ever see, around the outside of the stadium. Take an umbrella or hat, because most seats are not under cover, and it will either rain or be hot. (For more information on the three sports, refer to the Spectator Sports section in this chapter.) ■

inferior festival. The best and original Naadam Festival will always be held from 11 to 13 July in Ulaan Baatar.

## Tsagaan Sar

After months of enduring a bitter winter, Mongolians love to celebrate Tsagaan Sar (White Month), the start of the lunar new year, in January or February. Most travellers are unlikely to be in Mongolia at this time, but if you are, be prepared for a lot of food – especially steamed mutton dumplings known as *buuz*. (If you can't eat 10, you are deemed to be inadequate.) A cast-iron liver is also required to cope with the amount of airag and vodka which is normally consumed.

## Ovoo-Worship Festival

The *ovoo* is a shaman shrine (see Religion in the Facts about the Country chapter) to ensure auspicious riding across the vast distances of Mongolia. Traditionally the ovoos are places for libations, ritual offerings of airag and vodka, accompanied by songs telling of the beauty and power of the land.

An Ovoo-Worship Festival is mostly a small-scale, unofficial event held in rural areas. Monks say prayers, people give offerings and afterwards there is feasting and some traditional sports like horse racing. The rituals are held to celebrate the end of winter and pray for good rainfall, plentiful grass for the livestock and abundant fish and animals for hunting. Chances are you won't get to see it at all unless you have Mongolian friends who can take you to one. The festival, once prohibited and denounced by the communists as feudal, has been revived since the democracy movement of 1990.

## ACTIVITIES

This section provides a brief description of activities available in Mongolia and the best (or only) places to go for them. More details are provided throughout the book.

### Skiing

If you can bear the cold, Mongolia is a great place for cross-country skiing. Snow is often thin, but it's there throughout the long winter, sometimes for seven months a year. The Juulchin travel agency runs skiing tours near Ulaan Baatar, or if you have your own gear (there is nowhere to hire anything), go to Terelj or Nairamdal Zuslan, the best and most accessible places, and ask about some safe trails.

The best months for skiing are in January and February – but be warned: the average temperature in these months is about -25°C.

### Ice Skating

In winter, you won't have to worry about falling through the ice, as many lakes and rivers freeze right down to the bottom. Many Mongolians are keen ice skaters – at least those who live near water, or in big cities with rinks. To find the best spots, you will have to ask the locals where they go. Although it is possible to buy ice skates in Mongolia, don't count on it – if you're serious about this sport, bring your own equipment.

### Horse & Camel Riding

Riding on horses and camels (and even yaks) is part of many organised tours and great fun – if only for a few minutes. (Mongolians watching you will probably enjoy it more.)

---

**Tsagaan Sar**

Mongolians have been celebrating Tsagaan Sar for thousands of years, although it may have been held during the summer (possibly in August) when Chinggis was roaming the steppes. Now held over three days in January or February, Tsagaan Sar celebrates the end of winter and the start of spring, with plenty of eating and drinking vodka and airag (which has been frozen through the winter).

During the first day, the fattest sheep is killed and hundreds and hundreds of steamed dumplings called *buuz* are made. The tail, which is the most prized part of the sheep, is kept until the end of the celebrations. The days are filled with traditional songs, greetings called *zolgokh*, where younger people give their respect to the older generations, and visits to other gers and, these days, to monasteries. ■

Most ger camps can arrange horse riding – the prettiest (but not cheapest) places to try are the camps at Terelj and Khövsgöl lake.

If you are a serious rider, horses are everywhere; with some luck, guidance and experience, you should be able to find a horse suited to your needs. Mongolians swap horses readily, so there's no need to be stuck with a horse you don't like, or which doesn't like you. The only exception is in April and May, when all animals are weak after the long winter and before fresh spring plants have made their way through the melting snows.

The best time for riding is in the summer (June to September), though it is usually wetter then. See the Getting Around chapter for information about travel agencies which organise horse riding.

At touristy places like the ger camps at Terelj and in the south Gobi you can ride a camel, though these are more like photo sessions (and entertainment for local camel herders) rather than serious sport.

### Hiking

Mongolia has many outstanding opportunities for hiking, though very few locals do it and think foreigners are crazy for even thinking about it. The biggest obstacle faced by hikers is finding transport to the mountains once they get far afield from Ulaan Baatar. However, in the regions around Bogdkhan national park and Terelj, which are not far from Ulaan Baatar, there are enough mountains to keep hikers busy for months.

Way out west, you can break out the expedition gear and scale dozens of mountains with glaciers. Warm-weather hikers can head for the Gobi Desert, which despite its vast flatness also harbours a few rugged mountain ranges.

Essential survival gear includes a leakproof water bottle (take a minimum of two litres a day, preferably more during summer), emergency food rations, sunblock (UV) lotion, a compass, plaster (adhesive tape) for blisters and something to cut it with, sunglasses and a straw hat. You will need Chapstick or Vaseline. Don't forget about Mongolia's notoriously changeable weather – a sudden wind from the north will make you think you're in the Arctic rather than the Gobi. Only from June to August can you usually expect balmy temperatures, but this is when it rains most.

Decent maps are hard to come by. The ONC/TPC series, or the individual provincial maps available in Ulaan Baatar (refer to the Maps section earlier in this chapter), are your best bet. You will also need a working knowledge of appropriate phrases like: 'Where am I?' and 'Is that dog dangerous?'

Mosquitoes and midges are a curse. The situation is worst during spring and early summer. Mosquito repellent will make your life more comfortable. It's best to hike with at least one companion, always tell someone where you're going and refer to your compass frequently so you can find the way back. Unless you're planning a camping trip, start out early in the day so that you can easily make it back before dark.

### Mountaineering

Mongolia also offers spectacular opportunities for mountain climbing. In the western provinces, there are over 100 glaciers, and 30 to 40 permanently snowcapped mountains. You must have the necessary experience, be fully equipped and hire local guides. The best time to climb is from the start of July until the end of August.

While you don't need permits from the Ministry of Nature & Environment unless the mountain is in a national park, you should consult the undisputed experts in mountain climbing in Mongolia: the Mongol Altai Club (☎ & fax 55 246), PO Box 49-23, Ulaan Baatar. They run specially designed mountain climbing trips and have a fascinating collection of mementoes and photos at their office (which is often closed, so ring first) in room 107 (2nd floor) at the Central Sports Palace in Ulaan Baatar.

Mongolia's highest peaks are:

Otgon Tenger Uul (3905m) – in Zavkhan
Türgen Uul (3965m) – in Uvs; one of the most accessible and spectacular
Kharkhiraa Uul (4032m) – in Uvs

Sutai Uul (4090m) – on the border of Gov-Altai and Khovd aimags. This awesome mountain is accessible and dominates the road between Altai and Khovd city.

Altan Taban Uul (4150m) – has a 20km permanent glacier; in Bayan-Ölgii

Tsast Uul (4193m) – on the border of Bayan-Ölgii and Khovd aimags. It is accessible and the camping in the area is gorgeous.

Tsambagarav Uul (4202m) – in Khovd. In 1996 a Japanese man skied down this mountain in 24 minutes. It is relatively easy to climb.

Monkh Khairkhan Uul (4362m) – on the border between Bayan-Ölgii and Khovd aimags

Tavanbogd Uul (4374m) – in Bayan-Ölgii and virtually on the border of Mongolia, China and Russia. It is full of permanent glaciers.

## Kayaking & Rafting

Mongolia's numerous lakes and rivers are often ideal for kayaking and rafting. Rafting is organised along the Tuul and Khovd rivers by the Juulchin travel agency (see the Ulaan Baatar chapter for details). Boojum Expeditions (see the Getting Around chapter) has started kayaking trips on the Khövsgöl lake.

The best time for kayaking is in the summer (June to September); for rafting, July and August after some decent rain.

## Fishing

With Mongolia's large number of lakes and rivers, and its sparse population which generally prefers meat, the fish are just waiting to be caught. The best places to dangle your lines are at Khövsgöl lake in summer (June to September) and the nearby Five Rivers area in September and October. The region west of Khövsgöl lake known as Tsagaannuur and the Chuluut river in Arkhangai province are also excellent. Equipment is hard to rent anywhere in the country, so bring your own gear. In many places, all you need is a strong handline and a lure.

## COURSES
### Language Courses

Currently, there are no organised Mongolian language courses in the the country. You can learn Mongolian from someone who wants to learn or practise your language. (English,

French, German and Japanese are particularly popular.)

A few places to ask around for 'exchange lessons', or any possible future courses, are the various universities and colleges in Ulaan Baatar, particularly the National University of Mongolia (☎ & fax 324 385), PO Box 377, Ulaan Baatar, and the Institute of Foreign Languages, as well as the embassies and development agencies. Also check out the English-language newspapers for any ads about language courses.

If you are serious about learning Mongolian, contact The Mongolia Society Inc in the USA (refer to the Books section above for details) which produces a wide range of Mongolian language tapes and books.

### Religious Courses

Refer to the Facts about the Country and Ulaan Baatar chapters for courses in Buddhism, traditional medicine and thangka painting.

## WORK

Mongolia is certainly not somewhere you can just turn up and expect to get work – even for teaching English the demand is not high, and working regulations are fairly stringent for foreigners. Also, you will receive poor pay (possibly the same as locals), unless you can score a job with a development agency, but these agencies usually recruit their non-Mongolian staff at home, not from within Mongolia.

If you are keen to work in Mongolia and are qualified in teaching or health, contact the organisations listed in the Useful Organisations section above, or in the Volunteer Work section below. They will appreciate your contacting them *before* you come to Mongolia.

Officially, foreigners must get permission from the relevant ministry. (At the time of research, this was the Ministry of Population and Labour, but has changed following the recent shake-up of ministries. Your employer will know what to do.)

## Language Teaching

Some Mongolians want to forget Russian and learn a useful European language, particularly English, so there is a demand (albeit low) for teachers. Colleges and volunteer agencies are, however, on the lookout for qualified teachers who are willing to stay for a few terms (if not a few years), and not just for a week or two. Contact the voluntary service agencies in your home country or the ones listed below.

Informal, short-term work may be possible through smaller organisations, such as the many private universities which have sprung up, or you may be able to do freelance tutoring for a while, but don't expect to make much money. Try the Mongolian Knowledge University (☎ 327 165; fax 358 354), the Institute of Foreign Languages or the International School (☎ 52 959).

## Volunteer Work

Some organisations are anxious to receive help from qualified people, particularly in education and health. Unless you are particularly well qualified, or your expertise is in desperately short supply, you are asked to contact these agencies *before* you come to Mongolia.

They are more interested in committed people who are willing to stay two years or more. In most instances, you will be paid in local wages (or possibly a little more).

Australian Volunteers Abroad (AVA) has a handful of Australian volunteers; contact the AVA in your capital city.

Japan Overseas Cooperation of Volunteers (JOCV); contact the JOCV in Japan, or in Ulaan Baatar (☎ 325 939).

Peace Corps is well represented throughout the country. Contact your local Peace Corps office in the USA, or in Ulaan Baatar (☎ 311 520).

South Korean Youth Volunteers; contact the KYV office in Seoul, or in Ulaan Baatar (☎ 311 738).

United Nations Development Program (UNDP) is always on the lookout for committed and hardworking volunteers. Contact them at PO Box 49/207, Ulaan Baatar, or 7 Erkhuugiin St (☎ 32 7585; fax 326 221).

Voluntary Service Overseas (VSO) is a British-run organisation for Brits and EEC nationals (but they will take citizens from other countries, depending on their skills). In Ulaan Baatar, their address is PO Box 678, Ulaan Baatar 13 (☎ & fax 320 460), but they prefer you to contact their head office in the UK: 317 Putney Bridge Rd, London SW15 2PN (☎ (0181) 780 2266; fax 780 1326).

## ACCOMMODATION

Like most things about Mongolia, the accommodation situation in Ulaan Baatar is vastly different to what you will find anywhere outside of the capital city. In Ulaan Baatar, there is a wide range of accommodation, from dormitory-style places for T2750 a night to suites in the Chinggis Khaan Hotel which cost almost as much as Mongolia's Gross Domestic Product. Yet only 30 minutes by bus from the capital city, the hotels are decrepit, closed or offer very little comfort or service.

One unique option, particularly popular with organised tours, is to stay in tourist gers, like the ones used by nomads (except for the hot water, toilets, sheets and karaoke bars). The best type of accommodation is to bring your own tent and camp – it is free, and you really experience what Mongolia has to offer.

Except for upmarket hotels, which have caught on to the single/double room concept, all prices are per person – not per bed or per room. Always check for taxes and hidden extras. Remember that most hotels and ger camps will charge you a 'foreigners' price' (see Dual-Pricing earlier in this chapter).

If you negotiate a reasonable price with the management, try to pay immediately and get a receipt. Asking for a receipt sometimes drops the price dramatically; in some cases the staff will officially register you as a Mongolian, charge you the 'Mongolian price' on paper, charge you the 'foreigners' price' in reality, and pocket the difference themselves.

Hotel staff may ask for your passport as 'security'. It is not a good idea to leave your passport with them for three reasons: the common tendency for staff not to show up for work (the person with your passport cannot be found when you want to depart); once they have your passport, it leaves you open to extortion; or you may simply forget to pick it up and be 300km away before you realise it. An expired passport, student card or some other ID with your photo is a great alternative to leaving your real passport.

Security should be a consideration. Always keep your windows and door locked. Since the hotel staff may enter your room while you're not around, take any valuables with you or at least keep them locked inside your luggage and don't leave cameras and money lying around your room. Most hotels have a safe where valuables can be kept. When you retrieve things from it, they are often as anxious as you that you check everything on the spot, lest they be accused of sticky fingers.

## Camping

Mongolia is probably the greatest country in the world for camping. With 1.5 million sq km of unfenced and unowned land, spectacular scenery and freshwater lakes and rivers, it is just about perfect. The main problem is a lack of public transport to great camping sites, though there are some near Ulaan Baatar, such as Gachuurt, Khandgait and Terelj. Camping is also worth considering given the dire lack of hotels in the countryside and the expensive ger camps.

Local people (and even a few curious cows or horses) may come to investigate your camping spot, but you are very unlikely to encounter any hostility. Your jeep driver will have ideas about good places to stay, otherwise look for somewhere near water, or in a pretty valley. It is not hard to find somewhere to pitch your tent within walking distance of most aimag capitals and towns if you are hitching. You will need to bring your own tent and cooking equipment if you are not camping near main towns or want to avoid the food.

You can often get boiled water, cooked food, uncooked meat and dairy products from nearby gers in exchange for money or other goods, but don't rely on nomads, who may have limited supplies of food, water and fuel. It is best to bring a portable (petrol) stove – petrol is the only widely available fuel in Mongolia – rather than use open fires

which are potentially dangerous, use precious wood and are useless where wood is scarce anyway.

Be mindful of your security. If drunks spot your tent, you could have a problem – be especially careful of drunks around the 'tent city' at Yarmag, near Ulaan Baatar, during the Naadam Festival. If the owners (and their dog) let you, camping near a ger is a good idea for extra security from strangers – but not too close, because some of your bits and pieces may go missing, and your new neighbours may forget you are there when they have a midnight pee (or worse). Mongolians have little or no idea of the western concept of privacy. They will open your tent and look inside at any time – no invitation is needed.

Here are a few extra tips:

Burn dried dung if you are being eaten alive by mosquitoes (you may then have to decide which is worse: mossies or burning cow shit); bring strong repellent; make sure your tent is waterproof and always pitch it in anticipation of strong winds; rats and marmots are great for taking your food; keep your vehicle locked at night; don't pitch your tent under trees (because of lightning), or on or near riverbeds (flash floods are not uncommon).

**Minimum Impact Camping** If you are camping, please be aware of the fragile environment and take notice of a few guidelines:

- carry out all non-biodegradable items and deposit them at rubbish bins in the nearest town
- go to the toilet at least 50m from any water source, bury your waste, and bury or burn toilet paper, if possible
- do not use shampoo, soap or other washing liquids directly in water sources
- make friends with people at the local gers, and check that it is OK to camp there
- if building a fire, remember that it is sacred to Mongolians

## Traditional Gers

If you are particularly fortunate, you may be invited to spend a night or two out on the steppes in a genuine ger, rather than a ger camp set up for tourists. This is a wonderful experience, as it offers you a chance to see the 'real' Mongolia, but don't expect great meals, hot showers or flush toilets. In reality, you may be served a soupy mixture of hot water, flour, mutton, lumps of fat and some stray goat hairs and sand from the Gobi. There may be no way to wash at all, and going to the toilet will mean squatting behind the nearest rock, bush or camel (if you can find one). If a child comes to sleep with you at night, remember that they do not wear nappies (diapers).

In some cases, you may be expected to pay for this accommodation, but in many cases no payment is wanted if you stay for one or two nights. Indeed, your host may be insulted if you offer money. However, some sort of gift, especially food, would be greatly appreciated. See the relevant section in the Facts about the Country chapter for some suggestions about what gifts are more useful for nomadic families.

Please only stay one night (two, at the most) in any traditional ger (unless you have been specifically asked to stay longer). If you stay for longer, you will outstay your welcome and abuse their hospitality, making it less likely that others will be welcome in the future, as gers often have limited food supplies.

### Tourist Ger Camps

Tourist ger camps are springing up everywhere. It may seem touristy, and they are never good value, but if you are going into the countryside, a night in a tourist ger is a great way to experience some western-oriented, 'traditional Mongolian nomadic lifestyle' without the discomforts mentioned above. If on an organised tour, you will certainly stay in one for a few nights; if travelling independently, one or two nights in a tourist ger is often worth a splurge, particularly somewhere as remote as the south Gobi or as beautiful as Terelj.

A tourist ger camp is a patch of ground with a few dozen traditional gers, with separate buildings for toilets, showers and a restaurant/bar. Inside a ger, there are usually two to three beds, an ornate table, four tiny chairs and a wood stove which can be used for heating during the night – ask the staff to make it for you (though it may be with dried

dung). The beds are really just smallish cots – if you are built like an NBA basketballer or a sumo wrestler, you'll need to make special arrangements.

Toilets are usually the sit-down types, though they may be (clean) pit toilets; the showers should be hot. Expect to pay from US$35 to US$40 per person per night, including meals, which is a lot of money for an elaborate tent. Occasionally this price may include a trip to a nearby attraction, but normal activities, such as horse or camel riding, will cost extra.

Meals are taken in a separate restaurant (often in a ger). Although the food is western, and definitely better than in any restaurant anywhere in the countryside, it is rarely great. Sometimes you can pay about US$25 per person per night for the ger, and bring your own food, but they normally only accept this if they are not busy. Most camps have a bar (and, sometimes, even satellite TV and a blasted karaoke machine), but drinks will never be cold and they will always be expensive.

If you plan to stay in a ger camp you may want to bring a torch (flashlight) for nocturnal visits to the outside toilets; candles to create more ambience than stark electric lights (not all have electricity); towels (the ones provided are invariably smaller than a pygmy's handkerchief); and toilet paper (they usually run out).

If travelling around the countryside independently and you want to stay in a ger camp, it is best to book ahead to ensure that the camp is open and has decent food – but this is not always possible because they often have no telephone. Except for a handful of ger camps in Terelj catering to expat skiers, all ger camps are only open from 1 May to mid-September, a little later in the Gobi.

### Apartments

If you are staying in Ulaan Baatar for a week or more, it is cheaper and more convenient to rent an apartment – the hard part is finding one and arranging a short-term lease (refer to the Ulaan Baatar chapter for details). You must pay for the electricity and telephone.

Water and heating is free thanks to the unmetered centralised hot-water system installed by the Russians.

## Hotels

The hotels in Ulaan Baatar are generally pretty good, though they are all overpriced. Most places not in the bottom-end range cost at least US$50 per single room. This is very poor value – rooms with far better facilities cost less in most western countries. These rooms will be comfortable and clean, but have very little extra to justify the expense, except English-speaking staff and, perhaps, satellite TV – hot water and heating is standard for most buildings and hotels in Ulaan Baatar, and air-conditioning is never needed.

Staff at bottom-end places in Ulaan Baatar and anywhere in the countryside (except for ger camps) will speak no English. The 'foreigners' price' may be quoted in US dollars in an attempt to get the green stuff, but you should pay in tögrögs because it is now the law. A sleeping bag is generally not needed if you are staying in hotels unless the heating breaks down outside of summer, which is not uncommon. In bottom-end places, an inner sheet (the sort used inside sleeping bags) is handy if the sheets are dirty; blankets are always available, but are generally dirty or musty.

Most hotels have two types of rooms: a 'deluxe' *(büten lyuks)* room, which includes a separate sitting room, usually with TV, and a private bathroom; and a 'simple' *(engiin)* room, usually with a shared bathroom. Sometimes, dormitory-style *(niitiin bair)* beds are also available. Invariably, hotel staff will initially show you their deluxe room, which usually costs a ridiculous 'foreigners' price' of around T13,750 per person per night. Simple rooms are cheaper but generally still overpriced at about T5500 per person per night. Unless the hotel offers satellite TV, don't bother paying extra for a TV – it will only show distorted and incomprehensible Mongolian and Russian programmes.

It may be possible to make a deal with the cheaper hotels for a reduced price if you're renting by the month, especially during the off-season (October to May).

In the countryside, the hotels are generally empty and falling apart. They will normally be very cheap if you can get a 'Mongolian price' (about T1000 per person per night), but they have few facilities. You may have to find out where the manager lives to get the hotel opened; the hotel may have no food; the toilets may be locked or unbearable pit toilets; and the electricity will probably be turned off by midnight or may not work at all. The quality of hotels in the countryside is reason enough to take a tent, and camp.

As for service, it is generally very poor, except for upmarket places in Ulaan Baatar. Hotel receptionists are almost always sullen. You'll gain little by getting angry – just be businesslike and eventually you'll get what you want. If they haven't seen guests for a long time (very possible in the countryside), staff might have to search for some sheets, blankets, even a bed, washstand and water, and then rouse a cook to light a fire to get some food ready a few hours later.

## FOOD

Again, the quality and choice of food in Ulaan Baatar is vastly different from what you will find in the countryside. In the capital city, a reasonable choice of restaurants serve many types of food (though the menus will be limited) and the markets are reasonably well stocked. Less than 30 minutes by road from Ulaan Baatar, be prepared for a gastronomical purgatory. The vast majority of Mongolians eat little more than greasy boiled mutton, with lots of fat, and flour. The Kazak people in western Mongolia add variety to their diet with horse meat.

Mongolia is hell for vegetarians. If you don't eat meat, you can survive in Ulaan Baatar, but in the countryside you will need to take your own food (which you can buy in Ulaan Baatar). Vegetables are rare and usually pickled in jars, so the best way for vegetarians to get protein is from the wide range of dairy products. Yoghurt, milk, fresh cream, cheese and fermented milk drinks are normally delicious and available in the countryside and towns. It's hard to find bread or biscuits to put your cheese on. Eggs do exist, but they are also rare.

In restaurants in the countryside and the cheaper places in Ulaan Baatar, the one and only item on the menu (not that there is usually a menu) is mutton with spoonfuls of bland noodles, sometimes rice, but very rarely anything else. If that doesn't excite you, and you aren't taking your own food, add liberal doses of chilli or tomato sauce and pickled vegetables (both available in most markets in the country). It is amazing how these can hide the texture and taste of a plate of mutton.

If you are doing some extensive travelling in the countryside, you may wish to bring from home (or from China or Russia, if you came that way) dried fruits (limited supplies are available in Ulaan Baatar markets) for snacks and roughage, chutneys and sauces (a limited supply is available in most markets in the country), tea bags and coffee, curry powder, vitamin tablets, and packets of just-add-boiling-water pastas, noodles, rice and soups. A few of these will definitely add nutrition and taste to your diet; not to mention lift your morale. If you don't have a portable (petrol) stove, hot water is usually easy to get from hotels and restaurants.

An old Mongolian saying goes something like: 'Breakfast, keep for yourself; lunch, share with your friends; dinner, give to your enemies'. The biggest and most important meals for Mongolians are breakfast and lunch, though you are unlikely to find many places open for breakfast – which you may be glad about unless you can stomach a plate of greasy and fatty mutton at 8 am. Some staff may understand the word 'omelette', but this will be small consolation if no eggs are available.

### Guanzes

A guanz is an all-purpose word to describe a canteen. These guanzes are usually in buildings, gers or even train wagons, and can be found in most aimag towns, all over Ulaan Baatar and along major roads where there is some traffic. In the countryside, the ger guanzes are a great way to see a ger and meet a family without the lengthy stops and traditions expected with normal visits.

If a ger is within 50m of a main road, it is probably a guanz. A table and chairs outside, a picture of a knife and fork, or even a sign with the words ГУАНЗ, will make them easier to spot. Not surprisingly, they offer virtually nothing but mutton and noodles (about T400 a plate), either fried and on a plate, or boiled and in a soup. If you are lucky or prepared to wait, some steamed mutton dumplings *(buuz)* or fried mutton pancakes *(khuurshuur)* may be available. A bottle of sauce, and a jar of pickled vegetables, comes in very handy at these places. The supplies of salty tea is endless, or they will usually boil some hot water if you ask, and you bring your tea or coffee.

### Restaurants

In Ulaan Baatar, you can get pretty reasonable western food like pizzas, steaks and chicken, and there are Indian, Korean and Japanese restaurants. But things are vastly different in the countryside.

Except for upmarket hotels and restaurants in Ulaan Baatar, menus are rare; if there is one, it is usually hand-scrawled in Cyrillic and only lists a dozen varieties of beer, wine and vodka.

Two words which are often understood by Mongolian waiters and cooks are 'beefsteak' (a large mutton mince pattie, often topped with a fried egg) and 'schnitzel'. But normally requests for these will be met with a shake of the head and an offer of mutton, which goes under the English words of 'goulash' or 'meat' *(makh)*, and is served with squishy mashed potato, gluggy rice or pickled vegetables. Either way, what you will almost always get in restaurants in the countryside is greasy, fatty and often cold.

Service is usually as bad as the food, even in expensive restaurants in Ulaan Baatar. In some places, it can take ages to find anyone interested in cooking you anything; overcharging is not uncommon; many places are closed by about 9 pm; and you will either have to plead for the bill after you've finished, or it will be plonked onto your table 20 seconds after you've ordered – and you'll get nothing but snarls if you dare order anything else.

## Snacks

If you visit Mongolians in their gers or homes, you will invariably be served a snack from the hospitality bowl along with salty, milky tea. Some snacks are rather exotic, such as dried milk curds *(aaruul)*, which are as hard as a rock and often about as tasty. You may be served a very sharp fermented cheese called *aarts*, which will clear your sinuses. *Öröm* is a type of thick cream and, if fresh, is delicious with bread and jam.

Another standby for the Mongolian hostess with unexpected visitors is twists of deep fried bread. If you're offered a snack, it's most impolite to refuse. Nor is it necessary to consume it all.

## Traditional Food

Forget everything you ever learned about Mongolian hot pot, or the last time you ate in a 'Mongolian' restaurant back home. In cities all over the western world, Chinese restaurants try to differentiate themselves from their competitors by calling themselves 'Mongolian', but very little is Mongolian about them.

The most common dish is mutton (sheep, but possibly goat), served in various styles. It's best in the form of *shorlog* (the Mongolian barbecue, or shish kebab). Another delicacy is *khorkhog*, when an entire goat or sheep is slowly roasted from the inside out by placing hot rocks inside the carcass. (The preparation is not a pretty sight.)

Common are the steamed dumplings, buuz, with mutton filling which resemble Tibetan *momos*, or the Chinese variety, but the Mongolians use more meat, plenty of fat and less flour. Smaller boiled dumplings are called *bansh*. In the guanzes, you will probably be offered a mutton noodle soup *(guriltai shol)*. Another common dish is a pancake made with flour and mutton called a khuushuur. They can be large, fried and sit in your stomach like a lead brick, or small, deep-fried, crispy and tastier.

Most Mongolians prefer their mutton boiled, so the smell permeates everything – even Mongolian biscuits and butter smell like boiled mutton. Since there is no vegetable oil, mutton lard is used. When you try to wash the smell off, you may find the soap and towels smell like mutton too. Even old paper money and telephone receivers soon develop that distinct mutton fragrance. Foreigners who have spent a lot of time in Mongolia claim that it takes weeks to get rid of that mutton smell from their bodies after they get home.

## Self-Catering

Given the state of Mongolian restaurants, self-catering isn't a bad idea. In Ulaan Baatar, you won't save much money: a packet of noodles costs about T300 and a tin of ham about T700, whereas a plate of mutton and noodles in a guanz will costs about T400, and for about T1000, you can get a decent western meal in a good restaurant. However, buying your own food will provide some variety and nutrition and is ideal for vegetarians – especially if you have a portable (petrol) stove.

The markets *(zakh)* and shops *(delguur)* in Ulaan Baatar sell most things you need like jam, salami, noodles, bread, tinned fish, ham and sausages, pickled vegetables, tea, coffee, rice, flour and fruit and vegetables in season. The quality and variety is improving every day, but always check the expiry date.

Self-catering is almost essential when travelling in the countryside, unless you can live on fatty mutton and noodles three times a day. Take most of your supplies from Ulaan Baatar, because the markets in the aimag capitals are never as good as the ones in Ulaan Baatar, and the shops in the countryside are always poorly stocked.

Some markets and shops in Ulaan Baatar are still based on the old-fashioned Russian system: you chose what you want, pay for it at the cashier's desk, produce your itemised receipt at the counter, and only then are you given what you ordered. It means you need to know a few Mongolian words for basic items, so you can tell the cashier. These days most shops in Mongolia, however, do let you browse, inspect the goods, and then pay in the normal way.

## DRINKS
### Nonalcoholic Drinks
The Mongolians are big tea drinkers and they will almost never start to eat a meal until they've had a cup of tea first, as it aids digestion. However, Mongolian tea *(tsai)* tends to be of the lowest quality. In fact, it's mostly 'tea waste', which is made up of stems and rejected leaves that are processed into a 'brick'.

A classic Mongolian drink is salty tea, called *süütei tsai*, with or without milk and sugar. Some foreigners find it revolting but many learn to tolerate it. The taste varies by region, but tends to be best in western Mongolia. Many foreigners complain that drinking too much of this salty tea just makes them thirstier. If you see some unwanted lumpy bits (hairs, maybe even faeces) floating in your drink, calmly remove it before continuing.

(Mongolian tea must be slurped in the loudest possible way in accordance with an unwritten Mongolian tradition. You will never hear real slurping until you stop at a roadside guanz full of ravenous Mongolian truck drivers polishing off bowls of tea.)

If you can't get used to the salty tea, try asking for black tea *(khar tsai)*, which is like European tea, with sugar and no milk. (The word 'Lipton' is often understood and used in restaurants as an alternative to black tea.) Your best bet is to bring tea bags or coffee from Ulaan Baatar (or home) and ask for hot water (which may have a mutton tang to it).

Coffee is a popular drink. It is available in markets, shops and restaurants in Ulaan Baatar, and is invariably the 'three-in-one' packet of coffee, powdered milk and sugar. If you prefer it black and without sugar, bring your own and ask for hot water.

The Mongolians produce a variety of bottled fizzy soft drinks, some amazingly good, commonly called *undaa*. The ingredients vary, but it seems they use natural fruit flavours such as watermelon and little artificial colouring. Children sell these drinks on the streets and around the markets of most towns for about T80 a bottle – they are a cheap and safe way to quench your thirst. You must hang around the undaa seller and return the bottle when you finish. Major brand names of expensive soft drinks are available in the shops and markets of most larger towns.

### Alcoholic Drinks
Mongolians can drink you under the table if you challenge them. There is much social pressure to drink, especially on men, and men who refuse to drink vodka *(arkhi)* are considered wimps. The Russians can be thanked for this obnoxious custom, which started in the 1970s. The Mongolians manufacture vodka and used to export it to Russia, but now they drink it themselves, and in increasingly large quantities.

Cans and bottles of imported beers are expensive and usually only available in larger towns, but you can pick up a bottle of undrinkable Chinese ale at places along the Trans-Mongolian railway line. Except for decent restaurants in Ulaan Baatar, beer will always be served at room temperature. You can buy bottles of cheap Takhi beer, made in Inner Mongolia, or pints of home-brewed (warm) beer in bars all over Ulaan Baatar (but less so in the countryside where vodka remains the major drink).

### Airag
While in Mongolia, you should try a glass (or a gallon, if you like) of fermented horse's milk, called *airag*. First drunk in Mongolia over 1000 years ago, airag is still revered and enjoyed throughout the country. Since the days when Mongolian warriors lived on very little else, the method of collecting milk in huge leather bags and churning it has not changed.

Experts claim they can almost tell which aimag or valley the airag comes from by the taste. The provinces of Arkhangai, Bulgan, Övörkhangai and even Dundgov in the Gobi, are renowned for the quality of airag, because of the special grasses eaten by the horses there. ■

Herders make their own unique home brew, *airag*, which is fermented horse's milk with an alcohol content of about 3%. Although you aren't likely to get drunk from airag alone, many Mongolians distil it further to produce *shimiin arkhi*, which boosts the alcohol content to around 12%. Many Mongolians will insist that airag and shimiin arkhi are good for your health because both are milk products, which is rather like claiming that wine is good for you because it's made from grapes.

## ENTERTAINMENT

Except for the occasional Russian film at a cinema in Erdenet or Darkhan, every type of entertainment in Mongolia can only be found in Ulaan Baatar, so refer to that chapter for more details.

### Cinemas

Several cinemas operate in Ulaan Baatar, but in each aimag capital the cinemas (and drama theatres), which dominate most town centres, are mostly closed. In the past, most foreign films were Russian, but these days a few more flicks are coming from the USA, India, North and South Korea and Japan. They are often not dubbed, or badly dubbed, and virtually unwatchable.

### Nightlife

To cater for the nouveaux riches, a few discos are opening up (and closing down) in Ulaan Baatar. They play western dance music and have all the usual decor like mirror balls. To make money – but more to put off the poorer Mongolians – there is always a hefty entrance fee, equivalent to a week's wage for some Mongolians.

Don't expect any nightlife in the countryside. Some of the larger aimag capitals have a 'sports palace' in which occasional dances are held, usually to the accompaniment of badly recorded pirated tapes played on an equally precarious Russian cassette player. Nevertheless, they do help you meet the locals.

Ulaan Baatar has a few bars catering to trendy locals and rich foreigners, as well as thirsty and drunk Mongolians. The bars in the countryside are generally awful and should be avoided.

### Opera & Theatre

Opera and drama is still thriving in Mongolia, the various theatres being one worthwhile legacy of Russian domination. In Ulaan Baatar (but almost never in the countryside), local and foreign plays and operas in the Mongolian language are held, more regularly in summer. These energetic shows are often worth seeing, even if you don't understand anything.

### Traditional & Cultural Shows

One highlight of your trip should be a performance of traditional music and dance in Ulaan Baatar. These are regularly held during summer and should not be missed. Around the time of the Naadam Festival, there are occasional puppet shows. The State Circus in Ulaan Baatar is reasonably impressive, if a little amateurish, but probably not for animal lovers.

## SPECTATOR SPORTS

Mongolia is generally not passionate about sport, but wrestling, archery and horse racing, which dominate the Naadam Festival, are very popular.

### Wrestling

Mongolian wrestling is similar to wrestling found elsewhere, except there are no weight divisions, so the biggest wrestlers (and they are big!) are often the best. Mongolian wrestling also has no time limit – the bout will continue, with short breaks, until the first wrestler falls, and anything but the soles of his feet and open palms touch the ground.

Before each elimination bout, wrestlers limber up and honour the judges and their individual attendants *(zasuul)* with a short dance called a *devekh*, or 'eagle dance'. After the bout, the loser must take off his jacket and walk under the right arm of the winner, who then makes a lap of honour around the flag on a pedestal and does some more eagle dancing.

Wrestlers wear heavy boots called *gutuls* – similar to the traditional boots worn by ordinary Mongolians. The tight, unflattering pants are called *shuudag*, and the small vest across the shoulders is a *zodog*. Winners are bestowed glorious titles depending on how many rounds they win: Falcon (five rounds), Elephant (seven) and Lion (for winning the tournament). One renowned wrestler was given the most prestigious, and lengthy, title of the 'Eye-Pleasing Nationally Famous Mighty and Invincible Giant'.

You will see plenty of wrestling if you are in Mongolia during the Naadam Festival, or during the Ikh Sorilgo (Major Test) tournaments in the weeks before Naadam.

### Archery

Like horse racing, the sport of archery originates from the era of almost constant war, starting from around the 11th century.

Archers use a bent bow made of layered horn, bark and wood. Usually, arrows are made from willow and the feathers are from vultures and other birds of prey.

Traditionally dressed male archers stand 75m (women usually 60m) from the target. The target is sometimes a line of 360 round leather grey, red and/or yellow rings (known as a *sur*) on the ground, but usually there are only about 20 or 30. After each shot, special judges who stand near the target (but miraculously never get injured) emit a short cry called a *uukhai*, and raise their hands in the air to indicate the quality of the shot. The winner who hits the targets the most times is declared the best archer, or *mergen*.

### Horse Racing

Probably no people have more intimate understanding of, and pride in, their horses than Mongolians, who greatly depend on them for sustenance and transport.

There are normally six categories of horse racing, depending on the age of horses: for example, a two-year-old horse, called a *shudlen*, will race for 15km, and six and seven-year-old *azrag* and *ikh nas* horses go for up to 30km. There are no tracks or courses; it is just open countryside. Jockeys

Mongolian wrestling is a major attraction of the Naadam Festival.

– boys and girls aged between five and 13 years old – prepare for months for special races, particularly at Naadam, and horses are fed a special diet for weeks beforehand.

Before a race, the audience, all decked out in traditional finery, often sings traditional songs. The young riders sing a traditional anthem called a *gingo* before the race, and scream '*Goog*' at the horses during the race

The winner is declared *tümny ekh*, or 'leader of ten thousand'. The five winning horses are admired and talked about in reverence by the crowd, and traditional poems are read out extolling the virtues of riders and trainers. The five winning riders must drink some special airag, which is then often sprinkled on the riders' heads and on the horses backsides. During Naadam, a song is also sung to the two-year-old horse which comes last.

**Other Sports**

A football (soccer) competition is played in Ulaan Baatar, Erdenet and Darkhan but the game is still not as popular as in most countries. Boxing tournaments are held in major cities, and basketball is increasingly popular – it is not unusual to see a ring and backboard in the most remote places. Stadiums in Ulaan Baatar and various sports palaces around Mongolia sometimes hold live sporting events. The country's first golf course is just south of Ulaan Baatar, but it is probably a long time before we will see the start of the annual Mongolian Open.

## THINGS TO BUY

Except for a couple of shops in the south Gobi, and the Erdene Zuu monastery, just about every souvenir is for sale only in Ulaan Baatar. Refer to that chapter for more information and some examples of prices.

Be very careful about buying anything old. Customs officials are keen to stop any exporting of Mongolia's heritage, and may confiscate anything which looks old unless you have a receipt and/or document stating that it is not antique. Refer to the Customs section above for more information.

Many foreigners like to pick up traditional Mongolian clothing and boots. These are cheapest at the department stores and markets. Leather or nylon jackets with a sheepskin lining are a bargain if you don't buy them from touristy souvenir shops. Cashmere jumpers (sweaters) are an important export item, but hard to find except in expensive tourist shops.

The bright landscape paintings which you will see at most tourist stops around the country are ideal souvenirs: they are cheap, easy to carry and look great framed on your wall at home. Larger, more dramatic and nationalist paintings are for sale at several galleries in Ulaan Baatar. Tapes and compact discs of traditional music are also excellent mementoes of your trip, but a portable tape or CD player, to test the quality of recording before you buy, is a good idea.

If you are a philatelist, you can buy a range of extraordinarily bright and large stamps. These feature wildlife, religious dances, traditional costumes – just about everything. They are far more expensive than normal stamps but make good souvenirs. The stamps you are given for postcards and letters are very boring in comparison.

Other items which you may want to look out for are carvings, snuff bottles, Mongolian-style chess sets, and carpets and rugs from Muslim-influenced western Mongolia, and Erdenet.

# Getting There & Away

## AIR

Flying is the main form of transport into Mongolia; for foreigners, the only other way into the country is by train. Current airline schedules also allow you to fly from Ulaan Baatar to places in the wider Mongolia: Irkutsk, on Lake Baikal, and Ulan-Ude, capital of Buryatia (both in 'Russian Mongolia'), and Hohhot (Khokh Khot), the capital of the 'autonomous region' of Chinese Inner Mongolia.

Currently, all direct flights to Mongolia only go to the capital, Ulaan Baatar. Most people fly in from Beijing, Berlin and Moscow; for organised tours, there are also additional direct flights from Osaka (Japan) and Seoul. In July and August, most flights on most airlines are full, so book ahead, and confirm – and then confirm again.

The international Mongolian carrier is MIAT, which some wags claim stands for 'Maybe I'll Arrive Today'. Delayed and cancelled flights are common, and MIAT has also been getting a bad reputation for lost luggage. It seems that the aircraft is heavily overloaded by Mongolian traders who reckon this is a cargo flight. As a result, some luggage gets left behind despite being already checked in, and the longer it lies around unattended, the greater the chance of it being lost or stolen. As a precaution, put your most valuable items in your hand luggage.

High winds and fog are sometimes a problem, leading to delays and cancellations. Gales blowing in from Siberia affect smaller planes used for domestic flights more than the larger ones on international routes, but flights to Ulaan Baatar are sometimes diverted to Irkutsk (Siberia), where you could spend the night in the transit lounge (if you don't have a Russian visa) until the wind drops.

The international airport at Buyant Ukhaa, near Ulaan Baatar, is being extensively upgraded with the help of a loan from the Asian Development Bank.

## Discounts

Unless you hold a Mongolian or Russian passport, there are no discounts on flights going directly to/from Mongolia. However, there are heaps of discounts from other countries to Beijing or Hong Kong. Bargain fares are usually available from travel agents rather than airlines. Travel agents often hesitate to sell you the cheapest ticket, not necessarily because they want to cheat you, but because many budget tickets come with lots of restrictions which you may find inconvenient. If you want the cheapest ticket, be sure to say so and ask what restrictions, if any, apply.

There are plenty of discount tickets which are valid for 12 months, allowing multiple stopovers with open dates. These tickets allow for a great deal of flexibility.

Advance Purchase Excursion (APEX) tickets are sold at a discount but will lock you into a rigid schedule. Such tickets must be purchased two or three weeks ahead of departure, do not permit stopovers and may have minimum and maximum stays as well as fixed departure and return dates. Unless you really have to return at a certain time, it's best to purchase APEX tickets on a one-way basis only. There are stiff cancellation fees if you decide not to use your APEX ticket.

Round-the-World (RTW) tickets are usually offered by an airline or combination of airlines, and let you take your time (six months to a year) moving from point to point on their routes for the price of one ticket. The main restriction is that you have to keep moving in the same direction. One of the drawbacks is that because you are usually booking individual flights as you go, and can't switch carriers, you can get caught out by flight availabilities and may have to spend less or more time in a place than you want.

Some airlines offer discounts of up to 25% to student card holders. Besides having an International Student Identity Card (ISIC), an official-looking letter from your college is also required by some airlines. Many airlines also require you to be aged 26 or under to qualify for a discount. These discounts are generally only available on ordinary economy-class fares. You wouldn't get one, for instance, on an APEX or an RTW ticket since these are already discounted.

Frequent flier deals are available on most airlines flying to Beijing and Moscow. If you fly frequently with one airline, eventually you accumulate enough km to qualify for a free ticket or other goodies. If you fly a lot, contact the airlines for information before buying your ticket.

Airlines usually carry babies up to two years of age at 10% of the adult fare, and a few may carry them free of charge. For children between the ages of four and 12, the fare on international flights is usually 50% of the regular fare or 67% of a discounted fare. These days most fares are likely to be discounted.

### Direct Flights to Mongolia

**China** Air China and MIAT fly between China and Mongolia. Both have poor reputations for service (MIAT is marginally better), so don't be surprised if your luggage ends up in Bolivia or Yemen. When flying to/from China remember that during the summer (March to September) Mongolia has summer time, so it is one hour ahead of China.

MIAT flies from Ulaan Baatar to Beijing and back on Monday, Wednesday and Saturday. Air China flies from Beijing to Ulaan Baatar and back on Tuesday, Thursday and Friday. The times and days of these departures change regularly, especially during the summer. With both airlines, the fare for foreigners is the same. From Beijing to Ulaan Baatar, tickets are US$214/406 one way/return. (In Beijing, you can pay in Chinese yuan.) For some reason, Ulaan Baatar to Beijing is US$200/380. (In Ulaan Baatar, you must pay in US dollars.)

In Beijing, the MIAT office (☎ (010) 6507 9297; fax 650 77397) is in the China Golden Bridge Building (next to the China World Hotel Centre), East Gate, A1, Jianguomenwai. Air China (☎ (010) 6016 6667) is at the Aviation Building, 15 Xichang'an Jie, Xidan District.

MIAT also flies from Ulaan Baatar to Hohhot and back every Monday and Thursday for US$130/260 one way/return. There is a MIAT office in Hohhot (☎ (0471) 495 2026; fax 495 2015).

**Russia** The two carriers between Mongolia and Russia are MIAT and Aeroflot. MIAT flies to Moscow on Thursday and Sunday, and back to Ulaan Baatar on Friday and Monday. The cheapest fare from Ulaan Baatar to Moscow is US$390/700 one way/return. The MIAT office in Moscow (☎ (095) 241 3757) is at 1/7 Spasoperkovski Pereulok, 121002.

Aeroflot flies from Moscow on Monday night and arrives in Ulaan Baatar on Tuesday morning. It returns to Moscow on Tuesday afternoon. The tickets are slightly cheaper at US$350/690 one way/return.

To combine a trip to the stunning Lake Baikal, you could fly with MIAT from Ulaan Baatar to Irkutsk and back each Wednesday and Saturday for US$99/198 one way/return. In Irkutsk, there is a MIAT agency (☎ (3952) 286 778; fax 242 200).

Aeroflot flies between Ulaan Baatar and Ulan-Ude, in Russian Buryatia, every Thursday for US$119/238 one way/return.

**Germany** At the time of research, MIAT had just commenced weekly flights between Berlin and Ulaan Baatar on Sunday, with a brief stop in Moscow. For anyone in Europe, this is a better alternative than flying to, and getting a connection from, Moscow. However, the tickets are expensive at US$650/1200 one way/return. No other details were available at the time of research.

**Japan** To cater for organised tours from Japan, MIAT flies to and from Osaka on Saturday for US$695/1324 one way/return. MIAT (☎ (03) 3237 1851; fax 3237 1853) often schedules more flights in summer, depending on demand.

**South Korea** Both MIAT and Korean Air fly plane-loads of package tourists between Ulaan Baatar and Seoul for US$450/700 one way/return. Korean Air flies every Tuesday, but only in summer (early June to late September). They offer a free night in Seoul if you need to wait for a connection. MIAT (☎ (02) 592 7788; fax 592 7866) flies all year between Seoul and Ulaan Baatar on Friday.

**Kazakstan** Several years ago, MIAT flew between Ulaan Baatar and Almaty, the capital of Kazakstan, but this flight recently ceased because of the lack of passengers.

Kazakstan Airlines apparently still flies between Almaty and Ölgii, the capital of Bayan-Ölgii province, in western Mongolia, every Friday. However, these flights are possibly illegal, very unreliable, and almost certainly not available to foreigners (ie anyone who isn't Russian, Kazak or Mongolian) because Ölgii has no customs and immigration facilities. If the flight happens, and you can get on, the ticket will cost US$140 – refer to the Ölgii section for more details.

### Mongolia via Beijing & Hong Kong
Until there are more direct flights to Ulaan Baatar, you'll probably fly firstly to Beijing unless you are in Europe. You may also need to start in Beijing to collect your visa if you live, for example, in Australia, where there is no Mongolian embassy or consulate. You may find it cheaper to fly to Hong Kong and then pick up a cheap flight, or go by train, to Beijing.

**USA** The cheapest fares to Beijing are from San Francisco, Los Angeles and New York on Korean Air, Air China, Philippine Airlines and Thai Airways. US carriers Delta, Northwest and United also offer competitive fares. From the US west/east coast, return fares start at US$880/1460.

To Hong Kong, expect to pay about US$460/680 one way/return from the west coast and US$560/870 from the east coast.

**Canada** Canadian Airlines is worth trying for cheap deals to Hong Kong, although Korean Air may be cheaper. In general, fares from Vancouver will cost from 5% to 10%

more than from the west coast of the USA. The only direct flight to Beijing is the twice-weekly Air China flight from Toronto, via Vancouver and Shanghai.

**Australia** Generally, the cheapest way into China is via Hong Kong. The minimum one-way fare from Australia to Hong Kong is about A$840, or A$1100 return. Air China flies directly from Melbourne and Sydney to Beijing from A$1100 to A$1320 return (depending on the season). Malaysia Airlines flies from Melbourne and Sydney to Beijing for A$1300/1450 return in the low/high season, but you will have to stay overnight at your expense in Kuala Lumpur. Cathay Pacific and Qantas offer competitive fares and often have special deals.

**New Zealand** At the time of research, Garuda had the best fare to Beijing, NZ$1360 return during the low season. Singapore Airlines and Malaysia Airlines offer low season return fares to Hong Kong for NZ$1345. Qantas and Cathay Pacific have return fares from NZ$1400 to Hong Kong.

**UK** Air China offers the cheapest flights from London to Beijing for around £275/450 one way/return. Many airlines fly between London and Hong Kong for about £330/550. The competitiveness on this sector ensures that the flights occasionally cost as little as £420 return. It is still cheaper and quicker, however, to go through Berlin or Moscow.

**Continental Europe** Most Europeans would fly to Mongolia from Berlin or Moscow. Fares to Beijing and Hong Kong from Western Europe are similar to those from London. The Netherlands, Belgium and Switzerland are always good places to buy discount air tickets. Austrian Airlines offers a ticket which allows you to fly to Ürümqi (in Xinjiang province), travel overland to, and fly back from, Beijing. Air China has flights from Beijing to Berlin, Frankfurt, Milan, Paris, Rome, Stockholm and Zurich.

LOT (Polish Airlines) and JAT (Yugoslav Airlines) connect eastern Europe with Beijing.

### Mongolia via Moscow

Going via Moscow used to be the main option for Europeans, or people travelling from Europe or Russia, until the Berlin-Ulaan Baatar flights started. People in Asia, Australia/New Zealand and USA/Canada will probably come through Beijing, Osaka or Seoul. Moscow is connected every day to all major European, North American and Asian travel centres. A sample of the cheapest flights is listed below.

One interesting – but expensive – way to Mongolia is to fly from Niigata (Japan) or Shenyang (China) to Irkutsk, from where there are flights to Ulaan Baatar.

**USA** The cheapest return flight from Los Angeles is with LOT (Polish Airlines) for US$1308, which includes a free stop-over in Chicago, New York or Warsaw. From New York, the cheapest flight is US$910 return with CSA (Czech Airlines).

**Australia** Qantas, British Airways, Thai Airways and Aeroflot fly from Sydney and Melbourne to Moscow for A$2370 return with a change of aircraft in Bangkok, Singapore or Kuala Lumpur.

**UK** British Airways flies from London to Moscow for £325 return. Aeroflot is usually cheaper.

**Continental Europe** All of the several airlines which service the Paris-Moscow route cost US$807 return. The cheapest student return fare to/from Frankfurt is US$667 with Transaero (a new Russian airline); otherwise it is US$923 return with Aeroflot.

### Departure Tax

If you are leaving Mongolia by air, the departure tax is T4800. A small foreign exchange counter, next to the place where you pay your departure tax, will change US dollars into tögrögs if you don't have any left.

### LAND

Besides flying, the only way foreigners can enter and leave Mongolia is by train through Ereen-Zamyn-Üüd, on the Chinese-Mongolian border, and Naushki-Sükhbaatar, on the Russian-Mongolian border. You can take the Trans-Mongolian Railway (see below), which links Beijing with Moscow, or other trains.

At the time of research, foreigners could not travel on foot, by private vehicle or bus through any border with Russia or China (though there have been very occasional exceptions). The new Ministry of External Relations has promised, however, that foreigners will be able to cross by road at four other crossings 'soon':

Zamyn-Üüd-Ereen is pointless until foreigners are allowed to drive around China, and any bus service across the border will be inferior, slower and not necessarily cheaper than the existing train.

Sükhbaatar-Naushki are the two towns which you pass by train from Russia to Mongolia. Again, unless there are cheaper and better buses, the train will be better. If the border opens, you will be able to take a vehicle into Mongolia – but not further to China.

Altanbulag-Kyakhta is the main road border for Russians and Mongolians. If it opens to foreigners, they'll probably be able to drive their vehicles between Russia and Mongolia without actually taking the train across the border (see below).

Tsagaannuur-Tashanta is the border between the far western province of Bayan-Ölgii and Russia. This border would greatly open up western Mongolia and allow travel onto Kazakstan.

### China

**Train** You can take local trains and cross the border from Zamyn-Üüd (T3829/9409 for 'hard/soft seat' from Ulaan Baatar) in Mongolia to the Chinese border town of Ereen (also known as Erenhot or Erlian). Most travellers, however, catch the direct train between Beijing or Hohhot and Ulaan Baatar.

Schedules change from one summer to another, and services reduce in winter, or could increase in summer, depending on demand. Currently, the trains which travel between China and Mongolia are:

Beijing-Moscow (No 3)
This is a Chinese train with a good Chinese restaurant. It leaves Beijing on Wednesday and arrives in Ulaan Baatar the next day. In reverse, Moscow-Beijing (No 4) is a Russian train. It leaves Ulaan Baatar on Sunday and arrives in Beijing the next day.

Ulaan Baatar-Ereen (No 22)
This Mongolian train (no restaurant) leaves Ulaan Baatar on Monday and Thursday evenings and arrives in Ereen the next morning. In reverse, No 21 leaves Ereen on Tuesday and Friday evenings and arrives the next day. Tickets from Ulaan Baatar for 2nd/1st/deluxe class cost T14,094/19,093/23,692. The schedules of this train change regularly.

Ulaan Baatar-Beijing (No 24)
This is a Mongolian train (with a poor restaurant) which only runs in summer. It leaves Ulaan Baatar every Thursday and arrives the next day. From Beijing to Ulaan Baatar, train No 23 leaves on Saturday.

Ulaan Baatar-Hohhot (No 276)
This Mongolian service usually has a restaurant, but not always. It leaves Ulaan Baatar on Wednesday and Sunday and takes about 33 hours to reach Hohhot. No 275 leaves Hohhot on Sunday and Wednesday evenings and arrives in Ulaan Baatar two days later. Tickets from Ulaan Baatar for 2nd/1st/deluxe class are T25,636/34,965/45,445.

For more information on the above trains see the Trans-Mongolian Railway section below.

### Russia

**Car & Motorcycle** As a foreigner, you cannot currently cross the border between Mongolia and Russia in your own vehicle. You are allowed to bring *in* a vehicle, but you must personally cross the border by train. This may all change if the Kyakhta-Altanbulag and Naushki-Sükhbaatar borders are opened to foreigners.

The main road crossing is currently at Kyakhta-Altanbulag. You will have to leave your vehicle at that border (or ask a trusted Mongolian or Russian to drive across the border), return to Naushki or Sükhbaatar, cross the border by train and then pick up your vehicle. However, some travellers have been told by Russian border officials that they must place their vehicle on the same train as they travel on.

**Train** Besides the Trans-Mongolian Railway (see below) connecting Moscow and Beijing, three other trains run between Mongolia and Russia:

Ulaan Baatar-Moscow (No 5)
This has a reasonable restaurant and sleepers, but no deluxe class. The Mongolian train departs Ulaan Baatar on Monday and Saturday and arrives in Moscow four days later. The Russian train, No 6, departs Moscow on Wednesday and Thursday.

Ulaan Baatar-Irkutsk (No 263)
This is a Mongolian or Russian train with sleepers only and no restaurant or deluxe class. It leaves Ulaan Baatar every evening and arrives in Irkutsk two days later; No 264 does the reverse journey. (Be careful because the departure and arrival times listed in Irkutsk are on Moscow time, although Irkutsk is actually five hours ahead of Moscow.) These trains stop at every village, and the No 263 travels past Lake Baikal at night, so if you

are in a hurry or want to see the lake, take the Ulaan Baatar-Moscow (No 5) as far as Irkutsk.

Choibalsan-Chita

In 1939 the Russians built a train line from Choibalsan in Dornod aimag to Borzya, and onto Chita, in western Siberia, but this service now only runs once a week. Current regulations do not allow foreigners to cross the border on this train. See the Dornod section in the Eastern Mongolia chapter for more details.

### Trans-Mongolian Railway

Most people travel from Russia or China to Mongolia on the direct Trans-Mongolian Railway. (It can be done more cheaply by travelling in stages on local trains, eg from Ulan-Ude to Naushki, Naushki to Sükhbaatar, and Sükhbaatar to Ulaan Baatar, but it would involve more hassles.)

The names of the rail lines can be a bit confusing. The Trans-Siberian Railway runs from Moscow to the eastern Siberian port of Nakhodka – this route does not go through either China or Mongolia. The Trans-Manchurian Railway crosses the Russia-China border at Zabaikalsk-Manzhouli – also completely bypassing Mongolia. The Trans-Mongolian Railway goes from Beijing through Ulaan Baatar and onto a junction called Zaudinsky, near Ulan-Ude, where it meets the Trans-Siberian line and continues on to Moscow.

Only two trains traverse all of Mongolia and go to Beijing and Moscow:

Beijing-Moscow (No 3)

This is a Chinese train with a good Chinese restaurant. It leaves Beijing on Wednesday morning, passes through Ulaan Baatar the next afternoon, and arrives in Moscow on Monday afternoon.

Moscow-Beijing (No 4)

This is a Russian train, which has a Russian or Chinese restaurant – the restaurant cars change at the border. It leaves Moscow on Tuesday evening, passes through Ulaan Baatar on Sunday morning, and arrives in Beijing on Monday afternoon.

**General Information** The stations in Mongolia never have any food; in Russia, there may or may not be someone on the platform selling food; in the more entrepreneurial China, someone on the platform will have some delicious fruit and soft drinks for sale.

The restaurant cars on the Mongolian trains have almost no food – welcome to Mongolia! – while the Russian and Chinese trains have some decent, but expensive, food and drinks in their restaurant cars. On the Beijing-Moscow trains, good western meals cost from US$2 to US$4; a little less for Chinese meals. Restaurant staff will normally want US dollars, but you can pay in tögrögs while in Mongolia, and roubles while in Russia – but not vice versa. Staff will probably give you change from US dollars in local currency, but at an appallingly bad rate. Watch out: foreigners are fair game on this train.

Generally you are only allowed to take 35kg, but for foreigners, this is not checked, and never weighed. A lot of smuggling is done on this train, so never agree to carry anything across the border for anyone else.

Don't leave unattended baggage in your cabin. A few years ago, the Trans-Mongolian had a bad reputation for theft, but militia now ride the trains and security has improved. For added safety, lock your cabins from the inside and also make use of the security clip on the upper left-hand part of the door. The clip can be flipped open from the outside with a knife, but not if you stuff the hole with paper.

If you want to get off the Trans-Mongolian at Sükhbaatar, Darkhan or Sainshand, you will still have to pay the full fare to/from Ulaan Baatar. If you are not actually getting *on* the train in Ulaan Baatar, you should arrange for someone in Ulaan Baatar to tell the attendant that you will catch the train later, so your seat is not taken.

Tickets list the departure, not arrival, times. Get to the station at least 20 minutes before *arrival* to allow you enough time to find the platform and struggle on board, especially for the Beijing-Moscow trains, which only stop in Ulaan Baatar for about 30 minutes.

**What to Bring** Bring plenty of US dollars cash in small denominations to buy meals and drinks on the train, and to exchange for the local currency, so that you can buy things at the train stations. Stock up on munchies like biscuits, chocolate and fruit. You'd be wise to purchase your own alcohol before boarding the train because it is expensive on the train and the choice is limited.

Showers are only available in the deluxe carriages. In 2nd and 1st class, there is a washroom and toilet at the end of each carriage – which always get progressively filthy. It's a good idea to bring a large enamel mug (available in most Chinese railway stations) and use it as a scoop to pour water over yourself from the washbasin. A small urn at the end of each carriage provides constant boiling water which is a godsend for making tea and coffee, as well as meals from packets of instant noodles, pasta and soup.

**Classes** With a few exceptions, all international trains have two or three classes. The names and standards of the classes depend on whether it is a Mongolian, Russian or Chinese train.

On the Russian (and Mongolian) trains, most travellers travel in 2nd class – printed on tickets and timetables as 1/4 and known as 'hard-sleeper', 'coupe' or *kupeynyy* in Russian. These are small, but perfectly comfortable, four-person compartments with four bunk-style beds and a fold-down table.

On the Chinese trains, there is no 2nd class but only 1st class – printed as 2/4 and sometimes called a 'soft-sleeper', or *myagkiy* in Russian. It has softer beds but hardly any more space than (Russian) 2nd class and is not worth the considerably higher fare charged.

The real luxury (and expense) comes with the Chinese deluxe class, printed as 1/2: roomy, wood-panelled two-berth compartments with a sofa, and a shower cubicle shared with the adjacent compartment. The deluxe class on Russian trains, which is slightly cheaper than the Chinese deluxe, has two bunks but is not much different in size than the 2nd class and has no showers.

**Tickets** The international trains, especially the Trans-Mongolian Railway, are popular, so it's often hard to book this trip except during winter. Try to plan ahead and book as early as possible.

In Ulaan Baatar, tickets are only available at the International Railway Ticketing Office. Foreigners can supposedly get some assistance from English-speaking staff in room 212 at the station, but we never found anyone there. Staff at the counters who sell tickets to Beijing and Moscow speak enough English to ensure a smooth transaction.

You can buy tickets for all international trains (the exception is mentioned below) up to 10 days in advance from the ticket office in Ulaan Baatar. Advance booking adds T2400 to the ticket but is a very good idea when demand is high, especially in summer. Tickets are printed in Mongolian and Russian Cyrillic and in German, but destinations are typed in English.

If you are in Ulaan Baatar and want to go to Irkutsk, Beijing or Moscow, avoid going on the Beijing-Moscow or Moscow-Beijing trains; use the other trains mentioned above which *originate* in Ulaan Baatar. In Ulaan Baatar, you cannot buy tickets a few days in advance for the Beijing-Moscow or Moscow-Beijing trains, because staff in Ulaan Baatar don't know how many people are already on the train. For these trains, you can only buy a ticket the day before departure – ie on Wednesday for trains from Ulaan Baatar to Moscow, and on Saturday for trains from Ulaan Baatar to Beijing. You will need to get to the ticket office early and get into the Mongolian Scramble.

**Costs** The costs in tögrögs for major destinations in Russia and China from Ulaan Baatar are:

| Destination | 2nd class (1/4) | 1st class (2/4) | Deluxe (1/2) |
|---|---|---|---|
| Beijing | 30,749 | 42,326 | 55,273 |
| Ereen | 14,094 | 19,093 | 23,692 |
| Irkutsk | 18,706 | 26,401 | 35,647 |
| Krasnoyarsk | 27,036 | 35,439 | 43,889 |
| Moscow | 50,233 | 70,954 | 99,945 |
| Naushki | 10,516 | 15,169 | 21,950 |
| Novosibirsk | 30,802 | 44,661 | 62,537 |
| Omsk | 34,235 | 47,811 | 55,696 |
| Perm | 41,701 | 53,444 | 67,896 |
| Ulan-Ude | 12,211 | 19,214 | 25,995 |
| Yekaterinburg | 40,527 | 51,989 | 66,132 |

*From China* The best place to buy tickets in China is the China International Travel Service (CITS; ☎ (010) 6515 0232, ext 206; fax 6515 5292), in the Beijing Tourist Building, 28 Jiangwai St, Beijing. You can book up to one month in advance for trains originating in Beijing if you send a deposit of Y100; and you can collect your ticket from one week to one day before departure.

CITS will only sell you a ticket from Beijing to Moscow or Ulaan Baatar – no stopovers are allowed. Tickets to Ulaan Baatar cost Y651/1114 in 1st/deluxe class on the Chinese Beijing-Moscow train (No 3); more (Y707/1085) on the Mongolian Beijing-Ulaan Baatar (No 23) train.

You can buy train tickets privately; they will be more expensive than at CITS, but you may be able to arrange a stopover. See Organised Tours below for details of some companies which sell tickets and tours to Mongolia.

*From Russia* In Moscow, you can buy tickets at the building on ulitsa Krasnoprudnaya 1, next door to the Yaroslavl train station, from where the trains to Ulaan Baatar and Beijing leave. Travellers Guesthouse/IRO Travel (☎ (095) 974 1781; fax 280 7686), ulitsa Bolshaya Pereyaslavskaya 50, 10th floor, Moscow 129401, is one of the better private sellers.

*From Other Countries* Several agencies in western countries can arrange tickets on the international trains, but their prices will be considerably higher than if you bought them from the point of departure. They often only make the effort if you also buy an organised tour from them.

### USA & Canada
See Organised Tours for details.

### Australia
Gateway Travel
    48 The Boulevard, Strathfield, NSW 2135
    (☎ (02) 9745 3333; fax 9745 3237)
Red Bear Tours
    320B Glenferrie Rd, Malvern, Victoria 3144
    (☎ (03) 9824 7183; fax 9822 3956)

### New Zealand
See Organised Tours.

### UK
Regent Holidays
    15 John St, Bristol BS1 2HR
    (☎ (0117) 921 1711; fax 925 4866)
Progressive Tours
    12 Porchester Place, Marble Arch, London W2
    2BS (☎ (0171) 262 1676)
China Travel Service & Information Centre
    124 Euston Rd, London NW1 2AL
    (☎ (0171) 388 8838; fax 388 8828)

### Contintental Europe
Lernidee Reisen
    Berlin, Germany
    (☎ (30) 786 5056; fax 786 5596)
Travel Service Asia
    Kirchberg 15, 7948 Dürmentingen, Germany
    (☎ (7) 371 4963, fax 371 4769)
Scandinavian Student Travel Service (SSTS)
    117 Hauchsvej, 1825 Copenhagen V, Denmark

**Customs & Immigration** There are major delays of three to six hours at both the China-Mongolia and Russia-Mongolia borders. Often the trains cross the border during the middle of the night, when the alert Mongolian and Russian officials maintain the upper hand. The whole process is not difficult or a hassle – just annoying because they keep interrupting your sleep.

Your passport will be taken for inspection and stamping. When it is returned, inspect it closely – sometimes they make errors like cancelling your return visa for China. Foreigners generally sail through customs without having their bags opened, which is one reason why people on the train may approach you and ask if you'll carry some of their luggage across the border – *not a good idea*.

During these stops, you can get off the train and wander around the station, which is just as well since the toilets on the train are locked during the whole inspection procedure.

**Chinese & Mongolian Border Towns** You may have up to three hours to kill in Ereen. The market at the back of the station has a great range of fruit, drinks and bread. Stock up if you are heading into Mongolia, because

## Bogies

Don't be concerned if you get off at Ereen, on the Chinese side of the China-Mongolia border, and the train disappears from the platform. About two hours are spent changing the bogies (wheel assemblies) because the Russians (and, therefore, the Mongolians) and the Chinese use different railway gauges.

Train buffs may want to see the bogie-changing operation. Stay on the train after it disgorges passengers in Ereen. The train then pulls into a large shed about one km from the station. Get off immediately, before the staff lock the doors – they really don't want you in the train anyway. It's OK to walk around the shed and take photos, but don't get in anybody's way. ■

you won't see most of these things in the country. Upstairs in the terminal at Ereen station, a small bank is usually open. If heading into Mongolia from China, you can change half your unused Chinese yuan back to US dollars here if you have a receipt to show that you changed the money legally in the first place. You can also buy some yuan with US dollars, and possibly some Mongolian tögrögs. Otherwise, you can use US dollars in Ulaan Baatar until you get to a bank.

Zamyn-Üüd, on the Mongolian side, is not an interesting place, so you aren't missing anything if the train stops in the middle of the countryside (often in the middle of the night), and not at Zamyn-Üüd. Mongolian customs and immigration officials take about two hours to do their stuff.

### Russian & Mongolian Border Towns

Customs and immigration between Naushki and Sükhbaatar can take at least four hours. You can have a look around Naushki, but there is little to see, and the border crossing usually takes place in the middle of the night. Surprisingly, you may have difficulty finding anyone at the Naushki station to change money, so wait for Sükhbaatar or Ulaan Baatar, or somewhere else in Russia. Try to get rid of your tögrögs before you leave Mongolia, as almost no-one will want to touch them once you are inside Russia.

The train may stop for one or two hours

at, or near, the pleasant Mongolian border town of Sükhbaatar, but there is no need to look around. You may be able to buy some Russian roubles or Mongolian tögrögs with a moneychanger at the train station, but the rate will be poor. If there aren't any moneychangers, you can use US dollars cash to get by until you change money elsewhere.

**Trans-Mongolian Landmarks** The landmarks along the Trans-Mongolian Railway are listed below. Russia, Mongolia and China have their own km markers. In Mongolia, 0km is the border with Russia at Naushki; in China, 0km is Beijing.

**0km: Naushki** A small border town which serves as the Russian border post. The train stops here for at least two hours.

**21km: Sükhbaatar** You will be subject to Mongolian customs and immigration here.

**123km: Darkhan** Mongolia's second-largest city. You can get off here and detour by train to Erdenet, Mongolia's third-largest city, and then by road to western Mongolia.

**404km: Ulaan Baatar** The train only stops here for about 30 minutes. There is no time to see anything, and you shouldn't stray too far from the train anyway – it can leave when you least expect.

**649km: Choir** A former Soviet military base, Choir is a dismal place designated as a Free Trade Zone.

**876km: Sainshand** The capital of the Dornogov aimag, there is nothing to see from the station. No-one will sell any food, but you may be able to buy one of the fantastic bright Mongolian landscape paintings which you see around Ulaan Baatar. They make great souvenirs if you are just passing through Mongolia.

**1113km: Zamyn-Üüd** This is the Mongolian border post where you will have to deal again with Mongolian customs and immigration.

**842km: Ereen/Erlian/Erenhot** The Chinese border post is a good place to stock up on food and change some money. Bogies are changed here.

**415km: Fengzhan** Another largish and dull Chinese regional town.

**385km** You will see your first glimpse of the magnificent Great Wall of China.

**317km: Datong** Once Northern China's imperial centre, this is now one of the country's most depressing cities.

**193km: Zhangjiakou** Nothing much to get excited about here.

**82km: Kanzuang** There are spectacular views of the Great Wall nearby.

**0km: Beijing** There, at last!!

## ORGANISED TOURS

Most travellers visit Mongolia on an organised tour, and this trend is likely to continue as long as visas for independent travellers are difficult to get and extend. In addition, very few Mongolians in Ulaan Baatar, and virtually no-one outside it, speak anything but English and Russian (possibly, a smattering of German); and in the country-side, roads are little more than jeep trails and often atrocious, public transport is unreliable, infrequent and uncomfortable, and the food is bland, unappetising and, often, downright horrible.

Few foreign travel agencies specialise in Mongolia; they mainly sell tours organised and run by travel agencies in Mongolia (see the Ulaan Baatar chapter). Most tours will take you around Ulaan Baatar (possibly at the time of the Naadam Festival) and to one or all of the major tourist attractions: the south Gobi, Kharkhorin and Erdene Zuu monastery, Khövsgöl lake and Terelj. They will probably include a stay in a ger camp, some horse riding and a visit to a nomadic family. Very few agencies offer anything different – notable exceptions are listed below and throughout the book.

The costs of organised tours vary widely; they depend on the country of origin, length of trip, mode of transport, type of accommodation, current exchange rate and so on. However, you can assume that they are expensive. Below are a few places to contact about their current itineraries and prices.

### USA

Academic Travel Abroad
   3210 Grace St, NW, Washington, DC 20007
   (☎ (202) 333-3355)
Boojum Expeditions
   14543 Kelly Canyon Rd, Bozeman, MT 59715
   (☎ (406) 587-0125; fax 585-3474; email
   boojum@mcn.net) – specialises in excellent
   adventurous horseback, rafting and trekking
   tours.
Blue Sea Travel Service
   8929 Wilshire Blvd, Suite 420, Beverly Hills, CA
   90211-1953 (☎ (310) 659-4438; fax 659-4518)
Chinasmith
   324 West 42nd St, New York, NY 10036
   (☎ (212) 239-2410)

Distant Horizons
   619 Tremont St, Boston, MA 02118
   (☎ (1800) 333-1240) – specialises in cultural
   tours led by people with inside knowledge.
Inner Asia Expeditions
   2627 Lombard St, San Francisco, CA 94123
   (☎ (415) 922-0448) – runs some pricey tours.
Juulchin
   Princeton Corporate Plaza 1, 1 Deerpark Drive,
   Suite M, Monmouth Junction, NJ 08852
   (☎ (908) 274-0088; fax 274-9181) – the US representative of the major Mongolian travel
   company, Juulchin.
Nomadic Expeditions
   5 Independence Way, Suite 300, Princeton, NJ
   08540 (☎ (908) 329-8887; fax 329-1369; email
   nomadicexp@aol.com) – runs very good horse
   riding and palaeontological tours.
Tread Lightly Ltd
   One Titus Rd, Washington Depot, CT 06794
   (☎ (203) 868-17170; fax 868-1718)
Ulan Bator Foundation
   PO Box 3059, Venice, CA 90294
   (☎ (310) 821-3459; fax 821-5123)

### Canada

Exotik Tours
   1117 Ste-Catherine O, Suite 806, Montreal H3B
   1H9 (☎ (514) 284-3324; fax 843-5493)

### Australia

Australia-Mongolia Society
   Box 1091, Collingwood, Victoria 3006
   (☎ & fax (03) 9417 5953) – organises cultural
   tours, horse treks and soft adventure trips.
Classic Oriental Tours
   Level 4, 491 Kent St, Sydney, NSW 2000
   (☎ (02) 9261 3988; fax 9261 3320)
Gateway Travel
   48 The Boulevard, Strathfield, NSW 2135
   (☎ (02) 9745 3333; fax 9745 3237)
One World Travel Tours
   PO Box 34, Rundle Mall, Adelaide, SA 5000
   (☎ (08) 8232 2727; fax 8232 2808) – a division
   of Community Aid Abroad, it runs tours for those
   interested in development and the environment.
Red Bear Tours
   320B Glenferrie Rd, Malvern, Victoria 3144
   (☎ (03) 9824 7183; fax 9822 3956)

### New Zealand

Sun-Travel
   407 Great South Rd, Penrose, Auckland
   (☎ (09) 525 3074; fax 525 3065)

## UK
Equitour
> 41 South Parade, Summertown, Oxford OX2 7JP
> (☎ (01865) 511 642; fax 512 583) – specialises
> in horse-riding tours.

Exodus Expeditions
> 9 Weir Rd, London SW12 0LT (☎ (0448l) 675 5550)

Explore Worldwide
> 1 Frederick St, Aldershot, Hants GU11 1LQ
> (☎ (01252) 333 031; fax 343 170)

Progressive Tours
> 12 Porchester Place, Marble Arch, London W2
> 2BS (☎ (0171) 262 1676)

Regent Holidays
> 15 John St, Bristol BS1 2HR
> (☎ (0117) 921 1711; fax 925 4866)

Steppes East
> Castle Eaton, Swindon, Wiltshire SN6 6J
> (☎ (01285) 810 267; fax 810 693)

Voyages Jules Verne
> 21 Dorset Square, London NW1 6QG
> (☎ (0171) 723 5066; fax 723 8629) – runs
> upmarket tours.

## Denmark
Be-Eco Tours
> Teglgardsvej 601 3.tv, DK-3050, Humlebaek
> (☎ & fax (4542) 191 626)

Marco Polo Tours, Borgergade 16, 1300 Copenhagen
> (☎ 3313 0307)

## France
Air Sud
> 18 rue du Pont-Neuf, 75001 Paris
> (☎ 01 40 41 66 66; fax 01 42 36 38 89)

Orients
> 29 rue des Boulangers, 75005 Paris
> (☎ 01 46 34 29 00; fax 01 40 46 84 48)

Terres d'Aventure
> 6 rue Saint-Victor, 75005 Paris
> (☎ 01 53 73 77 77; fax 01 43 29 96 31)

## Germany
Juulchin
> Representative is at Arnold-Zweig Str 2-3R,
> 13189 Berlin (☎ (030) 478 2484; fax 471 8833)

Travel Service Asia
> Kirchberg 15, 7948 Dürmentingen
> (☎ (07) 371 4963; fax 371 4769)

Mongolia Travel Information Service
> Dudenstr 78, D-10965, Berlin 61
> (☎ (030) 786 5056; fax 786 5596)

## Italy
Nazionale por i Rapporti Culturali con la Mongolia
> PO Box 979, Viale 20 Settembre, 37, 1-34126
> Trieste (☎ (040) 362 241; fax 363 494)

## Norway
Kinareiser (China Travel Ltd)
> Hegdehaugshveien 10, 0167 Oslo
> (☎ 2211 0057; fax 2236 0544)

## Sweden
Eco Tour Production, Burge i Hablingbo
> 620 11 Havdhem, Gotland
> (☎ (498) 487 105; fax 487 115;
> email janw.nomadic@gotlandica.se)

Svensk-kinesiska Resebyran (Swedish-Chinese Travel Ltd)
> Humelgardsgatan 19, 114 87 Stockholm
> (☎ (8) 679 7000; fax 611 8126)

Häst-och Sportresor
> Norrgarden 2078, 760 10 Berghamra
> (☎ (176) 61 534; fax 61 542) – specialises in
> horse-riding tours.

## Switzerland
Kuoni Travel
> Zurich (☎ (1) 277 4444; fax 271 5282)

## Russia
BuryatIntour
> 12 Ranzhurov Sta, Ulan-Ude, 670000
> (☎ & fax (30122) 26 176)

Intourist Baikal
> 44 Gagarin Blvd, Irkutsk 664055
> (☎ (3952) 290 260; fax 277 872)

Lake Baikal Region Guides Association
> PO Box 3271, Irkutsk, 664000
> (☎ (3952) 461 164; fax 341 629)

Travellers Guesthouse/IRO Travel
> Bolshaya Pereyaslavskaya 50, 10th floor, Moscow
> (☎ (095) 974 1781; fax 280 7686)

## Japan
Juulchin
> Representative is at Room 802, Hon-Machi
> Tensho Building, 5–18 Utsubohon-Machi 1-chome,
> Nishi-ku, Osaka 550 (☎ (6) 441 7845; fax 441 7847)

MJT
> Also a Juulchin representative, 8/F, JBR Shibuya
> East, II 16-9, Higashi 2-chome, Shibuya-ku,
> Tokyo 150 (☎ (3) 3486 7351; fax 3486 7440)

## South Korea
Mongolia Travel Information Service
> Hyejung Building, 80, Nonhyon-Dong,
> Kangnam Ku, Seoul
> (☎ (2) 540 3928; fax (2) 542 1118)

## Hong Kong
Blue Sea Travel Service
> 1208 Silvercord Tower 1, 30 Canton Rd,
> Tsimshatsui, Kowloon (☎ 2375 1127; fax 2375 8475)

Moonsky Star
  Chungking Mansion, 36-44 Nathan Rd,
  Tsimshatsui, Kowloon
  (☎ 2723 1376; fax 2723 6653; email MonkeyHK
  @compuserve.com)
Phoenix Services
  Room B, 6th floor, Milton Mansion,
  96 Nathan Rd, Tsimshatsui, Kowloon
  (☎ 2722 7378)
Time Travel
  16th floor, Block A, Chungking Mansions,
  30 Nathan Rd, Tsimshatsui, Kowloon
  (☎ 2366 6222; fax 2739 5413)

**China**
Beijing Scene Publishing
  2-2-11 Qijiayuan, Beijing (☎ (010) 6592 2720;
  fax 6592 2714; email scene@well.com)
Monkey Business
  No 1 Building, Yu Lin Li, Room 406, 4th floor, Beijing
  Commercial Business Complex, Youanmenwai,
  100054 Beijing (☎ & fax (010) 6329 2244, ext
  4406; email MonkeyChina@compuserve.com)
Juulchin
  Golden Bride Mansion, East Door, Al Jin Guo,
  Men Wai Da Jie, Beijing
  (☎ (010) 6456 1225; fax 6507 7397)

# Getting Around

Travelling around the countryside independently is the best way to see the country and meet the people, but there are several matters you need to be aware of. Annual outbreaks of the plague in western Mongolia may affect your travel plans if there are quarantine restrictions. (In 1996 a cholera outbreak limited travel to some regions.) Forest fires are common, and in 1996 were devastating.

Generally, shortages of petrol and spare parts are rare except in remote regions. Accidents from negligence and drunkenness are not uncommon. Try to avoid travelling at night when unseen potholes, drunk drivers and wildlife can cause havoc. Lastly, if you think Ulaan Baatar is undeveloped and lacking in facilities, think again about travelling in the countryside.

## AIR

Mongolia, a vast, sparsely populated country with very little infrastructure, relies heavily on air transport. There are 81 airports, of which only 31 can be used permanently; only eight of these have paved runways. Pilots often use landmarks for navigation, so many flights are cancelled if there is a lot of fog.

## Flights

MIAT, the major internal airline, has flights to 17 *aimag* (provincial) capitals, major cities and tourist destinations – but not to Sükhbaatar, Erdenet, Darkhan or Sainshand, which are well serviced by train, or Zuunmod, a short drive from Ulaan Baatar. Of the 17 destinations, all but three are served directly to/from Ulaan Baatar, so it is impossible to fly, say, between Dalanzadgad and Altai without returning to Ulaan Baatar and catching another flight. Longer flights to the west stop to refuel, often at Mörön (or possibly Arvaikheer), so you can sometimes combine a trip to Khovd and Khövsgöl.

MIAT schedules change regularly, and almost weekly during the summer (10 June to 16 September). In summer, extra flights go to Khujirt, Kharkhorin (Karakorum) and Dalanzadgad, for the south Gobi ger camps.

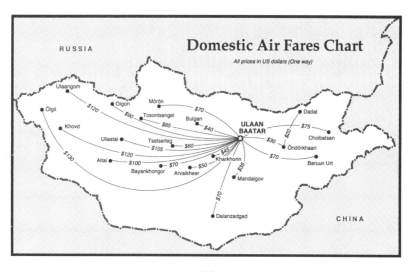

MIAT use ancient Soviet Antonovs, a couple of Boeing 727s (mainly for international flights), Chinese-built Y12s and a few helicopters.

The only company to give MIAT any competition is the relatively new Khangard airlines. For the same fares as MIAT, Khangard goes to Mörön, Uliastai, Khovd and Oigon (also known as Tudevtei). Khangard plans to provide a better service than MIAT (not difficult) by guaranteeing seats, departing on time and allowing 15kg of baggage (MIAT's limit is only 10kg).

Tengeryn Ulacech Airlines (☎ 379 765) sometimes offers flights or can be chartered. Tas Airlines (☎ 379 657) is a cargo service which may occasionally take passengers.

Here are a few tips on flying MIAT:

The most you get on any flight is a cup of warm fizzy cordial, so take your own food and water. There is no air-con, so dress lightly. Don't get over-concerned if there are no seatbelts. There is no visible safety equipment. Enjoy the views and try to forget about the lack of service. The planes have no toilets – cross your legs or have a leak at an airport if the plane stops for refuelling. Never lose your ticket – you'll possibly get a refund in Ulaan Baatar, but nowhere else. Try not to change the date of your ticket – it is just one more headache you don't need. A Mongolian (or anyone) can buy you a ticket, but you will always have to pay in US dollars.

## Reservations & Tickets

A MIAT reservation isn't worth diddly-squat until you have a ticket in your hand. In the countryside, buy your ticket as soon as you can – this is usually done at the airport or, sometimes, at the town bank. Confirm your ticket again, and again. In Ulaan Baatar, MIAT staff speak some English; in the countryside, they don't.

There is no computerised reservation system connecting the various airports around the country, so you cannot buy a return ticket in Ulaan Baatar. If you want to fly from Ulaan Baatar to Khovd and back, you will have to buy your Khovd-Ulaan Baatar ticket in Khovd. If you wish to fly in one direction and return by road in the other, to, say, Mörön, fly from Ulaan Baatar, where you are more likely to get a ticket and a seat,

and then return overland – otherwise you may wait days or more for a flight and ticket in Mörön.

## Costs

All foreigners must pay several times more than Mongolians for all MIAT (and Khangard) tickets. You must also pay in US dollars, and get a 'dollar-denominated ticket' or you won't get on the plane. Tickets range from US$35 to US$130 for a four-hour, 1380km flight to the far west – pretty reasonable, considering the distances. Children between five and 16 years pay half; under five, they fly for free.

One real hassle is that the baggage limit on internal MIAT flights is 10kg (15kg for Khangard), and MIAT will charge you for every extra gram when you check in. The cost for excess baggage ranges from T550 to T2750 per kg, depending on the distance of the flight. To avoid this carry some heavy stuff in your small, cabin luggage (which isn't weighed) or share the load among friends.

## Checking In

Go to all airports at least two hours before departure on the assumption that you will still have to struggle to get a seat on the flight, even if you have a ticket. In Ulaan Baatar, this is often less of a problem, but chaos still reigns supreme. (All flights from Ulaan Baatar leave between 8 and 10 am.) Even if you have a ticket, flight number and an allocated seat number, don't assume the plane won't be overbooked.

At the airport, you can start the Mongolian Scramble while queuing to exchange your ticket for a plastic docket, which you hand in when you finally get a seat on the plane. Then you have to scramble in another line to get your luggage weighed. After everyone sighs when the plane has finally arrived (if travelling from anywhere other than Ulaan Baatar), scramble past the guard and through the throng of arriving passengers and onto the tarmac. Then scramble on board and find a seat. Try to make certain your luggage has gone on the plane. The final scrambling takes place when you get off the plane, find your luggage (a good reason to take it with you as cabin luggage), plough through the throng of departing passengers, and find transport into town.

## BUS

Buses are an increasingly popular way of travelling around the country, but services are still limited, the buses are mostly old Soviet rust-buckets and the journeys are uncomfortable and slow. Allowing for stops, breakdowns and everything else, buses average around 30km per hour. They are generally safe, but drivers are sometimes drunk. Breakdowns can be expected on all long-distance trips.

All bus routes start and end in Ulaan Baatar; buses only travel between aimag capitals if they're on the way to or from Ulaan Baatar. For instance, buses go from Bulgan to Mörön as part of the Ulaan Baatar-Mörön trip, but not between Mörön and Uliastai. Buses go to all aimag capitals, major cities and tourist destinations except Sükhbaatar and Erdenet, which are connected by train, and to the far western aimag capitals of Khovd, Bayan-Ölgii and Ulaangom. Buses do not travel around western Mongolia; the furthest west they go is to Mörön and Altai.

The actual time that buses leave is rarely the same as the departure times listed on your ticket or on the timetable. As one reader noted, you should always get there early:

You get a computer ticket with the departure time of 8.30 am, and a request to show up at 8 am 'just in case'. Next morning, we found our bus and fought our way to a seat. The conductor showed up waving a piece of paper, and screaming loudly at everyone. I flashed my tickets at her, which was greeted with a smile, and she said something like 'Oh good, we can finally leave. We are late.' It was 7.30 am.

If travelling by bus, here are a few tips:

Avoid the back seats. Try not to worry about the land-speed record the drivers attempt during the rare times there is a good stretch of road. Don't expect any beg-your-pardons when getting a seat. Bring all your own food and drink – stops will be few and far between, or at *guanzes* (canteens), which have poor food. You may be charged extra for luggage, but it won't be much. Destination signs on the buses will be in Cyrillic. You can hail a long-distance bus from anywhere along the road.

### Reservations & Tickets

In Ulaan Baatar, it is a good idea to buy tickets in advance for all long-distance trips. In the countryside, you just get on the bus when it arrives and pay the conductor on board.

The schedule and costs listed below will certainly change by the time you read this, but the list gives you an idea of the frequency of buses to the major towns from Ulaan Baatar.

| Bus Schedule | | | |
|---|---|---|---|
| *Destination* | *Via* | *Days* | *Cost* |
| Arvaikheer | direct | daily except Sun | T3250 |
| Baganuur | direct | Mon, Wed, Fri, Sat & Sun | T1055 |
| Baruun Urt | Öndörkhaan | Mon & Wed | T4100 |
| Bayankhongor | Arvaikheer | daily except Sun | T4477 |
| Bulgan | direct | Mon | T1962 |
| Choibalsan | Öndörkhaan | Mon & Thur | T4610 |
| Dalanzadgad | Mandalgov | Mon | T2343 |
| Darkhan | direct | daily | T1200 |
| Kharkhorin | direct | Tue, Thu & Sat | T2760 |
| Öndörkhaan | direct | Mon, Tues & Fri | T3500 |
| Mandalgov | direct | Mon & Thu | T1970 |
| Mörön | Bulgan | Mon, Wed, Thu & Sat | T4700 |
| Tsetserleg | direct | Mon & Wed | T3720 |
| Uliastai | Tsetserleg | Mon | T6403 |

## MINIBUS

Minibuses regularly travel between Ulaan Baatar and towns in Töv aimag, and sometimes to popular spots such as Terelj, Kharkhorin and Khujirt, but very rarely to anywhere else in the country. Minibuses are slightly more expensive than buses, but you are usually guaranteed a seat, and they are always quicker and more comfortable. You can't reserve a ticket on a minibus; just get on and pay the driver or conductor.

## TRAIN

The 1750km railway is primarily made up of the north-south rail line, which is part of the Trans-Mongolian Railway, connecting China with Russia. (Both domestic and international trains use this same line.) In addition, there are two spur lines: to the copper-mining centre of Erdenet and the coal-mining city of Baganuur. Another train runs every week from Choibalsan, the capital of Dornod aimag, across the border and into Russia.

North of Ulaan Baatar, express trains travel every day to Darkhan, and onto Sükhbaatar or Erdenet. To the south, there are direct trains from Ulaan Baatar to Choir twice a week, and to Zamyn-Üüd, via Choir and Sainshand, daily. You can't use the Trans-Mongolian Railway for internal transport.

When travelling in hard-seat class (see below), you will almost certainly have to practise the Mongolian Scramble. If you're not travelling alone, one of you can scramble on board and find seats and the other can bring the luggage on board a little later. Young boys and girls usually travel around the train selling bread and fizzy drinks. Otherwise, there is nothing to eat or drink on local trains.

### Classes

There are only two classes on domestic passenger trains: hard seat and soft seat. In hard-seat class, the seats are actually padded but there are no assigned seats nor any limit to the amount of tickets sold, so the carriages are always crowded and dirty – sometimes reminiscent of the worst Indian and Chinese regional trains. If you get the hard-seat carriage but decide that you can't stand the mass of human bodies, walk to the soft-seat carriages and ask to upgrade – spare soft-seats are often available.

### Distance Table (by road in km)

|    |              | 1    | 2    | 3    | 4    | 5    | 6    | 7    | 8    | 9    |
|----|--------------|------|------|------|------|------|------|------|------|------|
| 1  | Ulaan Baatar |      |      |      |      |      |      |      |      |      |
| 2  | Tsetserleg   | 453  |      |      |      |      |      |      |      |      |
| 3  | Ölgii        | 1636 | 1220 |      |      |      |      |      |      |      |
| 4  | Bayankhongor | 630  | 214  | 1006 |      |      |      |      |      |      |
| 5  | Bulgan       | 318  | 289  | 1334 | 503  |      |      |      |      |      |
| 6  | Altai        | 1001 | 585  | 635  | 371  | 874  |      |      |      |      |
| 7  | Sainshand    | 463  | 855  | 1869 | 863  | 781  | 1234 |      |      |      |
| 8  | Choibalsan   | 655  | 1108 | 2291 | 1265 | 973  | 1656 | 531  |      |      |
| 9  | Mandalgov    | 260  | 500  | 1514 | 508  | 578  | 879  | 355  | 741  |      |
| 10 | Uliastai     | 984  | 531  | 830  | 459  | 820  | 195  | 1322 | 1639 | 967  |
| 11 | Arvaikheer   | 430  | 266  | 1206 | 200  | 348  | 571  | 663  | 1085 | 308  |
| 12 | Dalanzadgad  | 553  | 643  | 1583 | 577  | 725  | 948  | 516  | 1074 | 293  |
| 13 | Baruun Urt   | 560  | 1013 | 2196 | 1190 | 878  | 1561 | 340  | 191  | 613  |
| 14 | Sükhbaatar   | 311  | 629  | 1947 | 843  | 340  | 1312 | 774  | 966  | 571  |
| 15 | Khovd        | 1425 | 973  | 211  | 795  | 1271 | 424  |      | 2080 | 1303 |
| 16 | Mörön        | 671  | 413  | 981  | 627  | 353  | 583  | 1134 | 1326 | 913  |
| 17 | Öndörkhaan   | 331  | 784  | 1967 | 961  | 649  | 1332 | 302  | 324  | 417  |
| 18 | Zuunmod      | 43   | 496  | 1591 | 583  | 361  | 956  | 449  | 661  | 225  |
| 19 | Ulaangom     | 1336 | 883  | 301  | 988  | 1033 | 662  | 1738 | 1991 | 1383 |
| 20 | Darkhan      | 219  | 537  | 1582 | 751  | 248  | 1122 | 682  | 874  | 479  |
| 21 | Erdenet      | 371  | 357  | 1402 | 571  | 68   | 942  | 834  | 1026 | 631  |

Soft seats are only a little bit softer, but the conditions are much better: the price difference (usually at least double the price of the hard seat) is prohibitive for most Mongolians. The soft-seat carriages are divided into compartments with four beds in each. You are given an assigned bed, and will be able to sleep, assuming of course that your compartment mates aren't rip-roaring drunk and noisy. If you travel at night, clean sheets are provided for about T250, which is a wise investment since some of the quilts smell like mutton. Compared with hard-seat class, it's the lap of luxury, and worth paying extra for.

### Reservations & Tickets
If you're travelling from Ulaan Baatar, it is important to book a soft seat well in advance – it can be done up to 10 days before departure. There may be a booking fee of T60. Whichever class you travel in, booking ahead will save you doing the Mongolian Scramble at the ticket counter just before the train leaves.

### TAXI
Mongolia claims to have 46,700km of highway – of which only 1200km is actually paved. Taxis are only useful along these paved roads, eg from Ulaan Baatar to a few nearby places such as Zuunmod and Terelj. The general appalling quality of roads around the countryside means that most travel is by jeep.

### JEEP
The ubiquitous Russian khaki-coloured jeep is nicknamed *jaran yös*, which means 'sixty-nine' – the number of the original model. On the terrible Mongolian roads, these jeeps are an important form of transport, and mandatory when visiting more remote attractions. The large and comfortable Land Rover-type jeeps used by development agencies, embassies and very upmarket travel companies are not available to the general public.

Jeeps can typically travel only between 30 and 50km per hour. The distance table below may be helpful, especially when estimating the cost of a jeep per km. Along more popular routes, there are guanzes along the way.

### Hazards
Whether renting a jeep with a driver or travelling long distances by public shared jeep,

| 10 | 11 | 12 | 13 | 14 | 15 | 16 | 17 | 18 | 19 | 20 |
|---|---|---|---|---|---|---|---|---|---|---|
| 659 | | | | | | | | | | |
| 1036 | 377 | | | | | | | | | |
| 1544 | 990 | 856 | | | | | | | | |
| 1081 | 688 | 864 | 871 | | | | | | | |
| 442 | 995 | 1372 | 1985 | 1736 | | | | | | |
| 388 | 679 | 1056 | 1231 | 693 | 918 | | | | | |
| 1315 | 761 | 710 | 229 | 642 | 1756 | 1022 | | | | |
| 1027 | 385 | 518 | 566 | 354 | 1380 | 714 | 337 | | | |
| 529 | 1188 | 1565 | 1896 | 1373 | 238 | 680 | 1667 | 1379 | | |
| 989 | 596 | 772 | 779 | 92 | 1519 | 601 | 550 | 262 | 1281 | |
| 809 | 416 | 793 | 931 | 272 | 1339 | 421 | 702 | 414 | 1101 | 180 |

there are a few matters to note. Flat tyres are a time-honoured tradition. Insist that your driver bring a spare and a tyre patch kit consisting of rubber patches, glue, extra tyre valves and valve tool. Be sure the driver has a tyre pump, hydraulic jack and tyre irons. If the driver doesn't have a useable spare tyre, at least tell him to bring a spare inner tube.

The quickest distance between two points is a straight line, and the only thing which could (but not always) put off a Mongolian jeep diver from taking a shortcut is a huge mountain range or raging river. If renting a jeep by the km, you will welcome a shortcut, especially to shorten an uncomfortable trip. If you have an experienced driver, allow him to take shortcuts when he feels it is worthwhile, but don't insist on any – he is the expert. The downside of shortcuts is the possibility of breaking down on more isolated roads, and travelling over even more uncomfortable roads.

Serious mechanical breakdowns are a possibility. To be safe, it's necessary to bring tools and whatever spare parts are available. Should your vehicle break down irreparably in a rural area, you'll be faced with the task of trying to get back to civilisation either on foot (not recommended), by hitching (occasionally possible) or by whatever is available. The best solution is to travel with a small group using at least two jeeps.

Russian jeeps easily overheat. There is no easy solution, but it helps to travel during the early morning or late afternoon hours when temperatures are relatively low.

Most of Mongolia is grassland, desert and mountains. You might think that mountain driving would pose the worst problems, but forests cause the most trouble of all. This is because the ground, even on a slope, is a springy alpine bog, holding huge amounts of water in the decaying grasses, which are instantly compacted under tyres, reducing a wildflower meadow to slush.

Drivers in Mongolia enjoy a high status, and Mongolians are loath to dig – it's just not in their nomadic blood. This has been known to infuriate visitors, who expect a flurry of activity as soon as a vehicle becomes

bogged. Mongolians are more inclined to sit on their haunches, have a smoke and then send word to the nearest farm or town for a tractor to come and tow you out. Even in remote areas, there's usually someone passing by on a horse who can get a message through. Just be patient.

### Rental
Renting a jeep with a driver and/or guide from Ulaan Baatar is the best way to see the countryside, but you can save some money by using public transport to major regional gateways – that is Mörön for Khövsgöl lake, Khovd for the west, Dalanzadgad for the south Gobi and Baganuur for the east. From these places, you will be able to rent a jeep fairly easily. Don't expect to rent a jeep outside of an aimag capital. Most villages will have a jeep, but it may not be available or running, or the driver may be drunk.

In aimag capitals, jeeps are available at very negotiable prices. The charge for Mongolians at the time of research was from T120 to T130 per km. (This is about the same as the standard per km rate for taxis in Ulaan Baatar, so you can use the Ulaan Baatar taxi rate as a guide for the cost of jeep rentals in the countryside.) However, foreigners will be lucky to get one for less than T150 per km – more at touristy places like Kharkhorin.

This price will include a driver (you will soon realise that you would never be able to drive around Mongolia on your own), who almost certainly won't speak anything but Mongolian and Russian (so you may need a guide to translate). Avoid offers of 'all-inclusive' charges by 'the day' as you will almost certainly pay more than if you pay per km. You can pay up to T220 per km for more reliable jeeps and drivers from travel agents in Ulaan Baatar, or ger camps in the countryside. This charge may include a stove, tent and sleeping bag.

It is vital that you and the driver agree to the terms and conditions – and the odometer or speedometer reading – before you start. Ask about all possible 'extras' such as waiting time. Drivers are notoriously bad for assuming that you will feed them along the way. They will often not take enough food even if they have agreed to bring their own. Drivers will usually sleep in or near their jeeps, or in a ger, so you won't have to worry about, or pay for, their accommodation.

Three can sit in the back of the Russian jeeps, but it may be uncomfortable on longer trips. If you also take a guide, rather than just a driver, one less seat will be available. There is usually enough room at the back of the jeep for backpacks, tents, water and so on.

In the aimag capitals, jeeps hang around the market or the bus/truck stations. In Ulaan Baatar, the best place to start looking is outside the Ulaan Baatar Hotel or the various taxi stands, or ask at your hotel.

Here are a few tips when renting a jeep:

You decide which, if any, passengers you pick up along the way. If you arrange for a jeep to pick you up, or drop you off, agree on a reduced price for the empty vehicle travelling one way. Many towns and *sums* (districts) have identical or similar names, so make sure you both know where you are exactly going. Don't push the driver too hard; allow them (and the vehicle) to stop and rest. However, regular and lengthy stops for a chat and smoke can add to the journey. If you aren't taking a guide-cum-translator, hiring one just to negotiate the price and terms for a long and expensive trip is worthwhile.

### Public Jeeps

Public shared jeeps regularly travel between Ulaan Baatar and most nearby aimag capitals, and to tourist destinations. The frequency of departures depends almost entirely on demand. In more remote areas, there are some shared jeeps, but you may have to wait a day before it leaves. Shared jeeps are dearer, but quicker and more comfortable (and sometimes the only form of transport), than the public buses, though drivers will pack in as many people in the jeep as they can.

Trips generally cost about T10 to T20 per km per person for a long ride with about five others. There are usually at least three passengers in the back, and two, plus driver, in front. (At a petrol station in one isolated town, we saw 11 adults and three children stagger out of a shared jeep.) In most aimag

capitals, shared jeeps leave from the market or bus/truck station. You will have to ask around; listen to distorted announcements in Mongolian over the loudspeaker at the market; or check any noticeboards at the market.

### CAR & MOTORCYCLE

Travelling around Mongolia with your own, or rented, vehicle is not recommended. What looks like main roads on the map are little more than tyre tracks in the dirt, sand or mud. All maps are inadequate, and there is hardly a signpost in the whole country. Navigation is tricky – some drivers follow the telephone lines when there are any, or else ask for directions at gers along the way. Villages with food and water are few and far between, and no-one in the countryside will speak anything but Mongolian or Russian.

There is nowhere official in Mongolia to rent a car or motorcycle. If you want to buy one, you will have to ask around, or check out a couple of car yards below the bridge just south of the Bayangol Hotel in Ulaan Baatar. One traveller bought a new Ij Planeta – the Russian-made motorcycle you see all over the countryside – for the tögrög equivalent of US$900. After travelling 4000km, he was able to sell it for about US$800.

Travellers can use an international driving license to drive any vehicle in Mongolia; expat residents need to apply for a local license. If you buy a vehicle, inquire about registration at the local police station.

All aimag, and most *sum*, capitals have a petrol station. Supplies are regular, but you will probably have to come to terms with the hand pumps. Two types of Russian fuel are available: '93' is the best, but only generally available in Ulaan Baatar; all Russian-made vehicles use '76', which is all that is available in the countryside.

### BICYCLE

Now that Mongolia is opening up to the outside world, bicycles occasionally appear on the streets of Ulaan Baatar, but these are generally ridden by 'eccentric' expats. Most Mongolians don't see the point in bicycles:

all towns in the countryside are small enough to walk around; horses or motorbikes are the best form of transport between towns anyway; and buses run regularly around Ulaan Baatar.

Given the rough roads, a mountain bike would be a wiser choice than a more fragile 10-speed touring bike, but there are a few points to recognise: you will need to bring all your spare parts and tools; maps are inadequate; the roads are appalling; taking a bike on a bus or truck (it is better on a train) is fraught with problems, and airlines have luggage restrictions; dogs will cause you headaches; the notoriously fickle weather should be taken seriously; villagers will take a lot of interest in you and your bike; and Mongolians are terrible at estimating distance – they usually grossly overestimate.

## HITCHING

Hitching is never entirely safe in any country in the world and we don't normally recommend it. People who choose to hitch will be safer if they travel in pairs and let someone know where they are planning to go.

Mongolia is different, however. Because the country is so vast, public transport so limited and the people so poor, hitching (usually on trucks) is a recognised – and, often, the only – form of transport in the countryside. Hitching is seldom free, and it is *always* slow – after stopping at gers to drink, fixing flat tyres, breaking down, running out of petrol and getting stuck in mud and rivers, a truck can take 48 hours to cover 200km.

Hitching is not generally dangerous personally, but still hazardous and extremely uncomfortable. Don't expect much traffic in remote rural areas; you might see one or two vehicles a day on many roads, and sometimes nobody at all for several days. Along the road, just wave at the driver of any vehicle. In the towns, ask at the market, where trucks invariably hang around, or at the bus/truck/jeep station, police station or hotel. At the markets, sometimes there are announcements over the loudspeakers, and notices on a noticeboard, about imminent departures.

If you rely on hitching entirely, you will just travel from one dreary aimag town to another. You still need to hire a jeep to see, for example, the Gobi Desert, the mountains in Khentii or some of the lakes in the far west. Hitching out of Ulaan Baatar is difficult because you must find the right truck or vehicle at the right time, whereas in the smaller towns it is easier to ask around.

One traveller described the frustrations and discomfort involved in hitching:

We loaded our packs and spent the next few hours driving around town, loading sheep but mostly so the driver could have another vodka drinking session. We soon appeared to be on our way but every half a km the driver would enter a ger and we would sit there for ages.

The Mongolian passengers seemed to take it all for granted and seemed unperturbed by the fact that they had been sitting in the truck for ten hours and we still hadn't left the town environs. We went another 1km and approached a river. The driver headed for the worst trail across and of course we got stuck.

Everyone began making preparations to spend the night by the river. I nearly froze to death and got no sleep at all. The passengers had nothing to eat or drink for 24 hours. They had to urinate and defecate everywhere, including on everyone's luggage. They continued to make the ride interesting by urinating and defecating on everyone's legs and feet. We eventually reached Bayankhongor. It had taken 36 hours to cover 180km.

**Heidi Heinzerling, USA**

Truck drivers will normally expect some negotiable payment. Expect to pay at least T10 per km per person – which doesn't make it much cheaper than a long-distance bus or shared jeep, but in many places a truck is your only choice. Rather than cash, drivers may prefer vodka or cigarettes, or anything you have which could be of practical use to them. You'll need to speak either Mongolian or Russian, or have an interpreter with you. You never know what sort of vehicle you'll be riding in – you could be riding in the back of a truck along with sheep or pigs.

The most important thing to bring is an extremely large amount of patience, tolerance and time, and a high threshold of discomfort. You must carry a sleeping bag and, if possible, a tent, for the inevitable breakdowns.

Bring all your own food and water, though the truck may stop at guanzes somewhere along the way. One more good idea:

The only space for my luggage was an open tray on the roof used to store oily tool boxes and jacks. Add to that the rain and blood and guts from a dozen beaver carcasses which we carried for some hunters. You may want to slip the backpack into a large plastic bag first.

**Nick Winter, UK**

## BOAT

Although there are 397km of navigable waterways in Mongolia, the locals don't use rivers for transporting people or cargo. The only two boats we had heard of in the country are the *Sükhbaatar*, which occasionally travels around the Khövsgöl lake, and a customs boat which patrols the Selenge Gol on the border of Russia and Mongolia. Both can be chartered by foreigners.

## HORSE

Horses have provided reliable, albeit slow, transport for Mongolians for the past few thousand years. It worked for Chinggis Khaan and the Silk Road traders, not to mention countless nomads. In recent decades, many shepherds have also acquired motorcycles, but most still use horses. Travellers cannot see everything by horse, but it is the best way to travel around such places as Khövsgöl lake, Tsagaannuur and the muddy Khentii.

You can rent a horse for the day, week or month, or buy one for about US$200 – but you will need to know what to look for. Most foreign and local travel agencies also organise horse-riding trips. Like most forms of travel in Mongolia, there are a few things to know:

If you are taller than a Mongolian (most foreigners are), bring your own stirrup leathers. Use a Russian saddle, and not the Mongolian wooden saddle, unless you are a masochist. A versatile alternative to hiking boots is to combine lightweight hiking boots and half chaps. Bring a sense of balance and a love of horses. There is no need to treat horses roughly, like many Mongolians do, but the horses won't really respond to cuddles and sugar cubes either. Bring all your own

food and equipment. Watch and learn: Mongolians almost invented horsemanship. And be prepared for at least one good spill.

## CAMEL & YAK

Don't laugh: camels and yaks are recognised forms of transport. Camels, which can carry around 250kg but are a bit slow (about 5km per hour), carry about one-third of all cargo around the Gobi Desert. Yaks are also slow, but very useful for hauling heavy cargo, especially uphill.

A few travel agencies include a ride on a camel or yak in their programme. In more touristy areas such as the ger camps in the southern Gobi, Khövsgöl lake and Terelj you may be able to ride a camel or yak for an hour or so. Otherwise, you can always ask at a ger.

## LOCAL TRANSPORT
### Bus & Trolley-bus

In Ulaan Baatar, regular, and very crowded, trolley-buses and buses ply the main roads. Larger towns in the countryside will also have some local buses, but you are unlikely to need them because most facilities are located centrally.

### Taxi

Ulaan Baatar is the only place with a taxi service, though in the national capital any vehicle on the street is a potential taxi – just flag down the driver and agree on a price. The current rate is a standard T130 per km, but this will certainly increase. In the country towns there are no taxis, but you may be able to charter a local vehicle. Some taxi drivers are maniacs, but generally around Ulaan Baatar they drive safely. The main problem is drunkenness: if the taxi smells like a vodka distillery, don't get in.

## TOURS
### Organised Tours

Refer to the Ulaan Baatar chapter for details about recommended Mongolian travel agencies which organise tours around the country, and to the Getting There & Away chapter for information about foreign travel agencies which organise tours to Mongolia.

### Do-It-Yourself Tours

Easily the best way to see Mongolia is independently by rented jeep. If you can share the costs with others, it doesn't work out to be too expensive, so with enough time, tents, water and food, and a reliable jeep and driver, you will have the time of your life.

Refer to the Jeep section above about hiring a jeep and driver.

**Guides** It is safe to assume that no-one in the countryside speaks anything but Mongolian and Russian, so a guide-cum-translator is very handy, and almost mandatory. A guide will also explain local traditions, help with any hassles with the police, find accommodation, negotiate jeeps, explain captions in museums and interpret when you meet nomadic people.

A guide is less useful in Ulaan Baatar and major aimag cities, where it is easier to get around, and you are more likely to meet an English-speaking person – just as long as you carry the Lonely Planet guidebook, with its maps, and the Lonely Planet phrasebook. In Ulaan Baatar, a guide is helpful, however, to translate captions in museums and monasteries, and assist you if you have to deal with any bureaucracy.

Many Mongolians in Ulaan Baatar, from students up to professors, love to earn some real money as guides during the summer holidays. The most popular foreign language (besides Russian) is English, though some speak German after studying or working in the former East Germany, and other languages such as Japanese, Spanish and French. Standards of fluency may not be high: anyone who is fluent will get a comparatively well-paid job in an embassy, travel company and development agency.

Finding a guide is not easy. In Ulaan Baatar, ask travel agencies (where guides will be more expensive), talk to anyone who approaches you in the street for any reason, find some students at the universities or nearby cafés and hotels, or check out the classified ads in the English-language newspapers. In the countryside, there is nothing to do but ask, and ask, and ask – try the hotels and schools.

In Ulaan Baatar, a student or non-professional guide will cost a negotiable T5500 per day or more (and may want to be paid in US dollars). To take one around the countryside from Ulaan Baatar, expect to pay at least T6600 per day, plus expenses for travel, food and accommodation (the latter is considerably cheaper for the guide than for you). In an aimag capital, a guide (if you can find one) costs about T5500 per day, plus any expenses. For a professional guide who is knowledgeable in a specific interest, such as birdwatching, and very fluent in your language, the costs can go up to US$80 per day.

Here are a few final tips:

You can share a guide with up to four people – any more than that and it gets unwieldy. Test a guide for the day, before hiring one for a long trip. Guides are often little more than interpreters – they are not necessarily knowledgeable on the region you are visiting, or what you are interested in. Make sure the guide doesn't end up spending most of *your* time and money practising *their* English (or whatever language). Be careful that they don't demand expensive meals and accommodation if you are paying their expenses.

# Ulaan Baatar Улаан Баатар

Mongolia's largest city with over one-quarter of its population, Ulaan Baatar is also the transport and industrial centre of the country. Often called UB (you-bee) by foreigners, but not by locals, Mongolia's capital city still has the look and feel of a neglected European city from the 1950s. The old Soviet cars and buses are slowly being replaced by newer Japanese versions, but lawns remain unmowed and the paintwork is peeling badly. Occasionally cows wander the streets, even around the main square (so who needs a lawn mower?), goats often sift through the rubbish outside apartment blocks, and traditionally dressed men and women stroll along the streets together with Mongolia's nouveaux riches.

Built along the Tuul river and surrounded by lovely mountains, the centre of Ulaan Baatar is dominated by Soviet-style high-rise apartment blocks, but about 250,000 locals live in the extended ger suburbs on the outskirts of town. The gers are protected from the winds, which are especially fierce in spring, by wooden fences. The topography makes for good hillside views overlooking the city, but during winter the view is frequently obscured by pollution, exacerbated by temperature inversions caused by the burning of coal, which powers the Soviet-built heating system.

Despite being the national capital and Mongolia's largest city, Ulaan Baatar retains a relaxed, small-town atmosphere and is a

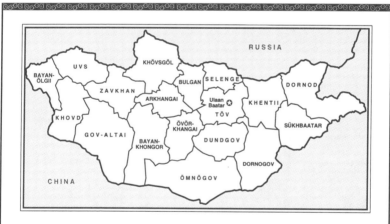

**Highlights**
- Gandan Khiid: largest monastery in the country, with enchanting ceremonies held every day; visit the university if you're interested in Buddhism
- Museum of Natural History: exhibits dinosaurs found in the Gobi in the 1920s
- Traditional & Cultural Show: a performance of traditional dance, *khoomi* singing, *morin khuur* violins and contortionists – not to be missed
- Naadam Festival: wrestling, archery and horse racing over three days in July; associated activities are also fascinating
- Winter Palace of Bogd Khaan: great collection of stuffed animals, thangkas and costumes

very pleasant place to visit and to base your-self for trips around the country. The city boasts good monasteries and museums, excellent cultural shows and several other attractions, so try to spend some time here before heading out to the glorious valleys, steppes or desert.

## HISTORY

The first recorded capital city of the recent Mongolian empire was created in 1639. It was called Örgöö and was originally located some 420km from Ulaan Baatar in the Arkhangai province at the Da Khüree monastery, the residence of the five-year-old Zanabazar, who had just been proclaimed head of Buddhism in Mongolia. The city was often moved (probably around 25 times) to various places along the Orkhon, Selenge and Tuul rivers and given other fairly unexciting official and unofficial names, including Khüree (Camp) in 1706.

In 1778 the capital was built at its present location and called the City of Felt because of the felt hats and gers. Later, the city became known as the Great Camp and was under the rule of the Bogd Khaan, or Living Buddha. (A map for sale along the streets of Ulaan Baatar provides an excellent idea of the layout of the city at that time.)

The Khangard – the official symbol of Ulaan Baatar

In 1911, when Mongolia first proclaimed its independence from China, the city became the capital of Outer Mongolia and was renamed Niislel Khüree (Capital Camp). In 1918 it was invaded again by the Chinese, and three years later by the Russians.

Finally in 1924, the city was renamed Ulaan Baatar (Red Hero) and declared the official capital of an 'independent' (from China, not from the Soviet Union) Mongolia. The Khangard (Garuda) was declared the city's official symbol. In 1933 Ulaan Baatar gained autonomy and separated from the Töv *aimag* (province) which surrounds it.

From the 1930s, the Soviets built the city in typical Russian style: lots of ugly apartment blocks, large brightly coloured theatres and cavernous government buildings. Tragically, the Soviets also destroyed almost all of the monasteries and temples. Ulaan Baatar is still young; unlike many Russian and European cities, there is very little that is old or glorious about the place.

## ORIENTATION

Most of the city spreads from east to west along the main road, Enkh Taivny Örgön Chölöö, also known as Peace Ave; the centre is Sükhbaatar Square, often simply known as the Square. The four majestic mountains which surround the city, Bayanzurkh, Chingeltei, Songino Khairkhan and Bogdkhan, as well as the Tuul river to the south, limit sprawling suburbia. Because they supply coal to Ulaan Baatar, two satellite towns, Nalaikh and Baganuur, are administratively under the capital's control, though both are in Töv province.

Useful landmarks include the tall Trade & Development Bank building to the north-west of the Square, the twin towers of the Bayangol Hotel to its south, and on top of the hill immediately to the south, the Zaisan Memorial. Around the Square are the Central Post Office and the Palace of Culture, and two blocks west of the Square is the State Department Store.

The city is divided into the following six major districts, but there's a multitude of subdistricts and microdistricts:

| | |
|---|---|
| Bayangol | Баянгол |
| Bayanzurkh | Баянзурх |
| Chingeltei | Чингэлтэн |
| Khan Uul | Хан Уул |
| Songino | Сонлино |
| Sükhbaatar | Cухбаатар |

Mongolians rarely use the western system of street names and numbers, so finding a place can be difficult. A typical address might be something like Microdistrict 14, Building 3, Flat 27. The problems are that you are unlikely to know which microdistrict you're in, most buildings are not numbered or signed and all street signs are in Mongolian Cyrillic. This is why most locals will give you an unofficial description like Flat 5, Floor 2, left-hand entrance of Blue Building No 44, behind the long-distance bus station. Perhaps the confusing addresses explain why mail delivery is incredibly slow and unreliable; not surprisingly, Mongolians prefer to receive their mail at post office boxes. To find your way around Ulaan Baatar, a map, phrasebook and sense of direction are vital.

In case you can't get your tongue and throat around some of the street names, they are listed in Cyrillic below. Some street names are sometimes translated into English. The main streets of Ulaan Baatar are:

**Maps & Magazines**

There are several maps of Ulaan Baatar, though not all are worthwhile. Besides the map in this guidebook, the best is the unnamed map produced by Nuudelchin, with the picture of the Palace of Culture on the front cover. It's also handy because it has photographs of many important buildings and landmarks which could be difficult to find as they are often not signed or named. The upmarket hotels sell this map for a ridiculous T2750; less touristy bookshops and street stalls charge less than half.

Worth picking up is the small, unnamed street map, identifiable by the red Mongolian

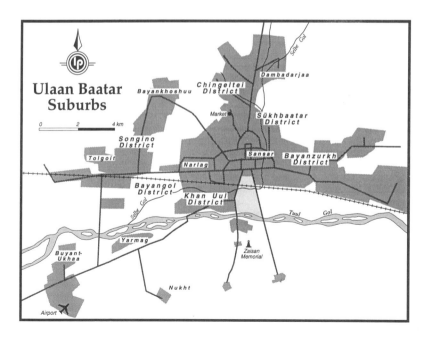

## Street Names

| Translation (if any) | Transliteration | Mongolian Cyrillic |
|---|---|---|
| Big Ring | Ikh Toiruu | Их Тойруу |
| Chinggis Khaan Ave | Chingisiin Örgön Chölöö | Чингисийн Өргөн Уөлөө |
| Karl Marx Ave | Marksyn Örgön Chölöö | Марксын Өргөн Уөлөө |
| | Khudaldaany Gudamj | Худалдааны Гудамж |
| | Khuvsgalchdyn Örgön Chölöö | Хувсгалчдын Өргөн Уөлөө |
| Natsagdorj St* | Natsagdorj Gudamj | Натсагдорж Гудамж |
| Peace Ave | Enkh Taivny Örgön Chölöö | Энх Таивны Өргөн Уөлөө |
| Small Ring | Baga Toiruu | Бага Тойруу |
| Sükhbaatar St | Sükhbaataryn Gudamj | Сухбаатарын Гудамж |
| | Teeverchidiin Gudamj | Тээвэрчидийн Гудамж |
| United Nations St | Negdsen Undestnii Gudamj | Нэгдсэн Үндэстний Гудамж |
| University St | Ikh Surguuliin Gudamj | Их Сургуулийн Гудамж |
| Zaluuchuudyn Örgön | Chölöö | Залуучуудйн Өргөн Уөлөө |

* Natsagdorj St is to be renamed Seoul St, or Seulyn Gudamj (СЭнлйн Гудамж).

script with light blue stripes. Also useful is the *Tourist Map of Ulaan Baatar* with the picture of the stupa on one cover. Both cost about T500 each.

The best places for these, and other maps of Mongolia, are the numerous stalls which line Enkh Taivny Örgön Chölöö, or in the bookshop immediately to the east of the State Department Store.

The Tourism Policy Department puts out a guide to Ulaan Baatar called *A Visitor's Guide to Mongolia*, which costs around T900 and is available in upmarket hotels. It looks impressive but is full of large advertisements, isn't detailed and is written in annoying 'Monglish'. Far more informative and detailed is the *Ulaan Baatar Survival Guide* (T1200), available at a few newspaper stalls near the Square, and at the Central Post Office.

### INFORMATION
### Tourist Offices

The Tourism Policy Department (☎ 324 026; fax 310 612) is in the Ministry of Infrastructure building, 11 Negdsen Undesnii Gudamj; PO Box 114, Ulaan Baatar 13. The department is far more involved in policy than providing information to tourists, but this may change in years to come.

The Biz Info Center (☎ 324 237) on the 4th floor of the Ulaan Baatar Hotel acts as a useful quasi-tourist office. Open from 6 am to midnight every day, it prints a weekly list of what's on, can book plane, train and cultural-event tickets (for a commission) and provide some other limited information. The Bayangol, Flower and Chinggis Khaan hotels also have business centres, but they are not as useful or handy.

### Embassies

A few countries are starting to open up embassies in Ulaan Baatar, though for most, the nearest embassies are in Beijing and/or Moscow. If your country has an embassy in Ulaan Baatar, it's a good idea to register with it if you're travelling into the remote countryside, or in case you lose your passport.

China
    5 Zaluuchuudyn Örgön Chölöö
    (☎ 320 955; fax 311 943)
    The consular section, at the front gate of the embassy, is a good place to get a visa for China. It is quick, efficient, the staff speak English and there is no need for the Mongolian Scramble (mainly because Mongolians don't need a visa). It is open from 9.30 am to 12.30 pm Monday, Wednesday and Friday.
    Transit visas (single or double entry) last up to seven days from each entry; single and double tourist visas can be issued for up to 30 days from the date of each entry. If you want to stay longer, you need an invitation from a tourist agency or business in China. Visa charges depend on your

country of origin (as an example, tourist visas cost US$30 for UK citizens, US$15 for Australians and US$25 for Americans). A visa takes a week to issue; if you want it within two days, add US$10; for same-day service, fork out an extra US$30.

Czech Republic
House 95, Apartment 58, Sixth Microdistrict, Chingeltei District (☎ 321 886)

Germany
7 Negdsen Undestnii Gudamj (☎ 323 325; fax 323 905) It has a library for German residents and selected Mongolians, but you'll have to make your way past the grumpy guards first.

Hungary
Large building 50m west of the Central Post Office (☎ 323 973; fax 311 793)

India
26 Enkh Taivny Örgön Chölöö (☎ 358 772; fax 358 171) It currently has a lama (monk) as an ambassador – possibly a world first.

Japan
On a side street behind the Ministry of External Relations (☎ 320 777)

Russia
Huge complex on the south side of Enkh Taivny Örgön Chölöö (☎ 326 037; fax 327 018) If at all possible get your Russian visa somewhere else; getting it here will give you severe headaches. Be prepared to practise the Mongolian Scramble to get through the huge throng of Mongolians hanging around the gate. (Mongolians now need Russian visas, and many have families in Russia, or study in Moscow.) The consular section is open for visas from 9.30 am to 12.30 pm and 2.30 to 5.30 pm on Monday, Wednesday and Friday.

The costs of Russian visas are different for each country, and at the time of research were due to increase. Currently, they are about US$15 for a transit visa and US$25 for a tourist visa. You will need three photos and an invitation or sponsor. A visa normally takes two days to issue or, if 'urgent', it can be issued within 24 hours for double the normal cost.

The embassy will also issue visas for former Soviet Central Asian republics (which are not represented individually), ie Kazakstan, Kyrgyzstan, Tajikistan, Turkmenistan and Uzbekistan.

South Korea
On the same street as the Japanese embassy, behind the Ministry of External Relations (☎ 321 548; fax 311 157).

UK
30 Enkh Taivny Örgön Chölöö (☎ 358 133; fax 358 036) The embassy handles normal consular duties for all Commonwealth countries (except India) and, alternating with Germany, handles consular duties for all member countries of the EEC.

USA
Just off the northern part of Ikh Toiruu (☎ 329 095; fax 320 776) There's a useful noticeboard, a library with books mainly about the US for Mongolians (but all foreigners are welcome) and film evenings, mainly for Americans – check with the embassy for details.

Other countries with embassies in Ulaan Baatar include Bulgaria (☎ 329 721), Cuba (☎ 327 709), Laos (☎ 321 048), North Korea (☎ 323 458), Romania (☎ 322 925) and Vietnam (☎ 358 923).

## Money
**Banks** The Trade & Development Bank (☎ 321 051; fax 325 449) – formerly known as the State Bank of Mongolia International – is the best place to change money. It's the large, modern building on the corner of Khudaldaany Gudamj and Baga Toiruu. The foreign exchange office, which is up some steps on the southern side of the building, is open during normal banking hours: Monday to Friday from 10 am to 5 pm (lunch from 1 to 2 pm) and Saturday from 10 am to noon.

The T&D Bank charges no commission for changing US dollar travellers' cheques (the only ones currently accepted) or US dollars and major European and Asian cash currencies into tögrögs. But it charges 2% commission for changing US dollar travellers' cheques into US dollars cash – it won't do a similar service for any other currency.

You can also get advances in US dollars on your Visa, MasterCard and American Express credit cards for a 4% commission. You cannot buy tögrögs with a credit card – you'll have to get US dollars, then convert them into tögrögs. Allow a few days for the authorisation to come through from Hong Kong or Beijing.

The Ardyn Bank (☎ 327 467; fax 310 621), along Khudaldaany Gudamj, between the Hotel Urge and the T&D Bank, also offers quick and easy foreign exchange. It will change US dollars cash and travellers' cheques into tögrögs, but you can't get credit-card advances or US dollars cash.

The bank on the 4th floor of the State Department Store and the Mongol Post

ULAAN BAATAR

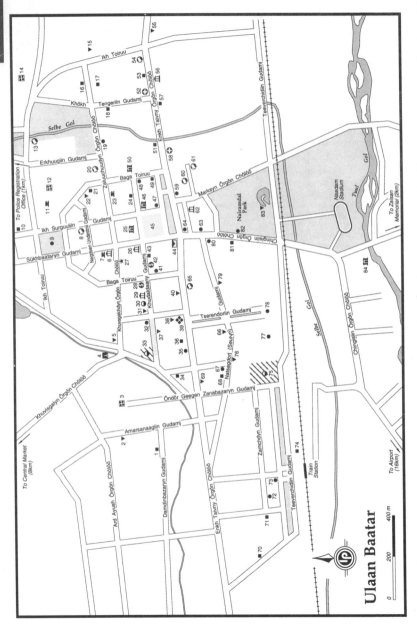

Ulaan Baatar

0    200    400 m

Bank, on your left as you enter the Central Post Office, are convenient, open normal banking hours and offer similar rates to the major banks.

At the airport, next to where you pay the departure tax, a small foreign exchange office changes US dollars cash into tögrögs at the standard bank rate.

**Moneychangers** At the time of research, a flourishing, open-air and legal money changing area known as the 'Dollar Market' (Долларын Зах) was situated at the eastern end of the mall on Khudaldaany Gudamj.

However, for some time local authorities have tried to move the moneychangers to other areas in the city or to stalls inside nearby buildings to curb associated crime and so that rent can be charged – so you may have to ask for the current location of the Dollar Market.

Also, because of the increasing desire for US dollars, moneychangers have started to move onto the main streets, and you may be approached near your hotel or other places frequented by tourists. They are probably not licensed, so it is best to stick to the licensed moneychangers in the Dollar Market.

**PLACES TO STAY**
1  White House Hotel
10  Narlag Hotel
16  Flower Hotel
17  Gegee Hotel
18  Chinggis Khaan Hotel
21  Zaluuchuud Hotel
24  Tuvshin Hotel
34  Kharaa Hotel
36  Mandukhai Hotel
43  Hotel Urge
49  Ulaan Baatar Hotel
51  Chadavchi Hotel
53  New Capital Hotel
57  Negdelchin Hotel
68  Shield Hotel
70  Baigal Hotel
71  Summer Garden Guest House
74  UB Station Hotel
81  Bayangol Hotel

**PLACES TO EAT**
2  Praha Restaurant
5  Hanamasa Restaurant
7  Cafe Good Food
11  Time Out Sports Cafe
15  Star II Bar & Restaurant
22  Ider Restaurant
23  Flamingo Coffee Shop
31  Tuul Restaurant
37  Europa Restaurant
38  Dulgunuur Tuya Restaurant
40  Elephant Restaurant
55  American Bar & Restaurant
66  Bogd Khangai

69  Nasan Fast Food
76  Solongo Bar & Restaurant
79  Pizza Place
83  Seoul Restaurant

**OTHER**
3  Gandantegchinlen (Gandan) Khiid
4  Geser Temple
6  Museum of Natural History
8  German Embassy
9  Mongolian Art Centre for Children's Creativity
12  Dashchoilon Khiid
13  US Embassy
14  Otochmaaramba Khiid
19  Zaluus Youth & Cultural Centre
20  Chinese Embassy
25  Government (Parliament) House
26  National Museum of Mongolian History
27  Police Headquarters
28  Trade & Development Bank
29  Zanabazar Museum of Fine Arts
30  Taxi Stand
32  Dollar Market
33  Truck Station
35  Peace & Friendship Building
39  State Department Store
41  MIAT Office
42  Ardyn Bank
44  Central Post Office
45  Sükhbaatar Square

46  Palace of Culture
47  State Opera & Ballet Theatre
48  Mongolian Art Gallery
50  Central Sports Palace
52  Russian Hospital No 2
54  UK Embassy
56  Ulaan Baatar City Museum
58  Yonsei Hospital
59  Ministry of External Relations
60  Japanese Embassy
61  South Korean Embassy
62  Monastery-Museum of Choijin Lama
63  State Central Library of Mongolia
64  Mongolian Artists' Exhibition Hall
65  Russian Embassy
67  Aeroflot Office
72  International Railway Ticketing Office
73  Domestic Railway Ticket Office
75  Long-Distance Bus, Jeep and Truck Station
77  Dalai Eej & Merkuri markets
78  State Circus
80  National Academic Drama Theatre
82  State Youth & Children's Theatre
84  Winter Palace of Bogd Khaan

Moneychangers are normally only interested in US dollars, Chinese yuan and Russian roubles. If you shop around you could get about 1 to 2% more for your cash than at the bank. If you know the current rate of exchange for the yuan or rouble, it's worth picking up some small change if you're taking the train to China or Russia.

Robberies of moneychangers are common (in 1995, two moneychangers were even murdered). Always be careful after changing money at the Dollar Market, as someone may follow you and try to rob you.

**Hotels** The Ulaan Baatar, Chinggis Khaan and Bayangol hotels have small bank branches which are open normal banking hours and offer the standard exchange rates. They will change US dollars cash and US dollar travellers' cheques into tögrögs with no commission, but if you are changing travellers' cheques (only US dollars are accepted) at a hotel reception desk – ie not at a bank's branch – you will be offered a lower rate than the bank branch. Just about all other hotels will change US dollars cash into tögrögs at a negotiable rate.

### Post & Communications
**Post** The Central Post Office (☎ 21 399), on the south-west corner of Sükhbaatar Square, is fairly quiet compared with other public places, but it can be just as confusing as elsewhere in Ulaan Baatar. Each district has its own post office, but it's easier and more convenient to use the Central Post Office.

As you enter from the main road, a door to your left leads to the Mongol Post Bank. The door to the right leads to the chaotic room for making interstate and international telephone calls.

Head for the room at the back with an English sign reading Postal Counter Hall, which contains the poste restante – it costs T30 to pick up anything, and you'll need to show your passport. There is also a good range of postcards, small booklets in English about Mongolia and Mongolian newspapers, including the *Mongol Messenger*, and you can send faxes from the same hall.

According to the sign, the hall is open from 7.30 am to 9 pm on weekdays and from 9 am to 8 pm on weekends, though in reality most services are almost nonexistent on Sunday.

**Telephone** Ulaan Baatar still has a rudimentary telephone system, but if you can find a telephone, it is not difficult to dial interstate or overseas, though it is expensive. For local calls, you can use the telephone at your hotel; it will probably cost nothing if you use the phone at the reception. Other hotels, including those with business centres, and some of the street stalls with telephones charge a standard T50 for each call. The unruly crowd at the small booth at the back, and to the left, of the front room at the Central Post Office is waiting to make local telephone calls for T20.

If you have access to a private telephone, the international operator (☎ 106) and domestic operator (☎ 107) may speak some rudimentary English and connect you to the right country, but not necessarily to the right number – your success may depend on how well you have learnt the Mongolian numbers. A Mongolian friend or guide who speaks your language would make it a whole lot easier.

For most Mongolians and foreigners, the only option for making interstate and international calls is to use the Central Post Office. Approach the small booth to your left as you enter from the main road, fill out the form (written in Mongolian) requesting the number you want to call, pay your money up front and then head to the chaotic room on the other side of the post office (to the right as you enter from the main road).

Give your form to the person behind the counter where everyone is frantically waving their forms, and wait for the announcement (in Mongolian) over the loudspeaker when your call has come through. Try to ask the person behind the counter to tell you when your call comes through (it may take an hour or two anyway), and which telephone booth to use; otherwise you'll wait forever.

**Fax** Most middle to top-range hotels have a fax machine which can be used by guests and anyone else who is willing pay the high rates. For similar prices, the business centres in the Flower (fax 358 330) and Ulaan Baatar (fax 324 777) hotels, and the Postal Counter Hall at the back of the Central Post Office can send your fax to anywhere around the world, and may charge you something nominal, perhaps T500, to receive a fax on your behalf.

**Email** Email is easily the most reliable, cheapest and quickest way of communicating with the outside world. The business centre at the Ulaan Baatar Hotel is the most convenient place to send a page of email anywhere in the world for a standard T1100 per page. If you are sending a lot of stuff, head to Datacom, which is currently the only service provider in the country – it charges by the kilobyte. Its office (☎ 326 259; email support@magicnet.mn) is at 49 Negdsen Undestnii Gudamj.

### Travel Agencies

Of the hundred or more travel agencies which have sprung up around Ulaan Baatar in the past few years, the dozen or so listed below in alphabetical order are recommended as generally reliable.

Postal addresses are not listed because the postal system in Mongolia is so unreliable; it is far better to communicate by fax, telephone or, even better (if possible), email. Some agencies run their businesses from home.

Bumbat Ord (☎ 327 859) is a new company, popular with expats, and has interesting tours around the Selenge province. Their office is in the New Capital Hotel.

Chono Travel (☎ & fax 324 232) runs all sorts of fishing and trekking tours, and trips by helicopter to remote spots, which are also popular with expats.

Eden Tours (☎ 310 803; fax 311 273) specialises in normal sorts of tours mainly for Swiss and French tourists. The staff speak French (and English) and it's on the 4th floor of the Marco Polo Hotel, which is a little east of the Dashchoilon monastery.

Federation of Mongolian Peace & Friendship Organisations (☎ 322 911; fax 320 045) arranges trips with other similar international organisations, but also handles the usual range of trips. (It no longer handles inquiries about work for foreigners.) Their office is in Room 20, 3rd floor, Peace & Friendship Building (about 200m west of the State Department Store).

Juulchin (☎ 312 095; fax 320 246; email jlncorp @magicnet.mn), the former government tourist agency, is now privatised and offers a wide range of tours all around the country, such as rafting, birdwatching, fishing, skiing, trekking and jeep trips around the Gobi. Their office is at the back of the Bayangol Hotel.

MIAT Tours (☎ 310 729; fax 324 992; email jargal @magicnet.mn) is more reliable than its parent company, MIAT. It caters more for the upmarket crowd and travels to the usual places in large, comfortable buses. Its office is next to the Seoul Restaurant, at the bottom of Nairamdal Park

Mongol Altai Club (☎ & fax 55 246) specialises in mountain climbing and runs some caving and rafting trips also. Refer to the Activities section in the Facts for the Visitor chapter for more details.

Mongol Tour OK (☎ 311 447; fax 311 441; email forbes @magicnet.mn) runs tours to the Gobi, Khövsgöl lake, Terelj and Kharkhorin, as well as more imaginative trips to Buir Nuur lake in the far east, and arranges caving, mountain biking and horse-back riding.

Mongolian Adventure Tours (☎ 312 255; fax 310 917; email advtour@magicnet.mn) specialises in more adventurous trekking, horse-back riding, mountain climbing, birdwatching and fishing trips. Their office is in Tower A of the Bayangol Hotel.

Nature Tour (☎ 312 392; fax 311 979; email nattour @magicnet.mn) runs the usual range of tours around the country and is reliable. It also offers ger camps in Terelj. Its office is in Room 212 of the Mongolian Youth Building (a little north of the Central Sports Palace).

Nomadic Journeys (☎ 323 043; fax 326 853; email nomadic@magicnet.mn) is a joint venture between Eco Tour Production in Sweden and Mongol Eco Tours and concentrates on low-impact tourism. It runs a few different trips, including probably the only one where you ride yaks and carry your own portable gers by yak cart.

Nomads (☎ & fax 328 146; email nomads@magicnet.mn) is an impressive outfit run by knowledgeable German, Australian and Mongolian staff. It has a range of tours including a popular horse-trekking trip in Khentii, jeep trips to more remote areas in the far west and treks by camel in the Gobi. Their office is in Room 21, 3rd floor, Peace & Friendship Building.

Shuren Travel (☎ 50 718; fax 323 363) is another impressive outfit which offers a range of interesting one to two-week trips to the Gobi, Kharkhorin, Terelj and Khentii, and to more obscure places by helicopter, on horseback and even on camel. Their office is in Room 707, Palace of Culture.

Terelj Juulchin (☎ 324 978; fax 342 535) runs a few fascinating tours to Terelj, Shargaljuut (in Bayankhongor province) and the Gobi.

## Bookshops

Unless you understand Mongolian or Russian you will be disappointed with the bookshops in Ulaan Baatar. For books about Mongolia in English (and sometimes in Italian, German and Japanese), which you may not be able to buy at home, try the souvenir shops at the Bayangol Hotel, the Monastery-Museum of Choijin Lama, the Museum of Fine Arts and the Winter Palace, or the 4th floor of the State Department Store. Naturally, these books will be priced for tourists. Nowhere can you pick up a novel in anything but Mongolian or Russian.

One bookshop which is good for maps of Ulaan Baatar and Mongolia, and possibly the occasional book in English, is immediately east of the State Department Store – look for the word 'book' in English. Another is the Nomin Bookshop – it also has a sign outside in English – just down the street from the Zaluuchuud Hotel. The numerous stalls along Enkh Taivny Örgön Chölöö, between the Central Post Office and the State Department Store, are good for maps, as is the (expensive) souvenir shop at the Winter Palace.

## Libraries

The State Central Library is on Chingisiin Örgön Chölöö, not far from the Bayangol Hotel. (A statue of Stalin once stood outside the library – the only statue to be removed since the fall of communism.) You will need some sort of 'permit' – from whom, no-one could say – to use the library, which is of no use unless you read Mongolian or Russian. One library which you can enter, but will also be of little use, is the Natsagdorj Library, which faces the street leading to the State Circus.

The library at the US embassy is open to all foreigners, but is full of stuff about the US for Mongolian students. If you read German, you could try the library at the German embassy.

## Film & Photography

Several places along the laneways around Sükhbaatar Square and on Enkh Taivny Örgön Chölöö develop print film – look for the obvious signs advertising major brand names. Costs are fairly standard – T350 for developing and T75 for each print – but the quality of developing varies from one place to another.

You can usually buy print, slide and even Polaroid film at the expensive hotels, souvenir shops around the Square, the major tourist attractions and at what used to be 'dollar shops' (see Things to Buy below). Costs vary, so shop around. For example, a roll of Agfa 36 print film costs T1500 but the same sort of film by Kodak costs T2600. A roll of Polaroid 600 Plus costs T6200.

Be careful when taking shots of something which may be considered important to the government such as Parliament House. Taking photos inside temples is almost always prohibited; outside the temples it is OK. There is often a charge for photographing inside a museum. Nairamdal Park and the Naadam Festival are excellent for people photos, but you should always ask before taking close-up shots of anyone.

## Cultural Centres

With a T500 million donation from South Korea, Natsagdorj Gudamj (soon to be renamed after the South Korean capital) will have, among other things, new walkways, bus stops and a South Korean Culture Centre. Building of the centre had not started at the time of research.

## Laundry

Almost all of the hotels in Ulaan Baatar offer a laundry service but they may not advertise it – so just ask. Naturally, the more expensive hotels charge more; laundry prices in the cheaper hotels like the Mandukhai, Zaluuchuud and the Gegee are lower and negotiable. If you can be bothered, it's not difficult to do some laundry yourself – the markets and shops sell detergent and bleach.

One of the very few dry cleaners in town is under the Xchange Restaurant, in the same shopping complex which houses the Hanamasa Japanese restaurant. They will clean shirts (T560), trousers (T790) and other things like sleeping bags (T3500), and are open from 9 am to 6 pm every day but Sunday.

### Medical Services

The South Korean-built Yonsei Friendship Hospital (☎ 310 945), a few hundred metres east of the Square on Enkh Taivny Örgön Chölöö, is still the best place to go. However, standards and facilities have recently dropped dramatically, and you cannot always assume that someone there will speak adequate English. The consulting rooms are open from 9 am to 12.30 pm and 1.30 to 5.30 pm on Monday, Tuesday and Wednesday, and from 9 am to 12.30 pm on Thursday, Friday and Saturday.

The only other place worth considering is the Russian Hospital No 2 (☎ 358 191), just before the UK embassy, on Enkh Taivny Örgön Chölöö. The best recommendation is one expat's comment: 'I know of someone who went there for pneumonia and survived'.

For any dentistry work, try the Evada Dental Clinic (☎ 327 336), about 200m east of the Square on Enkh Taivny Örgön Chölöö, the Arono Dental Clinic (☎ 342 609), about 100m north of the Winter Palace, or the Yonsei Hospital.

Pharmacies are poorly stocked, and you should always check the expiry dates. The hospitals mentioned above will have some supplies and there are a couple of pharmacies around the markets and the mall on Khudaldaany Gudamj, but you really should bring whatever you need from home.

### Emergency

If you are in an emergency, try to find a Mongolian who speaks English (or your language) to make the call, or to accompany you, because almost all of the people you need to speak to will only speak Mongolian or Russian. There are a few emergency numbers: Infectious Disease Emergency (☎ 100); fire (☎ 101); Emergency Aid or ambulance (☎ 103). Numbers also worth trying in a medical emergency are other hospital numbers (☎ 50 230, 50 554 and 50 296). If you have an embassy in Ulaan Baatar, it should be able to help in an emergency.

There is a general police emergency number (☎ 102), but if you need to make a general complaint you'll have to call one of the following telephone numbers depending on which district you are in:

| | |
|---|---|
| Bayangol District | ☎ 361 734 |
| Bayanzurkh District | ☎ 51 848 |
| Chingeltei District | ☎ 311 883 |
| Khan Uul District | ☎ 341 494 |
| Songino District | ☎ 331 669 |
| Sükhbaatar District | ☎ 320 341 |

### Dangers & Annoyances

Ulaan Baatar is a reasonably carefree and easygoing city, but this can draw you into a false sense of security. Treat the city as you would any other mid-sized European town, and be similarly conscious of the potential risks.

Beware of pickpockets and the occasional bag-slasher on the crowded local buses and trolley-buses, and at the train station and airport. Very rarely is violence attached to thefts, but unwary travellers, especially those straight off a long journey in a very foreign country, can be easy pickings. On public transport, carry your bags in front of you; money belts are mandatory. Recently, several travellers have had their passports and money stolen during busy ceremonies at the Gandan monastery – so take special care there.

You can come across a drunk at any time of the day and anywhere in the city. They are easy to spot and to avoid; they never travel in gangs and rarely cause problems. Women should avoid using a private car-cum-taxi after dark – take an official taxi. Everyone should be a little circumspect when leaving nightclubs or other places frequented by foreigners after dark – walk in a group, if possible – and when changing money on the street.

A torch (flashlight) can be very useful; it will save you from crashing down the stairways of apartments which are always pitch-black, even during the day. It's also handy when street lights go out during a blackout, but some expats still don't use one because it indicates that they are foreigners (only foreigners use torches) and thus feel more vulnerable. You should never walk around the ger suburbs and away from street lighting after dark; if the drunks don't get you, the stray dogs probably will.

Nestled in a valley, Ulaan Baatar suffers from high levels of carbon monoxide and other pollutants and, in the spring, terrible dust storms. Breathing the right amount and mixture of nitrogen, oxygen and carbon dioxide can sometimes be difficult.

## MUSEUMS

Ulaan Baatar has many museums of varying quality. Most captions are in Mongolian and guides often speak nothing else. There are three which you should visit; many others are open if you have a specific interest in what they display.

### Museum of Natural History

Байгалын Түүхийн Музей

Sometimes called the State Central Museum, this museum is worth a visit especially if you are heading out to the countryside. There are exhibits about Mongolia's geography, flora and fauna, including the requisite section with stuffed and embalmed animals, birds and even fish, and some displays about recent Mongolian history.

More impressive are the two complete dinosaur skeletons which were found in the Gobi – the giant flesh-eating *Tarbosaurus*, 15m tall and four to five tons in weight, and his first cousin, the little duck-billed plant-eating *Saurolophus* at 'only' eight metres. You can see them from above from the 3rd floor, or enter the room marked 'Tarbosaurus' on the 2nd floor – ask for it to be opened if it's locked. All captions in this section are in

English – which is not the case in the rest of the museum.

The museum (☎ 321 716) is old and disorganised, with doors and corridors going all over the place, so it's easy to miss something. It is located on the corner of Khuvsgalchdyn Örgön Chölöö and Sükhbaataryn Gudamj, one block north-west of the Square. The entrance fee is T350 and it's open daily from about 10 am to 4.30 pm, but closes a little earlier on Monday (the opening times seem to vary according to the whims of the staff, though).

The expensive art, souvenir and book shops inside the museum sell a pricey (T3850) guidebook in English (with photos) to the museum. This looks good value considering the ludicrous prices charged for photography: T5500 to T11,000 for still photographs, and T8250 to T16,500 for video cameras.

### Zanabazar Museum of Fine Arts

Занаъазарын Уран Зэргийн Музей

This museum has an excellent collection of paintings, carvings and sculptures, including many by the revered sculptor, artist and Buddhist, Zanabazar. It also contains other rare, and sometimes old, religious exhibits such as thangkas and Buddhist statues, representing the best display of its kind in Mongolia.

At the top of the stairs is a detailed explanation in English about Zanabazar and his work, and about other exhibits in the museum. Many captions in the museum are in English. Also worth checking out is the intricate painting, *One Day in Mongolia*, by renowned artist B Sharav, which depicts almost everything that is unique about Mongolia. The name and origin of the work are still the subject of much debate among experts, however.

The museum (☎ 326 060), facing the taxi stand on Khudaldaany Gudamj, is open every day from 9 am to 6 pm; entry is T450. The shops inside have a good, but expensive, selection of leather goods, souvenirs and paintings, and there is often a display of modern paintings and other art for sale on the ground floor. A handy little guidebook

(T2750) to the museum in English and French is for sale inside.

## National Museum of Mongolian History

Монголын Түүхийн Үндэснийн Музей

Still sometimes referred to by its previous name, the Revolutionary Museum, the National Museum of Mongolian History has three floors of interesting exhibits. The ground floor contains, among other things, a furnished ger, traditional farming and domestic implements, saddles, musical instruments and Buddhist items, including the controversial Ganlin Horn made from human bones.

The 2nd floor houses an outstanding collection of costumes and hats representing most major ethnic groups throughout Mongolia. With detailed captions in English, this is the highlight of the museum. The 3rd floor has a detailed, but less inspiring, display of Mongolian history, including many leftover exhibits from the recent communist past.

Keep your ticket when you walk around as staff will want to check it on every floor. The museum (☎ 326 802) is on the corner of Khudaldaany Gudamj and Sükhbaataryn Gudamj. It's open from 10 am to 4.30 pm daily except Wednesday, and closes a little earlier on Tuesday. Entrance fee is T200.

## Other Museums

The **Natsagdorj Museum** celebrates Mongolia's most famous poet and playwright, Dashdojiin Natsagdorj, who was also an ardent nationalist. The museum was supposedly built on the exact site where Natsagdorj lived. It's between the Choijin Lama monastery and the northern entrance of Nairamdal Park, but is often closed due to lack of interest.

Still referred to as Lenin's Museum (a huge bust of Vladimir Ilyich remains in the foyer), the new **Museum of Geology and Mineral Resources of Mongolia**, on Khuvsgalchdyn Örgön Chölöö, seems to be struggling for a purpose, and is almost always closed. The **Ulaan Baatar City Museum**, just east of the Nedgelchin Hotel, has a few exhibits of minor interest about the city, including some interesting old photos and a few leftovers exalting Lenin.

The **Ethnographical Museum**, located in the pink building in the middle of the lake at the southern end of Nairamdal Park, has a small collection of ethnic costumes and dolls, but the displays at the National Museum of Mongolian History are far better. If killing innocent animals is your thing, visit the **Hunting Museum**, on the street leading to the Gandan monastery. The **Railway Museum**, near the International Railway Ticketing Office, and other old engines located east of the station, may satisfy train buffs.

The **Mongolian Military Museum** is at the eastern end of Enkh Taivny Örgön Chölöö – you'll need to take a taxi to find it. The **Mongolian Theatrical Museum** is particularly worthwhile if you're interested in the theatre – the collection of puppets is wonderful. The entrance is on the northern side of the Palace of Culture; the museum is on the 3rd floor.

---

### Ganlin Horn

For centuries, Ganlin horns had been used by head monks throughout Mongolia to call, and exorcise, evil spirits *(lkham)*. The horns, which are about 18cm long and had to be kept hidden because of their powers, are no longer used, but they continue to create controversy.

Mongolian Buddhists claim that in Tibet the horn had to be made from the left thigh bone of a sacrificed 18-year-old unmarried female virgin, because the lkham (which is female) wouldn't respond to a call using a bone from a male. However, in Mongolia, the bone was apparently made from the thigh bone of (male) Buddhist monks who were already dead.

Examples of the Ganlin horn are found at the National Museum of Mongolian History and Monastery-Museum of Choijin Lama, the Manzshir Khiid monastery near Ulaan Baatar, and the museum in Sainshand, the capital of the Dornogov province. ■

## MONASTERIES

Around the start of the 19th century, over 100 temples (süm) and monasteries (khiid) served a population of only about 50,000 in Ulaan Baatar. Religious historians estimate that maybe over 50% of the population at the time were monks or nuns. Most of the temples and monasteries, along with their belongings, were destroyed during the Stalinist purges of the late 1930s. Several thousand monks were murdered, while many more fled or abandoned their Buddhist life. Only since the start of the 1990s have the people of Mongolia started to openly practise Buddhism again.

### Ninth Jebtzun Damba

The eighth Bogd Khaan (Living Buddha), Jebtzun Damba Hutagt VIII, lived in the Winter Palace in Ulaan Baatar until 1924. When he died, the communist government refused to allow any future reincarnations, so there were no further Mongolian Buddhist leaders.

After restrictions against religion were lifted in Mongolia, the Dalai Lama proclaimed the Ninth Khalkha Jebtzun Damba as the new spiritual leader for Mongolian Buddhism. (The title comes from Khalkh, the ethnicity of the majority of Mongolians, and Jebtzun Damba, which means 'lord of refuge'.)

The Ninth Jebtzun Damba was born in Tibet, and accepted as the ninth reincarnation at the age of four, but his identity was kept a secret from Stalin's thugs. In the early 1990s, he moved to Dharamsala, in north-west India, where he is close to the current Dalai Lama. ∎

### Winter Palace of Bogd Khaan

Болд Хааны Өвлийн Ордон

Built between 1893 and 1903, the Winter Palace of Bogd Khaan is where Mongolia's eighth Living Buddha, and last king, Jebtzun Damba Hutagt VIII, lived for 20 years. Depending on which version of history you read, the Bogd Khaan either enjoyed irreverent pleasures of the flesh and bottle and was almost blind with syphilis, or he was a great visionary and nationalist. When he died in May 1924, the Soviet-led communist government of Mongolia prohibited any ongoing reincarnations. For reasons that are unclear, the palace was spared destruction and turned into a museum.

There are six temples in the grounds. From the entrance, you immediately see the Temple of the Maharaja. A little further along the path is the Temple of the Applique to the left, and the Temple of the Thangka to the right, with the Temple of Mercy in the middle. At the end of the path is the Main Temple, flanked on the left by the Temple of the Many Gods, and on the right by a former temple, subsequently used as the Bogd Khaan's library.

The white building to the right as you enter is actually the Winter Palace itself. It contains a collection of gifts the Bogd Khaan had received from foreign dignitaries, such as a pair of golden boots from a Russian tsar, a robe made from 80 unfortunate foxes and a ger (ask the curator to open it up for you) lined with the skins of 150 snow leopards. The Bogd Khaan's penchant for unusual live animals – including an elephant which had to walk for three months from the Russian border to Ulaan Baatar – explains the extraordinary array of stuffed animals in the Palace.

The entrance fee is T520, but you'll need a permit for photo (T1650) or video cameras (T3850). The inside of the temples are often dark, and the exhibits always behind glass, so you are unlikely to get any great photos. The exceptions are the excellent thangkas, costumes and other items (in the open, and under good lighting) upstairs in the (white) Winter Palace. Maybe have a look around first, then if you want to take some photos or videos pay for your permit later.

A shop sells tapes, books, paintings, leather and cashmere products, and other souvenirs – it is one of the best places to pick up a memento. The selection is excellent, but the prices are high.

The Winter Palace (☎ 342 195), a few km south of the Square on Chingisiin Örgön Chölöö, is open every day except Thursday from 10 am to 6 pm, and on Wednesday from 10 am to 2 pm. It is a bit too far to walk, so take a taxi or catch bus No 7 or 19. A little

PAUL GREENWAY

PAUL GREENWAY

PAUL GREENWAY

**Ulaan Baatar**
Top: The National Academic Drama Theatre hosts Mongolian-language productions.
Middle: The Zaisan Memorial commemorates soldiers from various wars.
Bottom: A traditional ger in the middle of suburbia.

PAUL GREENWAY

RON GLUCKMAN

PAUL GREENWAY

**Naadam Festival**
Top: Archery originates from the era of almost constant war, around the 11th century.
Middle: Unlike most wrestling, Mongolian wrestling has no weight divisions or time limit.
Bottom: Young jockeys race their horses across the open countryside.

pamphlet (T260), available at the entrance, gives a very brief explanation of the temples in English, and includes a handy map showing the location of the temples. All captions in the Palace and temples are in Mongolian.

### Gandantegchinlen Khiid
Гандантэгчинлэн Хийд

Roughly meaning 'the great place of complete joy', Gandantegchinlen monastery is commonly referred to as Gandan. Still the largest and most important monastery in Mongolia, this is one of Ulaan Baatar's most impressive sights.

Building was started in 1838 by the fourth Bogd Khaan but was not finished until after his death by the fifth Bogd Khaan, Chultem Jigmid Dambijantsan. Like most monasteries in Mongolia, the purges of 1937 fell heavily on Gandan, but it survived because the communists decided to keep it as a showcase to impress foreigners. There are currently over 150 monks in residence.

As you enter the main entrance from the south, a path leads towards the right to a courtyard containing two temples. On the left, fronted by a lovely prayer wheel, is the Ochirdary Temple with an ornate roof (unfortunately covered by 150 years of pigeon poop). On the right is the smaller, golden Dedenpovaran Temple, where most ceremonies were being held at the time of research.

At the end of the main path as you enter is the magnificent white Migjid Janraisig Süm. This was closed at the time of research, but the temple and a huge statue inside should be ready for public viewing by 1997.

The Magjid Janraisig Süm houses the new 20-ton statue of Migjid Janraisig adorned with gold and jewels.

To the west of the temple is the Öndör Geegen Zanabazar Buddhist Monastery (☎ 363 831), established in 1970. If you have a genuine interest in Buddhism, you can visit the university and its library.

The souvenir shop, to the left as you enter the main southern gate of the monastery, sells non-touristy, religious artefacts, including miniature copper bowls for T2000 – but unlike other monasteries, there is not a postcard in sight.

You can take photographs around the monastery, but not inside the temples. The monastery (☎ 342 195), at the end of Öndör Geegen Zanabazaryn Gudamj, is open every day from about 9 am to 9 pm, and there is no

### Migjid Janraisig Statue
A 20m gold and bronze statue of Avalokitesvara, built by the Bogd Khaan in 1911, once stood in the main temple at Gandan Khiid. The magnificent statue was destroyed by the communists in 1937, and the metal taken to what was Leningrad and melted down to make bullets.

After nearly five years of work, a new statue, called Migjid Janraisig ('the lord who looks in every direction'), will be unveiled in 1997. The 25m-high, 20-ton copper statue is gilded with gold donated by Nepal and Japan, and contains nearly 200 precious stones. It will be covered with more than 100kg of clothes, including 36m of gold fabric and 500m of silk, one-fifth of which comes from India's holiest city, Varanasi. ■

entrance fee. Try to be there for the captivating ceremonies; they usually start at around 10 am, though you may be lucky and see one at another time.

Pickpockets are currently working overtime at the monastery, as one reader found out:

In the throng entering the temple to hear the lamas chant, smooth operators work the crowd to relieve you of whatever they can get their hands on. They use the crinkling paper technique also popular in Italy. I lost my passport, visas, money, etc. I was the third American victim that week ...

### Monastery-Museum of Choijin Lama
Чойжин Ламын Хийд-Музей

Also known as the Museum of Religion, the monastery was the home of Luvsan Haidav Choijin Lama ('Choijin' is an honorary title given to some monks), the brother of Jebtzun Damba Hutagt VIII, who built the Winter Palace. Construction of the monastery commenced in 1904 and was completed four years later. It was closed in 1938 and probably would have been demolished but it was saved as a museum in 1942 to demonstrate the 'feudal' ways of the past. Although religious freedom in Mongolia recommenced in 1990, this monastery is no longer an active place of worship and will probably remain a museum.

There are five temples within the grounds. As you enter, the first temple you see is the Temple of the Maharaja. The Main Temple, flanked by sculptures of the Buddha and of Luvsan Haidav himself, contains an impressive collection of thangkas and some of the best *tsam* masks in the country. The other temples are: the Zuu Temple, dedicated to one of the founders of modern Buddhism in Tibet, Skya Muni; the Temple of Yadam, which contains wooden and bronze statues of various gods, some created by the famous Mongolian sculptor, Zanabazar; and the Temple of the Amgalan, containing a self-portrait of the great Zanabazar himself and a small stupa apparently brought to Ulaan Baatar by Zanabazar from Tibet.

The museum (☎ 324 788) is only one block south of the Square. You pay T500 at the southern gate and there is no extra charge for photographs. Although not as good as the Winter Palace, there is still plenty to snap. A small booklet (T1000), written in English, is useful and available at the monastery entrance, or from the Winter Palace souvenir shop. A concrete ger inside the grounds has a good selection of reasonably priced souvenirs, and probably the best range of books about Buddhism and Mongolia in Ulaan Baatar.

### Other Monasteries & Temples

Part of the Gandan monastery, the **Geser Süm**, at the junction of Khuvisgalyn Örgön Chölöö and the western part of Ikh Toiruu, is also the home of several practitioners of traditional Buddhist medicine. The temple was closed to foreigners whenever we wanted to visit. The **Tasgany Ovoo**, about 300m behind the Geser temple, is worth a look if you haven't seen an *ovoo* (sacred pile of stones) before.

On the way to Gandan, the new **Lamrim Süm** temple was being completed at the time of research and should be interesting. **Dashchoilon Khiid** was originally built somewhere else in 1890, but was destroyed in the late 1930s. The monastery recently moved into two huge concrete gers which were once part of the State Circus and is now used by over 100 monks. You can get to the laneway running past the monastery from Baga Toiruu – look out for the orange and brown roof.

The **Otochmaaramba Khiid** can be easily seen from the north-eastern bend of Ikh Toiruu. Although not as interesting as the others, it's still worth a visit. The monastery is also the location of the **Manba Datsan** traditional medical clinic and training centre (refer to the Facts about the Country chapter for further details).

In the north-eastern suburbs of Ulaan Baatar the **Dambadarjaa Khiid**, built in 1765, was once home to 1200 monks. Only the ruins of a few of the 30 small temples have been restored, but it is worth a look. You have to take a taxi out there.

## ART GALLERIES

As well as music, Mongolians love visual arts, and there are a few galleries worth visiting.

### Mongolian Art Gallery

Монголын Уран Зургийн Үзэсгэлэн

This gallery, sometimes also called the Fine Art Gallery, opened as recently as 1989. It contains a huge and impressive display of modern and uniquely Mongolian paintings and sculptures. They are often nationalistic and always interesting, and are titled in English.

The gallery (☎ 327 177) has a better art collection than the Zanabazar Museum of Fine Arts, and is well worth a visit. Look for the signpost between the Opera & Ballet Theatre and the Ulaan Baatar Hotel. The entrance (T450) is in the courtyard of the Palace of Culture, and the gallery is open every day from 9 am to 1 pm and 2 to 4 pm.

### Mongolian Artists' Exhibition Hall

Монголын Зурадудьын Үзэсгэлэн Танхим

If you want to see more Mongolian art, and maybe buy some, head into the exhibition hall immediately south of the Square and opposite the Drama Theatre. This is a private collection of modern, and often dramatic, paintings, carvings, tapestries and sculptures. The displays often change, and there's a good souvenir shop. It's open from about 9 am to 5 pm every day but Sunday, and there is a nominal entry fee.

### Mongolian Art Centre for Children's Creativity

Монголын Хүүхдийн Урлан Бүтээс Урлагийн Төв

Housed in the ugly, bright blue-green building three blocks north of Government House, the centre was closed for renovations at the time of research. From what we saw, there were plenty of interesting paintings and sculptures by children and adults to impress the most jaded art lovers. Many exhibits are for sale and would make great (but heavy) souvenirs.

## SÜKHBAATAR SQUARE

СУХБААТАРЫН ТАЛХАЙ

In the centre of Ulaan Baatar in July 1921, the 'hero of the revolution', Damdiny Sükhbaatar, declared Mongolia's final independence from the Chinese. The square now bears his name and features a statue of the man astride his horse. The words he apparently proclaimed at the time are engraved on the bottom of the statue: 'If we, the whole people, unite in our common effort and common will, there will be nothing in the world that we cannot achieve, that we will not have learnt or failed to do.'

Sükhbaatar would have been very disappointed to learn that the square was also where the first protests were held in 1989 which eventually led to the fall of communism. Today, the square is occasionally used for rallies, ceremonies and even rock concerts, but is generally a serene place where only the pigeons and the photographers, standing in a straight line selling their services, are doing anything.

As you face north from the statue, the large grey building is **State Parliament House**, commonly known as Government House – which, like all gers, was built to face south. Directly in front of it is a **mausoleum**, built in 1921, which may or may not (depending on who you talk to) contain the remains of the two communist heroes, Sükhbaatar and Choibalsan.

To the north-east is the tall, modern Palace of Culture, a useful landmark containing the Art Gallery and several other cultural institutions. At the south-east corner of the Square, the salmon-pinkish building is the State Opera & Ballet Theatre. (See Entertainment below.)

On the north-western corner of the Square, the bright yellow building houses the Golomt Bank, with the grey National Museum of Mongolian History behind it. South of the Golomt Bank, the clay-red building (now with bright blue patches around the windows) is the **Mongolian Stock Exchange**, which was opened in February 1992 in the former Children's Cinema.

## NAIRAMDAL PARK
### НАЙРАМДАЛ ЛАРК

Also called the National Recreational Park, the Nairamdal (Friendship) Park is looking a bit sad and neglected these days, but is a nice enough place to walk around. It is particularly lovely in the early morning when the rest of the city is still asleep, and really photogenic on Sundays when hundreds of children enjoy the facilities.

There are the usual children's rides: dodgem cars (designed to teach the kids how to deal with the city traffic?); a popular (but not really scary) Mongolian Mad Mouse; a Ferris wheel (agonisingly slow, but with great views from the top); and, our favourite, the 'aerobicycle', a sort of tandem bike on a monorail track 3m high.

A dirty lake in the south of the park offers boat rides in summer and ice-skating in winter. The pink building in the middle of the lake is the Ethnographical Museum, and there's a concrete maze not far away. The nearby stadium has some wrestling during the lead up to the Naadam Festival, and other activities on some Saturday and Sunday afternoons in summer.

Several places around the park sell *khuurshuur* (fried mutton pancakes), éclairs and even passable fairy floss (cotton candy). There is sometimes a nominal T20 entrance fee to the park. You can enter from behind the Monastery-Museum of Choijin Lama, or opposite the Bayangol Hotel.

---

### Wedding Palace

The large, square building north of Nairamdal Park, and not far from the Monastery-Museum of Choijin Lama, is known as Khurimyn Ordon, or the Wedding Palace. Built in 1976 by the Russians, it has since been used for over 150,000 weddings.

At its peak in popularity, about 20 couples a day were married here. The cost for a wedding is T150,000 and includes wedding rings, video coverage, photographs and presents, but is becoming prohibitive for many young Mongolians. Visitors can get married here too: in the past six years, about 50 foreigners have married Mongolians at the palace. ∎

---

## ZAISAN MEMORIAL
### ЗАЙСАН ТОЛТОЙ

The tall, thin landmark on top of the hill south of the city is the Zaisan Memorial. Built by the Russians to commemorate 'unknown soldiers and heroes' from various wars, it offers the best views of Ulaan Baatar and the surrounding hills. The views are better at night, however, when you can't see the ugly power stations and the layers of dust and pollution, but there's no public transport there after 10 pm (when the sun sets in summer).

To get there, catch bus No 7, which goes past the Winter Palace. Get off at the Agricultural University, walk across the fields, up a goat trail to the car park and then up the steps to the top. A taxi would save some of the walk.

## ORGANISED TOURS

It is not particularly easy to get on an organised tour of Ulaan Baatar if you have arrived as an independent traveller and not as part of a packaged tour. You can try to contact one of the travel agencies listed earlier in this chapter and see what they have available, but seeing the sights of the capital city can be easily done without being on an organised tour. Although not really necessary, a guide-cum-interpreter, especially one who speaks your language if you're not confident in English, could be handy.

Most tours include the Gandantegchinlen Khiid monastery, the Museum of Natural History, the Zanabazar Museum of Fine Arts, the Monastery-Museum of Choijin Lama and Bogd Khaan's Winter Palace. Some will probably also include a day trip to the Manzshir monastery, Terelj and/or a visit to a nomadic family.

## SPECIAL EVENTS

The biggest event in Ulaan Baatar is undoubtedly the Naadam Festival, held between 11 and 13 July. It's a time when the city almost seems to wake up, before falling back to sleep again when it's all over. Some visitors may not find the festival itself terribly exciting, but the associated activities during the Naadam week and the general festive mood make it a great time to visit, though accommodation can be in short supply and prices higher. See the Naadam Festival boxed story in the Facts for the Visitor chapter for more information.

Around Naadam and at other times of the year such as public holidays, some special events are organised. They are for the benefit of locals so any promotion (often there isn't any) will be in Mongolian. It's worth reading the local English-language newspapers and asking a Mongolian friend, guide or hotel staff member to find out what may be on.

## PLACES TO STAY

There is a fairly good range of places to stay in the capital city, but rarely is there anywhere that could be regarded as good value. Prices are often higher, and accommodation may be in short supply, during the week surrounding the Naadam Festival.

### Places to Stay – bottom end

**Camping** There are no official camping grounds in Ulaan Baatar, and given that nobody owns any land in Mongolia, you can technically camp anywhere. If you wish to camp and visit Ulaan Baatar every day, catch a regular bus along the road to the airport and discreetly find a patch of ground away from the main road around Yarmag. During Naadam, Yarmag is where the horse racing takes place, and you can easily pitch your tent up in the fascinating, but very noisy, temporary 'tent city' there. Be careful of thieves and drunks during this time.

An even better place to camp is near Gachuurt, connected by regular bus to Ulaan Baatar. Just take your pick of the pleasant spots anywhere along the magnificent, but occasionally volatile, Tuul river. (Refer to the Töv aimag section in the Central Mongolia chapter for further details.)

**Hotels** Many of the really cheap places usually double as brothels and prefer to charge by the hour, but they will take your money anyway. They often charge Mongolian prices rather than foreigners' prices.

In a great location on the 3rd floor of a building just west of the Aeroflot office, the *Shield Hotel* (Бамбай Зочид) (☎ 326 920) has very basic rooms but is good value at T1500 per person. The deluxe rooms are worth a splurge at T8500 per person. Look for the sign 'Hotel Bar' in English above the entrance.

Only about 300m west of the Square, on Enkh Taivny Örgön Chölöö, the pink *Chadavchi Hotel* (Чадавчи Зочид) is identifiable by the 'Bar Hotel' sign. It charges T2500 per person for a very ordinary and noisy room, and is definitely a busy place during the night.

The only cheap dorm-style accommodation is in a kindergarten which is renamed the *Summer Garden Guest House* (☎ 367 209) during the summer holidays. It's not the most salubrious place – the beds consist of two or three children's beds pushed together – but it's cheap at T2600 per person. The advantages are that the owner speaks English, which is a bonus anywhere in Mongolia, and you'll probably meet other travellers there – but it is inconvenient, and closed by late August. The guesthouse is at the far western end of Zamchdyn Gudamj, near the train station – look for the telltale playground.

One of the best in this range is the *Narlag Hotel* (Нарлаг Зочид) (☎ 323 198) which primarily caters to occasional large youth groups. No-one speaks a word of English there, and it's a little inconvenient, but the rooms are large, clean and with attached bathroom – excellent value at T2600 per person. It is about 50m north of the intersection of Ikh Toiruu and the extension of Ikh Surguulin Gudamj, immediately past the kindergarten. Get there between 9 am and 5 pm on weekdays when the manager is around and you are more likely to get a room. Apparently, there is another place with the same name (but we couldn't find it), so if you take a taxi make sure you go to the right hotel.

Also recommended in this range is the *Mandukhai Hotel* (Мандухай Зочид) (322 204). Four-room dorms start at T3300 per person; tiny singles cost T6050; and four-bed suites, with TV, are good value at T14,520 per room. The service is good, the rooms are clean and some staff speak English and German. Three rooms on each floor share a bathroom. It's just west of the State Department Store, about 100m north of Enkh Taivny Örgön Chölöö – look for the yellow pagoda-style roof.

In a handy location on Enkh Taivny Örgön Chölöö is the *Negdelchin Hotel* (Нэг дэлчин Зочид) (☎ 53 230). At the time of research, small clean rooms with a shared bathroom cost T4950 per person; T7150 per person for the suite. However, renovations were going on, and during Naadam, prices went up dramatically, so it may no longer be good value. The restaurant is dreadful but has cheap beer.

At the top of Partizan Gudamj, just south of the truck station, the *Kharaa Hotel* (Хараа Зочид) (☎ 313 717) is good value in this range. The rooms are clean and the price of T8250 per person is negotiable. Look for the 'Hotel Bar Shop' sign in English.

The *Gegee Hotel* (Гэг ээ Зочид) (☎ 55 285), formerly known as the Zuul, is on the other side of the road from the Flower Hotel, hidden among a block of flats and inconvenient to the Square. You will probably have to ask for directions – there is only a small sign near the door. Standard rooms with bathrooms are reasonable value at T5500 per person. A suite, which cost T8250 per person (but which can be negotiated down), was aptly described by one traveller as reminiscent of a 'South London council flat' – but it does have satellite TV.

Another good option, if you can get any service from the surly staff, is the huge, grey *Zaluuchuud Hotel* (Залуучууд Зочид) (☎ 324 594) on Baga Toiruu, about 200m north of the Ulaan Baatar Hotel. Good singles, without bathrooms but with furniture which could almost be classed as 'antique', start at T4400 per person, but they will probably try to get you into their suite at a ridiculous T18,150 per person.

If you're waiting for the train or don't mind being woken up several times at night by approaching trains, try the *UB Station Hotel* (☎ 744 169), immediately east of the station. Rooms start from T8250 per person and very nice deluxe rooms, with bathroom, TV and sitting room, are T13,750 per person.

## Places to Stay – middle

Places in the middle range are not particularly good value, but they normally include breakfast. Ask whether the arbitrary government tax of 10% is included or not.

Deservedly popular because of its great location and cosy B&B feel is the *Hotel Urge* (Зочид Өргөө) (☎ 313 772; fax 312 712), at T27,500/38,500 a single/double. It's to the immediate west of Parliament House, at the start of Khudaldaany Gudamj. The restaurant and bar on the ground floor are quite pleasant.

Formerly called the Altai, the *Flower Hotel* (☎ & fax 358 330) has been nicely refurbished after plenty of Japanese investment. It's in a nice neighbourhood, with plenty of shops nearby, but is inconvenient to the Square. Standard singles/doubles are very comfortable but overpriced at T27,500/42,350 when you consider the showers are down the corridor (toilets are in the rooms). The Japanese bathhouse, with guaranteed warm water, is popular with Japanese tour groups. The Flower Hotel is on Zaluuchuudyn Örgön Chölöö, near Ikh Toiruu.

A good choice, more for the facilities than its location (about 20 minutes walk from the Square), is the *White House Hotel* (☎ 367 872; fax 369 973). Bill and Hillary aren't likely to be there, but the hotel has a classy English bar and French restaurant. Single/doubles start at T33,000/49,500. It's on Damdinbazaryn Gudamj, which heads west off Amarsanaagiin Gudamj.

Another reasonable place in this range – but, like the others, not worth the price – is the *New Capital Hotel* (☎ 358 235; fax 358 228) at T27,500/36,300 for a single/double. It's near the UK embassy, at the eastern end of Enkh Taivny Örgön Chölöö.

## Places to Stay – top end

All places in the top end include breakfast, but often they also include service and government charges of between 10 and 20%. Major credit cards are accepted and reservations are advisable in the peak season, especially around the Naadam Festival. These places should have their own supply of hot water and electricity, which is a real bonus if normal supplies are cut off to the rest of the city for weeks at a time.

Probably the most popular and convenient place in this range is the *Ulaan Baatar Hotel* (☎ 320 237; fax 324 485), just east of the Square, one of the very few which was built and flourished during the former communist days. Rooms have the facilities you would expect at T33,000/38,500 for a standard single/double and T66,000/88,000 for a deluxe. The hotel also has a sauna, billiard room and a useful business centre.

Popular with upmarket organised tours is the *Bayangol Hotel* (☎ 312 255; fax 326 880). Standard rooms start at T39,600/51,700 a single/double. While the rooms are a little ordinary for the price, the location and hotel facilities are very good. The twin towers are on Chingisiin Örgön Chölöö and are very hard to miss.

If you've been to Mongolia before you will be surprised to learn that the *Chinggis Khaan Hotel* (☎ 313 380; fax 358 067) has actually been completed, though it continues to be haunted by financial problems. The pink and black incongruous hotel has rooms starting at T49,500 (T44,000 in the low season) and suites at a ridiculous T115,500. It's located on Khökh Tengerin Gudamj – you cannot possibly miss it.

You may also wish to try the new, but small, *Tuvshin Hotel* (☎ 323 162), directly north of the Palace of Culture. Rooms range from T36,300 to T54,450.

### Places to Stay – apartments

If you are planning to stay in Ulaan Baatar for a while, you have a lot of gear or you are travelling in a small group, it's worth looking around for an apartment/flat to rent. Most owners or landlords obviously prefer long-term rentals, particularly to resident expats, but if business is slow (eg in winter) you may be able to arrange something with a short-term lease.

An apartment may also work out cheaper than a hotel if you stay in Ulaan Baatar for more than two or three weeks. For instance, a reasonable, furnished, two-bedroom apartment with a kitchen costs from US$200 per month. The price depends on demand, and will be more if you want TV or a good location.

Like most things in Ulaan Baatar, finding an apartment is usually a matter of asking around. Talk with expats, check the noticeboards at the US embassy and the UN Development Programme office (7 Erkhuugiin Gudamj), look for advertisements in the two English-language weeklies or visit the office of the Gegee Serving Foreigners Company (☎ 50 775), behind the State Department Store, which arranges a lot of rentals for foreigners.

One place which does rent out apartments by the night is the *Baigal Hotel* (Байгал Зочид) (☎ 366 881), to the west of the train station on the northern bend of Teeverchidiin Gudamj. It is hopelessly inconvenient to the centre of the city, and the restaurant serves nothing but mutton and vodka, but the apartments are clean and the furnishings OK. A two-bedroom apartment with kitchen (there's a stove, but no fridge), sitting room and TV costs T11,000/13,200/19,800/22,000 for one/two/three/four people.

## PLACES TO EAT

The days of food shortages are long gone, and there is now a reasonable choice of restaurants in the capital, but they still have a limited choice of food. At any place selling only Mongolian food, the menu (if there is one) will be written only in Cyrillic, and staff won't speak anything but Mongolian (and possibly Russian). Places catering mainly to foreigners will have menus in Mongolian and English; any change to this general rule will be noted below.

### Mongolian

For a plate of greasy mutton and noodles (for around T400) or, better, some buuz or khuurshuur for the standard price of T60 each, look for the ubiquitous sign Гуанз (pronounced guanz), which means canteen. Slightly more upmarket places will have the sign for restaurant (Рэсторан). Others will only have a sign showing a steaming cup of something, or a knife and fork.

Be careful because some of the rougher places are not hygienic. (In 1996 the health authorities closed down hundreds of guanzes in Ulaan Baatar.) The small lanes leading off Sükhbaatar Square and south of the Square on the other side of the road, and around Nairamdal Park, are good places to look for a cheap, Mongolian meal. One of the better guanzes is at the back of the Central Post Office.

There are several decent Mongolian restaurants which are cleaner, and have tables and waiters, but are a little more expensive (from around T500 to T800 a dish). The *Tuul Restaurant* (Туул Рэсторан) on Khudaldaany Gudamj has gone downhill recently, but the *Ider Restaurant* (Идэр Рэсторан), next to the Zaluuchuud Hotel, is worth a visit. The *Solongo Bar & Restaurant* (Солонго Бар & Рэсторан), almost opposite the Aeroflot office, is a huge cafeteria-style place, only open during the day.

The *Elephant Restaurant* on Enkh Taivny Örgön Chölöö, between the Central Post Office and the State Department Store, is certainly worth a try. Look for the sign in English; some of the staff can also speak a little English.

Also recommended is the small *Dulgunuur Tuya Restaurant* (Дулгунуур Туяа Рэсторан), in a light-green building directly behind the State Department Store – look for the sign in English: 'Restaurant Bar Shop'. Whatever you point to on the menu (which is handwritten in Cyrillic) will be delicious; the beef stew (T1100) will reawaken a love of meat after weeks of mutton in the countryside.

If you want to try some Mongolian food – but you are fussy about hygienic kitchens and want a menu in English – head for one of the middle or top-end hotel restaurants or a ger restaurant.

### Ger Restaurants

Two places cater for visitors on organised tours who want to taste some good – as opposed to truly authentic – Mongolian food, together with a traditional cultural show featuring some excellent music. A visit to a ger restaurant is often included in organised tours, but if you are travelling independently and want to come along anyway, give them a ring or visit them to find out when they have a show, and if they have a spare table.

The cost for food and the show (without drinks) is about T11,000. The incongruous *Chin Van Khanddorjiin Urguu* (no telephone) ger restaurant is on Natsagdorj Gudamj, a mock temple and ger in the middle of suburbia. Mongolia's biggest ger, near the US embassy, is a ger restaurant called *Abtai Sain Khani Orgoo* (☎ 53 118).

### Asian

To cater primarily for the increasing number of Korean and Japanese tourists, several good 'Mongrean' and 'Japagolian' restaurants have sprung up. Their all-you-can-stuff-down-your-throat buffets may seem expensive, but after weeks of boiled mutton in the countryside, or if you are hanging out for some vegetables, they are worth every tögrög. In the Zaluus Youth & Cultural Centre, on Zaluuchuudyn Örgön Chölöö, the *Korean Restaurant* serves a really good buffet for T4400. The *Seoul Restaurant*, in a building in the south of the Nairamdal Park, has lunch/dinner buffets for T5500/T6600.

For authentic Japanese cuisine, the *Hanamasa Restaurant* offers huge buffets from T4400 to T7700, and is popular with foreigners. It faces the Geser temple, in a big shopping complex on the corner of Ikh Toiruu and Khuvsgalchdyn Örgön Chölöö. The *Fuji Restaurant* in the Flower Hotel also serves pricey, but really tasty, sukiyaki and other Japanese treats.

Packed to the rafters on Friday nights with expats scoffing beers and pizzas, the *Green Club* is actually an Indian restaurant during the rest of the week. The quality of food is sometimes patchy, but you can usually get a good mutton korma – what else would you expect from an Indian restaurant in Mongolia? – for T770. Fish and chicken dishes cost more, and the pizza (T750) is so-so. Drinks are reasonably expensive. It's at the back of the Peace & Friendship Building, about

200m west of the State Department Store – look for the sign in English on the footpath.

It is surprising, and disappointing, that Ulaan Baatar still has no proper Chinese restaurant. The restaurant on the 3rd floor of the Mandukhai Hotel pretends to be quasi-Chinese (mainly because of the banquet tables), and the *Bogd Khangai* (Богд Хангай) on Natsagdorj Gudamj, near the road leading to the State Circus, serves some Chinese dishes (the menu is in English) for around T1500 – but both are poor excuses for the real thing.

### Western

Improved greatly over the past few years, the *Praha Restaurant* near the Gandan monastery serves Czech, Mongolian and other western food in pleasant surroundings. The service is good, but the servings are sometimes small and it's pricey – a two-course meal with a large bottle of Czech beer will set you back about T4000 per person. It claims to have a 'beer garden with views of the Gandan Monastery', which is stretching the truth, but the restaurant is still worth a visit for a splurge.

The *White House Hotel* has a classy French restaurant. Local frogs can breathe a sigh of relief because their precious lower limbs are not on the menu, but other authentic dishes are available from T2750.

Hidden among apartment blocks, just off the south-eastern section of Ikh Toiruu, is the *Star II Bar & Restaurant* – there is a sign in English on the footpath. It is expensive, but the service and food are pretty good.

Well worth the walk to Khudaldaany Gudamj mall is the *Europa Restaurant* (look for the sign outside in English). It is cosy and has about the best service and decor in town. Don't bother ordering fish from the menu – it's always 'unavailable' – but you can get a good steak with vegetables (T800), an excellent beefsteak (T1100), and a selection of salads, omelettes and soups from about T400. A 10% tax is added to your bill.

The *American Bar & Restaurant* is in, of all places, the Russian Polyclinic, at the eastern end of Enkh Taivny Örgön Chölöö – look for the big sign in English along the

road. It serves hamburgers with French fries (T1600), which impresses hard-to-please American expats, and other courses at around T2000 each. The decor and service are very good, and the bar is open until 6 am. There is a 10% tax.

### Fast Food

Big Mac and the Colonel haven't made it to Mongolia yet, but one traveller reported seeing a brochure at a hotel reception desk about a McDonald's franchise. The mind boggles – a McKhaan yakburger?

*Nasan* (Насан) *Fast Food*, on Enkh Taivny Örgön Chölöö, is one of the few places to sell fried chicken, hamburgers and hot dogs from around T500 – it's standing room only.

For pizza, try the unnamed place we have unimaginatively dubbed the *Pizza Place*. It is on the ground floor of a grey building on Natsagdorj Gudamj, opposite the Chin Van Khanddorjiin Urguu ger restaurant. There's a green sign outside with the word 'pizza' in English. Large pizza slices start at around T1100, and there's a selection of tasty salads (T250), frankfurters and French fries (T750) and cakes (not always available) for T250. They'll even deliver (☎ 322 859) if you order one day in advance and pay for the taxi. *Ejil's Pizza Delivery Service* (☎ 310 538) also delivers (from home), but only needs 90 minutes notice.

Complete with life-size posters of NBA basketball star Michael Jordan is the US-style *Time Out Sports Cafe*. The menu is limited at the moment to spaghetti, curry and rice, and...curried spaghetti (for around T600). It's open 24 hours, so it is good for breakfast (the French toast is excellent). The young and friendly staff speak English. It's near the Dashchoilon monastery – you can get there from any laneway near the corner of Ikh Surguuliin Gudamj and Baga Toiruu.

### Hotel Restaurants

Of all of the hotels listed in the bottom-end section, only four are worth trying. The restaurant at the *Gegee Hotel* gets varied reports. It serves a fairly limited selection of mutton and salads, but for breakfast may provide you with an omelette and porridge if you ask the day before.

The *Zaluuchuud Hotel* restaurant is nothing to write home about but serves reasonable, cheap meals and there's warm beer on tap. The *Kharaa Hotel* is one of the better places for Mongolian food; a cosy bar is attached.

The newly decorated restaurant on the 3rd floor of the *Mandukhai Hotel* serves cold drinks as well as good Mongolian dishes for around T600, plus western delights such as fried eggs and sausages (T800), as well as the usual assortment of soups and salads. One advantage is that the menu is in English.

The restaurant on the 1st floor of the upmarket *Bayangol Hotel* caters almost exclusively to guests on organised tours. We were turned away on three occasions before one of the staff grudgingly allowed us to have a meal. A decent spaghetti bolognaise cost T1200, and it is one of the cheapest places for beer (T500). There are several other expensive restaurants upstairs.

Far more accommodating to the public is the *European Restaurant* at the Flower Hotel, which serves tasty soups (T600) and real (not Mongolian-style) goulash (T1100). Other courses are more expensive at around T2500.

The most popular restaurant with foreigners is on the 1st floor of the *Ulaan Baatar Hotel*, affectionately known as The UB. This is *the* place to meet expats living and working in Ulaan Baatar. Tasty Mongolian pot soup (T700) and barbecue mutton (T1250) are good value, as are the western meals, such as fish and steak, for T1000-1500. Soft drinks and beer are expensive, and the service alternates between being very good and deplorable. It is a good place for à la carte breakfast as long as you avoid the occasional T3300 buffet. The restaurant on the 2nd floor offers *exactly* the same meals for two to three times more, and should be avoided.

Also recommended for western food (with menus in English) are the *Hotel Urge*, which also has reasonably priced drinks in a cosy, convenient location, and the *New Capital Hotel*, which has good service in a nice setting, but the meals are overpriced at T2750 and more.

### Cafés

In the summer, cafés spring up on any patch of ground in areas frequented by tourists and upper class Mongolians. These are great places to sip a coffee or Coke and watch Ulaan Baatar go about its business – but they have an annoying habit of being there one day and just when you are looking forward to another great coffee or pizza, they've disappeared or are closed for no reason.

Outdoor cafés congregate around Sükhbaatar Square, near the State Opera & Ballet Theatre, around the Drama Theatre and close to the Monastery-Museum of Choijin Lama. More permanent cafés, set up opposite the Bayangol Hotel, sell excellent (and safe) ice cream, cold drinks, kebabs and pizzas.

There are several good indoor cafés for cheap, western food: the *Holiday Coffee Shop* serves schnitzels (T800) and drinks, and is conveniently opposite (to the west) of the Ministry of External Relations on Enkh Taivny Örgön Chölöö; the *Flamingo Coffee Shop*, on the southern side of the State University, is popular with students and foreigners for cinnamon rolls, ice cream and pizzas (T800); and the popular *Cafe Good Food* (that's the name in English on the door) is north of the Museum of Natural History.

### Vegetarian

Vegetarians will have a dull time in Ulaan Baatar, and they will find it very difficult in the countryside, where fatty mutton dominates all meals. In the capital city, you can get passable lentil and rice-based meals at the *Green Club*, and vegetarian pizzas at the *Praha Restaurant* and *Pizza Place*. The buffets at the Korean and Japanese restaurants offer loads of vegetables among other things. Generally speaking, restaurants listed above under Western, and those in the middle and top-end hotels, will serve enough salads, soups and bread to fill you up. Alternatively, buy your own food and get to know the various markets.

## Self-Catering

If you are on a really tight budget, staying in an apartment with a kitchen, or are a vegetarian, then you will soon get to know the main markets (which are more like grocery stores) in Ulaan Baatar. The choice of food is still limited but is getting better each year. They are all open daily from about 10 am to 8 pm, and are worth a visit anyway for some atmosphere, fresh bread and tasty ice cream.

*Dalai Eej & Merkuri* (Далай Ээж & Мэркури) markets, at a convenient location next to each other about 100m west of the State Circus, have the best range of baked goods, meat, fruit and vegetables, and canned and packaged food, as well as tasty ice cream.

*Dorvon Uul* (дорвон Уул) is the red-and-white-striped building near the corner of Erkhuugiin Gudamj and the northern end of Ikh Toiruu. It has a good selection of the stuff you can get in other smaller shops, and plenty of fresh bread, but is a little inconvenient.

*KHID* (ХИД) is opposite (south of) the shopping centre with the Hanamasa Japanese restaurant. This market is convenient if you're staying in that side of town, and is less crowded than other places.

*State Department Store* (refer to Things to Buy) is often frequented by visitors, though it actually has a very poor selection of food. You have to pay a cashier, which is difficult if you don't speak Mongolian or Russian, and then give the receipt to the person behind the counter to eventually get what you want. Go somewhere else for your food.

## ENTERTAINMENT

Mongolians generally haven't yet learnt the power of advertising and promotion, so trying to find out what is going on in Ulaan Baatar can almost be a full-time job. You'll need to try a combination of the following: look at the 'Arts Diary' on the back page of the *Mongol Messenger* newspaper, or on the front page of *The UB Post*; check out the weekly entertainment guide at the counter of the Biz Info Centre on the 4th floor of the Ulaan Baatar Hotel; plead with a Mongolian friend, guide or hotel staff member to make some inquiries; walk past the various theatres or galleries and hope there is an advertisement

outside in English; or just buy a ticket anyway, and hope for the best.

## Cinema

The quality of films shown in the city is a great disappointment. Most are either kung fu classics or sleazy flicks (or both), and anything that isn't in the Russian language will be massacred by appalling overdubbing in Mongolian, making it unwatchable for foreigners. If that hasn't put you off, you can catch a flick at 4.30, 6.30 and 8.30 pm most days. The entrance fee is around T250.

The best cinemas around the inner city area are the *Ard* (Ард) on Baga Toiruu, almost opposite the MIAT office; the *Yalalt* (Ялалт), next to the Museum of Geology; and the *Sansar* (Сансар), near the Gegee Hotel.

## Discos & Nightclubs

Nick Middleton's book, *The Last Disco in Outer Mongolia*, written about his visits to Mongolia in the late 1980s, referred to what was Ulaan Baatar's only disco at the time – in the Bayangol Hotel. Now plenty of places with barmen in black bow ties, mirror-balls, expensive imported beer and thumping western music are springing up.

The following places charge a hefty entrance fee of T2750, and prices for drinks will be high – what you would expect to pay in the west. 'Closed for renovations' at the time of research (after only one year in operation), *Club Hollywood* may become 'bigger and better' than before. It's located in the Zaluus Youth & Cultural Centre on Zaluuchuudyn Örgön Chölöö.

If AC/DC is more your scene, you'll probably want to headbang at *Motorock* in the (light-blue) Saint Petersburg Centre, immediately south of the Square (it is signposted in English). Currently in vogue is the *Matisse Art Café*, a stylish bar with laid-back music and prints adorning the walls. It is in the basement of the theatre on Natsagdorj Gudamj opposite the Solongo Bar & Restaurant.

For live music, try Matisse's on weekends or, about 300m further west on Natsagdorj Gudamj, the *Emon Club* – there was a Bolivian

(Andean) band in residence there at the time of research!

### National Academic Drama Theatre

Үмдзсний Акадзмийн Драмын Тзатр

The large, bright orange-brown building on the corner of Natsagdorj Gudamj and Chingisiin Örgön Chölöö is the National Academic Drama Theatre (☎ 322 080). During most of the year, the theatre shows one of a dozen or so Mongolian-language productions by, among others, William Shakespeare and Jean-Paul Sartre, as well as various Mongolian playwrights. There are only between six and 10 performances, however, every month – maybe a few more in summer.

A list of upcoming shows is painted in Cyrillic on a board to the right as you look at the theatre. You can buy tickets in advance at the booking office (☎ 323 213), which is on the right-hand side of the theatre, between 9 am and 8 pm (lunch from 1 to 2 pm) every day but Tuesday. Tickets cost T2200.

### Traditional Music

A performance of traditional music and dance will be one of the highlights of your visit to Mongolia and should not be missed. You'll see outstanding examples of the unique Mongolian throat-singing, known as *khoomi*; full-scale orchestral renditions of new and old Mongolian music; contortionists guaranteed to make your eyes water; traditional and modern dancing; and recitals, featuring the unique Mongolian horse-head violin called a *morin khuur*.

The Traditional Song and Dance Company performs several times a week in summer at the National Academic Drama Theatre, or sometimes at the State Youth & Children's Theatre (☎ 327 916), opposite the Drama Theatre. You can buy tapes (T5500) of the performance after the show. If you have one, take a Walkman to check the quality of recording before you buy.

You can buy tickets at the Drama Theatre on the day of the performance. Get to the show 30 minutes early to ensure a good position at the front, because the seats are not numbered.

One company which performs on request – ie for large, pre-arranged groups – is the Tumen Ekh Song and Dance Ensemble. If nothing is going on at the two theatres mentioned above, try ringing them (☎ 327 279) to see where they are playing next.

### Puppet Theatre

Хүүхлдзй Тзатр

On the left-hand side of the National Academic Drama Theatre, as you approach it from the road, is a door which leads to a puppet theatre (☎ 321 669). Unfortunately, there are very few performances, but invariably something is organised during the week of the Naadam Festival, or can be especially arranged for a large group. If you're interested in puppets, have a look around the Mongolian Theatrical Museum.

### State Opera & Ballet Theatre

Built by the Russians in 1932, the State Opera & Ballet Theatre (☎ 322 854) is the salmon-pinkish building on the south-east corner of Sükhbaatar Square. Throughout the year on Saturday and Sunday evenings, and sometimes also on weekend afternoons in the summer, the theatre holds stirring opera and ballet shows (in Mongolian). Try to catch a performance.

One of the best operas is *Three Fateful Hills* – sometimes known as *The Story of Three Lives* – by Mongolia's most famous poet and playwright, D Natsagdorj. Other productions include an exhilarating (but long) rendition of *Carmen*, *Madam Butterfly* (sic) and *Swim Lake* (sic).

A board outside the theatre lists in English the shows for the current month. Advanced bookings are possible at the ticket office (☎ 323 881) – open from about 10 am to 5 pm every day but Tuesday – on the ground floor, and is worthwhile for popular shows and because tickets (T2200) *are* numbered, so you can get a good seat. If you are a little cheeky, you can have a look around inside the theatre during the day on weekdays (when there is no show in the evening).

A nightclub-cum-café on the 2nd floor opens after the evening show finishes.

## Palace of Culture
Соёлын Ордон
Also sometimes called the Central House of Culture (☎ 328 486), the Palace of Culture is the large, modern complex on the north-east corner of Sükhbaatar Square. Containing the Mongolian Art Gallery, the Palace of Culture is occasionally used by Mongolian and international orchestras and pop groups, but it's usually empty. Sometimes you may be lucky and find out what is playing there – a huge cloth banner outside, written in Cyrillic, may give you some idea; otherwise you'll probably never know unless you ask. There is a pleasant café (the menu is in Mongolian) upstairs with views of the Palace.

The State Philharmonic Society (☎ 325 553) performs classical and folk music at the Palace during most of the year, but not, unfortunately, during the summer holidays (between mid-July and 1 September). As this coincides with the major tourist season, the Society plans to change its performance schedule.

## State Circus
Улсын Чирк
Formed in 1940, the State Circus (☎ 320 795) is a bit of a misnomer: the circus has always been completely self-financed and receives no government assistance. Since 1971, the circus has been housed in the recognisable round building with the blue roof at the end of Tserendoriin Gudamj.

The circus is perhaps the most disappointing attraction in Ulaan Baatar. There are some impressive acrobatics and juggling, and extraordinary contortionists, but watching a poodle do the lambada in a tutu was not a highlight. Perhaps it is not surprising that the living conditions of the animals used in the show is poor. Although not apparently abused, the bears, wolves, goats, monkeys and yaks, among others, are muzzled, badly fed and neglected during the day, and forced to perform some amateurish jumping tricks

at night. Animal lovers may want to give the second half of the show a miss.

Advance bookings (☎ 324 517) are possible, but not really necessary, on the day of performance. Buy tickets (T2500) at the salmon-coloured building, south of the circus building. The circus is closed during August.

Performances usually start at about 5 pm, and sometimes matinees are held in summer (but not in August). Try to get there 30 minutes before the show starts to find a good seat. Nobody warns you, but flash photography is strictly prohibited. If you're caught, the usher will give you a very stern talking to – even if you don't understand, you'll certainly get the message!

### Contortionists
Make every effort to see a performance of traditional music and dance while in Ulaan Baatar. During this show, as well as at the State Circus and at tourist-oriented ger restaurants, you will see some pretty, young Mongolian girls bend their bodies in ways that will defy nature.

Contortionism has been a tradition in Mongolia for several hundred years. It was first performed in Mongolia during the Buddhist tsam mask dances, and then included in several famous Mongolian plays. Since 1941 it has been part of the programme at the State Circus, and by the 1960s it had became accepted as an art rather than acrobatics.

The girls are trained between the ages of seven and 14, and reach their peak between 14 and 25. The best contortionists tour internationally and can earn money they could only dream of as teenagers living in Mongolia. ■

### Bars
What may look like a café during the day often turns into a bar at night, selling beer (usually imported, expensive cans) to the younger crowds, and a dozen or so varieties of vodka to the older and drunker clientele. It's better to stick to bars in the main inner city area: in the suburbs, you may come across some aggressive drunks who are not used to comparatively rich foreigners.

For cheaper drinks in a safe place, try the *Solongo Bar & Restaurant* (Солонг о Бар &

Рэсторан), opposite the Aeroflot office, which has (believe it or not) a full-sized ger on the 2nd floor. The *Yangur Bar* (Янг ур Бар), south of the truck station on Khudaldaany Gudamj, serves pints of warm, drinkable beer for T300. A few reasonable places can be easily found on Ikh Surguuliin Gudamj and Sükhbaataryn Gudamj, running north from the Square – just look for a sign with a picture of a glass of foaming beer, or with the words Пиво, meaning beer (in Russian).

All of the hotels mentioned above have bars, but most are either dingy or expensive – rarely is there somewhere that is neither. Some of the better places for a drink are the bars at the *Negdelchin Hotel* (but avoid eating there), the *Zaluuchuud Hotel* and the *Kharaa Hotel*, which has a particularly cosy bar.

At the bars in the upmarket hotels, the drinks are expensive, the dreaded karaoke machines are loud and some 'ladies' aggressively ply their trade for hard currency.

## SPECTATOR SPORTS

Besides archery, horse racing and wrestling, and the popular game of outdoor, miniature *bilyard*, some of the local populace enjoy other sports. Fiery games of basketball are often held on summer evenings at the Central Sports Palace, which is the long, unsigned, yellowish building facing the lane behind the Ulaan Baatar Hotel.

Wrestling, boxing and dog-fighting (a curious mix of boxing and wrestling for humans, not dogs) are also held at the Central Sports Palace during the year. These tournaments are rarely advertised, so check the local English press or ask a Mongolian friend, guide or hotel staff member.

On weekends during the short summer (but not around the time of the Naadam Festival), the newly formed Mongolian Football League plays football (soccer) matches at the Naadam Stadium. In the lead up to Naadam, you should be able to catch some informal, but still competitive, wrestling at the Naadam Stadium, or at the stadium in the southern part of Nairamdal Park, on weekend afternoons. During

Naadam, you may also stumble across dog-jumping exhibitions and training at the stadium in Nairamdal Park.

For a swim, try the heated pool at the Zaluus Youth & Cultural Centre, on Zaluuchuudyn Örgön Chölöö. If golf is your game, you can play an expensive round at Mongolia's first golf course, south of the city (it was being completed at the time of research).

## THINGS TO BUY

The closest thing that Ulaan Baatar has to a shopping (pedestrian) mall is the western half of Khudaldaany Gudamj, which has several restaurants serving Mongolian food, plenty of good stalls and some useful shops, including hairdressers and pharmacies.

Ulaan Baatar's first and only true supermarket is opposite the Aeroflot office on Natsagdorj Gudamj. It contains a lot of useless and expensive items like salad dressings (you can't buy a lettuce in the whole country), but hopefully it will offer a better range in the future. Next door is the city's only shopping arcade – the Naran Arcade – with a few upmarket shops, including a Benetton franchise.

Cheap, easy to take home and unique to Mongolia are the bright landscape paintings which you will see in all the souvenir shops. The ones for sale (from T550 to T2750) from the art students who sometimes hang around the Square are far better and cheaper. Some days, the students may pester you a dozen times in one afternoon; then you won't see one for days. Other good places to buy these types of paintings are the Gandan monastery and the State Department Store.

If you want to pick up some Mongolian cashmere, the shops in the upmarket hotels and at the Winter Palace sell jumpers (sweaters), rugs and gloves – but prices are high and non-negotiable (so try other smaller shops). You may be able to arrange a tour of a cashmere factory, but this will be followed by a hard sell; you'll be expected to buy a few things. The major three cashmere factories are the government-owned Gobi Corporation (☎ 342 958; fax 343 081); Buyan (☎ 325 413;

fax 326 755) and Mon-Forte, a joint US-Mongolian company (☎ & fax 325 090).

## State Department Store
### Удсын Их Дэлгуур

Known as *ikh delguur*, or 'big shop', the State Department Store (☎ 320 506) is virtually a tourist attraction in itself, an anachronism from the communist days not so long ago. During the summer of 1996, the store was closed for many weeks while the staff exercised their new-found right to protest about, paradoxically, the store's privatisation. It is open between 9 am and 8 pm from Monday to Saturday and from 10 am to 6 pm on Sunday.

The 1st floor has a very poor selection of food. The 2nd floor has a reasonable selection of household goods of little interest to visitors. The 3rd floor sells normal clothes and has one of the best collections of traditional clothes. Here you could be fully decked out in the traditional *del* (long robe), *loovuuz* (hat) and *gutul* (boots) for a total of about T25,000.

Most visitors head straight to the 4th floor, which has one of the best collections of souvenirs in the country, many at reasonable prices. If you can't pick up one from an art student in the street, the landscape paintings here are still good value at T2600 to T5200. Other souvenirs you may wish to pick up include carvings from T11,000, wall hangings of the great Chinggis Khaan starting at T40,000, authentic Mongolian coats for around T11,000, incense bags and a good, but expensive, range of cashmere and leather products. This is also one of the better places to pick up some books in English, German and Japanese about Mongolia, postcards, and tapes and compact discs of traditional and new Mongolian music. A foreign exchange counter on this floor changes (only) US dollars at the standard bank rates.

## Central Market
### Төвийн Зах

The central market is actually called the Black Market (Khar Zakh), but it's not the sort of place where you go to change money illegally and smuggle goods – though this certainly happens there.

First established about 60 years ago, and run by Chinese traders in different parts of the city, the market is now north of the city. Although there are about 1.5 million sq km of land in Mongolia, the market is held in an area the size of a football field. Up to 60,000 people a day in summer squeeze in, while about 2000 vehicles travel along a narrow laneway to the market. This is where you can see, and be part of, the Mongolian Scramble at its worst; thousands of people pushing, and tripping over, each other. If you have experienced rush hour on a Bombay bus or Tokyo subway, you may have some idea of what to expect. Some visitors may find the crowds disconcerting.

Even if you can cope with the crowds, the market can still be disappointing. It caters entirely to locals, so there are rows and rows of boring things like toothpaste, sunglasses and stockings. You will be hard-pressed to find any great souvenirs. Prices are certainly lower than at the shops and markets in the city, but it's hardly worth the effort to come to this market just to save a few tögrögs. Don't even think about going to the toilet there.

And you can't even photograph the crowds. Some travellers have reported being abused, and even having rocks thrown at them, for taking photos. Hang on desperately to all your belongings; don't carry anything on your back, and strap your money belt to your body. This is a serious area for pickpockets and bag slashers; even Mongolians are scared of theft here.

To get to the market, catch one of the regular minibuses (T100) which cruise around town, or jump on one of the ramshackle yellow buses (T120) from outside the Ulaan Baatar Hotel or the Drama Theatre. If you want to walk, it'll take at least an hour from the centre of town (which still may be quicker than a bus), and it's uphill most of the way – just head up Khuvisgalyn Örgön Chölöö and follow everyone else. Don't get off at the first, smaller vegetable market along the road; carry on until the road and bus finally stop.

The market is open on Wednesday, Thursday, Saturday and Sunday from around 9 am to 6 pm. Try to avoid Saturday and Sunday afternoons, when the crowds can be truly horrendous.

### Dollar Shops

Only a few years ago, high-ranking communist officials were able to go to stores called 'dollar shops' which stocked imported 'luxury' goods (like edible food), unavailable to the ordinary masses. But these days with an open market economy, and because it is officially illegal to trade in US dollars, the concept of dollar shops is recent history. Expats still refer to these places as dollar shops, but most are little more than department stores selling beds, TVs and washing machines, while a few sell 'necessities' like Swedish chocolate, English baked beans and American breakfast cereals.

About 500m west of the State Department Store, on Enkh Taivny Örgön Chölöö, there are two shops in a grey building identifiable by the signs in English: 'Shop Shop' (so good, they named it twice) and 'Duty Free Shop' (which it isn't). They offer the best range of those tasty imported groceries which you may be craving, like crisps, real coffee and Corn Frosties (which don't taste so good with lumpy yak milk), as well as toiletries and film.

All upmarket hotels have small dollar shops, but these are expensive and have a very limited selection.

### Souvenir Shops

The art and souvenir shops in, and near, the Ulaan Baatar and Bayangol hotels are naturally more expensive than they should be, but they do have a reasonable selection of paintings, cashmere products, books, postcards, stamps and music. For price and selection, one of the best places to check out is in the yellow Golomt Bank building on the northwestern side of the Square – look for the word 'souvenir' painted on the window.

The Duty Free Shop (it isn't a duty-free place at all; see above) also has a large and reasonably priced selection of things to buy

for the folks back home. Other places to look around are the 4th floor of the State Department Store (see above), and the shops in the Winter Palace and the Monastery-Museum of Choijin Lama.

### GETTING THERE & AWAY
### Air

To get any service, let alone a ticket, in the MIAT office, you may need to sharpen your elbows and practise that traditional dance, the Mongolian Scramble. And it is important to always remember two golden rules: a MIAT ticket does not guarantee you a seat, and you can only book MIAT tickets from the point of departure.

The MIAT office is on the southern end of Baga Toiruu – there is a huge МИАТ sign on the roof, and a notice with the words 'ticketing and reservation office' in English by the door. The northern entrance leads to the room dealing with international flights; go to the next (southern) door for internal flights. Both offices are open on weekdays from 9 am to 5 pm (closed for lunch from 1 to 2 pm), and on Saturday from 9 am to 1.30 pm.

Most staff have a smattering of English (certainly Russian, and possibly German) so it is sometimes worth ringing them – arrivals/departures (☎ 119), international bookings (☎ 320 221) and internal bookings (☎ 322 144) – but you are far more likely to get what you want if you visit their head office.

There is also a MIAT office on the 1st floor of the Bayangol Hotel's Tower A, but the staff told us that they do not issue tickets or provide information about flights, which begs the question: What do they do? You may have more luck arranging a MIAT flight at the sales office (☎ 320 620), to the right of the reception desk as you enter the Ulaan Baatar Hotel.

If only as an alternative to the unreliable MIAT, the other internal airline, Khangard, is worth trying. Their booking office (☎ 311 333; fax 320 138), open every day (but Sunday) between 9.30 am and 1 pm and 2 and 5 pm, is on the 1st floor of the building still known as the Communist Party Headquarters (ie the large building immediately to the west of the Ulaan Baatar Hotel).

The office for Air China (☎ 328 838; fax 312 324) is in Room 201, 2nd floor, Tower B, of the Bayangol Hotel. Unlike the MIAT office, the staff at Air China are helpful and speak good English – it is almost worth flying on Air China just to avoid dealing with the MIAT office. The Air China office is open on weekdays between 9 am and 5 pm (closed between 1 and 2 pm) and on Saturday from 9 am to midday.

The Aeroflot office (☎ 320 720) (Аэрофлот) is on Natsagdorj Gudamj. Open from 9 am to 6 pm (lunch is the usual 1 to 2 pm) on weekdays, and 9 am to 3 pm on Saturday, the staff are also helpful, and speak English.

The staff at Korean Air (☎ 326 643; fax 326 712), on the 1st floor of the Chinggis Khaan Hotel, are also friendly and speak very good English. Their office is open Monday to Friday from 8.30 am to noon and 1.30 to 5 pm, and 8.30 am to noon on Saturday.

### Bus

From the long-distance bus station (Холын Уйлчилгээний Абтобус) at the southern end of Öndör Geegen Zanabazaryn Gudamj, buses travel at least once a week to all but the three provinces in the far west. The station is fairly chaotic; if you are new to Mongolia, don't speak the language and can't read Cyrillic, it may be a bit overwhelming at first. A Mongolian friend or guide would make buying a ticket, and finding your bus, a lot easier. Local bus Nos 15 and 20, and trolley-bus Nos 2, 4 and 7, link the long-distance bus station with Sükhbaatar Square.

The station is divided into several sections. Most buses park impatiently under specific destination signs – but not necessarily the *right* signs. Ask, and keep asking, other passengers where the bus is going (though passengers are often as confused as you will be), and look for destination signs (in Cyrillic) in the front window of the bus. Buses generally leave on time (if the driver can be found and he isn't too drunk).

Most departures are between 8 and 9 am. If you're taking a long trip, get to the station at least 90 minutes before your bus is scheduled to leave so you can find your bus, and scramble on board to get a seat when the driver finally decides to open the doors. Always remember that, as with MIAT airlines, a ticket never guarantees you a seat.

Tickets for places close to Ulaan Baatar – namely Nalaikh, Baganuur, Darkhan and Zuunmod – are bought on the bus, so jump on and get a seat; the conductor will find you after the bus has started. For longer trips, you can, and should, book as early as possible, which is, in fact, usually only one day in advance. The ticket office is hard to find: look for the sign for the café (Кафэ), which serves tea and excellent éclairs, in the eastern part of the middle section of the station.

### Minibus

Minibuses are usually a good alternative to the larger buses: minibuses are slightly dearer (only by a few tögrögs), but are more comfortable because you are usually guaranteed a seat. They are also far quicker. Minibuses run daily to nearby places like Zuunmod, Baganuur and Darkhan, and also less frequently to Bulgan city, Kharkhorin and Khujirt. Depending on demand, minibuses also travel as far as Bayankhongor, Ömnögov and Dundgov provinces, but don't rely on this.

Minibuses usually park near the larger buses which are going to the same places. The minibuses sometimes have a destination sign (in Cyrillic) in their windows, but usually it's a matter of asking the drivers and passengers where they are going. They mostly leave in the afternoon, catering for passengers who can't be bothered getting up early and scrambling on board the larger buses.

In summer, minibuses also go to Terelj and other nearby resort areas like Khandgait. They leave from the truck station on Khudaldaany Gudamj and have no schedule at all; getting a ride involves a lot of waiting, asking and then scrambling aboard when the damn thing arrives out of nowhere.

## Jeep

Public shared jeeps also congregate at a designated section of the long-distance bus station. They are not signed, so you will have to ask the driver and other passenger where they're going. Shared jeeps leave when full, and when we say 'full', we mean *really* full – they often resemble a sardine can on wheels. Sometimes, the jeep driver may surprise all on board by leaving with only five passengers; other times, 10 people and two goats may be a normal load.

Like minibuses, jeeps often leave in the afternoon. They travel to closer destinations like Bulgan city, Kharkhorin and Khujirt, and to other remote places where taxis cannot travel because of a bad road. Sometimes, shared jeeps also head up to Terelj.

Refer to the Getting Around chapter for information about renting jeeps for private trips around the countryside.

## Taxi

Taxis (shared or private) can only travel along paved roads, so they are only useful for trips around Töv province, to the towns along the main road to Russia (Darkhan, Erdenet and Sükhbaatar) and to the tourist site of Kharkhorin.

The cost of hiring a taxi to these places should be the same as the cost around Ulaan Baatar – currently T130 per km. Taxi drivers may want more for waiting if you are, for example, visiting the Manzshir monastery, or because they may return with an empty vehicle if dropping you off to somewhere remote. This is not unreasonable, but it *is* negotiable.

To avoid any argument about the final charge make sure that you and the driver have firstly agreed on the cost per km, and have discussed any extra charges. Then write down the number shown on the odometer or speedometer before you start.

## Train

The train station was, like the airport, undergoing extensive renovations at the time of research. The passenger terminal will be on two levels, and facilities will be vastly improved. Currently, there are two dismal restaurants selling vodka and mutton and little else (the restaurant upstairs is much better than the one downstairs), a small shop, and a post office. You can leave anything in the left-luggage lockers for as long as you like – ie there is no time limit – for T120.

From the capital city, daily trains travel to northern Mongolia and onto Russia, via Darkhan and Sükhbaatar, and south-east to China, via Choir, Sainshand and Zamyn-Üüd. There are also lines between Ulaan Baatar and the coal mining towns of Erdenet and Baganuur.

**Domestic** Tickets for domestic trains are available from a special office directly north of the square outside the train station – there is a helpful green sign outside in English: 'Ticket Office'. Unfortunately, no-one inside speaks English or any other European language. (Someone will speak Russian.) Boards inside the office list (in Cyrillic) the ticket prices for hard seats, but a timetable of departures and destinations (in English) is on the door of the information booth inside the train station.

The domestic ticket office (☎ 320 332) is one of those places where you will probably have to practise the Mongolian Scramble. It pays to firmly decide your destination and date of departure before you go in. If you look helpless, someone, maybe even one of the staff, may take pity on you and give you some special attention – but don't count on it. You can book a ticket up to 10 days in advance, which is not a bad idea if you have definite plans and want a soft seat during peak times (mainly July-August). If you speak Mongolian, there is an inquiries number (☎ 74 130). The booking office is open every day between 8 am and noon, and from 2 to 8.45 pm.

**International** Trains link Mongolia with its omnipotent neighbours, China and Russia. Getting a ticket in Ulaan Baatar isn't the ordeal it was, but you should still plan ahead.

About 100m west of the domestic train booking office, a bright orange building has the large, helpful sign in English on top:

'International Railway Ticketing Office'. Unlike its domestic partner, several staff, especially those selling tickets directly to Beijing and Moscow, speak some reasonable English. Inside the office, specific rooms sell tickets to Beijing, Irkutsk (Russia), Moscow, and Ereen and Hohhot (both in China).

You can book a ticket for international trains out of Ulaan Baatar up to one month in advance – but for the Moscow-Beijing or Beijing-Moscow trains you will have to scramble for a ticket on the day before departure. Refer to the special Trans-Mongolian Railway section in the Getting There & Away chapter for more details.

The booking office (☎ 322 994; fax 328 360) is open weekdays from 9 am to 1 pm and 2 to 5 pm, and from 9 am to 2 pm on Saturday and Sunday. In reality, however, no-one is usually around until about 10 am to sell tickets. Upstairs, in Room 212, there is supposedly a place with English-speaking staff, especially for foreigners – but we found this room to be permanently closed.

The booking office also boasts a currency exchange counter (which does not normally open when the trains arrive from China or Russia, and is a little inconvenient to the station), and a small, half-decent café. Complaints should be directed to the person (who should be able to speak English or German) in Room 109 on the 1st floor. There is also an inquiries number (☎ 74 133).

### Truck

Travelling by truck in the countryside is a necessary form of transport, but is less certain and more difficult to organise out of Ulaan Baatar. Most Mongolians get out of the capital city by bus, minibus, train or shared jeep/taxi, and hitch a ride on a truck for further trips around the countryside, where there is far less public transport. Refer to the Getting Around chapter for more information about hitching on trucks in the provinces.

In Ulaan Baatar, some trucks congregate around the station on the corner of Khudaldaany Gudamj and the south-west section of Ikh Toiruu. These primarily wait for cargo, but will take passengers if you are lucky

enough to be there when one is leaving. You can pre-arrange something, but you may be waiting for days and days. The trucks in the southern section of the long-distance bus station cater more for human cargo. They leave when they have packed in as many bodies (human and animal) as possible.

### GETTING AROUND
### The Airport

With the help of a US$38 million loan from the Asian Development Bank, the Buyant-Ukhaa (Буянт-Ухаа) airport was undergoing extensive renovations at the time of research to bring it up to international standards. The airport is 18km south-west of the city, in the dismal village of the same name.

Between the airport and city (T50), bus No 11 stops opposite the Bayangol Hotel and bus No 22 stops outside the Tuul Restaurant on Khudaldanny Gudamj. To find the bus stop near the airport, head out of the terminal, walk north for a few hundred metres and look for a group of locals mingling around a tin shelter.

If you have a lot of gear, or have just arrived in Mongolia and are not used to the Mongolian Scramble, it's worth paying extra for a taxi. Make sure that you pay the standard rate (currently T130 per km, but this is likely to be more in the future), and not the inflated price the taxi driver will probably ask.

### Bus

While old Soviet rustbuckets still rattle around the countryside, shiny new buses, donated by the Japanese government, travel around most of the capital city and as far away as the market and airport. The inner-city area is also serviced by a few trolley-buses.

Local public transport is reliable and departures are frequent, but buses can get extremely crowded. Sometimes, you can count yourself extremely fortunate if you even see a seat, let alone sit on one. The lady in the purple uniform who pokes you in the ribs and glares at you is the conductor. Pay her whatever she demands (currently T50 for any trip around Ulaan Baatar, including to the airport) or your life may be in peril.

Pickpockets and bag slashers occasionally ply their trade on crowded routes. It is not as bad as in China, but you should be careful.

All destinations of trolley-buses and buses will be in Cyrillic; the route number is next to the destination sign on the front of the trolley-bus or bus. Most public vehicles of use to visitors leave from opposite the Bayangol Hotel, or from the corner of Enkh Taivny Örgön Chölöö and Baga Toiruu, not far from the Ulaan Baatar Hotel.

Some of the useful buses and trolley-buses are listed below.

### Car & Motorcycle

There is nowhere in the city to rent a car or motorbike, and it's unlikely there will be for some time. If you can cope with the city traffic, or want to head out into the nearby countryside on your own, you can try to hire a car from a taxi driver or a local. You will have to pay at least T13,750 per day, plus petrol, but it is fairly pointless because you could probably get a car *and* a driver for the day at that price.

Motorbikes are few and far between, but you may be able to rent one (possibly with a sidecar) from a local for about T9000 per day, plus petrol.

### Taxi

In Ulaan Baatar, there are official and unofficial taxis; in fact, just about every vehicle is a potential taxi. They charge a standard T130 per km, but check the current rate as this will increase regularly. Don't agree to a set price because you will always pay more than if you pay the standard rate per km.

Taxi drivers are fairly honest, and within the city you won't be overcharged too much or too often. Don't be surprised if the taxi breaks down or runs out of petrol within a few metres of you getting in. (It certainly makes you realise how important a reliable vehicle is if you are travelling by rented jeep into the countryside.)

Getting a taxi is just a matter of standing by the side of a main street and waving your arms about. Within a minute or two a vehicle – either a taxi (some with a 'taxi' sign in English) or a private car – will stop. Alternatively, you can find them at designated taxi stands opposite the Zanabazar Museum of Fine Arts, outside the train station and at the car park in front of the Ulaan Baatar Hotel. Women should avoid using a private car, rather than an official taxi, after dark.

If you are in some remote part of the city, or want to book a taxi for a special trip (and speak Mongolian) you can ring for one: Zendmene 3 (☎ 341 795) has several minibuses; Ulaan Baatar Taxis (☎ 55 355) even has a few Mercedes; and Mon-Kor (☎ 313 450) has some newer vehicles. Some of these taxi services may not operate 24 hours a day.

Avoid using obvious landmarks such as the Ulaan Baatar and Bayangol hotels to catch, or get off, local taxis: taxi drivers will almost always assume that you are staying at these expensive places and can therefore afford to pay more than you should for your fare.

### Bicycle

Ulaan Baatar is reasonably flat and the streets are wide, so it's a good place for bicycles –

### Useful Buses & Trolley-buses

| Destination | Bus No | Trolley-bus No |
| --- | --- | --- |
| Airport | 11 & 22 | - |
| Enkh Taivny Örgön Chölöö (west) | 4, 17, 22 & 24 | 1 & 2 |
| Enkh Taivny Örgön Chölöö (east) | 2 & 13 | 1, 4, 5 & 6 |
| Flower Hotel | 9, 10 & 20 | - |
| Long-Distance Bus Station | 15 & 20 | 2, 4 & 7 |
| Train Station & booking offices | 15 & 20 | 2, 4 & 7 |
| Winter Palace | 3 & 19 | - |
| Zaisan Memorial | 7 | - |

except that almost no-one in the city rides them, or is interested in hiring any out. Mountain bikes in the nearby countryside would be excellent, but you will have to bring your own. You may be able to buy a Chinese-made bike, or find someone to do some repairs in Ulaan Baatar, but don't count on it – this is not India or China.

# Central Mongolia

The central aimags of Arkhangai, Töv and Övörkhangai are the most visited areas in the countryside for several reasons: the roads and transport are far better than the rest of Mongolia, the region is closer to Ulaan Baatar, and there is plenty to see, including several ancient monasteries, a stunning waterfall and some gorgeous lakes.

The central region has varied and dramatic scenery, from the Khentii Nuruu mountains in the north and the Khangai Nuruu range in the mid-west to the Gobi Desert in southern Övörkhangai. The rest is steppe with forests or desert, and there are several volcanoes, as well as many rivers, especially in the wet aimag of Arkhangai.

## Arkhangai Архангай

**Population:** 103,000
**Area:** 55,000 sq km
**Capital:** Tsetserleg
**No of Sums:** 17
**Elevation of Capital City:** 1691m
**Main Livestock & Crops:** horse, yak; potatoes, hay
**Ethnic Groups:** Khalkh, Oold

Arkhangai has astounding scenery: wide rivers full of fish (best times for fishing are in August and September), several volcanoes and volcanic lakes, forests covering one-sixth of the aimag and pastures (covering 70% of the aimag) where yak, including the

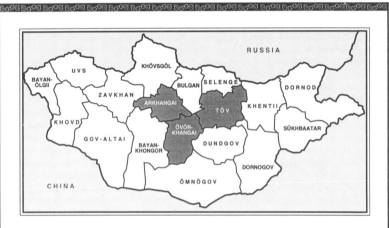

## Highlights

- Bogdkhan Mountain Strictly Protected Area: very close to Ulaan Baatar; hiking is superb; can stay in luxury ger camp
- Kharkhorin: home to magnificent Erdene Zuu monastery; site of Chinggis Khaan's former capital (Karakorum); stay at ger camps, hotels or camp
- Manzshir Khiid: the ruins of a small monastery; superb mountain and forest setting; stay at ger camp; horse riding can be organised
- Terelj: a popular area of ger camps; very good hiking and horse riding
- Terkhiin Tsagaan Nuur: one of the best lakes in the country, with a sandy beach; lovely sunsets; great camping and hiking

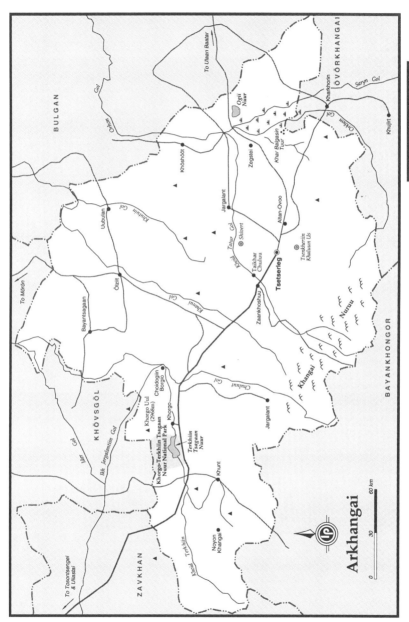

Arkhangai

0    30    60 km

ubiquitous long-haired Central Asian yak, thrive. It also boasts the stunning Terkhiin Tsagaan Nuur lake, ruins of ancient kingdoms and probably the nicest aimag capital in the country.

A lot of Arkhangai, which means 'north Khangai', is on the northern slope of Mongolia's spectacular Khangai Nuruu range. These are the second-highest mountains in Mongolia and are well watered. This means you can expect lovely forests, meadows and plenty of streams to quench your thirst while hiking, but it also means that flooded, muddy roads and snowfalls in the summer are not uncommon.

Another drawback·is that the aimag, particularly along the road between Tsetserleg and Ulaan Baatar, is notoriously bad for flies in summer – take repellent or you will live to regret it. If the flies make your life a misery, you can always get drunk on the fermented horse's milk, *airag*: Arkhangai is renowned for the quality of its airag.

One jeep road runs in an east-west direction through the aimag between Ulaan Baatar and Tosontsengel in Zavkhan aimag. The road is often bad, but the views are always spectacular. From the roads in Arkhangai look out for small rock formations, but please don't use these for toilet stops: they are ancient gravesites which may even predate Chinggis Khaan and his merry men.

## TSETSERLEG
ЦЭЦЭРЛЭГ

Tsetserleg is the only aimag capital in Mongolia which could, at a pinch, be called beautiful (tsetserleg means 'garden'). The town is ringed by scenic mountains, the streets are tree-lined and clean and a lovely little temple overlooks the town. These days, however, the town is looking neglected, and while it may retain some charm, a lot of things (and people) are not working.

Tsetserleg is a good place to break up your journey if you are combining a visit to Kharkhorin and/or Khujirt with a trip to Terkhiin Tsagaan or Khövsgöl lakes. Maybe it's the mountain air, but the people of Tsetserleg

seem to be friendlier than in other aimag capitals. There's even a huge, rusting sign in English, next to the main square, saying 'Welcome to Arhangai' (sic).

### Information
The bank in the bright green building, opposite the park, will change US dollars cash. The daily market just west of the post office is not particularly lively, but you can pick up some meat, rice and bread if you're camping. There is nowhere else in the aimag to buy food.

### Things to See
The complex which dominates the town from the top of the main street includes a monastery-museum and a temple. **Buyandelgeruulekh Khiid** (Буяндэлгэруулэх Хийд), just above street level, was first built in 1586 but was very small. A later expansion in 1679 brought the total to five temples, and up to 1000 monks were said to be in residence. Miraculously, the monastery escaped the Stalinist purges because it was made into a museum. The museum was closed at the time of our visit, but locals and expats say that it has a number of shaman costumes and *tsam* masks, and is well worth a visit. Religious services were being held at Buyandelgeruulekh Khiid while restoration work continued on the temple above.

Further up the hill, the **Zayayn Gegeenii Süm** (Заяын Гэгээний Сүм) temple was also closed and under restoration at the time of research. It is small, and did not look particularly interesting, but the setting under the cliffs, and overlooking the town, is spectacular. There is a trail up there for a jeep, or prepare yourself for a short but steep climb.

Behind the temple is a large, nearly vertical, rocky hill called Bulgan Uul. On the cliff face are some **Buddhist inscriptions**, which appear to have been damaged.

### Places to Stay
**Camping** If you head out north of Zayayn Gegeenii Süm, you'll find some good places to pitch a tent if you have one.

**Hotels** The two hotels in town are next to each other, opposite the square. Neither have reliable running water (all of the town suffers from this problem), so the toilets are fairly ordinary and the showers nonexistent.

The *Bulgan Hotel* (Булган Зочид) charges a reasonable T1200 per person for a simple room, and about triple that for a nicely decorated deluxe.

The *Khangai Hotel* (Хангай Зочид), identifiable by the little pagoda-style roof over the door, has simple/deluxe rooms for T1000/1800 per person.

### Places to Eat

Attached to the south side of the Bulgan Hotel is the large and clean *Bulgan Restaurant*, but there are no prizes for guessing the main (and, often, the only) dish on the menu.

The *Bayanberkh Restaurant* (Баяньзрх Рзсторан), just behind the square, is the only other restaurant in town. The food is nothing to write home about, but it offers a better selection of mutton than the Bulgan.

### Getting There & Away

**Air** MIAT flies from Ulaan Baatar to Tsetserleg and back every Wednesday and Saturday for US$60. The airport is only 1km south of town. There is no local transport; you'll have to walk there like everyone else.

**Bus** Overloaded and decrepit buses run between Ulaan Baatar and Tsetserleg every Monday and Thursday (T3720). The unofficial, and unsigned, bus/truck station is outside the shop-cum-canteen with the *delguur guanz* sign in Mongolian (Дэлгуур Гуанз).

**Jeep** Public shared jeeps go to Ulaan Baatar (T5000) when there is enough demand, but almost never go anywhere west. It is also hard finding jeeps for hire.

On the map, the most direct route between Tsetserleg and Ulaan Baatar (453km) is directly east through Zegstei. However, this road is falling apart and so are some of its bridges. The best road is via Kharkhorin, which adds 40km to the total distance but is in fact faster because almost all of the

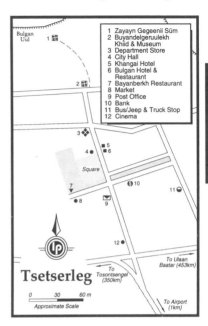

1 Zayayn Gegeenii Süm
2 Buyandelgeruulekh Khiid & Museum
3 Department Store
4 City Hall
5 Khangai Hotel
6 Bulgan Hotel & Restaurant
7 Bayanberkh Restaurant
8 Market
9 Post Office
10 Bank
11 Bus/Jeep & Truck Stop
12 Cinema

**Tsetserleg**

Kharkhorin-Ulaan Baatar leg is on a sealed highway – and you'll want to visit Kharkhorin anyway.

Heading west, the road from Tsetserleg to Tosontsengel (350km) initially goes through some wonderful mountain and wildflower scenery, and is in reasonably good condition. Between Terkhiin Tsagaan Nuur and Tosontsengel, however, it is one of the worst main roads in the country. Also, a few steep climbs along this section of the road will test the cooling system in your jeep, and the bridge over Khoid Terkhiin river is also in bad shape. There are a few guanzes along the way.

If you are travelling between Mörön (for Khövsgöl Nuur) and Tsetserleg, it's far better to go on the road through Ölziit (Θлзийт) in Erdenetandal (Эрдэнэтандал) *sum* (district), even if it means backtracking if you plan to visit Terkhiin Tsagaan Nuur (which you should). This will save you that awful stretch of road north-west of Terkhiin Tsagaan Nuur.

**Hitching** All types of vehicles go to and from Tsetserleg and, generally, along the main road through Arkhangai, but hitching opportunities are limited because the primary roads to the north-west (via Khövsgöl aimag) and to the south-west (through Övörkhangai) bypass Arkhangai. If you want to hitch, hang around the bus/jeep station and something will come along eventually.

## TSENKHERIIN KHALUUN US
## ЦЭНХЭРИЙН ХАЛУУН УС

This is a hot water spring 20km south of Tsetserleg, noteworthy because of its accessible location and is worth a detour if you have your own transport.

## SHIVERT
## ШИВЭРТ

If you want more hot springs to wallow in, Shivert is 35km north-east of Tsetserleg. As in Tsenkheriin Khaluun Us, there is nowhere to stay, but the camping is excellent.

## TERKHIIN TSAGAAN NUUR
## ТЭРХИЙН ЦАГААН НУУР

Known in English as the Great White Lake, this freshwater lake (and the volcanic area around it) is certainly the highlight of Arkhangai, and one of the best in a country full of beautiful lakes. Surrounded by extinct and craterous volcanoes (part of the Tarvagatain Nuruu range), Terkhiin Tsagaan Nuur is not as forested or as large as Khövsgöl Nuur, but it is closer to Ulaan Baatar, completely undeveloped and just about perfect for camping (though there are a few flies in summer).

---

**Khorgo Rebellion**

Khorgo is infamous in recent Mongolian history. In 1932 several hundred monks took the extraordinary step of starting a rebellion against the Mongolian communist government. Hopelessly outnumbered, the monks and their small band of supporters had no chance. The rebels were killed during battle or subsequent reprisals. Not surprisingly, nothing remains of their monastery. ■

---

The lake, birdlife and mountains are now protected within the 73,000-hectare Khorgo-Terkhiin Tsagaan Nuur National Park.

The lake, which was formed by lava flows from a volcanic eruption many millennia ago, is excellent for swimming, though a bit cold in the morning – try the late afternoon after the sun has warmed it up. The lake even has what may be Mongolia's only truly sandy beach. With a handline and lure, we caught a few tasty fish in an hour. Dramatic sunsets round off the day perfectly.

There are wonderful hiking opportunities around the north-eastern side of the lake, including (for the energetic) to Khorgo Uul volcano (2968m), about 900m above the lake. The volcano also has dozens of deep, and scary, caves – bring a strong torch (flashlight) and a load of courage.

The only problem with hiking in this area is crossing the wide river which runs into the eastern part of the lake. The closest bridge is at the nearby village of Khorgo (Хорго ) in the Tariat (Тариат) *sum*. From Khorgo, trails lead directly north to the volcano, but you'll need to ask directions to avoid getting stuck in swamp and mud.

**Organised Tours**

Surprisingly, Nomads (see Travel Agencies in the Ulaan Baatar chapter) is the only local travel agent to include a stop at the lake (for a day or two) on one of its tours heading west.

**Places to Stay & Eat**

**Camping** Except for a few annoying flies, the lake is one of the best camping spots in Mongolia. There is fish to catch, endless fresh water and flat ground for pitching a tent. The western end of the lake, where it joins the Khoid Terkhiin Gol, is muddy. The best place to camp is the eastern part where there are some pine trees (better for more discreet toilet stops) and even a guanz near the small hill. The area is cold all year round, so a good sleeping bag is vital.

**Hotels** There are no hotels right on the lake; the nearest accommodation is in. Khorgo village, about 6km east of the lake, and just a little off the main road. The one hotel in Khorgo is the unnamed, yellow building facing the main road. The rooms are huge, the landlady friendly and the place is good value at T900/1800 per person for a simple/ deluxe room. It also has a huge, and empty, restaurant. Khorgo is really too far to commute to the lake without your own transport (which is another reason to camp at this magical lake).

### Getting There & Away
The lake is right on the main road, so just pick your camping spot and get off your jeep, bus or truck. From the lake to Tosontsengel (179km), the main road climbs over Solongot Pass, a phenomenally beautiful area, which is also steep and very rough. You can see patches of permanent ice from the road. The road to Tsetsengel (171km) is in reasonable condition but fairly boring.

### NOYON KHANGAI
### НОЫОН ХАНГАЙ
A few intrepid souls push on to Noyon Khangai, a remote camping and hiking area in the mountains south-west of Terkhiin Tsagaan Nuur. It's a very difficult place to reach, but may be worth the effort if the jeep road, which is either muddy or potholed, is passable. From Khunt (Хунт), the capital of Khangai (Хангай ) *sum*, you need to follow the river west (upstream) into the mountains.

### CHOIDOGIIN BORGIO
### ЧОИДОГИЙН БОРГИО
To the east of Khorgo village and in Tariat *sum*, Choidogiin Borgio, where the Chuluut and Ikh Jargalantiin rivers converge, is a good hiking, fishing and camping area. Juulchin runs some fishing trips around the area. (See Travel Agencies in the Ulaan Baatar chapter.)

### TAIKHAR CHULUU
### ТАИХАР ЧУЛУУ
The nondescript town of Zaankhoshuu (Заанхошуу), in the *sum* of Ikh Tamir (Их Тамир), is about 25km along the main road west of Tsetserleg. You could stay at the 'hotel' by the barrier, where someone may ask

**Legends of Taikhar Chuluu**
Such an amazing rock formation is bound to be the subject of several legends. One legend involves a young man falling in love with a beautiful young woman. They were forced to elope, or commit suicide by jumping off the top of the rock (the legend varies at this point), after being shunned by their families. According to another legend, this enormous rock was carried to the current spot by a rather strong wrestler in an attempt to kill a huge and dangerous snake. ■

for some money for 'bridge maintenance', but this place mainly caters to truck drivers staying for an hour (or for however long it takes) with some local ladies. Camping along the Khoid Tatur Gol is better, or wait until Tsetserleg.

The reason to hang around here is to inspect the enormous Taikhar Chuluu rock formation, the subject of many local legends. Locals claim there are some ancient inscriptions on the rock, but we only saw the Mongolian equivalent of 'Kilroy wuz here '71' scrawled all over. There is even an *ovoo* (sacred pile of stones) on the top. Taikhar Chuluu is about 2km north along the river from Zaankhoshuu – you can see it from the main road.

### OGII NUUR
### ОГИЙ НУУР
On the road between Ulaan Baatar and Tsetserleg, near the border with Bulgan aimag, the Ogii Nuur lake is a truly wonderful place for birdlife – cranes and ducks, to name just a few, migrate to the area around late April. The lake is also renowned for its fishing. The lake and Khar Balgasin Tuur ruins (see below) can only be reached from the direct road linking Tsetserleg with Ulaan Baatar. You can visit them on a day trip from Khujirt or Kharkhorin if you have your own transport, but they're not easy detours.

### KHAR BALGASIN TUUR
### ХАР БАЛГАСЫН ТУУР
The black ruins of Khar Balgasin Tuur is in Khotont (Хотонт) *sum* on the banks of the

Orkhon Gol. With a guide and some luck, you'll see some limited ruins of what was the 8th century capital of the Uighur kingdom.

# Töv Төв

**Population:** 110,900
**Area:** 81,000 sq km
**Capital:** Zuunmod
**Elevation of Capital City:** 1529m
**No of Sums:** 26
**Main Livestock & Crops:** horse, cattle, sheep; potatoes
**Ethnic Groups:** Khalkh, Kazak, Barga

Ulaan Baatar is an autonomous municipality; the aimag which surrounds it is called Töv, which means 'central'. Just an hour's drive from Ulaan Baatar are restored monasteries in beautiful valleys and mountains with some wonderful hiking. You have a choice of simple hotels, tourist ger camps or unlimited camping spots. Marmots and squirrels abound in the mountains, while eagles and hawks hover silently in the valleys.

A large section of the aimag is part of the Gorkhi-Terelj, Khan Khentii and Bogdkhan national parks. Visitors to these parks will need a permit, but these are not difficult to obtain.

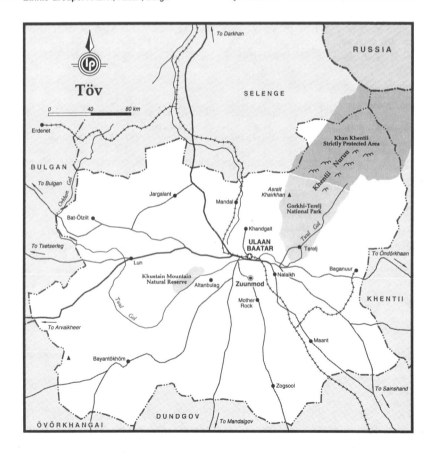

Töv may not be the wildest or most spectacular aimag in Mongolia, but it's an excellent place to start your exploration, or to see some of the countryside if your time is limited. It surrounds Ulaan Baatar and has a network of good and paved roads, so you can easily use public transport.

## ZUUNMOD
ЗУУНМОД

Nestled in a valley some 40km south of Ulaan Baatar, Zuunmod – the capital of Töv – is a laid-back city of about 17,000 souls. The town is much quieter and cheaper than the national capital, and that in itself might be a good reason for visiting. If travelling independently, you may need to stay in Zuunmod to visit the nearby Manzshir monastery or hike in the nearby mountains. Otherwise it's an easy day trip from Ulaan Baatar.

### Things to See

The chief attractions in Zuunmod are the two museums. The **Central Province Museum** is opposite the south-east corner of the park – look for the sign in English. Like most aimag museums, it gives a good summary of the local geology, flora and fauna, and has a

stuffed animals section– the moose is gigantic. Some traditional pottery is on display and there are some interesting B&W photos of Mongolia's military battles against Japan in 1939. The museum (tickets T500) is open every day except Tuesday from 9 am to 6 pm (closed from 1 to 2 pm).

The **Ethnography Museum** contains some interesting traditional artefacts and a fully furnished ger to peer in (some explanations are in English). It costs T500 (you'll be given 10 T50 tickets), is open from 9 am to 6 pm every day and is hidden down a laneway about 80m south of the park – look for the helpful sign in English.

Not in the same league as the Manzshir monastery but worth a visit anyway, the **Dashichoinkhorlon Khiid** (Дашучоыхнорлон Хийд) is a 500m walk directly east of the department store and across the creek. If you ask the monks, you can go inside the temple. Ceremonies start at around 9 am on most days.

### Places to Stay

You can camp anywhere near town, although Manzshir and the area around it is better than Zuunmod. The cheapest place is the

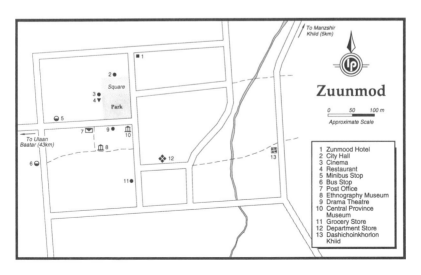

Zuunmod

0    50    100 m
Approximate Scale

To Manzshir Khiid (5km)

To Ulaan Baatar (43km)

1  Zunmood Hotel
2  City Hall
3  Cinema
4  Restaurant
5  Minibus Stop
6  Bus Stop
7  Post Office
8  Ethnography Museum
9  Drama Theatre
10 Central Province Museum
11 Grocery Store
12 Department Store
13 Dashichoinkhorlon Khiid

CENTRAL MONGOLIA

*Ethnography Museum*, which has a couple of basic rooms at the back for T500 per person. The only other place is the *Zuunmod Hotel* (Зуунмод Зочид). Reasonable rooms cost T2200 per person, though the staff (if you can find anyone) will probably try to get you into the deluxe room, with bathroom, for T3850 per person. The entrance to the hotel is at the back.

### Places to Eat

Zuunmod epitomises the poor choice of restaurants in the countryside: although the capital of one of the most populous provinces in the country, and only an hour's drive from Ulaan Baatar, Zuunmod has no decent place to eat. A few shops around the streets serve some milky tea and khuurshuur (fried mutton pancakes), but your best bet is the unnamed place with the sign 'Kafe', behind the yellow door in the orange building immediately south of the cinema. The decor is good, but the menu isn't: there is nothing but mutton and vegetables. The Zuunmod Hotel has no restaurant, but does boast a noisy bar.

### Getting There & Away

**Bus** Every day, buses run through the pretty countryside between Zuunmod and Ulaan Baatar (T250, one hour) about every hour between 8 am and 6 pm. Minibuses (T350) are quicker (45 minutes) and you are guaranteed some sort of seat. The road is paved and in good condition. The bus stop in Zuunmod is just a short walk west of the main streets.

**Taxi** Shared taxis (jeeps are not needed) ply the route between Ulaan Baatar and Zuunmod. They are more expensive (at around T400), but are far more comfortable than the sardine-can buses. You'll find shared taxis easily on the streets of Zuunmod; in Ulaan Baatar, they leave from the long-distance bus station.

However, it may be surprisingly difficult in Zuunmod to find a taxi, or any vehicle, interested in being chartered. The fare should be the standard rate paid in Ulaan Baatar – currently, T130 per km. Some drivers may want a waiting fee for hanging around the Manzshir monastery if you are going up there.

### MANZSHIR KHIID
### МАНЗШИР ХИЙД

Only 5km on foot to the north-east of Zuunmod, and 46km from Ulaan Baatar, is the Manzshir monastery. Established in 1733, the monastery had over 20 temples and was once home to at least 300 monks. Tragically, it too was reduced to rubble during the Stalinist purges of 1932.

The main temple has been recently restored and there are ruins of other buildings in the area. The monastery and museum are not as impressive as those in Ulaan Baatar – it is the spectacular setting which makes a visit worthwhile.

Manzshir Khiid overlooks a beautiful valley of streams and pine, birch and cedar trees, dotted with granite boulders. The monastery, and most of the area between it and Zunmood, is part of the Bogdkhan Mountain Strictly Protected Area, where wildlife, including wolves and foxes, is abundant and endangered species of hare and deer are (hopefully) protected from hunting. Hungry and cheeky marmots are everywhere, so keep an eye on your picnic lunch.

The only remaining temple is about 800m up a hill from the museum. Before you start climbing, look for the caretaker (who sensibly rides a horse) and make sure the doors of the temple are open. He is happy to show you around the temple and museum, but he speaks nothing but Mongolian. Many brochures about Manzshir, which you may pick up from travel agencies, still claim that religious tsam dances are held once a year at the monastery. In fact, they haven't taken place here for decades.

More interesting than the requisite animal trophies at the museum below the temple are the layout and some photos upstairs which clearly indicate what the monastery looked like before Stalin's thugs turned most of it into rubble. The museum also has several examples of the controversial Ganlin Horn made from human thigh bones, possibly from those of sacrificed virgin women.

If you have time, it is worth climbing up the rocks behind the main temple. At the top, the views are even more beautiful, and you'll find yourself in the midst of a lovely pine forest.

If you enter from the main road, you'll be required to pay an admission fee of T1000 per person and T500 for any car, including a taxi if you take one. The entrance fee also allows you into the Bogdkhan national park (though you are already in it). The monastery is open from May to October.

**Organised Tours**

Just about all foreign travel companies and local agencies include a trip to Manzshir as part of their one or two-week organised tours. Contact any of the travel agencies listed in the Ulaan Baatar chapter to see if you can pay to accompany a tour already going out there – but you may not have much luck.

Chono Travel sometimes runs an all-day bus trip out to the monastery with a Mongolian barbecue for about US$35 per person, and Shuren Travel runs a 400km two week horse-back trip all around the region.

**CENTRAL MONGOLIA**

Around Ulaan Baatar

## Places to Stay & Eat

**Camping** The area around the monastery is one of the best camping spots near Ulaan Baatar. It is located in a national park, so you can camp here for a small fee, but you'll need to get permission from the caretaker at the monastery.

**Ger Camps** If you've wanted to stay in a ger camp but have avoided it because it's expensive, the gers at the monastery may be what you're looking for. Only a handful are available at a comparatively reasonable T8250 per person, excluding meals. There's a restaurant in the grounds, but it may only be open if a tour group is staying there, so take your own food. The problem is that you can't book ahead, and the gers may be occupied, but it is worth asking anyway.

## Getting There & Away

The monastery is easy enough to visit in a day trip from Ulaan Baatar or Zuunmod.

**Taxi** From Ulaan Baatar, the only way to the monastery is by taxi (you don't need a jeep) or, cheaper, by bus to Zuunmod and then by taxi (7km). However, there are very few taxis in Zuunmod, so it may take some time to organise a ride. The fare should be the standard rate for Ulaan Baatar, with probably some negotiable extra charges for waiting. Once you're inside the gate, you can only drive about 1km before reaching a car park. From there, you walk uphill to the museum and monastery.

**Walking** From Zuunmod, you can either walk along the main northern road (refer to the map) or you can save about 2km if you walk directly north of Zuunmod and avoid the main road. Ask directions, if in doubt.

**Horse** The perfect way to get to Manzshir and explore the area is by horse, but finding one with all the right gear and, if necessary, a guide is not easy – Zuunmod is not set up for tourists. You could ask around the ger suburbs of Zuunmod, but it's probably best to arrange something from Undor Dov (see below), about 22km from Manzshir, though it won't be cheap.

## MOTHER ROCK

Near the village of Khöshigiin Ar (Хөшиг ийн Ар) in the *sum* of Sergelen (Сэрг элэн), about 15km south of Zuunmod, is the sacred rock known as Mother Rock. Mongolians often come here to seek solace and advice. Unfortunately, the area is now extremely dirty, with rubbish and broken bottles lying everywhere. Still, if you want to see something sacred or, indeed, seek some advice from the Mother Rock herself, try to get a taxi from Zuunmod, or include it in a day trip to Manzshir by taxi from Ulaan Baatar.

There is nowhere to stay near the Rock. You can camp but make very sure that you are well away from the drunks who congregate here.

## UNDOR DOV
УНДОР ДОВ

The *Undor Dov Tourist Camp* (☎ & fax 329 471) is about 8km directly west of Zuunmod. Opened in 1991, the camp contains a large

---

**Mother Rock**

A few years ago, rumours started about the healing powers of this rock, which could also provide advice and help the broken-hearted. The earth surrounding what is now called Mother Rock became sacred, so all rubbish which is dropped cannot be picked up; hence the rock's similarity to a rubbish tip, and the number of stray dogs in the area.

Visitors come to the rock and place the traditional silk scarf called a *hadag* (which you often see draped over ovoos) and other offerings, and then walk around the rock and pray. Vodka bottles are happily smashed on the rock; the contents are drunk, and the glass is left on the ground. What has only recently become a figure of hope is now a symbol of neglect. ■

Top: The Tibetan-influenced Lavrin temple at Erdene Zuu monastery in Övörkhangai.
Bottom Left: Shankh Khiid monastery is halfway along the main road between
    Kharkhorin and Khujirt in Övörkhangai.
Bottom Right: Detail from a door at Erdene Zuu monastery.

PAUL GREENWAY

PAUL GREENWAY

PAUL GREENWAY

## Landscapes of Mongolia

The southern third of Mongolia is dominated by the Gobi Desert, which, although barren-looking, has sufficient grass to support scattered herds of sheep, goats and camels. Much of the rest of Mongolia is covered by grassland, home to Mongolia's famed horses.

PAUL GREENWAY

PAUL GREENWAY

PAUL GREENWAY

## Landscapes of Mongolia

Mongolia is one of the highest countries in the world. In the west are the permanently snowcapped Mongol Altai mountains. The country's numerous freshwater lakes include the magnificent Khövsgöl lake, which contains up to 2% of the world's fresh water.

ROBERT STOREY

MICHAEL BUCKLEY

ROBERT STOREY

Top: A ger in winter near Kharkhorin in Övörkhangai.
Middle: Mongolians wearing the traditional *del*.
Bottom: Erdene Zuu monastery in Övörkhangai was the first centre of Lamaism in Mongolia.

concrete restaurant and a couple of dozen gers in a row. A night in a ger is T16,000 per person, but meals are extra.

If you are not staying here as part of an organised tour, there is little point in going to Undor Dov unless you happen to have a few golf clubs in your backpack and want to practise your swing on the golf driving range opposite the camp. (It's so windy here, you couldn't possibly hit a straight drive.)

The other attraction is a lovely horse ride from Undor Dov (inquire in the ger camp) to the Manzshir monastery (22km).

The only way to Undor Dov is by taxi from Zuunmod. There is an obvious turn-off on the paved road between Ulaan Baatar and Zuunmod. You may even want to walk from Zuunmod, either along the road or across the fields.

## FOUR HOLY PEAKS

The four peaks surrounding Ulaan Baatar are considered holy. Tsetseegun, Chingeltei, Songino Khairkhan and Bayanzurkh mountains correspond, more or less, to the four points on the compass. These peaks are great for hiking, and they're popular for their forests of larch trees, grasslands and stunning bird and other animal life, including ibex and sable. There is no shortage of thunderstorms in summer, so be prepared, and there's endless snow in winter.

Beware about hiking too close to the Presidential Palace, behind the Zaisan Memorial, as one reader warns:

There is a ring of army guards on the hills surrounding the palace. On my first hike, I had a couple of young soldiers with AK-47s running up the hill trying to catch me. They held me for a couple of hours before letting me go. But not before I was subjected to a stern 15 minute lecture in Russian, which ended with a sweep of the commanding officer's arms towards the hills and a shout of *nyet*!

## Tsetseegun Uul

Цэцээгүн Уул

Of the four, easily the most magnificent mountain is Tsetseegun. If you are hiking around this mountain, you need a permit – that is, pay an admission fee. You can do this at the gate to the Bogdkhan national park (see below) or at the Manzshir monastery. If you aren't hiking to the mountain through these entrances, you should get a permit from the Ministry of Nature & Environment (refer to the National Parks section in the Facts about the Country chapter).

At 2256m, Tsetseegun is the highest point in the Bogdkhan Uul range, which dominates the skyline to the south of Ulaan Baatar. From the city, you get no idea of just how beautiful this area is, but once you're in the forest it has a whole different feel. Some scrambling over fields of granite boulders is necessary, and the chance of slipping and injuring yourself should not be taken lightly.

The trip is only sensible from the beginning of June to the end of September. During the rest of the year, no matter how pleasant the weather is in the morning, sudden thunderstorms and icy winds can come out of nowhere (even during summer). It's important to take a compass and know how to use it, as it's easy to get lost in the forest. You'll need to make an early start, and as there is little or no water on top of the ridge, carry all you will need, plus extra food.

There are numerous approaches to the summit, some easier than others, and you may want to go up one way and descend by another route.

**Manzshir Khiid Route** This approach to Tsetseegun from the south side is the easiest route by far. As you face the monastery, cut over to your right (east) until you get to the stream. Just follow the stream until it nearly disappears and then head north. About three hours of walking should bring you out into a broad meadow which is close to the top. If you've walked straight to the north, the twin rocky outcrops of the summit should be right in front of you. If you can see Ulaan Baatar in the distance, you're on the highest ridge and close to the top.

There are two large ovoos on the summit, some spray-painted graffiti on the rocks, broken vodka bottles, empty cans and other detritus.

CENTRAL MONGOLIA

**Zaisan Route** This is the most scenic route of all, but also the most difficult. It's a good six hours each way and the boulders near the summit make it hard going.

From the Zaisan Memorial (see the Ulaan Baatar chapter), move past the huts and head up the valley 100m or so, then cut into the forest to your left. It's a very steep slope until you get to the top of the first ridge, about a 30 minute walk. On top of the ridge, you should find a large ovoo and an obvious path. From here, the slope levels off and becomes an easy walk through a pleasant forest for the next two hours. Eventually, the path disappears into an area of boulders, and you should come out to a point where you have a good view. You should clearly be able to see the summit at this point, but the climb is not yet half over.

Take a compass reading on the summit, then descend into a valley before climbing the final ridge. There is no path, though there are many false paths made by pine nut gatherers. You'll hit plenty of boulder fields on this last ridge, but you can avoid the worst of them by keeping a little to the east of the summit. Finally, you come out into a broad meadow, and the two rock pinnacles of the summit should be visible.

**Shavart Route** Shavart Uul, which appropriately means 'muddy mountain', is a lesser peak of 2003m on the south-east side of Tsetseegun. As you climb, you'll note seven large rocks on your left. This route takes five hours in each direction. Getting to the starting point requires a car or taxi.

**Khureltogoot Route** This is the easiest route on the Ulaan Baatar side, mainly because you hit the fewest boulders. However, this route is also the least interesting. The walk takes about three hours in each direction.

The problem is that getting to Khureltogoot is difficult. At about 8 am every morning a bus for workers at the Astronomical Building in Khureltogoot leaves from the long-distance bus station in Ulaan Baatar; you may be able to hitch a ride on this. Otherwise, you'll have to take a taxi.

### Chingeltei Uul
Чингэлтэй Уул
Chingeltei (1949m), on the north side of Ulaan Baatar, has some pretty forests near the top. You can reach the base of the mountain by bus Nos 3, 16 and 18 from the centre of Ulaan Baatar. By taxi, you can go all the way up to a gate from where it's a 2km walk to the summit.

### Songino Khairkhan Uul
Сонгино Хаирхан Уул
This small mountain to the west of Ulaan Baatar has the unusual name of 'onion mountain'. There is no bus there, so you need to take a taxi to the base, passing through a park with concrete animal statues. Getting back to Ulaan Baatar could be a hassle if you haven't made prior arrangements, though on Sundays it should be easy enough to hitch a ride.

### Bayanzurkh Nuruu
Баянзурх Нуруу
The name of this range of peaks to the east of Ulaan Baatar means 'rich heart mountains'. There's a little forest up here, and views from the summit are good. You can reach the base of the mountains by taking the bus to Nalaikh and getting off before the women's prison. Of the four holy mountains, these are the least impressive.

### BOGDKHAN UUL
БОГДХАН УУЛ
The Bogdkhan mountain was proclaimed a national park as far back as 1778, and some attempts at conservation in the area occurred in the 12th century. Now designated the Bogdkhan Mountain Strictly Protected Area (42,000 hectares), UNESCO has also proposed to establish a wildlife park in the region, perhaps up to 65,000 hectares in area. It seems that early legislation has ensured that the region won't become part of Ulaan Baatar's awful urban sprawl.

The national park is immediately south of the Tuul Gol, south of Ulaan Baatar and west of Nalaikh. It surrounds Tsetseegun Uul and contains the Zaisan Memorial, Nukht and the Manzshir monastery.

Entrance to the park costs T1000 for foreigners, and T500 for any type of vehicle. If you don't enter the park from the two gates – ie on the main road near the Chinggis Khaani Khüree or at the Manzshir monastery – you should get a permit from the Ministry of Nature & Environment.

One entrance to the park is near the turn-off to the left at the unlikely traffic light along the main road between Ulaan Baatar and Zuunmod. The cheapest way there is to catch the bus to Zuunmod, get off at the turn-off and walk a couple of km to the gate, where you pay for your permit. Otherwise, a taxi will take you there.

At this entrance, the *Chinggis Khaani Khüree* (Чингис Хааны Хүрээ) ger camp can justifiably claim to be 'different'. It goes the whole hog with the Chinggis Khaan theme: there's a museum with leftover costumes, weapons, armoury and ger carts from the movie about the great man. The restaurant has to be seen to be believed: each seat is an enormous throne, set inside a huge ger with a bear-skin welcome mat, and the walls are lined with the skins of 84 unfortunate snow leopards.

Considering the opulence, the meals are not unreasonable and worth a splurge at about T3300 a dish. At US$65 per person per night for a standard ger with three meals, it costs more than other ger camps, but if you don't mind paying more for something really different (though tacky and not for animal lovers), you can book at Tsagaan Shonkhor Holding Company (☎ 322 079).

## TERELJ
ТЭРЭЛЖ

Terelj, about 80km north-east of Ulaan Baatar, is a deservedly popular destination. At 1600m, the area is cool and the alpine scenery is magnificent, and there are great opportunities for hiking, rock climbing, swimming (in icy water), rafting, horse riding and, for the masochists, skiing in the depths of winter.

Terelj was first developed for tourism in 1964 and 30 years later became part of the 300,000 hectare Gorkhi-Terelj National Park. To the north-east, the park joins onto the Khan Khentii Strictly Protected Area, comprising over 1.2 million hectares of the Töv, Selenge and Khentii aimags. The Khan Khentii park is almost completely uninhabited but is home to endangered species of moose, brown bear and weasel, to name but a few, and to over 250 species of birds.

Parts of the tiny section of the Gorkhi-Terelj National Park developed for tourism are a bit touristy: some ger camps have concrete car parks, ugly electricity poles, TV antennae and discos at night; and locals overcharge for goods and services. But you can easily get away from all this if you want.

At any time of the year, the mosquitoes at Terelj can be appalling – at times, the worst in the country. Don't let this stop you coming to Terelj, or allow it to spoil your trip; just take all the necessary lotions, repellents etc.

There is a T1650 entry fee for each person and T300 for each car. If you don't enter on the normal road to Terelj, you should get a permit from the Ministry of Nature & Environment.

### Gunjiin Süm
Гунжийн Сүм

Surrounded by magnificent forests, not far from the lovely Baruun Bayan Gol, the Gunjiin temple was built in 1740 by Efu Dondovdorj to commemorate the death of his Manchurian wife. Once part of a huge monastery containing about 70 sq metres of blue walls, five other temples and a tower, Gunjiin Süm is one of the very few – if not the only – Manchurian-influenced temple in Mongolia to survive over the centuries.

Unlike most other monasteries in Mongolia, Gunjiin was not destroyed during the Stalinist purges, but just fell into ruin from neglect, vandalism and theft. Only the main temple, and some of the walls of the monastery, remain. Although you wouldn't know it, extensive restoration has been carried out – and is still being carried out – which gives you some idea of how damaged it must have been.

The temple is not a must – there are several better and more accessible temples and monasteries in Ulaan Baatar and Töv – but for hikers and horse riders, it's a great overnight trek from the ger camps at Terelj, or as part of a longer trip around the national park. Gunjiin is about 30km north of the main area where most of the ger camps are situated in Terelj. Follow the Baruun Bayan Gol to get there.

## Activities

**Hiking** If you have good maps, a compass and some experience (or a proper guide), hiking in Terelj is superb in summer, but be careful of the very fragile environment, and be aware of the mosquitoes and unpredictable weather. The fact that helicopters are sometimes used by travel agencies to start or finish treks in this area shows you how difficult the terrain can be.

For more sedate walks around the Terelj ger camp area, just follow the main road and pick a side valley to stroll along at your leisure. From the main road, look out for two interesting rock formations: Turtle (or Tortoise) Rock, in a side valley, which really looks like one at a certain angle, and the Old Man Reading a Book, on top of a hill.

Some suggested easier hikes are to the Gunjiin temple or along the Terelj or Tuul rivers towards the Khentii mountains. This is a great area for wildflowers, particularly rhododendron and edelweiss.

Places of interest on more difficult and distance treks in the Khentii mountains are:

Khagiin Khar Nuur, a 20m-deep glacial lake, about 80km up the Tuul Gol from the ger camps at Terelj.

Yestii hot water springs (up to 35°C), which are fed by the Yuroo and Estiin rivers. Yestii is about 18km north of Khagiin Khar Nuur.

Altan-Ölgii mountain (2656m), the source of the Akhian Gol.

Baga Khentii range, west from Gunjiin Süm.

**Horse Riding** Travelling on horse is the perfect way to see a lot of the park, including Gunjiin Süm and the side valleys of the Tuul Gol. To travel any long distances, you will need to have experience, or a guide, and to bring most of your own gear. Horses can be hired through any of the ger camps, but you'll pay high tourist prices. Alternatively, approach one of the Mongolian families who live around the park and hire one of their horses, but they will not be much cheaper.

At the entrance to the Terelj national park, a local nomad sometimes sells rides to tourists on a camel – but you won't go very far on one of those.

**Rafting** Tuul Gol, which starts in the park and flows to Ulaan Baatar and beyond, is one of the best places in the country for rafting. The best section of the river is a 40km stretch from an area known as Dorgontiin Gatsaa, north of the Terelj ger camp area, to Gachuurt, near Ulaan Baatar. Juulchin runs these rafting trips.

**Skiing** If you're unlucky enough to be in Mongolia during the -30°C winter, and can stand leaving your heated hotel (if there hasn't been an electricity failure), you might as well make the most of it and enjoy some outstanding cross-country skiing around Terelj. There are no set trails, so just take your own gear and ask the locals, or the (open) ger camps, for some good, and safe, areas to try.

## Organised Tours

Most foreign travel companies and local agencies include a night or two in a tourist ger at Terelj in their organised tours. Several local agencies (refer to the Travel Agencies section in the Ulaan Baatar chapter) also run some more interesting trips around Terelj:

Chono Travel often uses helicopters to get to more remote spots like Khagiin Khar Nuur and other places further north in the Khentii mountains.

Juulchin runs rafting trips down the Tuul Gol, treks to the Khentii mountains and skiing packages in the winter.

Mongol Tour OK runs some interesting trips around Terelj in combination with tours to Kharkhorin.

Nomadic Journeys organises low-impact trips in the region by yak and horse, with a cart carrying a portable ger.

Nomads runs treks on horse back (or, if you prefer, yak cart) to the Khentii mountains, through Terelj, visiting Gunjiin Süm.

## Places to Stay

**Camping** Camping around Terelj and the national park is possible, but not actively encouraged by park authorities for several reasons: the potential damage to the pristine environment; the genuine risk of forest fires from careless campers; and the fact that no money can be made from people who camp.

If you get permission to camp, and pay a small additional fee, pitch your tent away from the main road and other ger camps, don't use wood fires and please take all of your rubbish out.

**Ger Camps** During the peak season of July and August (and at more popular camps), it's not a bad idea to book ahead if you can (some places don't have telephones). Outside of the normal tourist season, it's also a good idea to ring ahead to make sure the camp is open and has food. A few places are open in winter, catering mainly to expats who want to ski.

Most ger camps mainly cater for organised tours and may not be so interested in independent travellers, but it is certainly worth asking anyway. The ger camps offer almost identical facilities and prices – about US$40, including three good, western meals.

Below is a selection of the better places. (If available, specific contact details are included; otherwise, refer to the Ulaan Baatar chapter for details about the travel agencies.)

*Bolor* has pleasant gers for a negotiable T6600 per person; extra for food. They don't mind if you take your own food, but the inexpensive meals are about the best in Terelj. They even cater for vegetarians (with notice), and serve up little treats like pancakes for breakfast if you ask. The camp is about 5km from the main gate, on your right before you hit the camp with the dinosaurs. If in doubt, ask; everyone knows the camp. No English is spoken there.

*Naiman Sharga* is easy to identify by the huge, concrete dinosaurs out the front. The camp has good facilities (including bar and disco), but after a few vodkas you're likely to dream about being in some scene out of *Jurassic Park*.

*Terelj-Juulchin* camp (☎ 324 978; fax 342 535), jointly run by Juulchin, is on the main road – you can't miss it. The camp looks like a few gers set up in the middle of a car park, but the camp facilities are good, or you can stay at the comfortable hotel nearby.

*Turtle Rock* camp (the exact name is unclear) is a lovely, clean and friendly place in a side valley, several km behind the Turtle Rock. You can bargain the owners down to about US$25 per person or, if you take your own food, to as little as US$10. Contact Bumbart Ord or Mongol Eco Tours for bookings.

## Getting There & Away

**Bus** The road from Ulaan Baatar to Terelj and through most of the national park is in pretty good nick. There's no scheduled public transport to Terelj, but in summer minibuses very occasionally surprise everyone at the truck stop, on the corner of Khuldaany Gudamj and Ikh Toiruu in Ulaan Baatar, and take passengers to Terelj.

**Taxi** A taxi from Ulaan Baatar is easy to organise; jeeps aren't necessary because the road is paved all the way. You should only pay the standard rate per km, but the driver may understandably want more because his taxi may be empty for part of the return journey. You can also arrange with your taxi to pick you up later. Naturally, it would be cheaper if you could share the cost of the taxi with other travellers.

When there's enough demand, shared taxis to Terelj sometimes leave from the long-distance bus station in Ulaan Baatar. This is more likely on summer Sundays when locals day-trip out here.

**Hitching** Hitching *out* of Ulaan Baatar can be difficult because vehicles going out to Terelj could leave from anywhere; try asking around the truck stations. The cheapest way to Terelj is to take the bus to Baganuur and get off at the turn-off to Terelj, where you are far more likely to get a lift.

Hitching *back* to Ulaan Baatar from along the main road through Terelj is not difficult, as almost every vehicle is returning to the capital.

**Bicycle** A mountain bike would be an excellent way of getting around some of Terelj if you could stand the 80km of uphill riding to get there and cope with the traffic in Ulaan Baatar along the way. There is nowhere to rent mountain bikes in the country, so you will have to bring your own.

## KHANDGAIT
ХАНДГАИТ
About 40km north of Ulaan Baatar, Khandgait is another lovely area of cow pastures, small mountains, pine forests and wildflowers surrounding the small village of the same name. Like Terelj, there is plenty of opportunity for hiking, rock climbing and fishing in the nearby Selbe Gol, and, in winter, ice-skating and cross-country skiing.

Khandgait is a cheaper and less touristy alternative to Terelj but, because of this, Khandgait suffers from a lack of transport and good facilities. Khandgait is not part of a national park, so no permit is required.

The first half of the road between Ulaan Baatar and Khandgait is paved; the second half is roughish. The road goes past Khandgait and continues north to smaller, lovelier, and more secluded, valleys.

On the road to Khandgait, you'll pass hundreds of wooden huts built in a haphazard fashion around the valleys. These were used by residents of Ulaan Baatar as summer houses – somewhere cooler and quieter to escape the heat. However, with the advent of capitalism, many Mongolians are now poorer and can no longer afford the huts so most of them lay abandoned. (They cannot be used by travellers.)

### Places to Stay
**Camping** This is great countryside for camping. Just pick any site, preferably near a river, and enjoy. Be careful about wood fires and make sure to take your rubbish out.

**Huts** In the Khandgait region, you'll see a few campsites with triangular (A-frame) huts; these mainly cater for groups of schoolchildren. Other types of huts, converted barracks and log cabins used in the past by Mongolian families are now often empty.

To find somewhere to stay, get off your taxi, truck or minibus at any group of cabins or huts which haven't been abandoned and ask the caretaker if you can stay. If you are unsuccessful, then hike one or 2km to the next group of huts along or just off the main road.

We had no difficulty finding rustic but comfortable rooms in some wooden huts for a reasonable T2500 per person. This also includes three meals of the usual mutton and noodles, so you may want to bring your own food.

**Ger Camps** Foreign tourism has brought some new hope to the depressed region. A few tourist gers were being built at the time of research and should have similar facilities to those in Terelj, but possibly at a lower price.

### Getting There & Away
**Minibus** There is no scheduled public transport to Khandgait, but if you hang around long enough at the truck stop on the corner of Khuldaany Gudamj and Ikh Toiruu in Ulaan Baatar, you may be lucky enough to catch a public minibus. Otherwise, take bus No 16 to the Zendmene terminal in the north of Ulaan Baatar and try to get a shared minibus further north. If that fails, you may need to charter one.

**Taxi** A taxi (jeeps aren't necessary) from Ulaan Baatar is easiest but, naturally, more expensive. You can arrange for the taxi to pick you up later.

**Hitching** Hitching *to* Khandgait from Ulaan Baatar is almost impossible. But it is fairly easy to hitch a ride *from* Khandgait within an hour or two – just about every vehicle going along the main road at Khandgait is going to Ulaan Baatar.

## GACHUURT
ГАЧУУРТ
The village of Gachuurt is nothing special but the area near the village is delightful. If

you're tired of the comparative hustle and bustle of Ulaan Baatar and crave some serenity and clean air, Gachuurt is definitely the place for you. You can hire horses from nearby gers, catch fish (and go rafting – refer to the Terelj section) in the Tuul Gol, hike in the nearby valleys and camp anywhere you want. And all of this is only 21km from Ulaan Baatar.

There is no hotel or restaurant in the village, so bring your own food and tent if you want to stay around Gachuurt. There are plenty of serene spots to pitch your tent about 2km before the village – just look for somewhere nice from the window of your bus or taxi.

The new Japanese-Mongolian ger camp called *Daisogen* (☎ & fax 358 373) is in a great location along the river. The cost is US$45 per person, including meals.

### Getting There & Away

Buses from the long-distance bus station in Ulaan Baatar travel along the good, paved road to Gachuurt village every 30 minutes to one hour during the day. You can also easily get a taxi from Ulaan Baatar. The road continues past Gachuurt, up the Gachuurt Gol as far as Sansar, but the public transport doesn't go this far.

### NUKHT
НУХТ

Another agreeable area for hiking and camping and only 10km from Ulaan Baatar is Nukht, also part of the Bogdkhan national park. The turn-off for the road to Nukht is south from the main road to the airport; on the corner are the remains of the tiny stadium used for the Naadam Festival in the 1940s.

The road leads to a gate of the national park. The gate has now been commandeered by guards working for the *Nukht Hotel* (☎ 310 421), so you may not be able to enter the park this way. Sometimes called the *Nukht EcoTourism Centre*, the hotel caters almost exclusively for organised tours. When we visited, all hotel staff were 'having

a day off' because there were no guests at the time. If you ask nicely, and business is quiet (and they are open), they may offer you a ger for as little as US$10 a night, excluding meals. Hotel rooms start at US$20, excluding meals, and go a lot higher if you want any luxuries. The place is sometimes booked solid by planeloads of Japanese golfing enthusiasts.

### KHUSTAIN UUL & NATURAL RESERVE
ХУСТАЙН УУЛ

Established in 1993, the Khustain Nuruu natural reserve is about 100km south-west of Ulaan Baatar. In the 90,000 hectare reserve, which includes the lovely Khustain Uul, the wild *takhi* horse and the steppe environment are being preserved.

### The Takhi Horse

The Mongolian wild horse is probably the most recognised and successful symbol of the preservation and protection of Mongolia's diverse and unique wildlife. The *takhi*, also known as the Przewalski's horse (named after the Pole who first took an interest in them), used to roam the countryside in great herds. In the 1960s they became nearly extinct after poachers killed them for meat and overgrazing by livestock as well as development reduced their fodder and breeding grounds.

At the time, only about a dozen takhi remained, living in zoos in Russia and Europe. After special breeding programmes in special parks in Australia, Germany, Switzerland and the Netherlands, the numbers of takhi outside of Mongolia increased to about 1000.

In the early 1990s, with assistance from international environmental agencies, many takhi were reintroduced into specially protected areas in Khustain Nuruu and Takhiin Tal (in the south Gobi). About 200 takhi now live in these parks or in the wild. They are successfully rearing their young and surviving the harsh winters.

If you are interested in the takhi breeding programme, or wish to stay at Khustain Nuruu, contact the Mongolian Association for the Conservation of Nature & Environment (MACNE) for details (See Ecology & Environment in the Facts about the Country chapter). ■

## NAIRAMDAL ZUSLAN
## НАЙРАМДАЛ ЗУСЛАН

Only 30km from Ulaan Baatar in the lovely Bayangol valley, the Nairamdal Zuslan International Children's Centre (☎ 332 776; fax 320 320) is an interesting alternative to Terelj. It may be full of hundreds of screaming kids from all over the world in summer, but you can easily avoid them and enjoy the serenity of the countryside.

The centre contains several buildings constructed in different styles, each representing cultures from Central Asia, Latin America, Scandinavia and the Balkans. The hotel is palatial, the rooms are spotless and the staff are courteous. The dining facilities are similarly impressive, and the skilful chef even makes the mutton palatable. You can enjoy some cultural displays, archery competitions and horse riding during the day. Cross-country skiing in winter is as good as in Terelj.

The centre (which is open all year) is sometimes full in July and August, so it's worth ringing ahead. Prices are high – they range from US$18 to US$35 for children and US$35 to US$80 for adults – but include all meals, guides and transport from the city. Nonguests are not particularly welcome, but you can have a look if you've got your own vehicle.

## NALAIKH
## НАЛАЙХ

The poor village of Nalaikh is part of the Ulaan Baatar autonomous municipality because it once jointly supplied the capital city with its coal. Coal is now primarily supplied by Baganuur; Nalaikh's coal mine has closed down, leaving the place with little purpose. Nalaikh is still worth a quick visit because it is one of the few places around Ulaan Baatar with regular transport; it gives you an idea of a typical, depressed country aimag town without going too far; and it has a significant minority of Kazaks.

In the 1950s many Kazaks, mainly from the far western aimag of Bayan-Ölgii, were 'persuaded' to work in Nalaikh's mine, supplying Ulaan Baatar with a lot of its coal. Many Kazaks worked hard, and got various mining qualifications, only to see the mine completely close down in 1990 when the Russians left. (In fact, some Kazaks first settled in the nearby *sum* of Erdene as early as the 1870s.)

To find Nalaikh's mosque, face the bright-blue town hall, turn 180° and walk about 25 minutes over a small hill. The mosque is a disappointment if you have been to Kazakstan or other Central Asian countries. On a building at the end of one of the two streets, there is a sign with the word 'Hotel' in English, but locals said this was not somewhere foreigners can stay; it is really just a bar.

There is no need to stay long in Nalaikh, which is about 35km south-east of Ulaan Baatar. Crowded buses leave Ulaan Baatar every 30 minutes (T230, 45 minutes) during the day.

## BAGANUUR
## БАГАНУУР

Technically, Baganuur isn't in Töv aimag; like Nalaikh, it's a district of Ulaan Baatar

---

### International Children's Centre

Built in the 1970s, the International Children's Centre was the brainchild of Filatova, the powerful Russian wife of former communist leader Tsedenbal. The idea was to enhance Mongolia's prestige by hosting international summer youth exchange programmes with both eastern bloc and western countries.

Filatova made this her personal pet project, and used her authoritarian connections to ensure that the camps received the best building materials, the best trained staff and the best food, all financed by generous state subsidies. When Tsedenbal lost power in 1984, the centre stagnated for several years, before being turned into a hotel. ∎

even though it's about 120km east of the capital city. This honour is bestowed upon Baganuur because it supplies the coal which fires Ulaan Baatar's power stations and heating system. It is not a bad place for an overnight trip from the capital city, or to hang around while organising onward transport to eastern Mongolia.

Although the Baganuur area has been inhabited for centuries, the present-day city (population 17,000) was only founded in 1978, a year before the mine commenced production. The old ger village on this site was previously named Gun Galuut Nuur (Deep Dark Lake) but was renamed Baganuur (Small Lake) about the time the coal-mining boom began.

The Soviets built their largest military base in Mongolia near Baganuur. It was closed in 1992 and is worth a look around if you like eerie ghost-towns.

1 Hospital
2 Urgo Bar & Restaurant
3 Erchim Hotel
4 Post Office
5 City Hall & Museum
6 Coal Miners' Hotel
7 Culture Palace
8 Department Store & Shops
9 Taxi & Bus Stand

To Former Soviet Military Base & Yonkhor Shadiv Darjaalan Khiid (16km)

Square

Baganuur

To Train Station (3km), Coal Mine (44km) & Ulaan Baatar (120km)

0    50    100 m

CENTRAL MONGOLIA

## Coal Mine

The former state-run coal mine, which is Baganuur's reason for existence, has now been partially privatised. The coal is strip-mined, meaning that the surface sand and rock (called 'overburden' in mining lingo) is simply removed rather than tunnelled under. Since the coal seam is about 20km long and 15 to 200m below the surface, there's a lot of digging in progress. At the present rate of consumption (six million tonnes a year) these coal reserves should last from about 60 to 100 years.

The mining company is sometimes (but not always) happy to show off its operation to foreign visitors – ask at the main entrance, but you'll need to speak good Mongolian or have a guide. We drove our jeep into the mine and had a look around; nobody cared. To get to the mine, simply turn right at the end of the road to Baganuur from Ulaan Baatar; the road to the left leads to Baganuur itself.

## History Development Museum

This small museum occupies one room on the right-hand side of the ground floor in the city administration building. There are no regular operating hours, but if you make it

known that you wish to visit somebody will open it for you.

There is a small display of dinosaur bones and old weapons, a layout of the local monastery, some musical instruments and a tribute to the locally born hero, Natsagdorj. Before leaving, you will probably be asked to record your impressions in the visitors' book.

## Yonkhor Shadiv Darjaalan Khiid

Ёнхор Шадив Даржаалан Хийд
This monastery was built in 1990 when Mongolians regained their freedom of religion. The original temple was just a ger but has now been replaced by a permanent building. The temple is still not large or rich enough to support its full complement of monks, so make local inquiries to find out exactly when the place is open and functioning. The monastery is about 16km north of Baganuur.

## Places to Stay

**Camping** Camping at Baganuur isn't great, but if you walk a km or two in any direction, you will find a secluded spot, but just don't let any drunk follow you.

CENTRAL MONGOLIA

## Natsagdorj, Mongolia's Celebrated Poet

Dashdorjiin Natsagdorj (1906-37) is Mongolia's best known writer, poet and playwright, and is regarded as the founder of Mongolian literature. He worked at the Leningrad Military Museum, studied journalism in East Germany, and then translated renowned works into the Mongolian language. His own writing included the dramatic nationalist poems *My Native Land* and *Star* and the play *Three Fateful Hills*.

Natsagdorj also worked for the Mongolian communist government churning out a military newspaper for the Ministry of Defence, and was secretary for the Stalinist puppet, Choibalsan. Natsagdorj was arrested in 1936 for reasons unknown, and died a year later in mysterious circumstances; his body and grave were never found.

There is a display dedicated to Natsagdorj in the provincial museum in Baganuur. His works are still performed, and you can buy copies of his poems and plays (translated in English) in Ulaan Baatar. ■

**Hotels** You don't have to be a miner to stay at what is known locally as the *Coal Miners' Hotel*, opposite the square (and a little hard to find). Simple rooms are overpriced at T5500 per person.

The only other place is known as the *Erchim Hotel* (Эрчим Зочид). Located on the 3rd floor of a building opposite the hospital, the hotel is not good value at T8250/13,750 per person for a simple/deluxe room. You may be able to stay for less in a local apartment – ask around at the shops.

### Places to Eat

The two hotels serve plates of unappetising mutton and rice. The best place to eat and get a drink is the *Urgo Bar & Restaurant* (Урго Бар & Рэсторан), in the round building on the way to the hospital. The reasonably well stocked shops in Baganuur are a good place to load up with food if you are heading out east. On Sunday, a market, not far from the hospital, sells clothes and other household items.

### Getting There & Away

The main road east of Ulaan Baatar is paved for only about 30km. At the time of research, the Japanese-funded roadworks made the journey fairly bumpy.

**Bus** Buses leave Ulaan Baatar every day but Tuesday and Thursday (T1055). Alternatively, catch the bus (which leaves Ulaan Baatar on Tuesday and Friday) to Öndörkhaan in Khentii aimag. It should stop at, or near,

Baganuur. Quicker, more comfortable but slightly dearer minibuses to Baganuur also leave from the long-distance bus station in Ulaan Baatar.

**Train** The train isn't particularly popular – most locals take the quicker bus or minibus. At 5.30 pm on Wednesday, Saturday and Sunday, the train to Baganuur leaves Ulaan Baatar and costs T997 for a soft seat and T274 for a hard seat. The train returns from Baganuur to Ulaan Baatar every Thursday, Sunday and Monday at 6 am.

**Jeep** Because of the current state of the road, a jeep is better for the trip to Baganuur, but a taxi would still make it. Public shared jeeps regularly travel between Baganuur and Ulaan Baatar (T1500) – departures depend on demand and how long it takes to squeeze everyone in. Very few public jeeps go anywhere east of Baganuur.

Baganuur is a useful starting point for trips to eastern Mongolia. Plenty of jeeps hang around the square and can be chartered. One worthwhile trip is to Delgerkhaan, about 130km away.

**Hitching** Hitching is possible, but the regular public transport makes it unnecessary. From Baganuur to places further north in Khentii, wait with everyone else at the top of the northern road between the coal mine and the town.

# Övörkhangai Өвөрхангай

**Population:** 112,900
**Area:** 63,000 sq km
**Capital:** Arvaikheer
**No of Sums:** 20
**Elevation of Capital City:** 1913m
**Main Livestock & Crops:** horse, cattle, goat, sheep; wheat
**Ethnic Groups:** Khalkh

Övörkhangai contains what is probably Mongolia's most popular attraction: the magnificent Erdene Zuu monastery, built from the ruins of the ancient Mongolian capital, Karakorum (now the modern town of Kharkhorin).

If travelling by rented jeep, it is easy to combine a visit to Kharkhorin with other places clustered near the borders of Arkhangai, Bulgan and Töv aimags: the Orkhon waterfall, Mongol Els sand dunes, Shankh Khiid monastery and the Batkhaan Mountain Natural Reserve. Paved roads, which almost reach Kharkhorin and go all the way to the aimag capital of Arvaikheer, are also definite attractions – but the road to the Orkhon waterfall is often atrocious.

Övörkhangai means 'south Khangai', a reference to the spectacular mountains of central Mongolia known as the Khangai Nuruu which dominate the north-western part of Övörkhangai. The southern part of the aimag, past Arvaikheer, is uninteresting desert steppe.

## ARVAIKHEER
АРВАЙХЭЭР
A nondescript but friendly aimag capital, Arvaikheer is of little interest except as a place to eat and rest, refuel the jeep or arrange onward public transport to places further west. Arvaikheer has the requisite hotel, bar, cinema, school and administrative building, and the monastery and museum are worth a look. The quiet, friendly, daily market is opposite the museum.

There is no need to go to Arvaikheer if you only want to visit Kharkhorin and other sights in northern Övörkhangai, because a paved road almost reaches Kharkhorin from Ulaan Baatar, and public transport there is far more regular.

### Gandan Muntsaglan Khiid
Гандан Мунтсаглан Хийд
This comparatively large monastery, about 150m north of the town square, contains a fine collection of thangka scrolls, including one depicting the original monastery, which was destroyed in 1937. The current monastery was opened in 1991, and now has about 50 monks in residence. Visitors are welcome and the friendly monks will probably offer you a cup of Övörkhangai's renowned airag.

### Museum
Since Övörkhangai lies partly in the Khangai (forest) region and the Gobi Desert, the museum boasts a better-than-average selection of stuffed mountain and desert animals. There are also some fossils and arrows, and leftovers from Karakorum. Upstairs are intricate carvings.

The museum is open from 9 am to noon and 2 to 5 pm, Monday to Saturday. Tickets are T400. The manager was extremely effusive and happily gave us a lengthy guided tour in Mongolian. Renovations were going on at the time of research. It is opposite the market and behind the post office.

### Places to Stay
**Camping** Like most aimag capitals, camping is a better option than the dreary hotel, but in Arvaikheer you'll have to walk a km or two to find a quiet place to pitch your tent. Best to head out to the area north of the monastery.

**Hotels** The *Khangai Hotel* (Ханг ай Зочид), a large Soviet-inspired structure on the west side of the town square, is looking very neglected these days, but it's the only place in town. Foreigners can stay in the small, simple rooms for a reasonable T1200 per person; the deluxe rooms cost about T5500 per person. The ornate painting of the Orkhon waterfall in the foyer is probably the finest thing about the hotel.

CENTRAL MONGOLIA

CENTRAL MONGOLIA

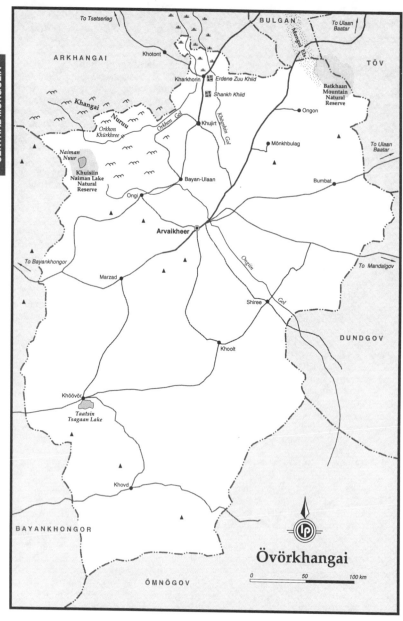

To Tsetserleg

BULGAN

To Ulaan Baatar

ARKHANGAI

Khotont

TÖV

Kharkhorin

Erdene Zuu Khiid

Shankh Khiid

Mongol Els

Batkhaan Mountain Natural Reserve

Khangai

Nuruu

Orkhon Khürkhree

Orkhon Gol

Khujirt

Kharzlin Gol

Ongon

Mönkhbulag

Naiman Nuur

To Ulaan Baatar

Khuisiin Naiman Lake Natural Reserve

Bayan-Ulaan

Bumbat

Ongi

Arvaikheer

To Bayankhongor

Ongiin

To Mandalgov

Marzad

Shiree

Gol

DUNDGOV

Kholt

Khöövör

Taatsin Tsagaan Lake

Khovd

BAYANKHONGOR

Övörkhangai

ÖMNÖGOV

0        50        100 km

## Places to Eat

The best place to eat is the *Khangai Hotel*, which has a small restaurant, a café and a comparatively well stocked shop with such goodies as chocolate and tinned meat. At the time of research, the *Ongi Bar & Restaurant* (Онг и Бар & Рэсторан) was closed through lack of interest and business. Maybe it will reopen again soon, but don't hold your breath.

## Getting There & Away

**Air** The airport is less than 1km south of town, but MIAT rarely flies to Arvaikheer. Sometimes you may be able to fly here for US$50 if a plane heading west stops to refuel.

**Bus** Buses run between Ulaan Baatar and Arvaikheer every day except Sunday (T3250). In summer, when demand is higher, buses often run more frequently.

**Jeep** You can travel quickly along the 430km paved road between Ulaan Baatar and Arvaikheer, which is just as well because the countryside is really boring. (There are plenty of guanzes along the way.) The paved road finishes just west of Arvaikheer; it is about another 200km along the usual rough road, with the occasional collapsed bridge, to the next aimag capital of Bayankhongor. With a jeep, an experienced driver and lots of time you could venture south to Dalanzadgad, 377km away in the Ömnögov aimag.

If you want to hire a jeep to see the sights around northern Övörkhangai, it is better to catch a bus to Kharkhorin and get a jeep there, rather than go to Arvaikheer. Shared and charter jeeps are rare in Arvaikheer, but you could try around the market.

**Hitching** The Ulaan Baatar-Arvaikheer road is one of the busiest in the country – at least one vehicle goes in both directions every minute. Hitching a ride on a truck or in a private car should be comparatively easy. Going further west along the main road won't be as easy, but is certainly possible. In Arvaikheer, trucks hang around the market opposite the museum.

## MONGOL ELS
МОНГОЛ ЭЛС

As you approach the border of Övörkhangai from Ulaan Baatar, one surprising sight which livens up a fairly boring stretch of road

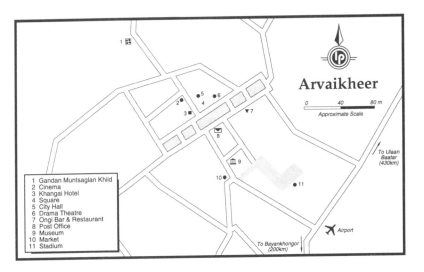

1 Gandan Muntsaglan Khiid
2 Cinema
3 Khangai Hotel
4 Square
5 City Hall
6 Drama Theatre
7 Ongi Bar & Restaurant
8 Post Office
9 Museum
10 Market
11 Stadium

Arvaikheer

0        40        80 m
Approximate Scale

To Ulaan Baatar (430km)

Airport

To Bayankhongor (200km)

are the Mongol Els sand dunes. If you don't have the time to visit the Gobi (where there are not a lot sand dunes anyway), these are certainly worth wandering around.

## KHARKHORIN (KARAKORUM)
ХАРХОРИН (КАРАКОРУМ)

In 1220 Chinggis Khaan decided to build the capital city of his vast Mongolian empire at Karakorum, 373km south-west of Ulaan Baatar. Building was completed by his son, Ogedei Khaan, after Chinggis' death, but Karakorum served as the capital for only 40 years before Kublai Khaan moved it to what is now Beijing.

Visitors at the time, including Marco Polo, reported that Karakorum had several ornate buildings, such as the 2500 sq metre Palace of Worldly Peace and a fountain designed by a French sculptor.

Following the move to Beijing, and the subsequent collapse of the Mongolian empire, Karakorum was abandoned and then later destroyed by hordes of Manchurian soldiers. Whatever was left of Karakorum was used to help build the Erdene Zuu monastery in the 16th century, which itself was badly destroyed during the Stalinist purges.

There is virtually nothing left of Karakorum; the modern and fairly dreary town of Kharkhorin was built on the same spot. But it is the remains of Karakorum, and the restored temples at Erdene Zuu monastery, which justifiably attract visitors.

### Information

Kharkhorin is not a tourist town, nor an aimag capital, so facilities are poor. A market is held every Sunday in a white-walled compound near the town square. There are some small shops around the square, and some better ones about 300m north-east of it. If you are camping around the area, stock up with provisions in Ulaan Baatar.

### Erdene Zuu Khiid
Эрдэнэ Зуу Хийд

Erdene Zuu (Hundred Treasures) was the first centre of Lamaism in Mongolia. The monastery was started in 1586 by Abtai

Khaan but wasn't entirely finished until about 300 years later. It had between 60 and 100 temples, about 300 gers were set up inside the walls and, at its height, maybe up to 1000 monks were in residence.

Like Karakorum, the monastery was abandoned and then vandalised by invading Manchurians. Attempts at restoration were made in about 1760 and, again, in 1808, but then came the Stalinist purges of the 1930s. All but three of the temples in Erdene Zuu were destroyed and an unknown number of monks were either killed or shipped off to Siberia and never heard from again.

However, a surprising number of statues, tsam masks and thangkas were saved from the monastery at the time of the purges – possibly with the help of a few sympathetic military officers at the time. These were buried in nearby mountains, or stored in local homes (at great risk to the residents). Many have been returned to the monastery, but tragically people have forgotten where many items were buried, so they remain lost forever.

The monastery remained closed until 1965 when it was permitted to reopen as a museum, but not as a place of worship. It was only with the collapse of communism in 1990 that religious freedom was restored and the monastery became active again. Today, Erdene Zuu Khiid still retains much of its former glory, though no doubt it's a shadow of what it once was. Restoration of the monastery is one of Mongolia's top cultural projects, but few funds are available from the government or international agencies.

The monastery is enclosed in an immense walled compound. Spaced evenly along each wall, about every 15m, are 108 stupas. (This is a lucky number for Buddhists.) The three temples in the compound, which were not destroyed in the 1930s, are dedicated to the three stages of Buddha's life: as a child, adolescent and adult.

The temple to the west, built by Abtai Khaan and his son, is dedicated to Buddha as an adult. Inside, on either side of the old Buddha, are statues of the two revered prophets of Buddhism: Sanjaa, to the left, and Jamba, to the right. Other items on display include some golden 'wheels of eternity', figurines from the 17th and 18th centuries, and exotic cakes made in 1965 and still well preserved (though probably not too tasty).

The main, central temple is called the **Zuu of Buddha**. The entrance is flanked by the gods Lham (on the left) and Gombogur (on the right). Inside, on either side of the statues of Buddha as a child, are (to the left) Otoch Manal, the god of medicine, and (to the right) Holy Abida, the god of justice. The temple also contains statues of the sun and moon gods, a few of the tsam masks which survived the purges, some carved, aggressive guards from the 16th and 17th centuries, and some displays from the revered sculptor and Buddhist, Zanabazar.

In the temple to the east, there's a statue depicting Buddha in his adolescence. The statue on the right is Bogd Lama, who spread Lamaism in Mongolia. The figure on the left is Janraisig, the god of peace.

Inside the monastery compound, there are several other interesting things to see. The **Dalai Lama Süm** was built to commemorate the visit by Abtai Khaan's son to the Dalai Lama in Tibet in 1675, but the temple is now irreverently used to store cleaning equipment. The large, white temple at the far end is the Tibetan-influenced **Lavrin Süm**, where ceremonies are held every morning.

You can also see the gravestones of Abtai Khaan and his son, and the main stupa, which is called the **Golden Prayer**.

In the centre are the base stones – now called the **Square of Happiness and Prosperity** – of a gigantic ger, once used for important meetings. The ger was reported to be 15m high and 45m in diameter and have 35 walls.

Entrance to the monastery (which is open from 9 am to 9 pm every day) is free. If you want to see inside the temples, however, you'll have to go to the administration office on your left as you enter the grounds, and ask them to open the museum (inside the temples). The museum is open from 9 am to 5 pm every day and costs T1500. The monastery is an easy 2km walk from the centre of Kharkhorin.

To appreciate what you're looking at, you may consider hiring a guide – ask at the administration office. (Or you may be able to stand discreetly within earshot of a guide speaking your language and showing other tourists around.) Ceremonies in the Lavrin Süm usually start between 9 and 11 am – the times vary (so ask at the office). Visitors are welcome, but photographs are not (for ceremonies). A shop next to the administration office sells some good but expensive souvenirs, and probably the only cold drinks outside of Ulaan Baatar – enjoy one if you are heading further west.

CENTRAL MONGOLIA

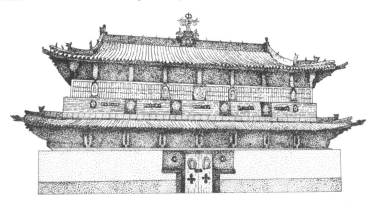

The Zuu of Buddha temple at Erdene Zuu Khiid is dedicated to Buddha as a child.

**CENTRAL MONGOLIA**

There are no set rules about the use of photography inside the temples, but please remember two important factors: continued flash photography inside a temple *does* over time affect the wall paintings and the coating on the statues; and the temples *are* very sacred places. Outside of the temples, you may take as many photos as you wish. The best time to visit is early morning and late afternoon to ensure some sensational snaps.

(One of our group continued to take photos inside a temple. Within five minutes, he had dropped his expensive camera, and it was irreparably damaged. Was it revenge of the gods?)

### Turtle Rocks

Outside the monastery walls are two 'turtle rocks'. Four of these once marked the boundaries of ancient Karakorum and apparently protected the Palace of Worldly Peace from floods. You'll probably need a guide to find them, or ask for directions. Often, an impromptu market, set up next to one of the turtle rocks, sells some beautiful stuff – usually better, and always cheaper, than the souvenir shop in the monastery (but please do not buy anything antique).

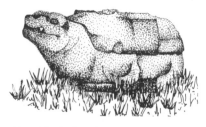

One of the 'turtle rocks' that once marked the boundary of ancient Karakorum.

### Phallic Rock

If you have some time, it is worth looking for the amazing 'phallic rock' which points erotically to something called a 'vaginal slope'. It is hidden in a small valley among the hills overlooking the monastery, about 30 or 40 minutes on foot. You will have to ask for exact directions at the monastery, or at your hotel – if you can describe in Mongolian what you want to see (and why!).

One traveller was told that, according to local tradition, all women who visit the rock must have sex within 24 hours. Enough said.

### Organised Tours

Almost all local and foreign travel agencies include a trip to Kharkhorin in their programmes, but most tours just visit the monastery, with possible side trips to the spa town of Khujirt and the Shankh monastery.

Three local agencies, however, offer something a bit different: Chono Travel sometimes uses a helicopter to link Kharkhorin with a visit to the Orkhon waterfall; Nomads goes to the waterfall on the way to the Gobi and nearby lakes, after visiting Kharkhorin; and Mongolian Adventure Tours runs a horse-riding trip around Kharkhorin and along the Orkhon river to the waterfall. (Refer to the Travel Agencies section in the Ulaan Baatar chapter for details about these agencies.)

### Places to Stay & Eat

**Camping** You could camp in the grounds of the *Orhon Hotel* and use their facilities for a negotiable T2750 per person, but it's very easy to find a perfect camping spot along the Orkhon Gol, only a km or two from Kharkhorin. From the road heading out west, just look for somewhere you like. The fishing in this part of the river isn't as good.

**Hotels** There are surprisingly few places to stay in Kharkhorin because most travellers stay in upmarket ger camps. Sometimes the water supplies in Kharkhorin are not reliable.

The cheapest hotel in town is the *Shankh Hotel* (Шанх Зочид), next to the unsigned bus station. Beds in an ordinary four bedroom dorm are T1000 per person. There is also a guanz and shop in the same building.

In the center of town, just north of the dusty town square, is the *Hotel Orkhon* – though the sign says 'Holel Opxon', you'll know what it is. A large, comfortable deluxe room, but with decrepit shared bathrooms, costs T3000 per person. At the *Khangbayin Hotel* (Хангбайин Зочид), next to the old cinema, you can get a pretty good deluxe room, including a TV (which doesn't work), for T3000 per person.

For a bit of a splurge, the *Orhon Hotel* (Орхон Зочид), along the Orkhon Gol, is a good option. The hotel is built in log-cabin style, and sometimes it sets up fancy gers during the summer. Lovely rooms (or a stay in the ger) cost US$25 per person, plus an extra US$15 if you want meals. The sign (in English) is in front of the entrance to Erdene Zuu, and you can see the hotel from the main road as you head west.

**Ger Camps** The travel company Juulchin jointly runs the *Karakorum Resort* (☎ 312 095), about 7km north of Kharkhorin. It costs about US$30 per person including meals, and is the usual standard ger camp.

In an excellent location in a lush valley, the *Chandmam* (Чандмам) camp is a better choice. It offers free lifts to/from Kharkhorin and Erdene Zuu, and a few interesting gimmicks like exhibitions for guests about how to make gers and wear traditional costumes. The price is a comparatively reasonable – and negotiable – US$30 per person, including meals. It is about 13km from Kharkhorin, on the main road to Khujirt.

**Getting There & Away**
**Air** Between 7 July and 1 September, MIAT flies between Ulaan Baatar and Kharkhorin for US$45, and then onto Khujirt (US$30), and back, every Tuesday, Thursday and Saturday. The landing strip is 3km from Kharkhorin, so you can either walk or take a jeep if available.

**Bus** Buses leave for Kharkhorin from Ulaan Baatar on Tuesday, Thursday and Saturday (T2760, seven to eight hours). As the road is all but sealed, this is one of the more bearable long-distance bus trips in the countryside. In summer, it's best to buy a ticket the day before departure.

The unofficial, unsigned bus/jeep/truck station in Kharkhorin is a large, dusty area about 1km north-east of the square, in front of the Shankh Hotel.

**Jeep** Several public shared jeeps travel between Ulaan Baatar and Kharkhorin every day for a little more than the price of the bus. You can also charter your own jeep from Ulaan Baatar, but you will be quoted an inflated tourist price; you should only pay the current taxi rate per km. A few jeeps are available for charter in Kharkhorin, but in the tourist season they may be hard to find. Ask around the jeep/truck station, or at the hotels.

The road from Kharkhorin to Khujirt (54km) is rough but scenic, and there are many hawks and falcons to admire and try to photograph. The aimag capital, Arvaikheer, is 138km to the south-east. Along the 160km road between Kharkhorin and Tsetserleg, there are some very rough patches, especially the 37km stretch between Khotont and Kharkhorin.

**Hitching** Hitching along the main road between Ulaan Baatar and Kharkhorin is fairly easy, but remember that a lot of vehicles will be carrying tourists, so they may not want to pick up a hitchhiker. Getting a lift between Arvaikheer and Kharkhorin is less likely, but if you're determined to wait something will come along.

Hitching between Khujirt and Kharkhorin shouldn't be too much of a hassle; many Mongolians take the Ulaan Baatar-Kharkhorin road to reach the popular spa town of Khujirt. In Kharkhorin, ask around the bus/jeep/truck station, or just stand by the road.

**SHANKH KHIID**
ШАНХ ХИЙД
The Shankh monastery, once known as the West Monastery, is the only one of many in the area which survived (other than Erdene Zuu). Shankh was renowned because of the visits by, and the donations from, the great Zanabazar. As elsewhere, the monastery was closed in 1937, temples were burnt and many monks were shipped off to Siberia. During

the years of repression, five monks secretly kept the monastery alive in a local ger at great risk to themselves.

The main temple is currently being slowly restored. Photographs are not normally allowed inside the temple, but if you ask, it may be possible. Ceremonies usually start at 10 am and visitors are welcome. There are presently 30 monks in residence, mostly young students.

There is nowhere to stay in the village, but it's easy enough to walk over the other side of the main road and find a discreet patch of ground to pitch a tent if you have one. Otherwise, you'll have to go on a day trip from Kharkhorin or Khujirt.

The monastery is exactly halfway along the main road between Kharkhorin and Khujirt, in the village of Shankh. If you have your own transport, it is a perfect place to stop between both places. There is no public transport going past the monastery, but with the amount of traffic along the road in summer it shouldn't be hard to hitch a ride. The monastery is now firmly part of the tourist trail, so don't be surprised to see a few coaches parked outside.

### KHUJIRT
ХУЖИРТ
Khujirt is a small, pleasant town noted for its mineral hot springs. There is a health resort for Mongolians who wish to spend their time soaking away arthritis and other aches and pains. Because it's a resort, Khujirt is a town of unusually orderly design and quite a contrast to the typical Mongolian village.

Khujirt is the place to organise onward transport to the Orkhon waterfall. Also worth visiting if you have a jeep is the area known as **Naiman Nuur** (Eight Lakes), which was created by volcanic eruptions centuries ago and is now part of the 11,500 hectare Khuisiin Naiman Lake Natural Reserve. The lakes are 70km south-west of Orkhon waterfall, but the roads are often virtually impassable.

The road between Kharkhorin and Khujirt (a bumpy 54km) is one of the best places in the country to see falcons and hawks, particularly the *saraa* (moon) hawk. If you are ever likely to get a photo of one of these birds, this is the place to do it.

### Spas
During the summer, Khujirt is chock-a-block with Mongolians enjoying the Russian-style all-inclusive spa resort which has apartments, a restaurant, a billiard room, parks and a resident health worker. If you want to wallow in a mud-bath or soak in some mineral hot springs (the water temperature can reach 55°C), head for the building with the sign КЛУБ (Club) at the end of the square. You'll probably need to speak Mongolian or Russian, or have a guide, to convince the officials that you're seriously contemplating a bath.

### Places to Stay & Eat
**Camping** There are no obvious camping spots, but if you walk 1km in any direction you will find somewhere secluded and decent.

**Hotels** We dubbed the grey building next to the ger camp the *No-Name Hotel*. It charges a fairly hefty, but negotiable, T8250 per person for a clean simple room, and T13,750 per person for the deluxe – the price includes three meals. The No-Name has a decent restaurant where you may be able to get something other than boiled mutton (but don't count on it) – the weird ger-style decor is worth checking out anyway. The ugly monastery-style building next door was a restaurant, but is now closed.

**Ger Camps** Someone thought it was a good idea to set up a ger camp in the middle of Khujirt. The ger camp has reasonable facilities, but the setting is poor compared with others nearby. The cost per person with meals is T16,500, or a reasonable T6600 per person without meals.

### Getting There & Away
**Air** During the summer (7 July to 1 September), MIAT flies between Ulaan Baatar and Khujirt for US$45, via Kharkhorin (Khujirt-

Kharkhorin is US$30), and back, every Tuesday, Thursday and Saturday.

**Hitching** With the number of Mongolians using the Ulaan Baatar-Kharkhorin road to get to Khujirt in summer, it shouldn't be hard to hitch a ride between Kharkhorin and Khujirt.

### ORKHON KHÜRKHREE
ОРХОН ХҮРХРЭЭ

Apart from the springs at Khujirt, the main attraction in the area is the Orkhon waterfall, situated on the Orkhon Gol, which flows an incredible 1120km to the north before it joins the mighty Selenge Gol. The waterfall, also called Ulaan Tsutgalan (Улаан Цутгалан), was formed by a unique combination of volcanic eruptions and earthquakes about 20,000 years ago. It is magnificent, especially after some heavy rain.

But the rains will also make the 82km road from Khujirt almost impassable; the river floods, the road is prone to mud slides and bridges often collapse. You should always ask around Khujirt for information about the current state of the road before heading out there.

A little way downstream from the waterfall, you can climb down to the bottom of the gorge. The gorge itself is only about 25m deep, but it is dotted with pine trees and is quite scenic from the bottom. Hardly anyone lives in the area near the falls, and the only sign of civilisation you'll see along the way are a few gers. There are plenty of opportunities to see and photograph yaks.

If you haven't brought a tent, you can stay at the *Orkhon Old Government House* set on

a gorgeous, secluded island. It is difficult to find: 500m before the bridge, turn left and drive parallel to the river (ie upstream) and ask for further directions. You can stay in the house (US$25 per person) or there may be a few gers (US$20) set up as well – prices include all meals. The people running the cabins are friendly and they can arrange fishing and horse-riding trips. It is always very cold at night up here, so be prepared.

The ruins of an ancient temple called **Tovkhoni Süm** are apparently within hiking distance of the waterfall. Ask the owners of the hotel for directions.

### BATKHAAN UUL
БАТХААН УУЛ

The *sum* of Burd (Бурд), in the north-east corner of Övörkhangai aimag, is host to some spectacular birdlife if you've timed your visit correctly. Some of the area is part of the 22,000 hectare Batkhaan Mountain Natural Reserve. The Mongol Els sand dunes are also nearby.

The area is just south of the main road between Ulaan Baatar and Arvaikheer, not far from the border of Övörkhangai and Töv aimags. With your own jeep, it is an easy day trip from Khujirt or Kharkhorin.

**Places to Stay**

To take advantage of this, and other sights, in the north-eastern part of Övörkhangai, Juulchin has a pretty good ger camp called *Bayangobi* – ask for directions from the town of Ongon (Онгон). It costs US$40 per person, including meals. Otherwise, just take your pick of unlimited camping spots if you have a tent.

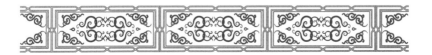

# Northern Mongolia

Hugging the Siberian border are the northern aimags of Bulgan, Khövsgöl, Selenge and Zavkhan. If you are going or coming by train to/from Russia, you'll pass through Selenge; if you are staying in Mongolia for a while, you will undoubtedly want to visit the stunning Khövsgöl lake, fast becoming the number one attraction in the country.

In the region around Khövsgöl aimag, the terrain is mainly taiga forest of Siberian larch and pine trees where there's plenty of rain, often about 40cm a year (falling predominantly in summer). The rest of northern Mongolia is steppe of mountains and forests. There are plenty of elk, reindeer and bears, and the rivers and lakes abound with fish.

## Bulgan Булган

**Population:** 63,300
**Area:** 49,000 sq km
**Capital:** Bulgan
**No of Sums:** 16
**Elevation of Capital City:** 1208m
**Main Livestock & Crops:** horse, cattle; potatoes, hay, wheat
**Ethnic Groups:** Khalkh, Buryat, Russian

Bulgan aimag is a curious mixture: the south is dry grassland and the north is green and has enough forest to support a small timber industry; among this are about 50,000 hectares of cereal and vegetable crops, and Erdenet, Mongolia's largest copper mine.

### Highlights
- Amarbayasgalant Khiid: a remote, but important, monastery being renovated; good camping, or stay at ger camp
- Bugat: a small, but accessible, region of forests and wildflowers; ideal for hiking and horse riding
- Khövsgöl Nuur: a gorgeous alpine lake; excellent for fishing, swimming, hiking among forests and mountains; stay in ger camps or camp by the lake

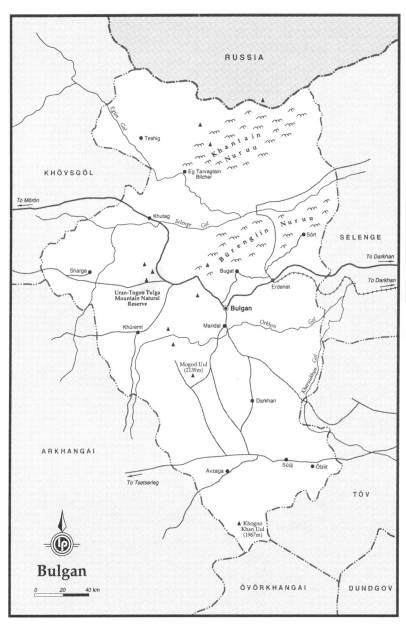

A small mountain range, the Bürengiin Nuruu, bisects the aimag, and though it only reaches a maximum altitude of 2058m, it provides plenty of lush habitat for wild animals and livestock. Herbs, often used for medicinal purposes, are being cultivated in the region with some success. Elk are abundant in this region. Mongolia's largest river, the Selenge Gol, crosses the aimag's north, and the Orkhon and Kharuukhyn rivers meander around the southern parts.

## BULGAN
БУЛГАН

A small aimag capital of 13,000, Bulgan city has long been known to foreigners as an overnight stop halfway between Ulaan Baatar and the ever-popular Khövsgöl Nuur. If you've been travelling in central or southern Mongolia, Bulgan city may impress you with its conifers, log cabins and absence of gers. Although there is little reason to linger, the town does have a certain run-down charm, but it is poor: there is a perennial lack of running water and the facilities are very limited.

### Orientation & Information
The bank along the main street will change US dollars. Alternatively, there may be a few moneychangers hanging about the market, just behind the bank. The daily market is small but interesting. Plenty of horses are hitched on poles outside the market and around town, as if from a scene in a wild west movie.

### Museum
The museum on the main street has some interesting photos and the usual stuffed animals. Even the local insects aren't spared: they are also mounted and displayed. The museum is open from about 10 am to 6 pm on weekdays and costs T120 to enter.

### Dashchoinkhorlon Khiid
Дашчоинхорлон Хийд

Like most monasteries in Mongolia, this one (built in 1992) replaces the original monastery called Bangiin Khüree, which was destroyed in 1937. About 1000 monks lived

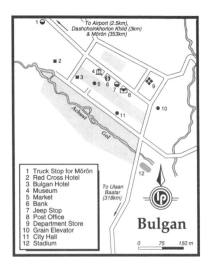

1 Truck Stop for Mörön
2 Red Cross Hotel
3 Bulgan Hotel
4 Museum
5 Market
6 Bank
7 Jeep Stop
8 Post Office
9 Department Store
10 Grain Elevator
11 City Hall
12 Stadium

To Airport (2.5km),
Dashchoinkhorlon Khiid (3km)
& Mörön (353km)

To Ulaan
Baatar
(318km)

**Bulgan**

0     75     150 m

and worshipped at Bangiin Khüree before they were arrested and, presumably, executed. About 30 monks now reside here.

Dashchoinkhorlon Khiid is about 3km north-west of Bulgan city and is hidden behind some hills.

### Places to Stay & Eat
**Camping** Camping is a good option considering the mediocre hotel. The best place to pitch your tent is over the southern side of the Achuut Gol. Go past the market, and find a discreet spot by the river.

**Hotels** The *Bulgan Hotel* (Булган Зочид), in the park, is the only hotel in town which is functioning (and only just). Large, clean rooms with bouncy beds, but no bathroom, cost T2200 per person. The deluxe room for T6600 per person is not worth the money, because the bathroom has no running water. Animal lovers may not be too impressed with the elk and moose heads which adorn the reception area.

The restaurant at the Bulgan Hotel may be able to rustle up some mutton and noodle if you can find anyone in the kitchen. As unappetising as this sounds (and is), there is nowhere else in town to eat. Bring some food from Ulaan Baatar or Mörön.

The *Red Cross Hotel* was closed at the time of research, but was due to reopen again soon. It should provide a cheaper alternative to the Bulgan.

### Getting There & Away

**Air** Each Friday, MIAT flies from Ulaan Baatar to Bulgan city (US$40), and very occasionally on to Khovd city for an extra US$45, and back again. Also the flight to Teshig, in the north-west of Bulgan aimag, stops at Bulgan city on Monday and Thursday. The airport is 2.5km north of town.

**Bus** A few buses go to Bulgan city. Direct buses leave Ulaan Baatar on Monday (T1962) and buses to Mörön (Monday, Wednesday, Thursday and Saturday) also stop at Bulgan city.

**Jeep** Locals say that a public shared jeep goes to Ulaan Baatar every Wednesday, but Bulgan city is not somewhere you want to hang around, so do what the locals do: catch a crowded public jeep to Erdenet, and then take the train to Ulaan Baatar. Jeeps hang around the main street, near the post office.

There are two routes between Ulaan Baatar and Bulgan city. The southern route is the most direct (318km), but it's mostly a dirt road, though not in bad condition as long as it isn't raining. Take this road if you are going straight to Khövsgöl Nuur.

The northern route (467km), through Darkhan (in Selenge aimag) and Erdenet, is on a good, often sealed, road except for the Bulgan-Erdenet leg. If you want to visit Darkhan, Erdenet or Amarbayasgalant Khiid (north of the Darkhan-Erdenet main road), the northern route is the way to go.

Bulgan city is 68km from Erdenet, 248km from Darkhan and 353km from Mörön.

**Hitching** Plenty of vehicles go along the Ulaan Baatar-Bulgan-Mörön road, including a few with foreign tourists, so it shouldn't be a problem hitching a ride. At a cafeteria near the bridge a few km south of Khutag

(Хутаг ) – which is about 80km north-west of Bulgan city – you will be able get some food and a bed for the night. A few trucks stop there, so it's a good place to hang around and ask for a lift.

To take advantage of the traffic between Erdenet and places to the west (which often bypasses Bulgan city), you need to hang around the petrol station about 500m north-west of Bulgan city.

## BUGAT
### БУГАТ

If you have rented a jeep with a driver, the best way to travel between Erdenet and Bulgan city is via Bugat village, in the *sum* of the same name. It is rough going, but the 40km jeep trail goes through some of the most picturesque forests and gorgeous wild-flowers in northern Mongolia. You will have to ask directions to find the start of the trail from Erdenet; it's easier to find from Bulgan city.

Mongolia's first hydroelectric dam will be built about 4km north of the convergence of the Selenge and Egiin rivers – about 40km north of Bugat. Besides the obvious environmental damage, and the question about whether the dam is really necessary, archaeologists are desperately concerned about the permanent loss of dozens of ancient Mongol and Uighur burial sites in the region. Try to visit the area before it possibly goes under water.

## ERDENET
### ЭРДЭНЭТ

In the autonomous municipality of Orkhon, and not actually part of Bulgan aimag, Erdenet is Mongolia's third-largest city with a population of 65,000. The reason for Erdenet's existence is the copper mine which employs about 8000 people and is the life-blood of the city. Erdenet is modern (built in 1974) and a bit soulless, but far nicer than most towns in the countryside. It is comparatively wealthy, so the facilities are the best outside of Ulaan Baatar. There is also a significantly large Russian community – up to 1000 Russians still work as technical advisers at the mine.

NORTHERN MONGOLIA

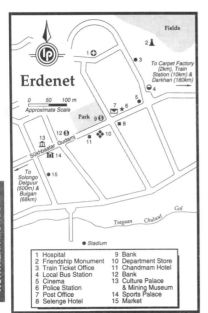

**Erdenet**

Fields

To Carpet Factory
(2km), Train
Station (10km) &
Darkhan (180km)

0    50    100 m
Approximate Scale

Park

To
Solongo
Delguur
(500m) &
Bulgan
(68km)

Sükhbaatar Gudamj

Gol

Tsagaan    Chuluut

● Stadium

| 1 Hospital | 9 Bank |
|---|---|
| 2 Friendship Monument | 10 Department Store |
| 3 Train Ticket Office | 11 Chandmam Hotel |
| 4 Local Bus Station | 12 Bank |
| 5 Cinema | 13 Culture Palace |
| 6 Police Station | & Mining Museum |
| 7 Post Office | 14 Sports Palace |
| 8 Selenge Hotel | 15 Market |

There is evidence that Mongolians were making copper pots in the Erdenet area at least 200 years ago. Russian geologists initially recognised the area's potential during the 1940s. The copper was first seriously prospected during the 1960s, and by 1977 a railway line to Ulaan Baatar was installed for hauling the ore. In 1981 an ore-processing plant was commissioned and Erdenet began exporting copper concentrate (30% copper), mostly to the former Soviet Union.

There are rumblings about privatisation, but the cash-strapped Mongolian government isn't keen to sell off the mine, as it currently generates about 70% of Mongolia's hard-currency earnings (depending on the current price of copper). In 1995, 208,000 tons of iron ore and 11,000 tons of molybdenum produced at the mine generated US$900 million for Mongolia. The mining and processing operation also consumes nearly 70% of Mongolia's electricity.

Travellers often bypass Erdenet and go straight from Ulaan Baatar to Mörön via Bulgan city. If you have the time, and want a little luxury, take the (soft-seat) train from Ulaan Baatar to Erdenet, with a stop-off at Amarbayasgalant Khiid if possible. From Erdenet, catch a jeep to Bulgan city – but then you'll have to wait for whatever comes along to Mörön.

### Orientation & Information

Erdenet is a sprawling city, though everything you will need is along the main street, Sükhbaatar Gudamj. Erdenet's railway station is inconveniently located more than 10km east of the centre.

The couple of banks along Sükhbaatar Gudamj are reluctant to change money, but many shops along the street will change money (US dollars cash only). Exchange rates are about 2% lower than in Ulaan Baatar, and differ from shop to shop, so check around. The daily market behind the Sports Palace is surprisingly small and scrappy – most locals buy their food in the selection of good shops along the main drag.

The Friendship Monument, about 200m north-east of the Selenge Hotel, is worth a look. A little further to the east, the *ovoo* is impressive (if you haven't seen too many before). The hills north of the monument, and south of the stadium, are great for short hikes.

### Mining Museum

This Soviet-built museum belongs to the copper-mining company, Erdenet Concern. It's on the 2nd floor of the Culture Palace, and is certainly worth a look. Entrance is free, and it is open weekdays from about 10 am to 5 pm.

### Copper Mine

The open-cut mine (thankfully, several km from the city) is one of the 10 largest copper mines in the world. Open-cut mining is more damaging to the environment but infinitely safer than digging mine shafts below the surface. Also, since this particular mountain is almost solid copper and molybdenum ore, this is the only practical way to reach it. The mine operates 24 hours a day, 365 days a year.

The mine is worth a visit if you've never visited one like this before. We were able to take a taxi to the mine and persuade the guard at the gate to take us on a guided tour. The views from the lookout over the gigantic open-cut mine, and of the city, are stupendous. A taxi to the mine from the town centre costs about T2500, including waiting time.

### Places to Stay
**Camping** Although the city is comparatively large, it is still possible to camp near Erdenet. The best places to try are north of the Friendship Monument, or south of the stadium, over the Tsagaan Chuluut Gol and among the pretty foothills.

**Hotels** Surprisingly, there are only two hotels in town, but both are pretty good. The *Selenge Hotel* (Сэлэнгэ Зочид) (☎ 20 474) has large, clean rooms with bathroom, TV and hot water for T5500 per person. It is in a good location, at the eastern end of the main street.

The *Chandmam Hotel* (Чандмам Зочид) (☎ 20 808) is better value than the Selenge. A clean, well-furnished room with bathroom and hot water costs T3300 per person. The hotel is a building on the main street, opposite the park – look for the sign in English: 'Bar Cafe Hotel'.

### Places to Eat
The *Selenge Hotel* has one of the best restaurants outside of Ulaan Baatar. It serves beefsteak with an egg on top (T850), schnitzel (T600), a delicious vegetable and beef soup and, maybe, fried chicken. You can top this off with a can of cold German or Filipino beer (T550). The café and bar at the *Chandmam Hotel* were being restored at the time of research, and should provide some good food and drinks when finished.

### Entertainment
The *Culture Palace*, on Sükhbaatar Gudamj, always has something on: a pop concert, some Russian and Chinese films, or a classical music recital. There is even a disco on the weekends.

If you have some time to kill, check out the impressive *Sports Palace*, also on the main street. Here you can plunge into the heated indoor pool, watch some wrestling or try some archery or, in winter, go ice-skating at the stadium at the back. The Sports Palace is open every day from 9 am to 9 pm.

### Things to Buy
If a couple of tons of copper is a bit inconvenient to carry around, a carpet would make a good souvenir. The city's carpet factory produces over one million sq m every year using machinery from the former East Germany. About 98% of the carpets are exported, mostly to Russia, but now increasingly to China and places beyond.

The carpet factory is closed during the summer (June-August) when staff take holidays and supplies of wool are scarce. If you are in Erdenet during the rest of the year, you can go on a tour and see the entire operation, from the processing of raw wool into thread to dyeing and weaving into finished products with exquisite patterns and colours (which you can buy, of course). The factory is just off the main road to the train station, about 2km from the Friendship Monument.

You can also buy carpets and rugs at the Solongo Delguur (Солонго Дэлгуур), about 500m west of the Sports Palace. A huge Chinggis Khaan wall carpet costs T78,000 and smaller, towel-sized carpets are T10,000 to T14,000.

### Getting There & Away
**Air** Although it is Mongolia's third-largest city, there are no flights to or from Erdenet; everyone travels by train, jeep and, to a lesser degree, bus. The airport is used almost exclusively by helicopters carrying executives to and from the mine.

**Bus** Because of the popularity of the train, buses from Erdenet to Ulaan Baatar, Darkhan and Sükhbaatar (T1000) only leave when there is enough demand. If there is a bus, it will leave from the market, or from the local bus station diagonally opposite the cinema.

**Train** The train between Ulaan Baatar and Erdenet goes through Darkhan, takes 14 hours and costs T1646 for a hard seat and T4103 in a soft-seat sleeper. The sleeper is definitely worth the extra tögrögs: the hard-seat carriages are packed to the roof. Departure times to Ulaan Baatar vary, so you'll have to check; sometimes they leave at 7.20 am, 6.50 pm or midnight.

The trip between Erdenet and Darkhan (five hours) goes through some lovely countryside. To Darkhan, the train costs T959 for the hard seat and T2540 for the soft seat. Trains to and from Sükhbaatar, in Selenge aimag, also change in Darkhan.

If travelling hard seat, get to the station a couple of hours before departure, sharpen your elbows and huddle outside the train – the doors of the carriages open about 30 minutes before departure.

Buses meet arriving trains, but the stampede of passengers quickly fills these to overflowing. Also, not every bus you see at the railway station is going to the centre – many are headed to industrial areas surrounding the city, so don't just get on any bus. It's best to get off the train as soon as you can and find a taxi (about T1200) before the crush starts. It is a little more sedate by bus *to* the train station; buses (T100) leave from the local bus station, south of the railway ticket office.

You can buy your tickets at the train station, but it's more convenient to queue on the day of, or before, departure at the railway ticket office in town. The office is open daily from 10 am to 1 pm and 3 to 6 pm – look for the small train sign on the side of an apartment block, north of the local bus station.

**Jeep** Reflecting the relative wealth of the populace, public shared jeeps are a common form of transport. Jeeps regularly go to Darkhan, Bulgan (T1000) and, when there's enough demand, Sükhbaatar and Ulaan Baatar. Shared jeeps, and ones for charter, congregate at the market, or in front of the department store along the main street.

The good but unpaved road between Erdenet and Darkhan (180km) will become fully paved with the help of a loan from, of all countries, Kuwait. The road between Erdenet and Bulgan city (68km) is unsealed and rough – or you could go via Bugat. Ulaan Baatar is 371km from Erdenet.

## URAN UUL & TOGOO UUL
УРАН УУЛ & ТОГОО УУЛ
About 60km directly west of Bulgan city are the extinct volcanoes of Uran and Togoo, now part of the 1600 hectare Uran-Togoo Tulga Mountain Natural Reserve in the *sum* of Khutar-Öndör (Хутар-Өндөр). You will have to hire a jeep from Bulgan city, and then find a trail to the top.

## MOGOD UUL
МОГОД УУЛ
At an altitude of 2139m, Mogod mountain is one of the highest peaks in the Bulgan aimag. There may be some sort of ger camp at the

---

### 1996 Fires
For several months in the middle of 1996, 14 of the 18 aimags were seriously affected by nearly 400 forest fires. In the hardest hit areas of Töv, Khövsgöl and Arkhangai, about 27 people died and nearly 600,000 precious livestock were killed throughout the country.

Tragically, the fires were almost certainly caused by human negligence: hunters smoking marmots out of their holes, nomads who had not extinguished their campfires properly, or children playing with matches. The disaster was prolonged by the country's severe lack of infrastructure to cope (for example, there are only four functioning helicopters in the country), vast distances, lack of qualified firefighters (90,000 professionals were brought in from Russia, Japan and the US) and delayed summer rains.

An estimated one-quarter (about 80,000 sq km) of the country's forests were destroyed. But from what we saw, the grass (fodder for so many animals) had grown back quickly, so there is some hope that Mongolia can recover. ■

base, but don't count on it. The peak is on the border of the two *sums*, Mogod and Khishig-Öndör (Хишиг-Өндөр). Access to the area is difficult.

## EG TARVAGTAIN BILCHER
### ЭГ ТАРВАГТАИН БИЛУЭР
This is a scenic area of rivers, forests and mountains, suitable for hiking and camping, though there are no tourist camps as yet. It is in the Teshig (Тэшиг) *sum*. Access roads are very poor in this region.

## KHOGNO KHAN UUL
### ХОГНО ХАН УУЛ
In the southernmost *sum* of Gurvanbulag (Гурванбулаг), near the border with Övörkhangai aimag, is the 1967m peak of Khogno Khan Uul. Nearby, there are ruins of some monasteries, destroyed by the armies of Jungar Galdan Bochigtu in the late 17th century – but you'll need a guide to find them.

Buses (T2090) travel from Ulaan Baatar on Monday and Friday to Gurvanbulag's capital, Avzaga (Авзага). From there to the mountain, it is a long and tough trek on foot or by horse.

# Khövsgöl Хөвсгөл

**Population:** 120,100
**Area:** 101,000 sq km
**Capital:** Mörön
**No of Sums:** 20
**Elevation of Capital City:** 1283m
**Main Livestock & Crops:** horse, cattle, sheep; hay
**Ethnic Groups:** Khalkh, Buryat, Tsaatan, Uriankhai, Darkhad

The northernmost aimag in the country, Khövsgöl is – with the possible exception of Arkhangai – the most scenic. This is a land of tall evergreen taiga forest, crystal-clear lakes, icy streams and lush grass. It does rain a lot during summer, but this only adds to the scenery: rainbows hang over the meadows dotted with white gers and grazing horses and yaks. The rivers abound with fish, especially in the south where five main rivers converge.

The aimag is dominated by the magnificent Khövsgöl Nuur, the highlight of the province and one of the most scenic spots in Mongolia. The lake is surrounded by several peaks near 3000m high, and to the west, there is the Darkhadyn Khotgor depression with plentiful forests and lakes. In this region, around Tsagaannuur, live the fascinating Tsaatan whose lives revolve around the domesticated reindeer.

## MÖRÖN
### МӨРӨН
This rather scruffy aimag capital of 28,000 is cooler than most Mongolian cities, and has relatively few gers because nearby forests supply abundant timber. Mörön (which means 'river') has few sights, but you may need to hang around here before you head to Khövsgöl Nuur or Tsagaannuur.

### Orientation & Information
The grey building north-east of the square is the Daatgal Bank. It will change only US dollars cash, between 9 am and 4 pm on weekdays, and from 9 am to noon on Saturdays. You may also have to buy MIAT tickets there.

The Hubsgul Travel Company (☎ 57 137; fax 324 620) is the only travel agency in Mörön or the Khövsgöl Nuur region. It can organise fishing, horse riding and jeep tours, and trekking trips around the lake and to the Tsaatan people. Seemingly well organised and with English-speaking staff, the office is immediately north of the square – there is a sign in English above the door.

### Museum
Given the variety of wildlife in the aimag, stuffed animals are, not surprisingly, the main feature of the museum. The collection includes a moose, an elk, a lynx, an ibex, an argali sheep, a wolf, a wild boar, a duck, a seagull and even a vulture. There's a large tusk from a woolly mammoth, but you won't see one of those – they haven't inhabited this region for over 40,000 years. Photos of the Tsaatan are also intriguing.

The museum is open from 9 am to 6 pm

every day but Monday, costs T500 to enter and is located about 100m west of the Ider Hotel. The depressing little zoo at the back has been thankfully removed.

### Danzandarjaa Khiid
Данзандаржаа Хийд

The monastery's history is unclear, but the original (Möröngiin Khüree) was built around 1890 and was home to 2000 monks. It was rebuilt, opened in June 1990, and now has 20 monks of all ages. It's a charming place, designed in the shape of a concrete ger, and contains a great collection of thangkas.

The monastery is just back from the main road, on the way to the airport. Visitors are always welcome.

### Places to Stay

**Camping** Mörön is not a great place to camp, so head up to Khövsgöl Nuur or into the countryside, as soon as you can. If you are hanging around for a lift, and want to camp, walk to the south-west of the town, and camp near the Delger Mörön river.

Twenty-seven km before Mörön, on the road to Bulgan city, a tiny, unmapped and unnamed lake is perfect for camping.

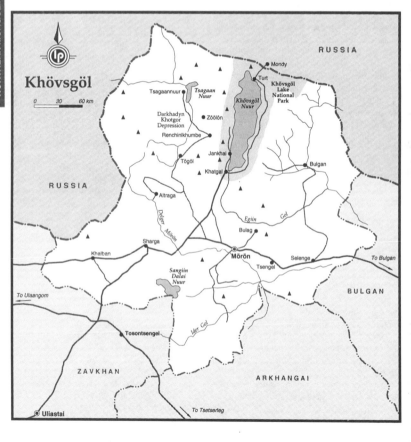

## Davaadorj

It seems that every aimag needs a local hero, and Khövsgöl gets Davaadorj. Unlike most heroes, he didn't fight in the 1921 revolution – he was too young. He was noted for his bravery while fighting the Japanese along Khalkhin Gol in 1939, although he must have been about 13 years old at the time.

Davaadorj didn't last long: he died in 1948, at the tender age of 22. Like Sükhbaatar, his death is a mystery. His statue now dominates the town square in Mörön. ■

**Hotels** Few people hang around Mörön. Consequently, all hotels are pretty dismal, or closed.

The cheapest place is unnamed, so we have called it the *Truck Drivers' Hotel*. Basic dorm-style accommodation costs from T500 to T800 per person. The hotel is the white, unsigned place with a yellow door, east of the market. Also in this price range (if you can find anyone working there), are a few rooms in the same building as the Hubsgul Travel Company.

The *Delger Mörön Hotel* (Дэлг зр Мөрөн Зочид) has some decent rooms from T2000 per person, but the toilets are often filthy and the showers nonexistent. The deluxe room, complete with ger-style furniture, TV and shower, costs a reasonable T3300 per person. If you ask firmly, they may agree to put you

up in an eight bed dorm for T1000 per person. The hotel is at the end of the street which starts north of the square.

At the time of research, the unsigned *Ider Hotel* (Идэр Зочид), 100m north-east of the square, was closed, but it planned to reopen soon and will provide a reasonable alternative.

### Places to Eat

The *Delger Mörön* has a restaurant, but it only serves the normal mutton-based dishes. The unnamed *restaurant* at the bottom of the same street as the Delger Mörön has supplies of excellent yoghurt, passable soup, and ...uggh...more mutton. The cheapest (but most unhygienic choice) is the *guanz* (canteen) at the market. The market has a reasonable choice of canned and fresh food, and plenty of *airag*.

**NORTHERN MONGOLIA**

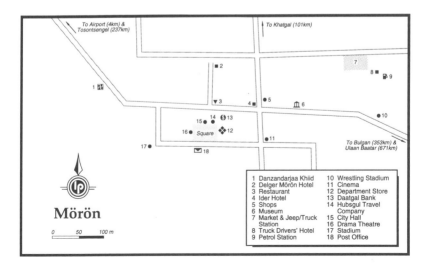

To Airport (4km) & Tosontsengel (237km)

To Khatgal (101km)

To Bulgan (353km) & Ulaan Baatar (671km)

# Mörön

0    50    100 m

| | |
|---|---|
| 1 Danzandarjaa Khiid | 10 Wrestling Stadium |
| 2 Delger Mörön Hotel | 11 Cinema |
| 3 Restaurant | 12 Department Store |
| 4 Ider Hotel | 13 Daatgal Bank |
| 5 Shops | 14 Hubsgul Travel |
| 6 Museum | Company |
| 7 Market & Jeep/Truck | 15 City Hall |
| Station | 16 Drama Theatre |
| 8 Truck Drivers' Hotel | 17 Stadium |
| 9 Petrol Station | 18 Post Office |

### Getting There & Away

**Air** There are direct flights between Ulaan Baatar and Mörön on Monday, Wednesday and Friday. Tickets, if you can get one, cost US$70. The other internal airline company, Khangard, flies to Mörön on Thursday for the same price as MIAT. Khangard can also arrange charters.

MIAT flights between Ulaan Baatar and Khovd city, and other places in the west, often stop at Mörön to refuel, so you can combine a trip to the west with Khövsgöl Nuur.

MIAT may schedule some infrequent flights between Mörön and Turt, at the northern end of Khövsgöl Nuur, but, like anything to do with MIAT, don't get too excited.

The Mörön airport is about 4km from the centre of town. You will have to charter a jeep there, or go on the crowded bus. The MIAT office is officially at the airport, but the staff may tell you to buy your ticket at the Daatgal Bank in town. If you don't have any luck at the MIAT office or the bank, try the Hubsgul Travel Company, where some staff speak English. Buy your ticket as soon as you can, and get to the airport in plenty of time. The dreaded Mongolian Scramble may well eventuate – this is a popular flight, as one traveller found out:

In Mörön, there were at least 24 people waiting for the 17-seater plane to Ulaan Baatar. We waited at the airport terminal door with a friendly hostess who identified our plane. The minute she gave us the go-ahead we sprinted across the tarmac, and flung our cases in the cabin, followed by a stampede of locals.

**Bus** Only one bus runs between Mörön and Khatgal every Friday (T800). From Ulaan Baatar, buses to Mörön leave Monday, Wednesday, Thursday and Saturday for T4700, and take around 25 hours. Buses come and go from the jeep and truck station at the market.

**Jeep** If there is enough demand, a public shared jeep may leave Mörön to places in the west, or to Khatgal, but they normally only go to Ulaan Baatar (T7000 per person). An announcement over the loudspeaker (in Mongolian, and distorted) will be made at the market when a jeep is planning to go somewhere. Otherwise, ask around at the jeep/truck station at the market.

If you are travelling by jeep between Khatgal and the western road towards Ulaangom and Uliastai, it is vital to note that you should go back to Mörön and take the main road to the west from there. We tried a direct, south-western route from Khatgal (bypassing Mörön) and had to drive across a branch of the Delger Mörön river – we got stuck, and very nearly drowned while sitting in the jeep.

Mörön is 273km north-east of Tosontsengel in Zavkhan aimag – it's a pretty road (albeit wet and mountainous) with plenty of marmots to entertain you. We even saw some wolves, foxes and hawks. It is 353km to Bulgan city (there are plenty of guanzes along the way), and 671km to Ulaan Baatar.

**Hitching** The Ulaan Baatar-Bulgan-Mörön road is fairly busy, so hitching a ride shouldn't be a problem. But be warned: the trip by truck between Ulaan Baatar and Mörön is a *very* tough 30 non-stop hours (expect to pay T5000 for a lift). Some travellers do it one way for the 'experience'; and then gratefully fly back.

To get any information about hitching a ride from Mörön, hang around the jeep/truck station, the Truck Drivers' Hotel (it's worth staying there if you are hitching) or the petrol station about 100m away.

### KHÖVSGÖL NUUR
ХӨВСГӨЛ НУУР

Try to imagine a 2760 sq km alpine lake, with water so pure you can drink it. Then add dozens of mountains 2000m high or more, thick pine forests and lush meadows with grazing yaks and horses, and you have a vague impression of Khövsgöl Nuur, Mongolia's top scenic attraction. In surface area, this is the second-largest lake (125km long and 30km wide) in Mongolia, surpassed in size only by Uvs Nuur, a shallow, salty lake in the western part of the country.

Khövsgöl Nuur is the deepest lake (up to 262m) in Central Asia, and the 14th-largest source of fresh water – containing between 1 and 2% of the world's fresh water. The lake is sacred to local Mongolians, who refer to it as 'Mother'. It is full of fish, such as lennok and sturgeon, and the area is home to argali sheep, ibex, bear and moose, as well as over 200 species of birds. The region also hosts three separate, unique peoples: Darkhad Mongols, Buryats and Tsaatan.

An amazing 90 rivers flow *into* the lake, while only one river flows *out* – the Egiin Gol, which flows into the Selenge Gol and finally reaches Lake Baikal in Siberia. The lake is now part of the Khövsgöl Lake National Park (established in 1986). Of its 838,000 hectares, 251,000 are forest (though some of the trees around the lake are now stumps.)

If you have been to Lake Baikal (only 195km to the north-east of Khövsgöl Nuur), you will see a lot of similarities with the scenery, lake and people. Baikal is the world's deepest (1500m), oldest (50 million years) and one of the largest in terms of water volume.

Khövsgöl Nuur freezes in winter (and may not completely thaw out until early June) with 120cm of ice, allowing huge trucks carrying fuel to cross from Siberia. This practice was officially prohibited in the 1980s (but still continues today) when it was realised that leaking oil from the trucks was polluting the lake.

Speleologists (cave explorers) are also interested in the area. There are numerous caves around the lake, though finding these in the thick forests will require a guide, considerable time and a lot of luck. Visitors also come to fish, swim in the icy water, watch the ducks, seagulls and other birdlife, hike or horse-back ride along the shoreline, or just find a comfortable spot to stay and soak in all the fresh air and natural beauty.

The best time to visit the lake is in spring (around April and May), when it rains less and the flowers and birdlife are often at their best – but it will still be very cold (there will be plenty of snow on the ground), and the

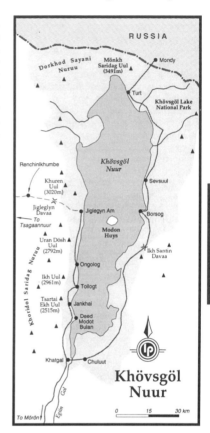

Khövsgöl
Nuur

0      15      30 km

lake may still be frozen. The summer (around July and August) is a little more crowded (not so much that it would spoil your trip), but it can still be cold, and it often rains.

**Permits**

On the main road a few km before Khatgal, you'll be required to pay an entrance fee at a gate to the Khövsgöl Lake National Park. The cost is T1000 per night for foreigners, and T300 for a vehicle driven by a Mongolian, but T3000 if driven by a foreigner. You'll be asked how long you intend to stay in the park, which is not always easy to estimate. If you are staying in a ger camp, or horseback riding to Tsagaannuur, you may want to stay two weeks or more. In addition, you may have to pay for a fishing permit and a video permit, the latter costing a whopping T5000 for every minute of film used!!

At the gate, you may be given a nicely typed pamphlet explaining the permits and the attractions of the lake. Unfortunately, it is written in Mongolian.

### Western Shore

From Khatgal, a reasonable road (across some initial dry river beds) goes for about 25km before you receive your first magical glimpse of the lake at **Deed Modot Bulan** (Дээд Модот Булан). The road continues past the gorgeous areas called **Jankhai** (Жанхаи) and **Toilogt** (Тоилогт), where there are some ger camps. The road then gets gradually worse. Very few vehicles venture past Toilogt, so no road maintenance is deemed necessary.

A jeep can carry on to **Jiglegyn Am** (Жиглэгын Ам), almost exactly halfway up the western shore, before the trail disappears into mud and forest. No vehicle can go further north, or along the western horse trail from Jiglegyn Am to Renchinlkhumbe, on the way to Tsagaannuur. There is no need to go past Toilogt by jeep, because there are plenty of agreeable, secluded and accessible camping sites between Deed Modot Bulan and Toilogt.

### Eastern Shore

The eastern shore is not as good because the road rarely hugs the lake, the scenery isn't as pretty, there are only a handful of gers between Chuluut and Borsog, almost no wildlife, and the flies can be appalling. If that doesn't put you off, it might if we said that this is the worse stretch of road we encountered in 15,000km of overland travel! There are some plans to improve the trail: we saw chain gangs of prisoners busily building pretty bridges which are likely to collapse after the first decent rain or heavy vehicle.

From Khatgal, head for the bridge over the Egiin Gol, where you may need to ask

directions. The trail meanders over some hills and past a collection of huts known as **Chuluut** (Чулуут) – if in doubt, follow the line of electricity poles. The trail continues past an interesting ovoo at **Ikh Santin Davaa** (Их Сантин Даваа) pass to a gorgeous spot called **Borsog** (Борсог ), six hours by jeep, and 103km, from Khatgal.

There are apparently some plans to establish a ger camp at Borsog, but this is very unlikely until the road improves. With a tent and your own food, you could have a lovely time in Borsog picking wildflowers, swimming, hiking and fishing. Just a few yaks, and a ger with a slightly loony family, for neighbours.

If your back hasn't suffered permanent damage by now, you could carry on further to a couple of gers known as **Sevsuul** (Сэвсуул). The road actually improves a little here, then hugs the lake and is usually passable all the way to Turt. Surprisingly, a few sand dunes dot the landscape. From Khatgal, allow at least 12 hours by jeep to travel the 200 or so km to Turt.

Remember that if you reach Turt, you will have to come *all* the way back along the same bone-crunching, eastern road: there is no way any vehicle could get from Turt to Jiglegyn Am, halfway up the western shore. At the moment going all the way around the lake is only possible by boat or horse.

### Activities

**Hiking** Hiking is one of the best ways to see the lake and the mountains surrounding it. You will need to be self-sufficient, though there are a few gers in the area to buy some meat or dairy products. The trails around the lake are easy to follow, or just hug the shoreline as much as you can.

Around the mountains in the southwestern (ie most accessible) region, hiking is excellent around Tsartai Ekh Uul (2515m), immediately west of Jankhai. Also, try the numerous other mountains in the Khoridol Saridag Nuruu range, such as Khuren Uul (3020m), not far north of the trail to Renchinlkhumbe; Ikh Uul (2961m), a little

Top: Two-humped Bactrian camels at a camel-breeding station in the Gobi Desert.
Bottom: A woman inside a tourist ger at Terelj, an area of magnificent alpine scenery in Töv.

Top: Tourist gers at Terelj in Töv, a popular destination for travellers.
Bottom Left: Ger doors face south and are always brightly painted.
Bottom Right: A child riding a yak near Khövsgöl lake.

north-west of Toilogt; and Uran Dösh Uul volcano (2792m).

Longer treks are possible around the Dorkhod Sayani Nuruu range, which has many peaks over 3000m. It is right on the border of Russia, so be careful.

Alternatively, inquire with travel agents in Mörön, Ulaan Baatar or in your own country regarding organised treks. These are naturally more expensive but are probably the best way to see specific wildlife, scenery and traditional people.

**Kayaking** Travelling by kayak would allow you to see the lake without the strain of driving along the appalling roads. The lake is full of glorious little coves for camping and fishing, there are a staggering 91 rivers connected to the lake to explore, and you could even check out the only island, **Modon Huys**, almost exactly in the middle of the lake. One agency (see below) is starting to organise kayaking trips.

**Horse & Yak Riding** All ger camps can arrange horse riding for guests and any other foreigner willing to pay high tourist prices. Expect to pay a ridiculous T2750 or more per hour for a horse from a ger camp, or from a normal ger near a tourist camp. If you ask someone who is not used to tourists (hard to find around the south-west part of the lake), you should be able to get a horse for T2750 per *day*. For serious long-distance riding, arrange things in Khatgal – refer to the Getting Around section below for details.

If you want something really different, challenging and uncomfortable, the Jankhai Resort can arrange some yak riding for about T1650 per hour.

**Fishing** If you love fishing, then you'll get excited about Khövsgöl Nuur. Bring your own fishing gear, or beg, borrow or steal some – there is nowhere in the country to rent anything. A rod would be better, but we had considerable success with a handline and a simple lure. You can fish from headlands along the shore, from bridges or, if you are keen, wade into the lake for a few metres.

After weeks of fatty mutton you'll be desperate for some fish – incredibly, none of the guanzes or restaurants in the aimag serve it.

Some of the best spots we found were the bridge at Khatgal (which leads to the road going up the eastern shore), Borsog, and at several coves where the eastern road meets the south-east shore, which we named 'Plague of Flies Cove' I and II for obvious reasons. Around 10 types of fish inhabit the lake, including salmon, (bony) sturgeon and lennok.

### Organised Tours
Almost every travel agency in Ulaan Baatar and overseas includes a trip to the lake in their programmes. Most, however, offer little more than a stay in a ger camp for a couple of days, and nothing more exciting than a few hours on a horse.

A few of the agencies organising something a little different are listed below. (Refer to the Ulaan Baatar and Getting There & Away chapters for details of these agencies.)

Boojum Expeditions, a US-based company, offers well-run kayaking and horse riding trips.
Mongolian Adventure Tours has interesting trekking and horse-riding trips around the lake, and fishing tours.
Mongol Tour OK runs pony treks around the lake, sometimes looking for shaman relics.
Nomads arranges jeep tours to the lake, via the magnificent Terkhiin Tsagaan Nuur in Arkhangai aimag, and visits to the Tsaatan people by horse.

### Places to Stay
**Camping** Khövsgöl Nuur is possibly the best place in Mongolia to camp. No-one owns any land, so pitch your tent anywhere you want (preferably a little way from ger camps and other gers). Also, the water is endless and drinkable; there are plenty of fish; and the hiking is outstanding. On the down side, it often rains in summer and flies abound.

The best camping spots on the western shoreline are anywhere between Deed Modot Bulan and Ongolog (Онг олог), 10km north of Toilogt. Any further north is unnecessary because the road gets bad, and transport is rare. If you have your own jeep, and want to experience one of the worst roads in Mongolia, the best spot to camp on the eastern shoreline is at Borsog.

**Hotels** There are currently no hotels on or near the lake, but this might soon change. All accommodation is in ger camps, though the Jankhai Resort (see below) is the closest thing to a hotel in the region.

**Ger Camps** There are several ger camps in stunning locations on the western shore (none on the east). These ger camps have no running water or sewerage – pit toilets and 'outdoor plumbing' only – but they do have electricity. Most places will offer a lower price if you don't take meals there, so you can save money (and probably eat better) by bringing and cooking your own food.

At Deed Modot Bulan, just after the road meets the lake for the first time, the *Deed Modot Bulan Ger Camp* (it has no name, so we named it) is in a majestic location on a headland, surrounded by pine trees. Part of the main resort at Jankhai, a night in one of the six gers costs US$30 per person including meals.

From there, it is another 5km to the *Jankhai Resort*, which has the best range of good-value accommodation on the lake. Although on the western side of the road, the setting is excellent and it is still only less than 100m to the shore. At the time of research, no gers were set up, but there may be some later. Large, comfortable rooms in a wooden hotel cost US$30/15 per person with/without meals. Simple rooms without meals for US$5 to US$10 are good value.

Another 5km north of Jankhai, two other ger camps are set up at Toilogt, around two lovely, tiny lakes immediately adjacent to the larger Khövsgöl Nuur. *Toilogt I* (named by us, again) is run by the Hubsgul Travel Company (in Mörön) and costs US$30 per person including meals – look for the sign in English on the main road.

The other one, *Toilogt II*, is set up on an isthmus linking the two tiny lakes – follow the main road a little further north of Toilogt I

camp. This second camp is co-run by Juulchin. Wooden gers, and normal felt ones, cost US$35/20 per person with/without meals.

### Getting There & Away
**Air** Khatgal has a dirt runway, often rendered unusable when it rains heavily. There are no scheduled air services to Khatgal, only a few chartered flights (maximum of 30 people) from Mörön.

MIAT may also fly between Mörön and Turt; they offered us a price (US$30) but no schedule.

**Bus** A bus runs between Khatgal and Mörön once a week only – on Friday (T800).

**Jeep** Occasionally, a public shared jeep (about T2000 per person) may leave Mörön for Khatgal – but don't count on it. A chartered jeep is probably the best way to get to Khatgal and back. You could waste precious days waiting for a lift or a bus when you should be enjoying the lake.

A chartered jeep should not cost more than the normal T130 per km and, with some bargaining, you may be able to get it for a little less, perhaps T10,000 per jeep one way. The other option is to ask other travellers in Mörön if they want to share a jeep. Khatgal is a rough 101km from Mörön – allow about three hours.

**Hitching** Every one or two days, a truck, specifically for passengers, will travel between Mörön and Khatgal for about T1000 per person. For lifts from Mörön, hang around the market, the Truck Drivers' Hotel or the petrol station – and keep asking. In Khatgal, most trucks will stop in front of the post office.

### Getting Around
**Jeep** The Hubsgul Travel Company in Mörön can organise a chartered jeep for about T220 per km, or a negotiable US$40 to $50 for a one-way trip to their ger camp at Toilogt. If you are prepared to wait and haggle, you can get a jeep in Mörön for about

T130 per km. In the peak season of July and August, it may be difficult to charter a jeep for a reasonable price. It is also important to find a reliable jeep which can handle the terrible roads.

The lake may only be 125km long, but the road meanders considerably, especially along the eastern shore. From Khatgal to Turt, which is not at the top of the lake, it is about 200km. You need to be aware of this if you are chartering a jeep by the km.

**Boat** Most ger camps can arrange the rental of a boat for high tourist prices. The Jankhai Resort charges T2750 per person per hour, and the Juulchin camp at Toilogt claims to have a boat which costs T5500 per person per hour.

A large cargo/passenger boat called the *Sükhbaatar* used to travel the length of the lake between Khatgal and Turt, but at the time of research it could only be chartered at negotiable prices. In Ulaan Baatar, one foreign travel agent was quoted US$60 for the whole boat between Khatgal and Turt; in Khatgal, we were quoted T1000 per person, with a minimum of 20 people, for the same trip.

The post office in Khatgal seems to be the best place to start negotiating. If you charter the *Sükhbaatar*, you'll still have to share it with a boatload of nonpaying passengers who have been waiting for some tourist or trader to fork out the money.

**Hitching** There is no public transport around the lake, so without a jeep you'll have to hitch or hike. Hitching a ride from Khatgal to Jankhai or Toilogt wouldn't be difficult in summer, but you'll probably end up paying a fair bit for a lift anyway.

Hitching around the lake as far as Toilogt (on the western shore) and Borsog (on the eastern shore) is not impossible. If you are self-sufficient with tents and food, then you can wait a day or three for something suitable to come along.

**Horse** The only place to organise a horse trek around the lake is at Khatgal. Go to the

unnamed hotel in Khatgal and tell them that you want a horse and, if necessary, a guide and saddle. The folk at the hotel are becoming used to travellers and understand their requirements; they can arrange everything within 24 hours. Prices are negotiable, of course, but expect to pay about T1500 per horse per day, and about T2000 per day for a guide. You would pay a lot more at a ger camp.

One Swiss couple we met left their guide in the middle of nowhere and rode their horses back to Khatgal on their own, because the guide was always drunk. Another thing to keep in mind is that guides will expect you to provide the food.

A return trip by horse from Khatgal to Tsagaannuur, and a visit to the Tsaatan people, will take from 10 to 12 days. You can get from Khatgal to Renchinlkhumbe, or even Tsagaannuur, without a guide if you're experienced and speak Mongolian, but to find the Tsaatan you will definitely need a guide. In any event, a guide is recommended for any trips by horse in the region.

### Khatgal
Хатгал

As the southern gateway to Khövsgöl Nuur, Khatgal is the largest town on the lake. It is usually ignored by visitors who just go straight through the town on the way to a ger camp or camping spot. The town looks neglected these days and the facilities are poor. It is on a tiny inlet, so you don't get any impression of the enormous size of the lake from here.

**Places to Stay & Eat** If you have a tent and are hanging around for a lift to the lake or to Mörön, you can camp along the shores of the Egiin Gol in the middle of town, as long as the town drunk doesn't know you're there.

The only hotel in town has no name, so we called it the *No-Name Hotel*. Large, comfortable rooms cost T700 per person, but bring your own sleeping bag because the sheets are dirty and it is always cold. The staff can rustle up some mutton and noodle soup, or will cook your fish if you've been lucky.

(We caught some fish from the bridge nearby.) The hotel is near the sign for the (closed) guanz, opposite the first Chinggis Khaan poster on the main road from Mörön.

For some reason, someone installed public showers in Khatgal – look for the sign in English from the main road. There is no hot water, but if you don't want a swim in the lake or river, cold showers are available. Food supplies in Khatgal are very limited, so stock up in Mörön or Ulaan Baatar.

**Getting There & Away** All road transport to and from Khatgal stops at the large vacant area just in front of the post office, near the large statue which you can see from the main road. See Getting There & Away under Khövsgöl Nuur for more details about transport to/from Khatgal.

### Turt
Турт

Turt (often called Khank – Ханк – which is the name of the *sum*) is the village on the north-east shore of Khövsgöl Nuur, connected by the appalling eastern road from Khatgal. Turt is more Buryat and Russian than Mongolian, because it is closer to its northern neighbour than to Ulaan Baatar. Don't stray too far from Turt; nearby is the Russian border, where smugglers can get arrested or shot.

There is nowhere to stay or eat, so you will have to be completely self-sufficient.

### TSAGAANNUUR
Цагааннуур

About 50km west of Khövsgöl Nuur, in Renchinlkhumbe (Рэнчинлхумбэ) *sum*, is a large depression called Darkhadyn Khotgor, often referred to as Tsagaannuur (White Lake), after the main village in the area. This is one of the best-watered regions in Mongolia; the aimag has about 300 lakes, over 200 of them in this area alone. The difficulty in reaching the region ensures that the unique Tsaatan people who inhabit the valleys are able to continue with their traditional lifestyle – but tourism is slowly making an impact.

The lakes are a vital part of Mongolia's very limited commercial fishing industry – white carp and trout are packed in salt and flown out to Ulaan Baatar to be served in the fancier hotels. Salmon can be found in the rivers and are a big hit with the local bears. One definite drawback to visiting the region is the insects which invade the area. Be warned: these little critters have insatiable appetites for foreign skin and will ruin your trip if you are not fully prepared with mosquito nets and repellent.

### Permits

Tsagaannuur and the region inhabited by the Tsaatan is not part of the Khövsgöl Lake National Park. However, one traveller in 1995 (when permits in the countryside were required) reported real hassles with local police – but in 1996 we heard of no such problems:

---

**The Tsaatan**
Not far from Khövsgöl Nuur live the Tsaatan people, named from the Mongolian word for reindeer, *tsaa*. Their entire existence is based on the reindeer, which provides milk, skins for clothes, transport and, occasionally, meat.

The Tsaatan are part of a Tuvan ethnic group which inhabits nearby Russia, and they speak a Turkic language, different to Mongolian. There are only about 200 Tsaatan people, spread over 100,000 sq km of northern Mongolia. They are extremely nomadic, often moving their small encampments (called *ail*) every two or three weeks while looking for special types of grass and moss loved by the reindeer. The Tsaatan do not use gers, preferring tents made from reindeer skin.

Visiting the Tsaatan people is truly difficult and exhausting. Also, the mosquitoes are legendary and the climate is exceedingly harsh, so the handful of tourists who currently make the effort have a negligible effect on the Tsaatan people and the environment. But anthropologists are worried about the negative impact of increasing tourism. ■

My interpreter brought me to a friend of her sister's. We were just sitting down to a nice cup of tea when enters the local policeman who confiscates my passport and then demands that I pay a fine because one is supposed to get a permit from the police in Mörön to go to Tsagaannuur because it is close to the Soviet border. They assume that travellers have psychic abilities and are supposed to know this... He tells me that it costs T5000 per day just for permission to visit the Tsaatan people....'

**Heidi Heinzerling, USA**

Authorities in Ulaan Baatar are currently considering a plan to limit the effects of tourism on the Tsaatan by implementing a permit system. These permits are likely to be expensive and only available to organised tour groups.

At the time of research, there were no restrictions on travelling to Tsagaannuur, but this may change in the future. It is best to check with the police in Mörön before starting the long trek out there.

### Places to Stay

There is a tiny hotel in Tsagaannuur, but it was closed at the time of research Until it reopens, you'll have to take a tent. Make sure there are no holes, otherwise those miserable little biting midges will turn you into a screaming lunatic. Bring all your own food; there are plenty of lakes and rivers with fresh water and fish in the area.

### Getting There & Away

**Air** Tiny, chartered planes can land at the dirt runway at Tsagaannuur, but it will still take a couple of days on horseback to reach the Tsaatan. Khangard airlines occasionally flies to Tsagaannuur – it may be worth ringing them.

Staff from foreign embassies and development agencies in Ulaan Baatar sometimes take a helicopter directly to the Tsaatan encampments, and land there like some spacecraft from outer space.

**Jeep** By chartered jeep, you can get to Tsagaannuur from Mörön (but not from Khatgal) in a bone-crunching 12 to 15 hours, depending on the state of the road. You will

have to negotiate hard and long. There are no scheduled public, shared jeeps to Tsagaannuur.

**Hitching** Traffic between Mörön and Tsagaannuur is extremely sparse, but if you have your own tent and food, and don't mind waiting for a day or two, something may come along during summer. But getting from Tsagaannuur to the Tsaatan settlements can only be done on foot or by horse – and with a reliable guide.

**Horse** There is really only one way to get to Tsagaannuur and, particularly, to visit the Tsaatan: by horse. It is best to arrange things at Khatgal.

From Khatgal to Jiglegyn Am, about halfway up the western shore of Khövsgöl Nuur, will take three leisurely days (about four hours riding each day). From Jiglegyn Am, there are several easy-to-follow horse trails to Renchinlkhumbe – just make sure you are heading west. You will need to allow two days to get from Jiglegyn Am and over the Jiglegyn Davaa pass (2500m). From the pass, the trail is easy to Renchinlkhumbe, and then it heads north-west to Tsagaannuur. From Tsagaannuur, it will probably still take a couple of days to reach some Tsaatan encampments.

A trip from Khatgal to Tsagaannuur and back, including a visit to the Tsaatan, will take from 10 to 12 days. You could go directly from Khatgal to Tsagaannuur on an easy trail, bypassing Jiglegyn Am, in about five days, but your back would not appreciate the hard ride, and you wouldn't see the magnificent Khövsgöl Nuur.

The region is lush and rain is common, so you will have no problems finding enough grass and water to satisfy your horse. There are plenty of gers along the way at which to buy some milk, butter and meat – otherwise, bring your food from Mörön.

### TARIALAN
ТАРИАЛАН

The *sum* of Tarialan, on the border of northeast Khövsgöl aimag and Russia, is particularly wet. Our guide assured us that pike, and other fish, from the Khokh, Arig and Artag Kheven rivers are just begging to be caught. The Hubsgul Travel Company in Mörön organises trips to the best fishing spots in the area.

## FIVE RIVERS

About 50km south of Mörön, on the border with the Arkhangai aimag, is an area where the Ider, Bugsei, Selenge, Delger Mörön and Chuluut rivers converge. Here, our guide *definitely* assured us that the fish, especially in September and October, will jump into your frypan before you can find your fishing line. It wasn't *quite* that easy, but we were very successful.

---

# Selenge  Сэлэнгэ

---

**Population:** 102,900
**Area:** 42,800 sq km
**Capital:** Sükhbaatar
**No of Sums:** 17
**Elevation of Capital City:** 626m
**Main Livestock & Crops:** potatoes, hay, wheat, fruit
**Ethnic Groups:** Khalkh, Buryat, Dorvod, Oold, Russian

Selenge is the first – or last – aimag seen by train travellers shuttling between Ulaan Baatar and Russia. There is not a lot to attract visitors to Selenge except the majestic, but remote, Amarbayasgalant monastery.

Buryats, Kazaks, Russians and even Chinese live in wooden huts in villages hugging the rail line and the main road which both bisect the aimag. They look after some of the 300,000 hectares of grains, fruits and vegetables. Many others live in Darkhan, Mongolia's second-largest city. In the south-east, the open-pit coal mine at Sharyn Gol produces about two million tons of coal each year to provide electricity for the Erdenet mine in Bulgan aimag.

The mighty Selenge Gol starts from the mountains of western Mongolia and flows into Lake Baikal in Siberia, draining nearly 300,000 sq km in both countries. The other great river, the Orkhon, meets the Selenge near the aimag capital of Sükhbaatar. Selenge aimag is one of the more famous historically: it is where 'revolutionary ideals', more recently against the Chinese, often seem to have sprouted.

## Organised Tours

The only travel agency to organise tours

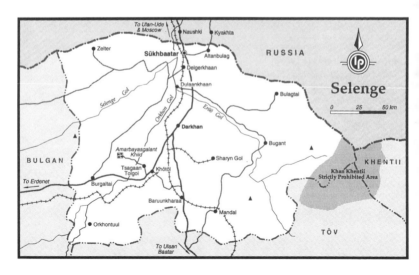

around Selenge aimag is Bumbat Ord (see the Ulaan Baatar chapter). It runs imaginative trips by train and jeep, visiting horse-breeding families, a bow and arrow factory and Altanbulag; and you may even get a chance to ride on one of two known boats in the whole of Mongolia – a patrol boat along the Selenge Gol (the other boat is on Khövsgöl Nuur lake).

Incredibly, no foreign or local travel agency arranges tours to the Amarbayasgalant monastery.

## SÜKHBAATAR
СУХБААТАР

Near the junction of the Selenge and Orkhon rivers, the capital of Selenge aimag, Sükhbaatar, was founded in the 1940s. Although Mongolia's chief border town, it is a quiet, pleasant place with about 20,000 people. There is little reason to stay, however, unless you want to break up the train journey to or from Russia, you want to save money by travelling on local trains rather than on the more expensive international train, or you are smuggling.

### Orientation & Information

Just north of the train station is the centre of town, where the main hotel, market and town square are. The daily market, behind the Selenge Hotel, is lively and friendly and, as a border town, well stocked. The cold fizzy drinks and *khuurshuur* at a building at the back of the market are recommended. The hills north-east of the square look great for hiking, but don't go too far because Russia is only a few km away.

### Money

When the international train arrives and stops for an hour or two, a few money-changers come out of the woodwork. They will change Mongolian tögrögs, US dollars and Russian roubles. Otherwise, the bank, which is open during normal banking hours, which is not when the train normally arrives, is in a round, orange building just south of the train station.

If you are leaving Mongolia, get rid of your tögrögs – they are worthless anywhere

in Russia (including on the Trans-Mongolian train in Russia).

### Places to Stay

**Camping** Selenge aimag is particularly pleasant for camping. At Sükhbaatar, the best place to try is across the train line, and among the fields, just west of town. Alternatively, there are great spots among the hills north-east of the market.

**Hotels** Probably the best place in town is the *Selenge Hotel* (Сэлэнг э Зочид), a yak's spit

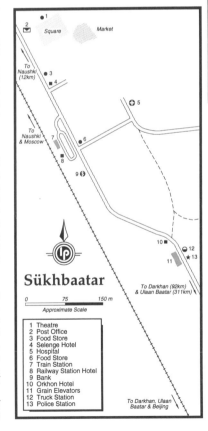

**Sükhbaatar**

```
0        75        150 m
Approximate Scale
```

1  Theatre
2  Post Office
3  Food Store
4  Selenge Hotel
5  Hospital
6  Food Store
7  Train Station
8  Railway Station Hotel
9  Bank
10 Orkhon Hotel
11 Grain Elevators
12 Truck Station
13 Police Station

from the railway station. Musty and dark rooms with a toilet (but little or no running water) go for T6000 per person.

The *Orkhon Hotel* (Орхон Зочид) is in the southernmost corner of town, next to the grain elevators. These generate a lot of noise, but the rooms are nicer than at the Selenge. Beds in a dorm cost T1000 per person; individual rooms cost T5500 per person. You may have to spend half a day looking for someone who works there, and then persuade them to give you a room. The *Railway Station Hotel*, at the station, is really grotty but comparatively good value at T800 per person.

### Places to Eat

The restaurant on the ground floor of the *Selenge Hotel* serves barely edible mutton goulash and undrinkable Chinese beer. The only decent place to eat is the *guanz* above the train ticket office at the station. Here you can dine out on a reasonable mutton and noodle dish for T400, and the beer is tasty, but warm.

### Getting There & Away

**Train** Sükhbaatar is the first (or last) Mongolian stop on the regular Ulaan Baatar-Irkutsk, Ulaan Baatar-Moscow or Beijing-Moscow services. Trains stop here for two or more hours while Mongolian customs and immigration are completed. Most of the time, this takes place late at night or very early in the morning – not the best time to wander around Sükhbaatar. Refer to the Trans-Mongolian Railway section in the Getting There & Away chapter for details about the international trains which stop in Sükhbaatar.

Direct, local trains travel between Ulaan Baatar and Sükhbaatar, with a stop at Darkhan. Tickets from Ulaan Baatar to Sükhbaatar cost T1492 for a hard seat and T3847 for a soft seat. Trains leave Ulaan Baatar every day at 10.30 am and return from Sükhbaatar at 4.15 pm.

**Taxi** The road to Ulaan Baatar (311km) through Darkhan (92km) is well paved, so jeeps are not necessary. Because of the popularity and regularity of the train, public shared taxis between Sükhbaatar and Darkhan (T1000), and onto Ulaan Baatar, are not regular, and only leave when there is enough demand.

If you want to explore the nearby countryside, the best place to hire a taxi or jeep is outside the train station.

**Hitching** Because of the regular public transport along the main road between Ulaan Baatar and Sükhbaatar, you'll get a lift pretty easily along this road. From Sükhbaatar, trucks, which congregate outside the grain elevators, could give you a lift to Ulaan Baatar – but definitely not across the Russian border.

### DULAANKHAAN
ДУЛААНХААН

This tiny village, in the *sum* of the same name and about 62km south of Sükhbaatar, is worth a stop if you have your own vehicle. Dulaankhaan is home to Mongolia's only bow and arrow factory. Bows and arrows are made from ibex, reindeer horn, bamboo and, even, fish guts. Only 20 sets (for about

---

#### The Buryats
Half of the 420,000 Russian Buryats live in Buryatia (around Lake Baikal), while many more Buryats live in northern Mongolia. Some believe that Chinggis Khaan's mother was a Buryat from near Lake Baikal, and many Buryats joined Chinggis' hordes which invaded Europe.

The Buryats have a separate language, which is not widely spoken, and there are attempts to revive the Buryatian script (written, like Mongol, from top to bottom). The Buryats have always been Buddhists (except during the communist reign), but have never fully given up their shamanist beliefs. ∎

US$400 each) are made every year because they take about four months to complete.

There is nowhere to stay in the village so carry on to Sükhbaatar or Darkhan, or camp nearby.

## ALTANBULAG
АЛТАНБУЛАГ

Just 24km to the east of Sükhbaatar is Altanbulag, a small, peaceful border town in the *sum* of the same name. Just on the other side of the border is the Russian city of Kyakhta. From the border, you can easily see the abandoned, but once opulent, Kyakhta Cathedral. The Mongolian government recently decided to allocate 500 hectares at Altanbulag as a Free Trade Zone for the development of trade with Russia. Hopefully, this will be more successful than the Free Trade Zone in Choir, in Dornogov aimag.

Altanbulag is worth a look if you have some spare time in Sükhbaatar. Don't go too close to the Mongolian border: the guards are trigger-happy. Buses run between Sükhbaatar and Altanbulag at various times during the day. There is no fixed schedule, so make local inquiries. Otherwise, charter a taxi.

At the time of research, foreigners could not cross the border by road through Altanbulag; you can take a vehicle over the border, but you have to personally go through customs on the train between Naushki and Sükhbaatar. However, there are future plans to open the road border at Altanbulag for foreigners. (Refer to the Getting There & Away section for more details.)

Both Kyakhta and Altanbulag are of some historical importance to Mongolians. In 1915 representatives from Russia, China and Mongolia met in Kyakhta to sign a treaty granting Mongolia limited autonomy. This was later revoked when China invaded again in 1919. At a meeting in Kyakhta in March 1921, the Mongolian People's Party was formed by Mongolian revolutionaries in exile, and the revolutionary hero Sükhbaatar was named minister of war.

### Sükhbaatar, the Hero

It won't take long before you wonder who Sükhbaatar is – his statue astride a horse dominates the square named after him, his face is on many currency notes and there is a provincial capital and aimag called Sükhbaatar.

Born in 1893, probably in what is now Ulaan Baatar, Sükh (which means 'axe'), as he was originally named, joined the Mongolian army in 1911. He soon became famous for his horsemanship but was forced to leave the army because of insubordination. In 1917 he joined another army, fought against the Chinese and picked up the added moniker of *baatar*, or 'hero'.

By 1921 Sükhbaatar was made commander-in-chief of the Mongolian People's Revolutionary Army, which defeated the Chinese again, and, later, the White Russians. In July of that year, he declared Mongolia's independence from China at what is now known as Sükhbaatar Square.

He packed a lot in a short life; he was dead at the age of 30. The exact cause of his death has never been known, and he did not live to see Mongolia proclaimed a republic. ∎

## DARKHAN
ДАРХАН

With a population of 90,000, Darkhan is the second-largest city in Mongolia. This city is, in fact, not part of Selenge aimag, but an autonomous municipality, Darkhan-Uul. Fortunately, Darkhan's designers put a little thought into urban planning, so the industrial smokestacks are on the south side of town and the pollution is carried away from residential areas by the relentless northern wind. The Russians designed the city in their image – from the matchbox apartment blocks to the Lenin statues. A sizeable Russian community still lives in Darkhan.

Darkhan was built in the middle of nowhere in 1961 as a satellite town to take pressure off the sprawling Ulaan Baatar, and as a northern industrial centre. Darkhan, which means 'blacksmith', is a modern, stagnant place. It is not somewhere you would rush to see, but you may need to stay here while you arrange transport to the Amarbayasgalant monastery.

If your time is limited, and you want to see

some pretty countryside, you could travel by train from Darkhan to Ulaan Baatar and return by shared taxi or bus and stay overnight in Darkhan.

## Orientation & Information

Darkhan is spread out. The city is divided into four main sections: two industrial districts (one in the north and another in the south); an old town near the train station; and a new town to the south of the old town. Near the Central Post Office in the new town is Darkhan's pride and joy: a 16 storey building, still Mongolia's tallest.

The modern Khorshoo Bank in the suburbs, just behind the museum, will change US dollars cash. You can also change US dollars and Russian roubles at the market.

Hiking in the hills directly behind the Darkhan Hotel is a pleasant diversion. The hike up to the radio relay station offers magnificent views of the whole city and surrounding area.

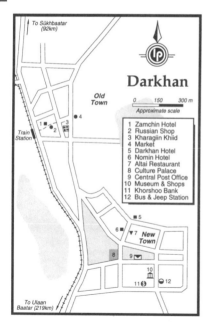

To Sükhbaatar
(92km)

**Darkhan**

Old
Town

0        150        300 m
Approximate scale

Train
Station

1 Zamchin Hotel
2 Russian Shop
3 Kharagiin Khiid
4 Market
5 Darkhan Hotel
6 Nomin Hotel
7 Altai Restaurant
8 Culture Palace
9 Central Post Office
10 Museum & Shops
11 Khorshoo Bank
12 Bus & Jeep Station

New
Town

To Ulaan
Baatar (219km)

In the unlikely event that you would call someone in Darkhan from outside Mongolia, the telephone area code for international (but not internal) calls is 37.

## Kharagiin Khiid
Харагийн Хийд

Probably the most interesting sight (but not the friendliest place) in Darkhan is the Kharagiin monastery. Housed in a pretty log cabin in the old town, the monastery has recently become very active. As elsewhere, photography is forbidden inside unless special arrangements are made. It was closed at the time of our visit, and the head monk made it known that advance notice is required if foreigners want to visit the monastery.

## Museum

The museum is grandly named the Traditional Museum of Folk Art. It contains a fairly dull collection of archaeological findings, traditional clothing and instruments and, of course, plenty of stuffed animals. Upstairs in a building in the shopping square, opposite the bus/jeep station, the museum is open between 10 am and 5 pm on weekdays and costs T500 to enter.

## Places to Stay

**Camping** Despite the size of Darkhan, it isn't hard to get away from the town and find a nearby secluded spot to camp. South of the train station are some empty fields – but get away from the drunks which hang around the station. The fields to the north of the Darkhan Hotel are also good. You can easily camp, and use the facilities in town.

**Hotels** The best place to stay is the *Zamchin Hotel* (Замчин Зочид), a friendly place where a room with clean, shared bathrooms costs T1000 per person. The hotel is in a laneway about 100m up from (and east of) the train station. You may have to knock loudly because the landlady is a little deaf, or wait awhile for her to come back from the market.

The next cheapest option is the *Nomin Hotel* (Номин Зочид), on the 5th floor of a building opposite the Altai Restaurant. A basic and noisy simple room is T1500 per person, the deluxe T3500 per person, but they may charge foreigners extra.

The *Darkhan Hotel* (Дархан Зочид) charges T5500/7700 for a pleasant simple single/double – but the attraction is a private bathroom with hot water. The deluxe at T16,500/22,000 is very good, but way too expensive. Pay for your room when you register to avoid a possible increase in the price when you check out. The hotel is a large, modern building, and not hard to find.

If you are desperate, and don't want to walk in the middle of the night to catch that damned connection to Erdenet, you could try one of the dorm beds at the train station for T700 per person. As you enter the terminal, the doors to the right lead to this grimy 'hotel'.

### Places to Eat

Easily the best place to eat in Darkhan, and one of the best in northern Mongolia, is the restaurant at the *Darkhan Hotel*. It actually has a choice (but no menu), including beefsteak and schnitzel (T800 each) – although the latter was not available when we were there. The bar also serves cold beer. The best combination is to stay at the Zamchin Hotel and eat at the Darkhan.

The only other alternative is the cheap *Altai Restaurant* (Алтаи Рэсторан), which is just down the street from the Darkhan Hotel. It has a nice decor, but nothing nice can be said about the choice of food: the only available dish is mutton, noodles and squishy, cold mashed potatoes.

The train station has a half-decent restaurant.

### Entertainment

The *Darkhan Hotel* has the town's liveliest bar, with cold drinks, while the dingiest place is just opposite the main entrance to the hotel. The *Culture Palace* shows some films, and occasionally features some wrestling. The *stadium*, just behind the Culture Palace, sometimes has archery tournaments.

### Things to Buy

Although not a shopper's paradise, Darkhan makes some of Mongolia's best leather products, including fine suede jackets, winter coats with sheepskin lining, gloves and mittens. These are mainly for export, so it is difficult to find any for sale in Darkhan.

A grocery and department store run by, and catering for, local Russians is directly opposite the Zamchin Hotel. You can stock up on vegetables and vodka, and there's even fish for those Russians who are just a little fed up with endless mutton.

The market is dusty and fairly unexciting, but you may need to go there if you want to buy food, arrange a shared taxi to Erdenet, or change some money (several money-changers will change US dollars and Russian roubles). The market is in the old town, a few hundred metres up from the train station.

### Getting There & Away

**Bus** The daily bus between Darkhan and Ulaan Baatar (T1200, five hours) is faster than the train. The bus leaves Ulaan Baatar at 8 am, and should leave Darkhan at about 1.30 pm. The road between Darkhan and Ulaan Baatar is paved and in good condition. Many guanzes along the way sell airag and basic meals.

The road between Darkhan and Sükhbaatar is one of the best in the country, but there are no scheduled buses along this route – so take the train. Surprisingly, there are also no scheduled buses between Darkhan and Erdenet – so, again, the train is your best bet. The road between Darkhan and Erdenet will be improved further with the help of some donations from Kuwait.

In Darkhan, buses stop at the bus/jeep station opposite the shopping square. Unscheduled minibuses also travel to Erdenet, Sükhbaatar and Ulaan Baatar, and are more comfortable and quicker (but dearer) than the bus or train.

**Train** Darkhan is the only railway junction in Mongolia: all northern trains to/from Ulaan Baatar, and all trains to/from Erdenet, stop here. If your time is short, and you want to see some scenery in comfort (ie in soft seat), take the train between Darkhan and Ulaan Baatar: the train travels during the day, the trip is short and the scenery is interesting in Töv (but gets a little boring in Selenge).

All trains to Ulaan Baatar and Erdenet are jam-packed, reminiscent of the worst squalor you'll see on regional Indian and Chinese trains. It is definitely worth spending a few extra tögrögs for a soft seat. At the Darkhan train station, there is a timetable, but it is in Cyrillic.

The five hour daily trip between Erdenet and Darkhan (T959/2540 for hard/soft seat) goes through some lovely countryside, but you miss it going the other way because the train often leaves Darkhan at the ungodly hour of 2 am.

The daily Ulaan Baatar-Sükhbaatar train leaves Darkhan for Sükhbaatar at 5.40 pm (T520/1345 for hard/soft seat). Between Darkhan and Ulaan Baatar, there are also three daily express trains. Tickets cost T1228/3499. Refer to the Trans-Mongolian Railway section in the Getting There & Away chapter for details about international trains to/from Russia and China which stop at Darkhan.

**Taxi** Constant demand ensures that public shared taxis regularly go to Ulaan Baatar (T2000). They go less often to Sükhbaatar (T1000) because of the popularity of the train. Shared taxis, and taxis and jeeps which can be chartered, normally hang around the bus stop. Shared taxis to Erdenet are very infrequent. Occasionally, they leave from the market, following an incomprehensible announcement (in Mongolian) over the loudspeaker. A chartered taxi to Erdenet will cost T20,000.

Being a major city, Darkhan enjoys the privilege of having a paved road to Ulaan Baatar (219km) and Sükhbaatar (92km). The road to Erdenet (180km) is not paved but in good condition.

**Hitching** Hitching is easy along the busy roads to Sükhbaatar and Ulaan Baatar, but is only necessary to save a bit of money; it is

quicker and more comfortable by bus, train, shared taxi or minibus.

### Getting Around
Darkhan is spread out, so you will probably have to take a taxi or two. The local taxis, which are mostly fascinating old Soviet khaki jeeps, charge a reasonable T200 per person between the Darkhan Hotel and train station.

### BUGANT
БУГАНТ
Most of Selenge consists of fields and flood plains, but Bugant is an area of birch and pine forests, mountains and abundant wildlife. At one time, the town was known for its sawmill and nearby gold mine, but these industries are on their way out. The crystal-clear Eröö Gol flows through the town, and one possible journey on horseback would be to follow the river upstream to its source in the Khentii Nuruu range. Trekking is a possibility, but if you go wandering through the forest during the hunting season, wear bright colours to avoid being mistaken for an elk.

Bugant is in Eröö (Эрөө) *sum*, a remote area about 110km south-east of Dulaan-khaan. Access is strictly by jeep or truck over a bad, and often muddy, road.

### KHÖTÖL
ХӨТӨЛ
There is no reason whatsoever to visit the tiny, depressing mining town of Khötöl, in the *sum* of the same name, except that you may need to come here to reach Amarbayasgalant monastery if relying on public transport. Khötöl gained some unwanted notoriety in the summer of 1996 as the centre of a serious outbreak of cholera. It is now currently clear of any disease.

If you need to stay in Khötöl, the unnamed *hotel* charges between T600 and T1200 per person for a basic room. Khötöl is on the Darkhan-Erdenet train line (T1189/3058 for hard/soft seat from Ulaan Baatar), but the arrival and departure times at Khötöl are often lousy. The bus would be better: apparently it leaves Darkhan for Khötöl every day at 8 am (T500), but it was nowhere to be seen when we tried to catch it.

If you have a jeep and an experienced driver, he will be able to find a useful, and pretty, shortcut from the Ulaan Baatar-Darkhan road to Khötöl. Otherwise, it is safer to get to Darkhan and then follow the main Darkhan-Erdenet road to Khötöl (56km).

## AMARBAYASGALANT KHIID
## АМАРБАЯСГАЛАНТ ХИЙД
The star attraction of Selenge aimag, this monastery is considered the second most important in Mongolia after Erdene Zuu Khiid in Kharkhorin. Besides being one of the largest monasteries, Amarbayasgalant is also one of the most beautiful.

Although it is under restoration (and will be for many more years) with the help of UNESCO, Amarbayasgalant is worth visiting on the way to or from Khövsgöl Nuur or other areas in northern or western Mongolia. It is very difficult to get to, however, and probably not worth the effort to come especially from Ulaan Baatar, where there are several good monasteries – particularly if you have seen Erdene Zuu and Manzshir monasteries.

Amarbayasgalant Khiid was originally built in 1737 by the Manchurian king Kansu, who dedicated it to the great Mongolian Buddhist and sculptor, Zanabazar – this explains the unusual Chinese script above some of the gates and doors. The communists found a way out here in the late 1930s, but 'only' destroyed 10 out of the 37 temples and statues, possibly because of sympathetic and procrastinating local military commanders. These days, 32 monks live in the monastery.

The temples in the monastery are normally closed, so you'll have to ask the head monk to find the keys and open them up if you want to see any statues or thangkas. To help with the restoration work, foreigners are charged T1500 to see the daily ceremony, which starts at around 10 am. For the ceremony, you should enter and pay at a side entrance (on the left as you face the front gate) but if you don't, someone will chase you for your donation anyway. Photos inside

the temple are allowed for a negotiable extra donation; around the monastery, photos are OK and free.

Our guide said that the lovely hills which surround the monastery are full of elk during the late evening. Thankfully, he (and his rifle) didn't find any.

### Places to Stay
**Camping** This is a great camping area, but avoid spots, particularly near the ger camp, which are infested with midges, guaranteed to drive you to despair. If you camp near the monastery, find somewhere secluded to avoid any unwelcome visits from the drunks who live in the nearby huts.

**Ger Camps** The *Juulchin Ger Camp* is about 7km south of the monastery – you can see it from the main road. The midges around this sight are appalling in summer; they seem to penetrate every orifice. The camp charges the standard US$40 per person including meals, and is sometimes full of tour groups. You can eat there (for US$5 for dinner, for example) if you are camping nearby.

### Getting There & Away
**Jeep** To go on a day trip from Ulaan Baatar would take an horrendous 15 hours (there and back, including time to look around). It's far better to take your time, stop off at Darkhan if you want, and stay near the monastery so you can witness a ceremony in the morning and appreciate (and photograph) the place at sunset.

Even with an experienced driver you may need directions to find the monastery. From Khötöl, on the Darkhan-Erdenet road, drive 18km west (towards Erdenet) and look for a rusty, buckled yellow sign on the right indicating an obvious (northern) sandy trail. The trail continues for 14km to Tsagaan Tolgoi (Цагаан Толгои). From there, head left (west) as you approach the petrol station and continue on that trail for a very rough 54km to the monastery. It's best to ask directions at the petrol station to make sure you are on the correct trail.

**Hitching** Vehicles to the monastery are few and far between, but with a tent, enough food and water and some determination, you will get there. The cheapest and best way from Ulaan Baatar is to catch a train to Khötöl, hitch (which is easy) from there to the turn-off, then hitch another ride (less easy) to Tsagaan Tolgoi. From there, hang around the petrol station for a further (and infrequent) lift to the monastery.

### Zanabazar
You will see a lot of Zanabazar's creations in monasteries and museums in Mongolia, such as at the Gandan Khiid, the Erdene Zuu Khiid and the Winter Palace of Bogd Khaan. A museum of fine arts in the national capital is also named after him.

Born in about 1635, Zanabazar is Mongolia's earliest Buddhist leader, and a renowned sculptor. At the tender age of three, he was deemed to be a possible *gegeen*, or saint, so he studied Buddhism with the Dalai Lama in Tibet. Zanabazar returned to Mongolia to spread Tibetan Buddhism and created many famous bronze statues of Buddha. ∎

# Zavkhan Завхан

**Population:** 105,800
**Area:** 82,000 sq km
**Capital:** Uliastai
**No of Sums:** 22
**Elevation of Capital City:** 1760m
**Main Livestock & Crops:** cattle, goat, sheep; potatoes
**Ethnic Groups:** Khalkh

The eastern edge of Zavkhan aimag is the western flank of the Khangai Nuruu, the second-highest mountain range in Mongolia, and a spectacular area of forests and lakes, dotted with snow-clad peaks, white-water streams and hot and cold springs.

The southern and western parts of Zavkhan, usually ignored by visitors and Mongolians because of poor roads and transport, is a sharp contrast – a land of vast deserts, salt lakes and sand dunes where rain falls once or twice a year. Most of the border with the Gov-Altai aimag is the Zavkhan river, which flows from Khangai Nuruu to the Khyargas Nuur in Uvs aimag and drains an area of over 71,000 sq km.

Zavkhan is in an unfortunate location; very few travellers are likely to pass through much or any of the aimag. If going from Khövsgöl to the western provinces, you'll quickly pass through the northern part of Zavkhan, via Zür; travelling from Ulaan Baatar to the west along the better, southern roads, you'll miss the aimag entirely; heading from Khövsgöl to the Gobi region, it's far better to go through Arkhangai and Övörkhangai aimags.

Zavkhan's isolation is unfortunate, because the scenery is some of the most dramatic and varied in the country; one minute you are travelling through lush valleys and hills which could come straight out of a scene from *The Sound of Music*; a few km further, you are in something from *Lawrence of Arabia*.

## ULIASTAI
УЛИАСТАЙ
Uliastai is wedged in by mountains on all sides, and has a brisk but dry climate. It is

one of the most remote aimag capitals in Mongolia, but is pleasant and quiet, and a logical place to stay while you consider the direction of your plunge into the Mongolian wilderness.

## Orientation & Information

The town is divided into two main districts: west of the river (Chigistei Gol) is the central area with the hotels, restaurants and other life-support systems; across the bridge on the eastern bank is the industrial area, which you are unlikely to visit. Like most Mongolian cities, the hillsides are dotted with ger communities.

The tree-lined main street is full of friendly people, doing very little. The daily market has a surprisingly good selection of groceries such as rice, bread and meat, as well as 'necessities' like Coke and Snickers, so stock up if you're heading into the remote countryside. You can also buy these, and other goodies, at a shop inside the post office.

The bank is the two storey pink-and-white building behind the main square. If you can find the manager upstairs, he will change US dollars. It is open between 9 am and 5 pm from Monday to Saturday.

## Museums

The two museums – the Museum of Famous People (ie from Zavkhan aimag) and the History Museum – are next to each other on the main street. The former contains plenty of photos and memorabilia, as well as an interesting display of religious artefacts. Both are open from 9 am to 6 pm every day but Sunday, and the entrance fee for each is T500. Ask someone to open up the museums for you; they will probably be closed and the lights may not be working anyway.

## Dechindarjaa Khiid

Дэчиндаржаа Хийд

This small, well-appointed monastery reopened in 1990 and now has 20 monks.

NORTHERN MONGOLIA

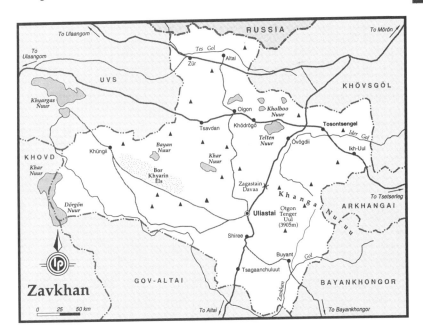

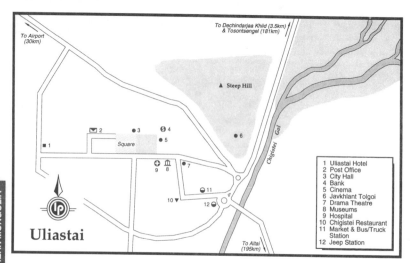

The history of the original monastery is unknown, but the recent destruction is sickeningly familiar. The monks are very friendly, and you are allowed to watch their ceremonies, which start at about 9 am every day. The monastery is in a ger district, a pleasant 3.5km walk north of the town centre – you'll notice the blue tin roof as you enter from the north.

### Javkhlant Tolgoi

Жавхлант Толгои

This hilltop near the river, and just to the north of the main street, features a pavilion and three concrete animals: an elk, ibex and argali sheep. The views from the top aren't spectacular, but it's worth the short climb to get some notion of how the city is laid out.

### Places to Stay

**Camping** Along the lush valley which hugs the Chigistei Gol for 15km from town, and parallel to the northern road to Tosontsengel, there are some gorgeous (though a little busy) camping spots. Just get off the bus, truck or jeep at somewhere you like.

**Hotels** Like most aimag capitals these days, there is only one hotel to choose from. The *Uliastai Hotel* (Улиастаи Зочид), which now incorporates the defunct Dayan Hotel, has simple rooms for T2200 per person. The rooms are OK, but avoid the ones facing the small square, which is full of screaming kids during the day and screaming drunks during the night. Deluxe rooms cost from T4400 to T7700 per person. There are no showers in the hotel.

### Places to Eat

The *Uliastai Hotel* has a restaurant, but it is often closed. The *Chigistei Restaurant* (Чиг истэи Рэсторан), identifiable by the blue panes and the knife-and-fork sign outside, offers a better range of mutton dishes than the hotel – which is still not much of a recommendation. Your best bet is to take advantage of the reasonable market and buy your own food.

### Getting There & Away

**Air** MIAT flies between Ulaan Baatar and Uliastai on Tuesday, Thursday and Saturday for US$105. For the same price, Khangard flies between Ulaan Baatar and Uliastai on Friday. The absence of level ground in the region means that the airport is 30km to the west of town. You'll have to charter a jeep to get there.

**Bus** Because Uliastai is not on the way to anywhere important, there is only one bus service from Ulaan Baatar (or anywhere else). It leaves Ulaan Baatar on Monday and takes around 45 hours to get to Uliastai (T6403). Hitching and public shared jeeps are the normal way to get around this part of the country.

If, or when, a bus arrives, or is about to leave, there will be an inaudible and incomprehensible (unless you speak fluent Mongolian) message over the loudspeaker at the market.

**Jeep** A surprising number of jeeps are available in Uliastai. They congregate at the roundabout near the bridge, not far from the market. If you are chartering one, their fares are naturally very negotiable.

Every day, several public shared jeeps leave Uliastai for Tosontsengel (181km, T3000), usually in the morning. The road between Uliastai and Tosontsengel is unpaved, but pretty reasonable and easy to follow – except that the turn-off to Tosontsengel is unmarked: the turn-off is 148km north of Uliastai and 33km west of Tosontsengel.

Along the road between Uliastai and Altai (195km), in Gov-Altai aimag, the bridge across the Zavkhan Gol, at the town of Tsagaan-Olom (Цагаан-Олом) is sometimes in a bad state. Very few shared jeeps travel between Uliastai and Altai.

**Hitching** The road between Uliastai and Tosontsengel is fairly busy, so hitching wouldn't be difficult, but as it rains a fair bit in summer, hanging around for a lift may not be pleasant. Hitching to anywhere else from Uliastai is really hard, because Zavkhan's isolated location ensures that few vehicles come this way.

### ZAGASTAIN DAVAA
### ЗАГАСТАИН ДАВАА
Forty-eight km north-east of Uliastai on the Uliastai-Tosontsengel road is a spectacular

mountain pass with the unusual name of Fish Pass. At the top, there are sensational views, a large ovoo and the largest collection of flies in northern Mongolia. Between the pass and Uliastai, the road is paved, indicating that it suffers badly from rain and blizzards, which can start as early as October. This section of road is a great place to pitch your tent and hike around.

### OTGON TENGER UUL
### ОТГОН ТЭНГЭР УУЛ
Hard-core mountaineers may want to travel to Otgon Tenger Uul, about 40km east of Uliastai. At 3905m, it is the highest peak in the Khangai Nuruu range and is now part of the 96,000 hectare Otgon Tenger Strictly Protected Area.

### TOSONTSENGEL
### ТОСОНЦЭНГЭЛ
Tosontsengel is the second-largest city in Zavkhan and perhaps should have been the aimag capital, as it has more economic justification for its existence than Uliastai: Tosontsengel is the centre of the timber industry in western Mongolia.

Tosontsengel is a poor, dusty, '20-horse' town with no market or regular transport. Nevertheless, it is a useful stop-over if you are travelling between Khövsgöl and Arkhangai aimags, though Tosontsengel is 33km east of the main Mörön-Uliastai road. There are two main roads between Mörön and Tosontsengel: one is via Sharga (Шарга) in the Tsagaan-Uul *sum* (Цагаан-Уул), and the other goes via Orgil (Оргил) in the Jargalant (Жаргалант) *sum*. These two roads are rough, but extremely pretty and worth exploring and camping if you have a good jeep and tent.

### Places to Stay
**Camping** Tosontsengel is another reason why you should have a tent with you. From the town square, head south for a few hundred metres to the Ider Gol river, on which the town is based, and find a quiet spot.

NORTHERN MONGOLIA

**Hotels** At the time of research both hotels, on either side of the town square, were in a permanent state of disrepair (and no refurbishments seemed imminent). Neither place had a name, so we gave them the obvious monikers, the *Pink Hotel* and *White Hotel*. Both have musty rooms for a bargain T500 to T800 per person.

### Places to Eat

The *guanz* at the petrol station serves some reasonable mutton and noodles. If that doesn't excite you, then it's best to stock up with food in Mörön or Uliastai.

### Getting There & Away

**Air** MIAT flies between Ulaan Baatar and Tosontsengel on Monday, Wednesday and Friday for US$85.

**Jeep** The only form of regular transport to/from Tosontsengel is a public shared jeep from Uliastai. In Tosontsengel, all public transport leaves from the petrol station north of the square.

From Tosontsengel, it's 181km south-west to Uliastai (the turn-off to the south is at the 33km point); 273km north-east to Mörön; 533km north-west to Ulaangom and a *long* 803km south-east to Ulaan Baatar. The first half of the 350km south-east stretch towards Tsetserleg, as far as the magnificent Terkhiin Tsagaan Nuur lake, is one of the worst roads in the country.

**Hitching** If you hang around the petrol station in Tosontsengel, you should be able to get a lift to Uliastai; to anywhere else, you will have to wait a long time.

### OIGON
ОЙГОН

The only claim to any fame for Oigon, in the *sum* of Tudevtei (Түдэвтэй), is that some flights go there because of its apparent central location. MIAT flies between Oigon (usually referred to as Tudevtei on schedules) and Ulaan Baatar on Wednesday and Friday for US$90, and Khangard on Saturday for the same price.

### NÖMRÖG
НӨМРӨГ

This *sum* has two beautiful lakes, Telten Nuur (Тэлтэн Нуур) and Kholboo Nuur (Холъоо Нуур), which are accessible by a bad jeep road from Khödrögö (Хөдрөгө ), the *sum* capital. Access to the area, which starts about 50km west of the Tosontsengel-Uliastai turn-off, is very difficult.

### BAYAN NUUR
БАЯН НУУР

This salt lake, among the Bor Khyarin Els sand dunes, is in the remote western part of Zavkhan and difficult to reach. The scenery is fascinating and locals claim there is good fishing.

# Eastern Mongolia

Nestled along the borders of China and Russia are the three provinces of Dornod, Khentii and Sükhbaatar, which were all part of the giant Tsetsenkhaan aimag before it was split up in 1921. Except for the spectacular Khentii Nuruu range, and some forests surrounding it, eastern Mongolia is pure steppe. The area is almost uninhabited by people, but home to thousands of Mongolian Gazelle and birdlife, such as the ubiquitous Demoiselle Crane and the Steppe Eagle – all of which are under threat from increases in potential mining.

Most travellers head out west from Ulaan Baatar, but the eastern part of the country does offer some stunning scenery and has the advantage of being closer to Ulaan Baatar, meaning shorter trips and less arduous travel.

## Dornod Дорнод

**Population:** 84,600
**Area:** 123,500 sq km
**Capital:** Choibalsan
**No of Sums:** 15
**Elevation of Capital City:** 747m
**Main Livestock & Crops:** sheep; hay
**Ethnic Groups:** Khalkh, Buryat, Barga, Uzemchin

Dornod, which means 'east', is not the most remote aimag in Mongolia, but it probably receives the least visitors. If you have the time, and a jeep to cross the vast treeless and sparsely populated steppes, there are a few places of interest: Buir Nuur and Khalkhin Gol – both the scenes of fierce fighting against the Japanese; Khokh Nuur, the

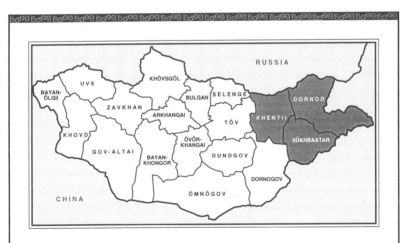

**Highlights**
- Dadal: majestic streams and forests; Chinggis Khaan was born here; stay in a cheap resort by the lakes; great hiking
- Dariganga: superb area of lakes, sand dunes and grasslands; stay in a cheap resort or ger camp; plenty of domestic animals to photograph; birdlife
- Shiliin Bogd Uul: a sacred mountain near the Chinese border; awesome views across to China

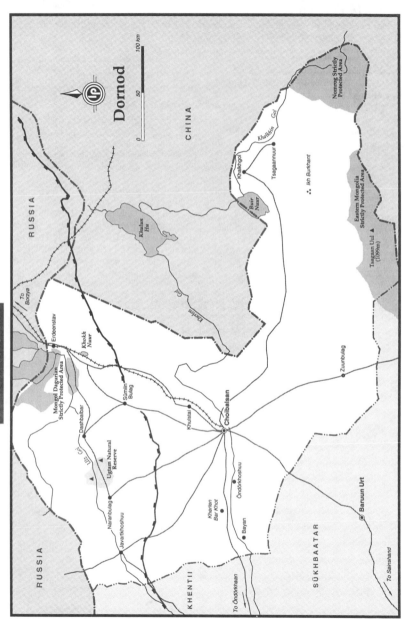

EASTERN MONGOLIA

lowest point in the country; a few remains of the Wall of Chinggis Khaan; some scattered ruins from the days of Manchurian rule; and even a uranium mine (but you won't be able to visit this).

Before the Stalinist purges of the 1930s, eastern Dornod had a staggering number of monasteries. Finding ruins of the monasteries will involve a lot of effort and you'll need an experienced driver. The best ruins are at **Ikh Burkhant**, 350km south-east of Choibalsan. A large map in the City Museum in Choibalsan shows the locations of the ruins, and several photographs give you some idea about how splendid the monasteries once were.

### National Parks

Thankfully, authorities have been convinced that the area's fragile environment and endangered fauna and flora need to be conserved. Three large strictly protected areas have been established in the aimag: Eastern Mongolia (570,000 hectares), which includes Tsagaan Uul (1099m), a sacred peak to Buddhists; Nomrog (311,000 hectares), which contains rare species of moose, cranes, otter and bears; and Mongol Dagurian (103,000 hectares), which includes wetlands full of cranes along the Ulz Gol. More of the aimag is being considered for additional national reserves.

Theoretically, you need a permit to visit these areas (see National Parks in the Facts about the Country chapter), but if you forget or can't get one in Ulaan Baatar, don't worry – you can get one in Baruun Urt.

## CHOIBALSAN
ЧОЙБАЛСАН

Named after the Stalinist stooge Khorloogiyn Choibalsan, this charmless aimag capital of 45,000 is easily Mongolia's largest (after the autonomous cities of Ulaan Baatar, Darkhan and Erdenet). Centuries ago, the city was a trading centre and part of a caravan route across central Asia. It grew into a town in the 19th century, and is now the major economic centre for eastern Mongolia.

Choibalsan is inhabited by a large number of dark-skinned people, a legacy of centuries of intermarriages between Buriads, Bargas, Uzemchins and Chinese from Inner Mongolia.

From the ruins of many houses, it looks like Choibalsan once suffered a horrendous earthquake. In fact, these houses were built by Russians (who have now left), and heated using special Russian fuel. As this fuel is no longer available in Choibalsan, the houses have been abandoned and the bricks, windows, gates and anything useable have been removed to help build new houses.

### Orientation & Information

Although the city is spread out along a narrow 5km corridor north of the Kherlen Gol, most of the facilities needed by visitors are near the park and around the Kherlen Hotel. The market, known as the Black Market, is 3km west of the park, about halfway between the town and the train station.

The Mongolian Heroes' Memorial is one of the more dramatic pieces of Stalinist architecture in Mongolia. It is a large arch

**EASTERN MONGOLIA**

### Gazelles & Antelopes

One of the most magnificent sights in Mongolia, especially in the flat and dull eastern provinces, is the hundreds of Black-tailed gazelles and Saiga antelopes, which almost seem to float across the plains.

In one year alone (1942), 100,000 gazelles and antelopes were slaughtered for meat by Russian troops. While wholesale slaughter is now outlawed, they are still at risk from development and mining, but endangered antelopes and the gazelles are being preserved in national parks such as the Eastern Mongolia Strictly Protected Area.

Antelopes are especially prized by Chinese and Mongolians for their meat, skins and horns – each one fetches from 70 to 100 yuan (US$8.50 to US$12). Mongolia has about 300,000 antelopes, but hunting – illegal and legal – continues: in 1996 several Mongolian and Chinese poachers armed with submachine guns were arrested in Dornod. ∎

## Khorloogiyn Choibalsan

Choibalsan was born in the Dornod aimag, north-east of what is now the city of Choibalsan. A great hero of the 1921 revolution, he became Mongolia's leader in 1928, probably purging or assassinating rivals in the process. Like his Russian mentor, Joseph Stalin, Choibalsan was ruthless, and is credited with launching a purge in the 1930s which reportedly cost about 27,000 lives. Although Choibalsan's regime has been heavily criticised by modern Mongolians, statues of him remain, and his name is still used for streets, cities and *sums*. ■

with a soldier on horseback charging towards the enemy. A Soviet tank next to the monument adds a quaint reminder of who was really boss. Presumably, they are too big to destroy.

### Museums

The **City Museum**, in the park, is probably the best of its kind outside of Ulaan Baatar. It contains some interesting paintings, fascinating old photos, stuffed animals (of course), some memorabilia about Choibalsan and a giant bowl, made in 1825, which is large enough to boil mutton for 500 people. (The mind boggles, the stomach churns.) The museum is open from 9 am to 5 pm every day but Monday and Tuesday (T350).

The **Khalkh Golin Museum** chronicles the war with the Japanese along the Khalkhin

river in 1939. The museum was closed at the time of research, but should reopen soon. It is in the ger suburbs, about 200m north-east of the Drama Theatre.

### Danrag Danjalan Khiid

Данраг Данжалан Хийд

According to the chief monk, this monastery was built around 1840 and was once very active. It contained three northern temples and four southern temples, but less than half the monks could be accommodated at one time, so most had to pray outside. The rest of the temple's history is sickeningly familiar. The Mongolian security forces descended on the place in 1937, destroyed all records and arrested most of the monks, none of whom has ever been heard from since.

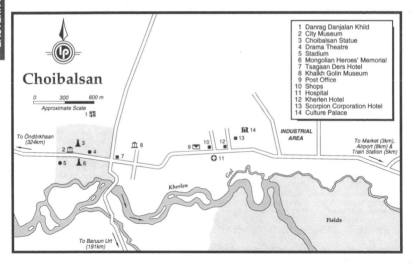

Choibalsan

0    300    600 m
Approximate Scale
1

1 Danrag Danjalan Khiid
2 City Museum
3 Choibalsan Statue
4 Drama Theatre
5 Stadium
6 Mongolian Heroes' Memorial
7 Tsagaan Ders Hotel
8 Khalkh Golin Museum
9 Post Office
10 Shops
11 Hospital
12 Kherlen Hotel
13 Scorpion Corporation Hotel
14 Culture Palace

To Öndörkhaan
(324km)

INDUSTRIAL
AREA

To Market (3km),
Airport (8km) &
Train Station (5km)

Kherlen

Gol

Fields

To Baruun Urt
(191km)

In June 1990 the monastery reopened and it now has two small temples where about 20 monks worship. The monks are particularly friendly; we were warmly welcomed and allowed to watch a ceremony. The monastery is north of the park in the ger suburbs, identifiable by its familiar yellow roof.

### Places to Stay

**Camping** The best place to camp is anywhere south of the main street – a few hundred metres' walk, and you will be sharing some great spots along the Kherlen Gol with a few curious cows.

**Hotels** The cheapest place to try is the *Tsagaan Ders Hotel* (Цаг аан Дэрс Зочид), on the main street just a little to the east of the park. It was being renovated at the time of research and the owners weren't sure of the foreigners' price, but it is bound to be far cheaper than the alternatives.

The *Kherlen Hotel* (Хэрлэн Зочид) is *the* place to avoid, though currently the choices are limited. The rooms are comfortable enough, but foreigners have to pay a ridiculous T8800/13,750 per person for a simple/deluxe room – and they demand US dollars. None of the rooms have showers, which doesn't really matter because the city has a permanent lack of hot water anyway.

Unfortunately, the only other functioning place is also expensive, but it's certainly better value. The unlikely sounding *Scorpion Corporation Hotel* is part of (and located behind) the grandly named, and very quiet, Business Development Center of Eastern Mongolia. The hotel has large and pleasant double rooms for T13,750 per person, and two-room apartments for T15,400 per person including TV, and (would you believe it?) a swimming pool – which presumably doubles as an ice-skating rink for eight months of the year.

### Places to Eat

For a hotel which charges an exorbitant price for foreigners, the restaurant at the *Kherlen Hotel* is lousy. The staff could only offer mutton and rice, and looked really put out when we

ordered bread. A few other places along the main street serve the same sort of food.

Better meals and choice can be found at the *cafeteria* on the ground floor at the front entrance of the Business Development Center. The shops in Choibalsan are in a sorry state. They sell loads of expensive things, which nobody can afford, like laundry detergent, stockings and Tiger Beer (imported from Singapore), but no tinned food or vegetables.

We were initially excited by a hamburger joint on the road to the airport but, predictably, they had run out of supplies.

### Getting There & Away

**Air** MIAT flies between Ulaan Baatar and Choibalsan three times a week – Monday, Wednesday and Friday – for US\$75. Choibalsan boasts a top-notch airport (by Mongolian standards), a legacy of the large Soviet military base which existed until 1990. The airport is about 8km east of the centre; jam-packed buses sometimes go there.

**Bus** From Ulaan Baatar to Choibalsan, buses leave on Monday and Thursday and cost T4610 – though the fare for the return journey is T6000. Buses returning to Ulaan Baatar leave from the market and from outside the Kherlen Hotel.

**Train** A direct rail line from Choibalsan to Russia was built in 1939 to facilitate the joint Soviet-Mongolian war effort against Japan. It still functions, albeit only weekly. As a foreigner, you can go as far as Erdeenstav (Эрдээнстав) on the Mongolian side of the border (there seems very little point) – but not any further into Russia.

In case the border reopens for foreigners, the international train leaves Choibalsan every Thursday at 4.30 pm, and arrives from Russia on Saturday at 8 am. To Borzya, 80km past the Russian border, tickets cost T8000.

The train station is about 5km north-east of the centre, near a still-functioning gold mine. You can reach the station by bus, but go early, because close to departure time the buses make a sardine tin look spacious.

**Jeep** When there is enough demand (which isn't often) public shared jeeps to Ulaan Baatar and, less frequently, to Öndörkhaan and Baruun Urt leave from the crowded Black Market. Quite a few jeeps hang around the market and can be chartered to visit the national parks and lakes in the aimag.

Choibalsan is 191km north-east of Baruun Urt, 324km north-east of Öndörkhaan and 655km north-east of Ulaan Baatar. The roads in the northern part of Dornod are often buried under mud, but to the other eastern aimag capitals, the roads are OK.

**Hitching** Choibalsan is a large city by Mongolian standards, so hitching a ride on a truck or any other vehicle in or out of the city should not be difficult. Hang around the market and keep asking.

## WALL OF CHINGGIS KHAAN
Stretching over 600km from Khentii aimag to China, through all of Dornod, are the ruins of the Wall of Chinggis Khaan. This is not promoted by Mongolian tourist authorities because it was not built, or used, by Chinggis Khaan, but almost certainly created by the Manchurians to limit (unsuccessfully) frequent raids from rampaging Mongolian hordes.

---

### Erdes Uranium Mine
In northern Dornod, the Erdes uranium mine was built by the Russians and under the control of the puppet Mongolian Ministry of Public Security. The USSR wanted uranium for its warheads during the mid-1980s, so a mine producing one million tons a year and a city for 25,000 people (huge by Mongolian standards) were planned for the year 2000.

In 1990, however, finance dried up and the Russian government pulled out. Uranium is still in demand, but transport to Erdes, which still produces about 180,000 tons of uranium ore each year, is the problem. Some US mining companies have shown interest, but nothing has eventuated. About 250 Russian and 60 Mongolian families still live in this very remote section of the country. ∎

---

You will need a guide and jeep to find what remains from the ravages of vandals and time. The best place to start looking is about two-thirds along the northern road from Choibalsan to the Russian border, near the village of Sümiin Bulag (Сумийн Булаг) in the *sum* of Gurvanzagal (Гурванзагал).

## UGTAM UUL
УГТАМ УУЛ
Ugtam mountain is part of the Ugtam Mountain Natural Reserve (30,000 hectares), which also includes the nearby Khairkhan Uul and the ruins of some monasteries. The park is situated along the Ulz Gol in the north-west of the aimag, near the village of Naranbulag (Наранбулаг) in the *sum* of Bayandun (Баяндун).

## KHOKH NUUR
ХОХ НУУР
The lowest point in Mongolia is Khokh Nuur (Blue Lake), a small salt lake at 560m altitude. Other than the thrill of standing in the lowest part of the country, there isn't much to keep you here, though you could combine it with an exploration of the Wall of Chinggis Khaan.

Khokh Nuur is in the northern part of the Choibalsan *sum*, just off the main road from Choibalsan city and about 60km south of the Russian border.

## BUIR NUUR
БУИР НУУР
This beautiful lake is the largest in eastern Mongolia (the northern shore is actually in China). The surrounding countryside is mostly grassland, though there are a few trees. The lake has a maximum depth of 50m and, if you're equipped with the proper paraphernalia, is a good place to fish. The area is especially popular with mosquitoes. Bring lots of repellent, or you'll need a blood transfusion.

For war buffs, several foreign (mainly Japanese) travel companies organise tours to the region by chartered plane. One Mongolian company, Mongol Tour OK (see the Ulaan Baatar chapter) runs tours to Buir Nuur and the Khalkhin Gol, 90km away.

The nearest town to Buir Nuur, Tsagaan-nuur (Цагааннуур) in the *sum* of Sümber (Сумбэр), has an unnamed *hotel* with basic facilities. An occasional *ger camp* on the shore of the lake caters for organised tour groups.

Small chartered aircraft can land near the lake shore, though rain can create problems on the dirt landing field. The only other way there is by chartered jeep from Choibalsan, 285km away over a flat, dirt road which occasionally gets flooded.

## KHALKHIN GOL
ХАЛХИН ГОЛ

The banks of the Khalkhin Gol, in the far eastern part of Dornod, are of particular interest to war historians because of the battles against the Japanese in 1939. The dry, unpolluted air ensures that most of the relics, which are just lying around, have been well preserved.

Numerous war memorials line the banks of the river. The memorials, which were dedicated in 1984, are real socialist master-pieces, built to honour the Russian and Mongolian soldiers who died here. The largest memorial is the 50m **Khamar Davaa**. A small **museum** in Tsagaannuur (near Buir Nuur), and a larger one in Choibalsan, offer some explanations (in Mongolian) about the history of the battles.

## KHERLEN BAR KHOT
ХЭРЛЭН БАР ХОТ

Kherlen Bar Khot is the location of some small-scale ruins from a 12th century city, once part of an ancient state called Kitan.

There are also some '**man stones**' (unexplained ancient rocks shaped like men) and, predictably, a Chinggis Khaan memorial of sorts: a rock called the '**Chinggis Bed**' which commemorates his stay here.

Kherlen Bar Khot is about 120km west of Choibalsan, in the *sum* of Tsagaan Ovoo (Цагаан Овоо). It is on the main road between Choibalsan and Öndörkhaan, and is worth a look if you have your own vehicle.

# Khentii Хэнтий

**Population:** 75,200
**Area:** 82,000 sq km
**Capital:** Öndörkhaan
**No of Sums:** 23
**Elevation of Capital City:** 1027m
**Main Livestock & Crops:** horse, sheep, cattle; hay, wheat
**Ethnic Groups:** Khalkh, Buryat

Khentii is named after the impressive Khentii Nuruu range, which covers the north-west corner of the aimag and is part of the giant 1.2 million hectare Khan Khentii Strictly Protected Area (most of which is in the adjoining Töv aimag). Although none of the peaks are over 2000m, these mountains are well watered and heavily forested. The aimag has over 70 rivers, including the Kherlen Gol, which flows through the aimag capital of Öndörkhaan, and the Onon in the far north-east. There are also over 30 sources of mineral water, which often overflow.

All this means that the scenery is lush and the travelling is very difficult. Jeeps have a hard time and often get bogged; access

EASTERN MONGOLIA

---

**War at Khalkhin Gol**

After the Japanese moved into north-east China in 1931 to create the puppet state of Manchukuo, hundreds of thousands of Soviet troops and 80,000 Mongolian soldiers moved into Dornod. When the Japanese attacked the banks of the Khalkhin Gol in May 1939, the Russians were ready.

Until September 1939, battles involving tanks, bombers and ground troops resulted in about 61,000 Japanese killed, wounded or captured; about 10,000 Russian and over 1000 Mongolians suffered the same fate. War historians believe the result probably prompted the Japanese generals to change their strategies and avoid further war with Russia, and concentrate instead on eastern Asia and the Pacific region. ■

through the thickly forested regions is mainly on horseback or on foot. The water attracts an abundance of wildlife and is responsible for the stunning wildflowers which seem to carpet hills and valleys with a profusion of purple, red and yellow in season.

Given the lovely environment, you would think that the local officials responsible for tourist development would promote the aimag's great natural beauty. However, this is not the case. Khentii is believed to be the birth and burial place of Chinggis Khaan, and the authorities have decided that this is the aimag's greatest tourist attraction. Local officials have so far identified 43 historical sites relating to Chinggis Khaan.

### Organised Tours
Khentii's proximity to Ulaan Baatar and its natural beauty are reasons enough for some local travel companies to offer organised tours around the aimag (see the Ulaan Baatar chapter for details):

Juulchin organises horseback trips from their resort at Delgerkhaan.
Nomads runs excellent, popular trips by horse or yak cart through the wildflowers of the Khan Khentii national park.

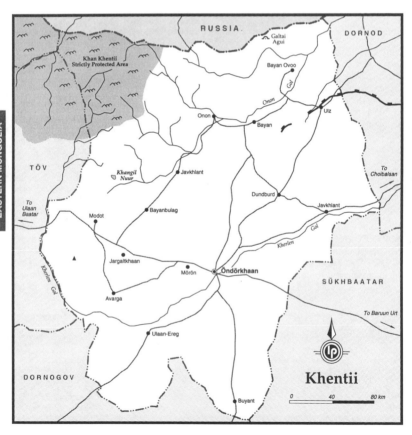

Shuren Travel offers interesting trips to remote spots in the Khan Khentii national park, often by helicopter.

## ÖNDÖRKHAAN
ӨНДӨРХААН

Öndörkhaan, which means 'high king', is in one of the flattest and driest parts of Khentii aimag. The Kherlen Gol flows through the southern part of town, however, providing the cows with water and grass, and the locals (and brave foreigners) with a good swimming hole (in summer). Most of the residents live in wooden buildings, so gers are relatively few in number.

Öndörkhaan, a sleepy place with about 17,000 people, is far nicer than the other two eastern aimag capitals. It is perfectly located as a gateway to eastern Mongolia, so you may need to stay here to arrange onward transport, to break up a journey if you are heading to/from Dadal or other places in the east, or to wait a few days if MIAT has off-loaded you.

### Orientation & Information

The town is fairly compact and centred on a desolate central park. At a counter to your right in the bank opposite the Kherlen Hotel you can change money – US dollars only. There are no further funds to complete the enormous wrestling stadium which dominates the southern part of town, so it will probably never be finished.

### Museums

The **Ethnic Museum** is one of the best of its kind in the country, and is certainly worth a look. It contains a few ethnic costumes and some religious artefacts, such as statues, thangkas and books which must have been rescued from Stalin's thugs in the late 1930s. Previously an 18th century monastery, the museum is actually four temples in a pleasant park. It is officially open from 8 am to 1 pm and 2 to 6 pm, and on Saturday morning (T200) – but it is often closed during the day, so ask someone at the hut at the back to open it up. The museum is next to the City Hall.

The **City Museum**, north of the park, was

closed at the time of research, but is probably also worth a look.

### Gundgavirlan Khiid
Гундгавирлан Хийд

The original Gundgavirlan monastery was built in 1660 and housed the first Buddhist philosophy school in Mongolia. At its peak, the monastery was home to over 1000 monks. In the spring of 1938, the Stalinist purge reached Khentii and the monks were all arrested and, presumably, sent to their deaths. The buildings remained standing until the 1950s, when they were torn down.

In 1990 the monastery reopened in a ger. Two years later, the present monastery was opened on the same site as the original one. Although all photos of the original monastery were burned, some of the old people – relying on memory alone – worked with a painter during the 1960s to recreate a portrait of what it looked like. This painting has been

1 Bus & Truck Station
2 Bayan Bulag Hotel
3 Shops
4 Sports Palace
5 City Museum
6 Drama Theatre
7 City Hall
8 Department Store
9 Ethnic Museum
10 Kherlen Hotel
11 Market
12 Bank
13 Post Office
14 Stadium
15 Gundgavirlan Khiid

Öndörkhaan

0    50    100 m
Approximate Scale

To Choibalsan (324km)

To Ulaan Baatar (331km)

To Airport (2km)

To Baruun Urt (229km)

preserved and hangs in the temple. The monastery is only about 100m south of the main street. The 70 monks who worship there are friendly, and foreigners are welcome to see the ceremony which takes place most mornings.

### Places to Stay

**Camping** If you want to camp, head south past the incomplete wrestling stadium, and walk along the Kherlen Gol to the west until you've found a quiet spot.

**Hotels** Both places in town are decent and good value. The *Kherlen Hotel* (Хэрлэн Зочид) has dorm-style rooms for a bargain T700 per person, and the deluxe rooms for T1200 per person are also very good value. It is on the main street and above some shops – enter from the laneway on the western side.

The *Bayan Bulag Hotel* (Баян Булаг Зочид), still sometimes known as the Nedgelchin Hotel, is even better value. Good simple rooms (not dorm-style) cost T1500 per person, and the deluxe is T1800 per person. The staff are friendly, which is often unusual. The Bayan Bulag is on the western end of the main road.

### Places to Eat

The only places to eat are the two hotel restaurants. They both serve the usual mutton-based dish, but the Bayan Bulag is probably the better if only because it has a bar with vodka, warm Pepsi and beer to wash down the barely edible meal.

The shops and market along the main street are well stocked compared with other towns in eastern Mongolia, so it is not a bad idea to buy your own food, considering the dismal choice of restaurants.

### Getting There & Away

**Air** On Tuesday and Friday, MIAT flies to/from Ulaan Baatar for US$30. When there is enough demand, MIAT sometimes continues on to Onon, in Binder *sum*, and/or Dadal. Öndörkhaan's airport is 2km west of the city. MIAT in Öndörkhaan is sometimes unreliable – we met several unhappy foreigners on

an organised tour with confirmed tickets who had just been bumped off a flight from Öndörkhaan to Ulaan Baatar.

**Bus** A comparatively large number of buses go from Ulaan Baatar to Öndörkhaan, and on to the other two aimag capitals in eastern Mongolia. Direct buses leave Ulaan Baatar on Monday, Tuesday and Friday (T3500) and return the next day. You can also get a ride on the buses from Ulaan Baatar which go through Öndörkhaan on the way to Baruun Urt (on Monday and Wednesday) and Choibalsan (on Monday and Thursday).

The bus station is currently about 100m west of the Sports Palace, but locals say that it will be moved to somewhere north of the Drama Theatre. The exact location was not known at the time of research.

**Jeep** Öndörkhaan is well serviced by public shared jeeps. One or two leave most days for Ulaan Baatar (T3500; or T4600 with luggage), but go less regularly to Baruun Urt, Choibalsan and other places in Khentii. Shared jeeps, and ones which can be chartered, hang around the two main streets in the town, but may soon congregate at the new bus station.

Öndörkhaan is 331km east of Ulaan Baatar, 324km south-west of Choibalsan and 229km west of Baruun Urt. The roads to these places are unpaved but fairly reasonable.

**Hitching** Öndörkhaan is the gateway for eastern Mongolia, so all vehicles heading to Dornod and Sükhbaatar aimags will come through here. Getting a lift on a truck, or anything else, going to Ulaan Baatar, Choibalsan and Baruun Urt is comparatively easy. Hitching to other places – for instance, along the main north-east road towards the Russian border – is far harder.

At the time of research, most trucks just parked along the two main streets in Öndörkhaan, but they will probably have to move to the new bus station.

## DADAL
ДАДАЛ

As written in *The Secret History of the Mongols*, it is now generally accepted that the great Chinggis was born at the junction of the Onon and Balj rivers (though his date of birth is still subject to great conjecture). The assumed spot is in the Dadal *sum*, near the *sum* capital of Bayan Ovoo (Баян Овоо).

Dadal is a gorgeous area of log huts (very few people live in gers), lakes, rivers and forests – reminiscent of Siberia, which is only 25km to the north. Even if you are not a Chinggisphile, there is no shortage of scenery to admire and hike around. It wouldn't be hard to stay here a few days (which may be necessary anyway unless you have rented a jeep). The downside is that it often rains here in summer.

### Things to See

Three km north of Bayan Ovoo is a collection of hills known as **Deluun Boldog**. On top of one of the hills is the unimpressive **Chinggis Khaan Statue**, built in 1962 to commemorate the 800th anniversary of his birth – the inscription states that Chinggis was born here in 1162. Some historians may not be entirely convinced about the exact date or location of his birth, but it's a great place to come into the world: the scenery and hiking around the valleys and forests are superb.

About 1km west of the statue is the **Khajuu Bulag** (Хажуу Булаг) mineral water springs, where the great man once drank. Take your water bottles and fill them to the brim, because this is the freshest (flowing) spring water you will ever taste. (Presumably, it is only a matter of time before the Chinggis Khaan Mineral Water bottling factory opens up nearby.)

### Places to Stay & Eat

**Camping** If you have your own tent and food there is no need to stay in a hotel or ger camp; this is perfect camping country. Just walk about 200m in any direction from Bayan Ovoo and set up camp.

**Hotels** The village of Bayan Ovoo has one hotel. It was closed when we visited, but locals said that it's normally open. They charge T400 per person.

**Ger Camps** Several ger camps and resorts, once built for holidaying Communist Party officials, now cater for tourists. (In this part of the country, locals use wooden houses; only tourists stay in gers.) None of them have running water or sewerage, and the pit toilets are often fairly unpleasant. You can eat at the ger camps or resorts if you give them a bit of notice and are willing to pay their foreigners' prices. There are no shops in the village.

One km from Bayan Ovoo, the *Onon* (Онон) ger camp was probably nice a few years ago but has been neglected. The prices are lower than normal: US$10 per person in a ger, but the extra US$15 for three meals is way too much. Nearby, the *Santkhaan* (Сантхаан) ger camp will open soon and offer similar prices, standard and facilities in their gers.

The *Gurvan Nuur* (Гурван Нуур) (Three Lakes) resort is in the nicest location, and is

**EASTERN MONGOLIA**

---

### Chinggis Khaan Statue

The statue at Deluun Boldog is odd, if only because it was built at the time of the communist reign and never torn down by the communists. Construction of the statue was authorised by Tomor-Ochir, a high-ranking member of the Central Committee of the Mongolian Communist Party in 1962. He was considered a loyal communist and an ardent nationalist. After the statue was constructed, he lost his official position and was expelled from Ulaan Baatar.

He went to work in a timber mill in Zavkhan aimag and later became museum director at Darkhan. Years later, he was clubbed to death and the killer was never found. The sculptor who carved the statue also lost his job. Why the statue remained, and what happened to those involved with the construction of the statue, is another mystery. ■

## Search for Chinggis Khaan's Grave

Mongolians, and some historians, have agreed that the birthplace of Chinggis Khaan is at Deluun Boldog, in northern Khentii. But where was he buried?

Chinggis' grave is probably in Khentii aimag, and not too far from his birthplace, but the exact location is not known. According to diaries kept by Marco Polo, the Mongols at the time wanted to keep the location of the grave a secret – which they have managed to do to this day. According to legend, the 2000 or so people who attended Chinggis' funeral were killed by 800 soldiers, who were in turn slaughtered themselves – so total secrecy was ensured.

Various expeditions, often with Japanese and US assistance and technology, have failed to shed any light on the mystery. His tomb may contain millions, if not billions, of dollars worth of gold, silver, precious stones and other priceless religious artefacts (which obviously weren't destroyed during the Stalinist purges), so the search is sure to continue.

However, the vast amount of money spent so far, which could be better used to assist regional development, and the fact that discovery of the grave is against the obvious wishes of Chinggis Khaan himself, also causes resentment among many Mongolians. ■

the best value. On the shore of a lake about 2km from Bayan Ovoo, the setting in a pine forest is superb. A basic but clean room (there are no gers) costs a negotiable US$5 per person but, again, the meals are too expensive at US$15 per day (so take your own food). The camp contains another Chinggis Khaan statue, which is far more impressive than the one at Deluun Boldog.

### Getting There & Away

**Air** To Dadal, there are occasional chartered tourist flights, and the twice-monthly postal plane. According to its schedule, MIAT flies between Dadal and Ulaan Baatar (US$50) (with a possible stop at Onon in Binder *sum* nearby), via Öndörkhaan, on Tuesday and Friday. These flights are only likely to take place with sufficient demand, but it is certainly worth checking with MIAT – it would save a long, tough ride by jeep and/or truck. The airport has a hard surface, which is essential in this moist climate, and is 14km from Bayan Ovoo.

**Jeep** As there is no public transport to Dadal, chartering a jeep or hitching is the only way to go. In summer, along the road between Bayanbulag (Баянбулаг), in Ömnödelger (Өмнөдэлг эр) *sum*, and Dadal (about 236km) you'll see plenty of nomadic families moving home with heavily laden carts pulled by camels or yaks (the best form of transport in muddy Khentii).

The road to Dadal via Ulz (Улз), in the *sum* of Norovlin (Норовлин), which is on the main road between Öndörkhaan and northern Dornod, takes longer from Ulaan Baatar. A new bridge over the Onon Gol, just south of Dadal, has replaced the dicey pontoon used in the old days.

As there are virtually no vehicles available for hire in Bayan Ovoo, the only option is to contact the Onon ger camp. It rents jeeps with drivers for T165 per km which is not unreasonable for this part of the country. Guides can also be arranged at the camp for T3300 per day.

Dadal is 254km north-east of Öndörkhaan; 301km north-west of Choibalsan; and 585km north-west of Ulaan Baatar – or exactly 500km if you have an experienced driver who knows the right shortcuts.

**Hitching** Hitching to Dadal from Ulaan Baatar is difficult and will take several days, but is great fun. Quite a few vehicles travel between Baganuur and Bayanbulag every day, so this stretch shouldn't be difficult. (At Baganuur, wait at the top of the northern road between the coal mine and the town; something will come along.) A few guanzes along this road serve good *khuurshuur* (fried mutton pancakes).

From Bayanbulag (a pleasant village with wooden huts and a hotel), fewer vehicles travel to Javkhlant (Жавхлант), in the *sum* of Bayan-Adraga (Баян-Адрага), another pretty, forested area. From Javkhlant to Dadal, you could even trek (about 60km) along the Onon Gol river to the north-east. Otherwise, a vehicle to Dadal will eventually come along, but it might take a few days.

Alternatively, you could try to hitch a ride from Öndörkhaan to Ulz, along the north-east road heading to the Russian border, but the traffic along this road is also sparse and there is nowhere to stay along the way.

## GALTAI AGUI
ГАЛТАЙ АГУЙ

Seventy km north-west of Bayan Ovoo is the Galtai cave. It is an amazing 80m deep; apparently the deepest in Mongolia. Be careful because the cave is very close to the Russian border. You'll need a good driver or guide to find it.

## DELGERKHAAN
ДЭЛГЭРХААН

Locals, and some historians, claim that Avarga, not Karakorum, was the first capital of the Mongolian empire. In Avarga, Chinggis Khaan apparently established his armies which tore through Europe, and Chinggis' third and favourite son, Ogedei, was later proclaimed king of the Mongolian empire. The ancient capital of Avarga is now apparently underground, 14km from the modern village of Avarga (Аварга), in the *sum* of Delgerkhaan.

Chinggismania has gone a little overboard in Delgerkhaan, but even if you have no interest in the man, there is some enchanting scenery in the area. Delgerkhaan is an easy detour to or from Öndörkhaan, and not far from Baganuur.

### Things to See

The biggest and most impressive of the various statues and monuments in the area is the **Chinggis Statue**, 13km south of (the modern) Avarga village. It was built in 1990 under the sponsorship of UNESCO, to commemorate the 750th anniversary of the writing of *The Secret History of the Mongols*. The symbols on the side of the statue are the

brands used by about 300 different clans in the area for marking their livestock.

One km east of the statue is the **Avarga Toson Mineral Spring**, from which Ogedei drank and was cured of a serious stomach ailment. Locals, who claim the water can cure up to 13 known diseases including ulcers, hepatitis and any pancreatic problem, will encourage you to drink from the spring – even though it looks like a fetid pond from the top. In newly found capitalist style, the water is being bottled (in recycled and very distinctive green bottles from a famous European brewery).

About 1km north-east of the statue, the ruins of the **ancient city of Avarga** lie under the hills and rocks. Locals showed us western media reports about computer findings from a Japanese-Mongolian expedition which proved the existence of an entire capital, including nine temples and a palace belonging to Chinggis' first wife, under the rocks. (This seemed a little far-fetched, but future excavations will doubtless impress the sceptics.)

If you've had enough of Chinggis, you can always go for a swim in the tiny **Avarga Toson Nuur** lake, not far from the village.

### Places to Stay & Eat

**Camping** You can camp anywhere near the lake (but away from the ger camp and resort) and still use the lake, enjoy the scenery and visit nearby attractions. The village of Avarga has very limited supplies of food, so bring your own, or ask the ger camp or resort if you can buy an (expensive) meal at their restaurant.

**Ger Camps** On the shore of Avarga Toson Nuur is the *Avarga Resort*. Set up for Mongolian families, the resort is often full in summer. The owners weren't sure of the price for foreigners, but a bed in a rustic but clean wooden hut shouldn't cost more than about T8250 per person, including three (Mongolian) meals.

Juulchin co-runs a new ger camp called *Khuduu Aral*, which means 'country island'.

It's in an agreeable position overlooking a valley, about 4km west of Avarga village. The facilities (food, toilets and showers) are good. The price of US$35 per person includes (western) meals and a tour of all the Chinggis attractions.

### Getting There & Away

The major advantage of Delgerkhaan is its proximity to Ulaan Baatar (260km) and the regional centres of Öndörkhaan (124km) and Baganuur (95km). However, there are no flights or public transport to Delgerkhaan or Avarga.

**Jeep** Chartering a jeep to Delgerkhaan from Ulaan Baatar, Öndörkhaan or Baganuur is easy – you could even go on day trips from the latter two places. No jeeps are for hire in Avarga, but the Khuduu Aral camp can probably arrange one for about T200 per km.

**Hitching** Delgerkhaan is not a tourist region, nor near any main road, so not a lot of vehicles come here. The best idea is to get off the bus to Öndörkhaan at the southern turn-off to Avarga, just south of Modot. And wait.

### MODOT
МОДОТ

Modot is the capital of Tsenkhermandal (Цэнхэрмандал) *sum*, on the border of Töv aimag. The Russians operated a logging camp near Modot using prison labour. Though the activities of the Russians were not glamorous, they did leave behind some lovely log cabins and a hotel in this unremarkable town. Some developers plan to convert these empty buildings into another tourist camp, but there is nothing in the area to particularly attract visitors.

Modot is just north of the main road between Ulaan Baatar and Öndörkhaan. It's an interesting place to break up a journey if you are hitching and have a tent, or to have a look at if you have chartered a jeep.

# Sükhbaatar Cүхъаатар

**Population:** 59,100
**Area** : 82,000 sq km
**Capital:** Baruun Urt
**No of Sums:** 13
**Elevation of Capital City:** 981m
**Main Livestock & Crops:** cattle, sheep
**Ethnic Groups:** Khalkh, Dariganga, Uzemchin

At the eastern edge of the Gobi Desert, Sükhbaatar aimag is one of the least visited and most uninteresting parts of Mongolia. Almost the entire aimag is flat grassland – there are no forests at all, and only a few hills masquerading as mountains. The sparsely populated aimag is named after Sükhbaatar, the canonised hero of the communist revolution of 1921. Sükhbaatar didn't actually live in this part of the country – it was his father who came from here.

The best thing about the aimag is the far south-eastern region known as Dariganga, and the Shiliin Bogd mountain nearby. Both are definitely worth a visit, but getting there will involve some effort. Try to avoid the dreary capital, Baruun Urt.

### BARUUN URT
БАРУУН УРТ

Baruun Urt gets our vote as the most depressing and uninteresting aimag capital in Mongolia. The small, dusty town was built in the middle of nowhere, probably because it is a central point in the aimag. Most of the 15,000 people live in large, ugly apartment blocks and a lot seem to be permanently drunk in the town square. A Soviet-built factory keeps a few locals occupied, and a coal mine 34km to the north-west employs a few more. Some maps refer to the town as Sükhbaatar, which is confusing because this is the name of the capital of Selenge aimag.

### Museum

If you are stuck in Baruun Urt, the museum in the dusty, southern part of town is worth a look. It has a reasonable collection of costumes representing the three ethnic groups which inhabit the region: the majority

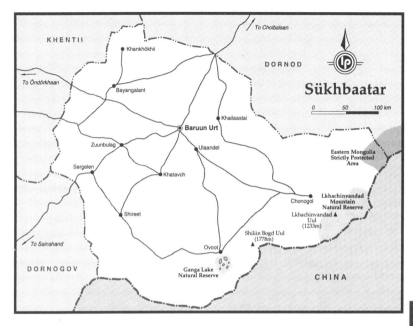

Khalkh, Dariganga (30,000 live in the south of Sükhbaatar aimag) and Uzemchin (about 2000 live in Dornod and Sükhbaatar aimags).

There are also fine examples of products from Dariganga's renowned silversmiths and blacksmiths, some stuffed gazelles (which is probably about as close as you will ever get to one), a map showing the locations of the 'man' and 'woman' statues in the aimag and some memorabilia of Sükhbaatar, the hero. The museum is open every weekday from 8 am to 5 pm (T250).

### Erdenemandal Khiid
Эрдэнэмандал Хийд

According to the monks at the monastery, Erdenemandal Khiid was originally built in 1830, about 20km from the present site. At the height of its splendour, there were seven temples and 1000 monks in residence, but the Stalinist purges of 1938 had the same result as elsewhere. Two of the monastery's deities, Gombo and Sendem, were secretly hidden and are now on display in the new temple. The monastery is about 200m west of the square.

### Places to Stay

Baruun Urt is the only aimag capital where camping is not a good idea; staying in a hotel is strongly recommended. The town is in the middle of dusty plains, there is no river nearby, and the abundance of aggressive drunks can easily ruin your night.

For such a dismal town, the two hotels are astoundingly good. The simple rooms at the *Sharga Hotel* (Шарга Зочид), next to the town square, are good value at T2400 per person, while the deluxe rooms, which comprise a sitting room, TV room, bedroom and private bath (but no hot water), cost only T3200 per person. Try to get a room which doesn't face the square because it is full of loud drunks during the evening.

The *Ganga Hotel* (Ганга Зочид) is the square, crimson building, about a 10 minute walk north-east of the centre. The rooms are far better and cheaper than at the Sharga: T1800 per person for the simple and T2700 for the deluxe, with a bathroom. Incredibly, the Ganga is one of the best hotels outside of Ulaan Baatar.

### Places to Eat
The *Sharga Hotel* is the best place to eat: it actually serves up an edible mutton and potato dish and, if you ask nicely, they will provide some hot water for tea, coffee or soup. The *Ganga Hotel* has a plush-looking restaurant, but doesn't offer anything to get excited about.

The two other alternatives are the *Zotol Restaurant* (Зотол Рэсторан), on the eastern side of the square, and an unnamed *restaurant* on the north-western side. The town has no market, and the shops are very poorly stocked.

### Getting There & Away
**Air** MIAT has flights to and from Ulaan Baatar on Monday, Wednesday and Friday for US$70. The airport is 1km south of town.

**Bus** Buses leave Ulaan Baatar every Monday and Wednesday (T4100) and return about two days later, depending on how long it takes to get to Baruun Urt.

**Jeep** Don't expect to be able to charter a jeep in Baruun Urt. The town is very poor, so there are no public shared jeeps; everyone hitches or takes the bus.

Baruun Urt is 191km south-west of Choibalsan, 229km south-east of Öndörkhaan and 560km south-east of Ulaan Baatar. The roads in eastern Mongolia are in pretty good condition, but the scenery in Sükhbaatar aimag is monotonous. Only the sight of thousands of gazelles galloping across the steppes can liven up a dull trip.

**Hitching** Hitching is difficult because few vehicles come here. Still, with some patience you'll get a lift to Choibalsan, Öndörkhaan or Dariganga. In Baruun Urt, ask around at the hotels or the police station.

### DARIGANGA
ДАРИГАНГА
Dariganga *sum* in the south-east of Sükh-baatar is the only region in the aimag worth

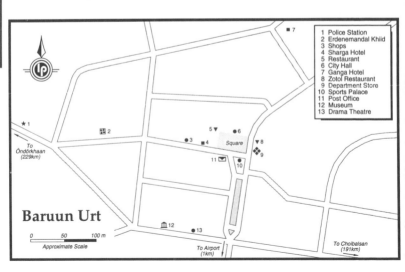

1 Police Station
2 Erdenemandal Khiid
3 Shops
4 Sharga Hotel
5 Restaurant
6 City Hall
7 Ganga Hotel
8 Zotol Restaurant
9 Department Store
10 Sports Palace
11 Post Office
12 Museum
13 Drama Theatre

To Öndörkhaan (229km)

**Baruun Urt**

0    50    100 m
Approximate Scale

To Airport (1km)

To Choibalsan (191km)

EASTERN MONGOLIA

visiting. Famous for its silversmiths and blacksmiths, Dariganga is also where the sand dunes of the Gobi and the grassy plains of the northern steppe converge to create what looks like thousands of hectares of perfect, natural golf courses (but don't let any developer know!).

To reach the sights in the area you will need a jeep and a good driver or guide. It's the only way to, firstly, get to Dariganga, and then to explore the lakes, 200 or so extinct volcanoes, mountains, sand dunes and ancient stones. And the sacred mountain of Shiliin Bogd isn't too far away.

### Things to See
There are six lakes in the vicinity; all are part of the 28,000 hectare Ganga Lake Natural Reserve. The three main lakes, Kholboo Nuur, Tsagaan Nuur and Ganga Nuur, are good for swimming, though a bit muddy.

The magnificent **Ganga Nuur** is about 10km south-east of the *sum* capital of Ovoot (OBOOT). When we visited, hundreds of horses were washing and drinking in the lake – very photogenic. Between the start of August and the end of October, the lake is also home to thousands of migrating swans. Along the shore, in a fenced compound, there is some fresh, delicious and safe spring water. The sand dunes in the region are known as **Kholboogiin Els**.

The skyline of Ovoot is dominated by **Altan Ovoo** (Golden Ovoo), a wide hill topped by a new **stupa** which only men are allowed to visit. The stupa was built in 1990 on top of the ruins of a monastery which was destroyed in 1937. In the area around Altan Ovoo, there are dozens of broken **statues** – their exact origins are not clear.

### Places to Stay
**Camping** There is nothing stopping you camping anywhere you want as long as you stay away from the ger camp and resort. If you have a vehicle, camp on the shores of Ganga Nuur.

**Resorts** There are no hotels in Ovoot, but at the time of research there were plans to open one near the town square. One km north of the village, the one and only resort is a collection of quaint blue and white huts along the tiny Dagshin Bulag Nuur. Beds in a large dorm-style room cost T850 per person and they serve reasonable mutton soup dishes for T350.

**Ger Camps** About 10km east of Ganga Nuur, Juulchin plans to open a new ger camp. The price will be about US$40 per person including meals; the standard and facilities will be the same at its other ger camps.

### Things to Buy
Dariganga is renowned throughout Mongolia for the kettles, plates, jewellery and other products made by its blacksmiths and silversmiths. Examples of their excellent work can

---

**Legends of Dariganga**

The word Dariganga comes from the Dar volcano (many volcanoes in the region were thought to be sacred and never named in public by locals for fear of upsetting the spirits) and the Ganga Nuur lake. Some of the local legends include:

- Chinggis Khaan made a sword which he dipped into Ganga Nuur, giving the lake special powers of healing.
- In the late 19th century, a local herdsman nicknamed Toroi-Bandi annoyed Manchurian rulers by stealing their horses, but eluded them by hiding near Shiliin Bogd Uul.
- The statues around Altan Ovoo are probably from a 10th or 13th century Mongolian pagan festival. Each represents a man on a throne, with a glass in his left hand resting on his knee. According to local tradition, you should place an offering of food in the 'glass'. ∎

be seen in the museum in Baruun Urt, or you can buy some from a few shops in Ovoot. One tiny factory, Darsan (Дарсан), can make anything you want if you are prepared to wait. If you're interested, make inquiries around town.

### Getting There & Away

At the height of the tourist season, chartered flights for organised tours may come to Dariganga. Your best bet is to catch the weekly bus (the day of departure varies) which connects Ovoot with Baruun Urt (153km), or you could hitch a ride from Baruun Urt to Ovoot without too much problem in summer.

The road between Baruun Urt and Ovoot is not bad, but the region is surprisingly barren of gers and animals. One or two jeeps are available for charter in Ovoot – ask at the ger camp, or around town.

### SHILIIN BOGD UUL
### ШИЛИЙН БОГД УУЛ

At 1778m, Shiliin Bogd, about 50km east of Ovoot, is the highest peak in Sükhbaatar aimag. The mountain is sacred to many Mongolians: the spirit of any man (sorry, again, ladies) who climbs it, especially at sunrise, will be revived. The region is stunning, isolated and close to the Chinese border – so be careful.

A jeep can drive about halfway up the mountain, and then it's a short, but blustery, walk to the top. There are plenty of ovoos and awesome views of craters across the border to China. (The empty, tiny Chinese hut in the distance must represent one of the world's most isolated postings for a border guard.) If you are camping, Shiliin Bogd offers one of the greatest sunrises in a country full of great sunrises.

### Permits

It wasn't until we had travelled about 40km from Chonogol on the way to Shiliin Bogd that the senior officer from the local military border patrol caught up with us and demanded to see our permit. He forced us to return to Chonogol, confiscated our pass-

ports and questioned us for four hours. Then he made a few telephone calls to Ulaan Baatar, gave us a permit and 'persuaded' us to spend the evening as their 'guests' in the barracks.

The upshot is that according to authorities in Chonogol and Ovoot (but not in Ulaan Baatar), foreigners need a permit to visit Shiliin Bogd because it is so close to the Chinese border. (Nobody can tell how close: there are no border signposts whatsoever.)

Authorities in Chonogol and Ovoot prefer that you get a permit in Baruun Urt, but they will issue you one if you have turned up in Chonogol or Ovoot without one. The permits are free but may take a day or two to process unless some extra fee is offered.

### Getting There & Away

The only two roads to Shiliin Bogd start from Chonogol (75km away) and Ovoot (55km). It's better to go to Ovoot first, where you are more likely to find a jeep for rent or get a lift.

### AROUND SHILIIN BOGD

Assuming that you have a jeep to get to Shiliin Bogd in the first place, there are a few other places to see in the area. The **Taliin Agui** (Талийн Агуй), 5km north of the mountain, is one of the largest caves in Mongolia. If you can squeeze through the narrow entrance, the large, and a little claustrophobic, cave has seven chambers to explore. You'll need a torch (flashlight) to see anything, and be careful on the icy floor. A small sign in Mongolian identifies the entrance.

In **Khurguin Khundii** (Хург уин Хундий), a valley 35km north of Shiliin Bogd, a dozen or so ancient (pre-Chinggis Khaan) stone statues lay on the ground. The origin of these statues varies: they either represent famous people from the region, or they were built to commemorate local women who jumped off a nearby mountain because they were forced to marry men they didn't love. You will have to rely on your driver to find the statues and to locate **Bichigtiin Skhakhaa** (Буүуг тийн Схахаа), a pretty canyon about 2km away.

## CHONOGOL
ЧОНОГОЛ

The nearest hotel (or, indeed, building) to Shiliin Bogd is 75km away at Chonogol village in the *sum* of Erdenetsalan (Эрдэнэтсалан). There is almost nothing in the village to see or do, except visit the two monasteries and a quaint stadium on top of the hill. The ruins of the biggest monastery in the aimag are reportedly nearby, but you'll have to take a guide and a jeep to find them. The monastery was built in 1886 and destroyed in 1946.

The unnamed and unsigned *hotel* in Chonogol has clean rooms with a black and white TV for T1000 per person. You'll have to ask locals where it is. If the only jeep in the village is available, working, full of petrol and the driver is not drunk, you may be able to charter it to Shiliin Bogd – but you are better off trying in Ovoot.

## LKHACHINVANDAD UUL & NATURAL RESERVE
ЛХАЧИНВАНДАД УУЛ

If you are visiting Shiliin Bogd by jeep, you may wish to carry on east for another 120km to the 60,000-hectare Lkhachinvandad Mountain Natural Reserve, on the border with China. This reserve contains the Lkhachinvandad mountain (1233m) and is full of gazelle and elk.

EASTERN MONGOLIA

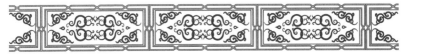

# Western Mongolia

In 1931 the giant western aimag of Chandmani was divided into three: Bayan-Ölgii, Khovd and Uvs. The dominant feature of western Mongolia is the Mongol Altai Nuruu, Mongolia's highest mountain range, which stretches from Russia through Bayan-Ölgii and Khovd and on to the adjacent Gov-Altai aimag. It contains many challenging and popular peaks for mountain climbers, and is the source of several rivers which eventually flow into the Arctic and Pacific oceans.

There are some important points to note when travelling in western Mongolia. Transport between western Mongolia and Ulaan Baatar is mainly by plane – so flights are often very full. No long-distance buses travel from Ulaan Baatar to these three aimags, or between the aimags. The only form of travel around western Mongolia is by shared or private jeep, or truck. As the three capitals are joined by road, it is easy to see all the sights by jeep. In the future, foreigners may be able to travel by road from western Mongolia to Russia, and onto Kazakstan – check the current situation.

Western Mongolia is on a different time zone than Ulaan Baatar, ie one hour earlier than the rest of the country. In some parts, especially Bayan-Ölgii, Kazak is a dominant language. At the time of research, all three aimag capitals suffered from serious electricity and water shortages in summer. You should also be aware that an occasional outbreak of the plague can restrict travel, and that rabid dogs are not uncommon in the region.

In the summer of 1995, when foreigners needed permits to travel into the countryside,

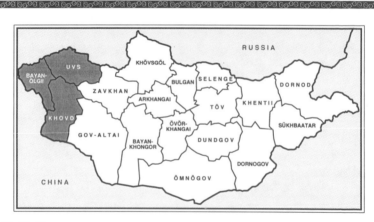

**Highlights**
*   Achit Nuur: pleasant swimming, fishing and camping; superb sunsets; birdlife
*   Kazaks: visit a brightly decorated ger; learn about eagle-hunting
*   Kharkhiraa Valley: a stunning area of forests and streams; stay in a cheap resort; superb hiking
*   Üüreg Nuur: a lovely, accessible freshwater lake; excellent camping and hiking
*   Uvs Nuur: Mongolia's largest lake; birdlife is vast (but hard to find); explore nearby sand dunes and mountains

several travellers reported real hassles with police and security officers in the three aimags. In 1996, when permits were no longer required, we heard of no-one who had any problems. Hopefully, this is a thing of the past, but if the border with Russia is opened for foreigners, security in the area may tighten up a little.

# Bayan-Ölgii Баян-Өлгий

**Population:** 90,100
**Area:** 46,000 sq km
**Capital:** Ölgii
**No of Sums:** 13
**Elevation of Capital City:** 1710m
**Main Livestock & Crops:** goat, sheep; hay, wheat
**Ethnic Groups:** Kazak, Khalkh, Dorvod, Uriankhai, Tuva

The Mongol Altai Nuruu is the backbone of Bayan-Ölgii. The highest peaks, many over 4000m, are permanently covered with glaciers and snow, while the valleys have a few green pastures which support about two million livestock, as well as bears, foxes and lynxes. These valleys are dotted with small communities of nomadic families enjoying the short summer from mid-June to late August. The lower regions are mostly arid, rocky hills. Like Tibet, this aimag is almost totally devoid of trees, but the stark beauty of rock, ice and desert makes up for it.

The only national park in the aimag is the Khokh Serkh Strictly Protected Area, on the border with Khovd. Environmentalists hope that further sections of Bayan-Ölgii will become national parks to preserve the argali sheep, ibex and snow leopard, as well as the important sources of lakes and rivers in the Great Lakes Depression in the Uvs and Khovd aimags.

Unlike the rest of Mongolia, which is dominated by the Khalkh Mongols, about 90% of Bayan-Ölgii's population are Kazak, almost all of them Muslim. The remaining

## The Kazaks

Kazak nomads first started to come to what is now Bayan-Ölgii in the 1840s (and a few made it all the way to Töv in the 1860s). The nomads came to graze their sheep on the high mountain pastures during summer, and spent the winter in Kazakstan or Xinjiang province in China. After the Mongolian revolution in 1921, a permanent border was drawn by agreement between China, Russia and Mongolia, but the Kazaks remained nomadic until the 1930s, crossing the border at will.

The word *kazak* is said to mean 'free warrior' or 'steppe roamer'. Kazaks trace their roots to the 15th century, when rebellious kinsmen of an Uzbek khaan broke away and settled in present-day Kazakstan. In Kazakstan, but less in Mongolia, Kazak women wear long dresses with stand-up collars, or brightly decorated velvet waistcoats and heavy jewellery. The men still wear baggy shirts and trousers, sleeveless jackets, wool or cotton robes, and a skullcap or a high, tasselled felt hat.

Kazaks generally adhere rather loosely to Sunni Islam, but religion is not a major force because of the distance from the centre of Islam, their nomadic lifestyle, and the suppression of Islam by Stalinism. Islam is making a comeback in Bayan-Ölgii following the lifting of restrictions against religion, aid packages from other Muslim countries, the construction of a mosque in Ölgii, and the first *hajj*, or pilgrimage, to Mecca, in 1992.

Kazaks speak a Turkic language with 42 Cyrillic letters, similar to Russian and a little different from Mongolian. The Mongolian government is trying to placate the Kazak minority and stop them from returning to Kazakstan by encouraging the Kazak language in schools in Bayan-Ölgii – but it has not been successful. ■

RUSSIA

UVS

Ulaangom

Tsagaannuur

Nogoonnuur

Achit
Nuur

Sogoog

Gol

Tsagaan

Gol

Tavanbogd
Uul
~(4374m)

Bilüü

Ölgii

Tsagaantüngi

Tsul-Ulaan

Khovd

Gol

Khöshööt

Gol

Khoton
Nuur

Khovd

Tsengal
Uul
(3943m)

Tsast Uul
(4193m)

Tsambagarav
Uul
(4202m)

Buyant

Tolbo
Nuur

Khurgan
Nuur

Tolbo

Dayan
Nuur

Tal
Nuur

Khokh Serkh
Strictly Protected
Area

Khovd

Khar Us
Nuur

Sagsai

Gol

Mongol

Altai

Rashaant

KHOVD

Nuruu

CHINA

Tögrög

Bayan-Ölgii

0     40     80 km

Jargalant

WESTERN MONGOLIA

10% are mostly obscure minority groups, including the Uriankhai, Dorvod and Tuva. Many people in the aimag speak Kazak, so if you have spent time perfecting some conversational Mongolian, you may be devastated because many Kazaks won't be able to understand you. Someone nearby, however, will speak Mongolian and, possibly Russian, but certainly nothing else.

## ÖLGII
ӨЛГИЙ

Ölgii, the capital of the aimag, is a Kazak city which happens to be in Mongolia. You can

certainly feel that you are in a Muslim-influenced Central Asian region, rather than in Mongolia: many places have squat toilets; in the city, there are more signs in Arabic and Kazak Cyrillic than in Mongolian script; the market, which is called a *bazar* rather than the Mongolian *zakh*, sells kebabs *(shashlyk)*; and some women wear headscarves.

Ölgii is a depressed city, suffering from the outflow of Kazaks to Kazakstan following the breakup of the Soviet Union. Ölgii is the only aimag capital to have a serious decline in population: like most of Mongolia, the population rose steadily from 19,700 in 1980 to

29,400 in 1990, but fell to 21,400 in 1995 – about 9000 Kazaks left the city in 1992/3.

Maybe we were unlucky, or it was hot and late (so a lot of drinking had taken place), but Ölgii was the only place in Mongolia where we felt uncomfortable. While walking around the market for 10 minutes, we were mildly assaulted several times by drunks. Around town, and especially in the market, it is wise to hang on to your valuables and avoid eye contact with any drunks. Women, especially on their own, may need to be more circumspect than normal.

The **museum** is not the best in Mongolia, but it does give an indication of the abundant wildlife in the aimag – probably the grandest exhibit is the huge, stuffed snow leopard. The 2nd floor is devoted to history, and the 3rd floor has some interesting displays of Kazak culture. Entrance to the museum costs T500. It is open on weekdays from 9 am to 1 pm and from 2 to 6 pm, and is located in a large, modern building between the two town squares and the market.

### Places to Stay

**Camping** Ölgii is not as safe for camping as other aimag capitals because of the number of drunks in the town; a hotel might not be a bad idea. If you want to camp, walk east of the square to Khovd Gol and then head south-east, away from the market and ger suburbs.

**Hotels** Opposite the National Theatre, the Kazak-run *Tavanbogd Hotel* (Таванъогд Зочид) is currently the only hotel in town. All rooms are comfortable and clean, and

have a toilet and sink (though the plumbing, if there is any water, has seen better days). Foreigners pay from T2640 to T4000 per person – the owner couldn't really decide. Some travellers have reported being charged another price when they leave, so pay in advance and get a receipt, or agree on the price in writing. This is one of the few hotels to keep your passport while you stay there.

### Places to Eat

The restaurant in the *Tavanbogd Hotel* serves rice with meat, and little else. On the plus side, the atmosphere is not bad and the service is friendly. A large Kazak restaurant at the western end of the main street and another east of the post office are worth trying for some Kazak boiled mutton rather than Mongolian boiled mutton (unfortunately, there is no difference).

Otherwise, try the five or six *shaykhana* (teahouses) in abandoned train wagons around the market and town squares. They usually serve delicious tea (*shay* in the Kazak language) – not the milky and salty stuff loved by Mongolians – and some khuurshuur (fried meat pancakes). The kebabs at the market are a tasty change.

### Entertainment

The best place to while away some time, and maybe ask about a lift (and watch your driver get drunk), is the bar next to the Tavanbogd Hotel – look for the sign 'Disco Bar' in English. It gets rowdy at night, but the service is friendly and the setting is pleasant – even if the Coke and beer are warm.

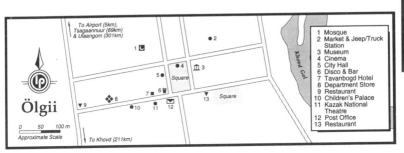

1 Mosque
2 Market & Jeep/Truck Station
3 Museum
4 Cinema
5 City Hall
6 Disco & Bar
7 Tavanbogd Hotel
8 Department Store
9 Restaurant
10 Children's Palace
11 Kazak National Theatre
12 Post Office
13 Restaurant

The incongruous, ochre-coloured Kazak National Theatre dominates the town centre. Some occasional performances of ethnic songs, dances and plays are held, but it stands empty and unused most of the time.

## Things to Buy
The Kazak influence in Ölgii makes the market far more interesting than others in the countryside. There is not a lot of food to buy (and some of the drunks there are aggressive), but you can get kebabs (mutton, of course), Chinese tea and expensive bread.

You can also pick up some traditional Kazak clothing, including skullcaps worn by Muslim men, boots and sheepskin coats, magnificent hand-woven carpets and various leather products. If you have a local guide, you may be able to look around the small Kazak factories in Ölgii which churn out these products.

## Getting There & Away
**Air** MIAT flies between Ölgii and Ulaan Baatar, with a refuelling stop (often at Mörön), every Tuesday, Thursday and Saturday for US$130. The four hour flight provides breathtaking views of glacier-capped peaks as you approach Ölgii.

The airport is 5km north of the centre, on the opposite side of the river. There is no bus, but it's usually possible to hitch a ride in a truck or on the back of a motorcycle.

MIAT has stopped flying between Ulaan Baatar and Almaty (the capital of Kazakstan), via Ölgii, after losing T180 million in one year. Each Friday, Kazakstan Airlines apparently still flies between Almaty and Ölgii – but this flight (US$140) is unreliable, probably illegal and almost certainly not available for foreigners. If you want any information, there are a couple of numbers to ring in Ölgii (☎ 712 161 or 712 056).

**Jeep** The road from Ölgii to Khovd city (211km) is pretty good. The 301km road to Ulaangom, via Tsagaannuur, is also good. Some vehicles take a shortcut via the bridge just south of Achit Nuur, bypassing Tsagaannuur, but the road north of Achit Nuur is rough.

Ölgii is not blessed with a lot of jeeps for hire. For a trip around western Mongolia, it's better to start from Ulaangom or Khovd city. Public shared jeeps to Tsagaannuur and, less frequently, to Khovd city and Ulaangom leave from the Ölgii market.

**Hitching** A few vehicles, mainly petrol tankers, travel the road between Ölgii and Khovd city. The Ölgii-Ulaangom road is not as busy because most vehicles head east towards Ulaan Baatar and use the southern road via Khovd city. Some vehicles travelling between Ölgii and Ulaangom will bypass Tsagaannuur and take the shortcut via Achit Nuur.

### Hawking
While travelling around Bayan-Ölgii, you may come across Kazaks living in slightly larger and darker-coloured gers. Some are eagle-hunters who train eagles, falcons and hawks to collect marmots, small foxes and wolves and return them to the ger, where they are used for food by the Kazaks. If you ask nicely, the Kazaks may proudly show you their birds.

In the Kazak tradition known as hawking, which dates back about 2000 years, young birds of prey are caught in nearby valleys, fattened up and washed. The birds' training involves being kept awake for weeks at a time, sitting on a pole called a *tugir*, and catching small-animal skins called *shirga* thousands of times. Some of the tools of the trade are a *tomaga* (hood), *bialai* (gloves) and *khundag* (blanket to keep the bird warm). If well trained, a bird can live and hunt for about 30 years.

When we asked how a vicious hunting bird can be trained to collect, but not eat, small animals, the patriarch, or *aksakals*, of the clan, smiled without teeth and answered with ambiguity that 'it is just like teaching a child'.

The best places to find some Kazak eagle-hunters are at Buyant near Khovd city, the Tsast Uul region between Khovd and Bayan-Ölgii and in most of Bayan-Ölgii province. ∎

Check out the noticeboard at the market for information (in Mongolian, Kazak or Russian) about lifts around the aimag. If you can't read the notices, just ask around anyway. A lot of Russian trucks hang around the market, waiting for cargo to take to Russia via Tsagaannuur. The other place to ask is the Disco Bar next to the Tavanbogd Hotel.

## TSAGAANNUUR
ЦАГААННУУР

Yet another town called White Lake, Tsagaannuur is less famous for its lake (there are several bigger and nicer ones nearby) than as the starting point for travel by road into Russia, and then onto Kazakstan. See the Kazakstan via Russia boxed story in the Getting There & Away chapter for details about this border.

The Ölgii-Ulaangom road is generally not busy, and some vehicles take a shortcut via Achit Nuur, but you can get a ride on a truck to Tsagaannuur easily enough – a truck takes about 18 hours from Khovd city and about five from Ölgii. There are no hotels in Tsagaannuur, so if you are waiting for a lift, ask some Russian drivers, or someone at the petrol station, about a place to stay.

## TSAST UUL
ЦАСТ УУЛ

The two *sums* of Altaitsögts (Алтайнөгтс) and Bayannuur (Баяннуур) are about 50km south-east of Ölgii, on the border with Khovd aimag. They are full of lush valleys with friendly Kazak and Mongol nomads in summer, dozens of tiny, unmapped lakes and soaring, permanently snow-capped peaks, such as Tsast Uul (4193m).

If you have your own vehicle and tent, take a detour between Khovd city and Ölgii and spend a few peaceful days around Tsast Uul. It is always cold up here (it only stops snowing between about mid-June and late August), so be prepared. Just to the south, in the Khovd aimag, Tsambagarav Uul (4202m) is slightly higher and equally as stunning (see the Khovd section for details).

## TAVANBOGD UUL
ТАВАНБОГН УУЛ

Tavanbogd (Five Saints) mountain rises 4374m above the borders of three nations, and for this reason it is also known as Nairamdal (Friendship) Peak. If you sit on the summit, you can simultaneously be in Mongolia, China and Russia.

Tavanbogd was long believed to be Mongolia's highest mountain, but there is a dispute with officials in Khovd aimag who now claim that Mönkh Khairkhan (at least 4362m) is higher. Nevertheless, Tavanbogd is one of Mongolia's most spectacular peaks, and the only one in Bayan-Ölgii to be permanently covered with large glaciers and of interest to professional climbers. It's fairly dangerous, and to climb it you need to be with an experienced group properly equipped with ice axes, crampons and ropes. Don't even consider attempting it solo.

To get to the mountain, you should be able to hitch a ride to Khöshööt (Хөшөөт), in the *sum* of Tsengel (Цэнгэл), but from there you will have to trek about 110km along the Tsagaan river. If you have your own vehicle, you can drive to within about 40km of the base of the mountain. Once you reach the end of the road, it's a 15km trek to the first glacier, where most climbers set up base camp. The climb up the glacier is about 25km, and you can expect to encounter icy temperatures, crevasses and, maybe, even a snow leopard or two.

Two local travel agencies, Mongolian Adventure Tours and the Mongol Altai Club, organise treks up the mountain in July and August. See Travel Agencies in the Ulaan Baatar chapter and Activities in the Facts for the Visitor chapter for more details.

## TSENGEL UUL
ЦЭНГЭЛ УУЛ

At 3943m, Tsengel mountain is not the highest peak in Bayan-Ölgii, but it's a beautiful, albeit strenuous, climb. The approach is usually by jeep to Khöshööt, followed by a trek south along Kharganat creek.

> **Falcons**
> Falcons, for centuries revered by Mongolians, have greatly decreased in number in the past few decades because of poaching. The falcon will, however, make a comeback. It may be resurrected as the country's national symbol, and Saudi Arabia and Kuwait have agreed to donate US$2 million to establish a Falcon and Bustard Protection Centre in conjunction with the Mongolian Bird-Watch Foundation. ■

## TOLBO NUUR
ТОЛБО НУУР

Tolbo lake is about 50km south of Ölgii, on the main road between Ölgii and Khovd city, so it's an easy day trip or stopover. The saltwater lake is high (2080m), large and eerie, but a bit disappointing because the shoreline has no trees. There are a few gers around the lake, and the water is clean enough for swimming if you don't mind icy temperatures. If you want to see, and camp at, some better lakes, keep travelling on to Uvs aimag.

## DAYAN NUUR
ДАЯН НУУР

This remote and high (2212m) lake is in the far western part of the aimag. Dayan Nuur (as well as Khurgan Nuur nearby) is the source of the Khovd Gol and the starting point for rafting trips downriver. During the five day trip by boat from Dayan Nuur to Ölgii, you can fish and explore nearby mountains. Juulchin is the only agency to organise this rafting trip (see Travel Agencies in Ulaan Baatar).

You can reach Dayan Nuur by trekking on foot or horse upstream from Khöshööt, or from Buyant (Буянт).

# Khovd Ховд

**Population:** 90,400
**Area:** 76,000 sq km
**Capital:** Khovd
**No of Sums:** 16
**Elevation of Capital City:** 1406m
**Main Livestock & Crops:** camel, sheep, goat; potatoes, wheat, melons
**Ethnic Groups:** Khalkh, Kazak, Uriankhai, Zakhchin, Myangad, Torguud, Oold, Khoton

Khovd is one of Mongolia's most heterogeneous aimags, with a Khalkh majority and minorities of Khoton, Kazak, Uriankhai, Zakhchin, Myangad, Oold and Torguud peoples. It is the most visited aimag in western Mongolia and the most popular place for tourists west of Khövsgöl Nuur, though some visitors can become disconcerted by the attention in the more remote *sums*:

I've been stranded in a remote sum in Khovd. No-one speaks English, and I am being stared at and followed by a large group of children as if I'm from outer space. For the first time in two days there hasn't been a tremendous gaggle of people in my hotel room gawking at me.
**Heidi Heinzerling, USA**

Khovd aimag is almost cut in half by the mighty Mongol Altai Nuruu range, and the northern and southern sections are barren and dotted with salt lakes and smaller mountain peaks. The melting snow from the mountains recharges the water table every spring, providing Khovd with more than 200 fast-moving rivers (and dozens of lakes), none of which has an outlet to the sea. All the rivers simply disappear beneath the sands or run into large saltwater marshes which serve as giant evaporating ponds.

Subterranean water runs beneath the desert, bubbling to the surface in springs, and creating oases and green pastures surrounded by sand. The rivers and lakes provide sufficient water to support over a million head of livestock and an abundance of wild animals and birdlife.

### National Parks
There are several national parks in Khovd aimag, and attempts are being made to establish

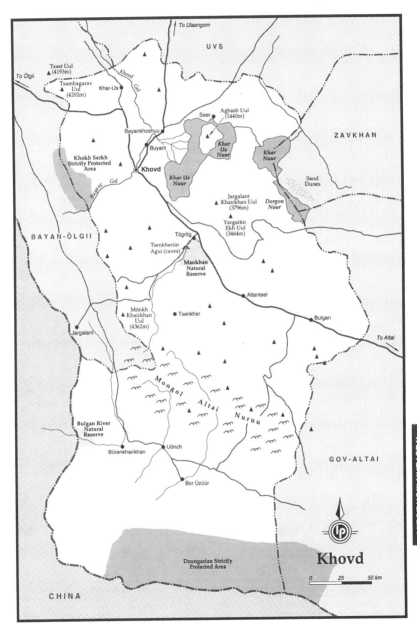

To Ulaangom

UVS

Tsast Uul
▲ (4193m)
To Ölgii
Tsambagarav
Uul
▲ (4202m)
Khar-Us

Khovd Gol

ZAVKHAN

Seer

Agbash Uul
(1440m)

Bayankhoshuu

Buyant

Khar
Us
Nuur

Khar
Nuur

Khovd

Khokh Serkh
Strictly Protected
Area

Sand
Dunes

Khar Us
Nuur

Buyant Gol

Jargalant
Khairkhan Uul
▲ (3796m)

Dorgon
Nuur

Yargaitin
Ekh Uul
▲ (3464m)

BAYAN-ÖLGII

Tögrög

Tsenkheriin
Agui (caves)

Mankhan
Natural
Reserve

Altanteel

Bulgan

Mönkh
▲ Khairkhan
Uul
(4362m)

Tsenkher

To Altai

Jargalant

Mongol Altai Nuruu

Bulgan River
Natural
Reserve

Bürenkhairkhan

Uönch

GOV-ALTAI

Bor Üzüür

Khovd

Dzungarian Strictly
Protected Area

0    25    50 km

CHINA

another around the salt lakes of Khar Nuur and Khar Us Nuur, because they are the breeding grounds for antelopes and rare species of migratory pelicans, falcons and bustards.

Bulgan River Natural Reserve, on the south-western border with China, was established to help preserve beavers.

Dzungarian Strictly Protected Area (also known as 'Gobi B') was created to protect *khulan* wild asses, gazelles, jerboas and *takhi* wild horses.

Khokh Serkh Strictly Protected Area, on the north-west border with Bayan-Ölgii, helps protect argali sheep, ibexes and snow leopards.

Mankhan Natural Reserve, directly south-east of Khovd city, preserves an endangered species of antelope.

### Organised Tours

The attractions for visitors to Khovd are its lakes, mountains and Kazak culture, though there are better examples of all three in Bayan-Ölgii and Uvs aimags. However, there's more regular and reliable air transport from Ulaan Baatar to Khovd.

Several Mongolian companies run tours around Khovd aimag and other parts of western Mongolia. Refer to the Travel Agencies section in the Ulaan Baatar chapter for details of these agencies, and to the Activities section in the Facts for the Visitor chapter for information about mountain climbing.

Juulchin runs an interesting birdwatching and trekking trip around Khar Us Nuur, and treks up Mönkh Khairkhan Uul. It is the only company which organises rafting trips down the Khovd Gol in Bayan-Ölgii.

Mongol Altai Club is the specialist in mountain climbing treks of all major peaks in Khovd aimag and the other two western provinces.

Mongolian Adventure Tours also does trekking trips up and around Mönkh Khairkhan Uul.

Nomads runs fascinating tours to Khovd aimag, sometimes to coincide with the Naadam Festival (as an alternative to seeing it in Ulaan Baatar). These tours include horse riding and walking along several valleys, including to Tsambagarav Uul, visits to Kazak families and exploration of the magnificent Üüreg, Achit and Uvs lakes.

### KHOVD
ХОВД

Once a small farming community, and later a centre for Russian and Mongolian trading, Khovd city is, not surprisingly, the capital of the aimag, as well as the major industrial centre of western Mongolia. A pleasant and easygoing city of 35,000 people, built near the fast-flowing Buyant Gol, Khovd is a good place to start a trip around western Mongolia. One of the most bizarre sights (and sounds) in Mongolia are the flocks of seagulls which inhabit the city – it must be thousands of km to the nearest sea.

The city is fairly depressed but survives on an agricultural economy, food processing and some light manufacturing of building materials. It also boasts an agricultural institute and a teachers' training college. The tourist potential is considerable, but Khovd city will need a lot more infrastructure. At the time of research, a decrepit power station and unpaid debts of about T200 million have resulted in severe shortages of water and electricity in summer.

### Information

The Daatgal Bank, next the police station, changes US dollars and also doubles as the MIAT office. It is open from 8 am to 3 pm

WESTERN MONGOLIA

## Aldanjavyn Ayush

In the square in front of the city hall in Khovd, a small statue honours Aldanjavyn Ayush (1859-1939). In 1903 he wrote a petition to oppose excessive taxation and debt, and presented it to the Manchurian rulers in Khovd, all to no avail. In 1912, after the Manchu dynasty was overthrown in China, he again wrote a petition to oppose feudal privilege and ask the Mongolian government to cancel previous debts and lower taxes – but he was later arrested.

Ayush joined the 1921 revolution which succeeded in overthrowing the monarchy and bringing socialism to Mongolia. He was rewarded by being made head of the Tsetseg *sum* in Khovd aimag, where he is a local hero. ■

(with lunch from noon to 1 pm), and on Saturday morning. Alternatively, you can change US dollars, Chinese yuan or Russian roubles with a couple of moneychangers who hang around the market.

### Museum

The museum in Khovd city is one of the better ones in the countryside. It has a relatively good geology exhibit, the usual collection of stuffed wildlife, including an ibex with its distinctive corrugated antlers, some ethnic costumes and artefacts, and a snow leopard pelt tacked up on the wall. One of the more interesting exhibits are the re-creations of the cave paintings at Tsenkheriin Agui (see later in this chapter). All the explanations are in either Mongolian or Latin.

According to the sign above the door, the museum is open from 8 to noon and 1 to 5 pm on weekdays, and on Saturday morning – but it was often closed. Tickets cost T500. It is on a corner, near the police station.

### Sangiin Kherem (Manchu Ruins)
Сангийн Хэрэм

At the northern end of the city are some rapidly disappearing ruins built in about 1762 by the Manchu (Qing dynasty) warlords who once conquered, and brutally governed, Mongolia. The walled compound once contained several temples, a Chinese graveyard and the homes of the Manchu rulers.

The compound was 40,000 sq metres in area, and the walls were about 4m high, and 2m thick. At one time, there was a moat (2m deep and 3m wide) around the compound, but this has been completely filled in, and three enormous doors provided access. The compound was abandoned after the 1911 Chinese Revolution which overthrew the last emperor.

These limited ruins, and the area around them, are now used to grow vegetables, practise football and volleyball, and as landfill – but are still worth a look. The one legacy of Manchurian rule which has remained are the magnificent 200-year-old trees which line the streets of Khovd city.

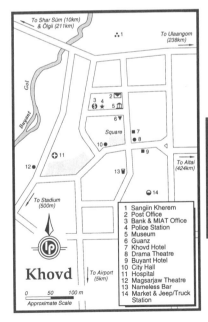

| | |
|---|---|
| 1 | Sangiin Kherem |
| 2 | Post Office |
| 3 | Bank & MIAT Office |
| 4 | Police Station |
| 5 | Museum |
| 6 | Guanz |
| 7 | Khovd Hotel |
| 8 | Drama Theatre |
| 9 | Buyant Hotel |
| 10 | City Hall |
| 11 | Hospital |
| 12 | Magsarjav Theatre |
| 13 | Nameless Bar |
| 14 | Market & Jeep/Truck Station |

Khovd

WESTERN MONGOLIA

## Shar Süm
Шар Сүм

The original Shar Süm (Yellow Temple) was built in the 1770s but was completely destroyed during the Stalinist purge of 1937. In 1990 the temple was rebuilt and today is an active place of worship. It is open every day until about 2 pm, but the best time to visit is from 9 to 10 am when a ceremony usually takes place. The temple is 10km north-west of the city.

## Hiking

The dry, rugged hills north of the Manchu ruins offer some good opportunities for hiking. The views are naturally great from up there – just be careful of the rocks.

The Buyant Gol is a swift river on the west side of town. The locals go swimming here, and it's a great place to hike around either upstream or downstream. However, from around mid-September until the cold weather sets in, clouds of mosquitoes make this an area to avoid. You may be tempted to drink from the river, but thinking about the livestock upstream may quench your thirst altogether.

## Places to Stay

**Camping** Some of the best camping in western Mongolia is along the Buyant Gol. Just walk south from the town for about 10 minutes (or take a jeep) to the interesting, Islam-influenced Naadam Stadium. The area is fairly crowded with cows and gers, but you will be left alone. If you have your own vehicle, try further along the Buyant, on the road to either Ulaangom or Ölgii.

**Hotels** If you are going to stay for a while, the best option is to try to get a room in a local ger or flat. If you ask around, or look lost, someone may take you under their wing and offer you a bed for about T500 per person.

The *Buyant Hotel* (Буянт Зочид) is the place to avoid: it charges a hefty foreigners' price of T8250 per person (and the staff wondered why no tourists stay there). There is no sign; it is opposite the Drama Theatre.

The effusive staff at the *Khovd Hotel* (Ховд Зочид) will probably try to palm you off with their comfortable, but overpriced, deluxe room with bathroom for T6600 per person, but if you ask again, they will reluctantly give you a bed in a pleasant simple room for T2750 per person. The Khovd Hotel is north of the Drama Theatre; it is easier to find than the Buyant.

## Places to Eat

If the staff can be bothered to open it, the *Buyant Hotel* has a restaurant, but if the prices of the rooms are any indication, this may be a good place to avoid. The *Khovd Hotel* serves ordinary mutton dishes, and is nothing special.

The best place to try during the day (it is closed in the evening) is the friendly, unnamed *restaurant* in the city hall building. During the evening, the bar we have dubbed the *Nameless Bar*, south of the square, is more interested in serving drinks than food, but will rustle up something 'muttonish'. The *guanz* just south of the museum is OK. It is unsigned, but you can find it by the music blaring from the window. Several guanzes are located in train wagons around the town.

## Entertainment

The *Magsarjaw Theatre*, on the way to the Naadam Stadium, often holds cultural shows, but very rarely during the summer holidays.

## Things to Buy

One traveller bought some fantastic camel-hair jumpers (sweaters) from a tiny factory in town. We couldn't find any camel-hair products or the factory, but saw many goat-skins and sheepskins, and skins hanging from other unrecognisable carcasses, at the market.

The daily market, south of the town centre, is large, lively and well stocked. It is a good place to buy noodles, rice, tea, meat and bread, as well as other 'necessities' like chocolate bars and soft drinks. Khovd aimag is justifiably famous for its watermelons (normally best in late summer), which are also available at the market. One or two shops in the town sell some basic supplies, but generally the best place for food and supplies is the market.

### Getting There & Away

**Air** The four hour MIAT flight between Ulaan Baatar and Khovd city leaves on Tuesday, Thursday, Friday (via Bulgan city) and Saturday. Tickets (if you can get one) cost US$120 for Ulaan Baatar-Khovd. You may also get a flight from Khovd city to Bulgan for a cheap US$45, so if you want to save money, and also see the northern part of Mongolia, this is a good option – but double-check the price first. Khangard airlines flies to Khovd city on Wednesday for the same price as MIAT: US$120.

Flights to Khovd city always stop somewhere to refuel. If it stops at Mörön, this flight is the only one in the country where you can combine two trips – to Khövsgöl Nuur and to western Mongolia – without returning to Ulaan Baatar. The airport is 5km south of the city. There may be a bus there when you arrive, but otherwise you will have to charter a jeep.

Khovd-Ulaan Baatar flights (and in reverse) are popular, so it is vital to buy tickets in advance at the Daatgal Bank in Khovd city. The MIAT office and staff do not enjoy a great reputation. Get to the airport at least two hours before departure (three hours if you don't have a ticket).

To buy a ticket on the day of departure, check in your luggage and to get onto the plane, be prepared for that traditional dance, which you may have forgotten after leaving Ulaan Baatar: the Mongolian Scramble. Travellers have also reported being charged double for normal 'foreigners' tickets' – all 'rich' foreigners are fair game to MIAT here.

**Jeep** There are several jeeps for hire in Khovd city, which makes it the best place to start a trip around western Mongolia. Jeeps cost from T100 to T130 per km, but you will be hard-pressed to get one for less than T150

per km. They hang around the market. Bargain hard.

The road from Khovd city to Ölgii (211km) is pretty good; to Altai (424km) it is rough and boring in patches; and to Ulaangom (238km) the road is often marred by broken bridges and flooded rivers after heavy rain.

**Hitching** The road between Altai and Khovd city is not really busy, but something will come along. Less traffic goes to Ölgii from Khovd city, and very few vehicles travel along the Khovd-Ulaangom road because vehicles head east from Ulaangom or Khovd towards Ulaan Baatar.

To find a lift in Khovd city, ask the truck drivers who hang around the market, and check the noticeboard at the entrance to the market.

### BULGAN
### БУЛГАН

Along the main road, about halfway between Khovd city and Altai (in Gov-Altai aimag), Bulgan, in the Dariv (Дарив) *sum*, is the quintessential Mongolian ghost-town. There is no need to stop at all, except to check out what a busy regional centre used to look like. There is a decrepit hotel, a barely functioning guanz and plenty of people wondering what to do with their time.

### BUYANT
### БУЯНТ

Only about 25km north-east of Khovd city is the small town of Buyant in the *sum* of Dund-Us (Дунд-Ус). If you are not going onto Bayan-Ölgii, or have no private transport, Buyant is an accessible place to visit a Kazak community and, if you are lucky, see some eagle-hunters. You can hire a jeep there from Khovd city, or hitch a ride. There is nowhere to stay; you can camp or go on a day trip from Khovd city.

### KHAR US NUUR
### ХАР УС НУУР

About 40km to the east of Khovd city is Khar Us Nuur (Black Water Lake), the second-largest freshwater lake (15,800 sq km) in

Mongolia – but with an average depth of only 4m. Khovd Gol flows into this lake, creating a giant delta with what could be described as an island – the 270 sq km Agbash Uul mountain (1440m) – to the north-east of the lake.

Khar Us Nuur is the perfect habitat for wild ducks, geese, wood grouse, partridges and seagulls, including the rare Relict Gull and Herring Gull – and a billion or two common ol' mosquitoes by late summer. Be prepared for the blighters, otherwise your life will be a misery.

Khar Us Nuur (and Khar Nuur) are proposed sites for a national park to protect the breeding areas for antelopes, as well as rare species of migratory pelicans, falcons and bustards. The best time to see the birdlife is in May and late August.

As at Uvs Nuur, birdwatchers may be a little disappointed: the lake is huge, difficult to reach because of the marshes, and locals know very little, if anything, about the birdlife. The best place to start looking is where the delta of Khovd Gol enters the lake.

## KHAR NUUR
ХАР НУУР

The outflow from Khar Us Nuur goes into a short river called Chono Kharaikh, which flows into another freshwater lake, Khar Nuur (Black Lake), home to some migratory pelicans. There is a dispute about which lake is the deepest in Mongolia: it is either Khar Nuur or Khövsgöl Nuur. The southern end of Khar Nuur flows into Dorgon Nuur, which is a large, salty pond. The east side of Dorgon Nuur is an area of bone-dry desert and extensive sand dunes.

Just to the south, and between, the Khar and Khar Us lakes, are the twin peaks of Jargalant Khairkhan Uul (3796m) and Yargaitin Ekh Uul (3464m). You can see both as you drive to Ölgii from Altai in Gov-Altai aimag.

## TSENKHERIIN AGUI
ЦЭНХЭРИЙН АГУЙ

The Tsenkheriin Agui caves are reasonably attractive but the drawcard is the cave paint-

ings inside which are approximately 15,000 years old. (There is also about 15,000 years' worth of bird dung in the caves, so watch where you step.) There are numerous passages to explore, with the largest cavern being about 15m high with the floor measuring around 12m by 18m. Unfortunately, some recent graffiti has marred the cave paintings. Recent controversy has erupted among experts about the interpretation of the paintings.

The caves are in an attractive setting next to a stream, in the *sum* of Mankhan (Манхан), about 90km south-east of Khovd city. You could hitch a ride to the village of Tögrög (Төргөр ), just south of the Khovd city-Altai road, or rent a jeep there and walk to the caves. Bring a strong torch (flashlight), lots of warm clothes and high, dung-proof boots.

If you can't make it to the caves, the museum in Khovd city has an interesting display re-creating the cave paintings.

## MÖNKH KHAIRKHAN
МӨНХ ХАИРХАН

An argument continues about which mountain is Mongolia's highest. Tavanbogd (4374m) in Bayan-Ölgii aimag was thought to be Mongolia's highest point while Mönkh Khairkhan was measured at 'only' 4204m. A more recent survey concluded that Mönkh Khairkhan is 4362m, which is still 12m lower than Tavanbogd (so the argument seems a little pointless).

No matter which is higher, both are beautiful, but Tavanbogd is more difficult to climb thanks to its glaciers. You can walk up Mönkh Khairkhan if you approach from the north side. There is plenty of snow and ice on top, so crampons are called for, and an ice axe and rope probably wouldn't go amiss either. Two travel companies in Ulaan Baatar – Juulchin and Mongolian Adventure Tours – run trekking trips up Mönkh Khairkhan. Refer to the Ulaan Baatar chapter for details.

Mönkh Khairkhan is on a remote part of the western border with Bayan-Ölgii. A jeep trail runs to the base from Tögrög.

## TSAMBAGARAV UUL
ЦАМБАГРАВ УУЛ

Tsambagarav mountain, in the far north-west *sum* of Bayannuur (Баяннуур), is one of the most glorious snowcapped peaks in Mongolia. Despite its altitude of 4202m, the summit is relatively accessible and easy to climb compared with Tavanbogd.

In Ulaan Baatar, the museum run by the Mongol Altai Club, the Mongolian specialists in mountain climbing, has some photos of a Japanese man who *skied* down Tsambagarav Uul in 1996. It took him 24 minutes.

Tours around western Mongolia, run by Nomads, reach this part of Khovd aimag (see Travel Agencies in the Ulaan Baatar chapter for details).

---

# Uvs УВС

---

**Population:** 101,900
**Area:** 69,000 sq km
**Capital:** Ulaangom
**No of Sums:** 18
**Elevation of Capital City:** 939m
**Main Livestock & Crops:** sheep, goats; hay, millet
**Ethnic Groups:** Dorvod, Khalkh, Bayad, Khoton

One of the least visited of Mongolia's aimags, Uvs is dominated by the Ikh Nuuruudin Khotgor – the 39,000 sq km Great Lakes Depression stretching from the enormous Uvs Nuur to the Khovd and Zavkhan aimags. Other geographical features of Uvs aimag, which are definitely worth exploring, are the Böörög Deliin Els sand dunes, east of Uvs Nuur; a cluster of other lakes (which are nicer than Uvs Nuur) –

Achit, Khyargas and Üüreg lakes; the 4037m Kharkhiraa Uul; and the gorgeous Kharkhiraa Valley.

Uvs aimag was originally named Dorvod after the main ethnic group which inhabited the area. The Dorvod people, who still represent just under half of the population of Uvs, speak their own dialect. Other minority ethnic groups include the Bayad and Khoton.

Uvs is a good place to organise and start a trip around western Mongolia. It is one of the few places where you could justify renting a jeep to explore lakes, mountains, valleys and sand dunes – all within a day or two by jeep from Ulaangom.

## ULAANGOM
УЛААНГОМ

Ulaangom, which means 'red sand', is a pleasant, tree-lined town of 29,600 inhabitants. It is a good place to hang around while you explore the countryside, or to plan a trip around western Mongolia: there are good shops, reasonable hotels and a fantastic market.

In 1995 one or two travellers reported hassles with the police in Ulaangom. However, we have heard nothing similar since then, most probably because foreigners currently no longer need permits to travel around the Mongolian countryside.

Like the other western aimag capitals, Ulaangom suffers from power shortages due to unpaid (and unpayable) debts to the nearest power station – across the border in Russia. At the time of research, electricity (and, therefore, water supplies) was only working between 9 am and 2 pm. Russian officials mercifully allow the electricity to return to normal during the winter.

WESTERN MONGOLIA

---

### Tsedenbal & Givaan

In Uvs, two famous communists are still revered. Yumjaagiyn Tsedenbal, who ruled Mongolia for about 40 years until 1983, was born in Ulaangom – there is a bronze statue in front of the city hall. His Russian wife still lives in Moscow.

Opposite the town square in Ulaangom, a statue honours Givaan, who was born in Ulaangom in 1926. He became a sergeant in the Mongolian army and was assigned to patrol the area in southern Khovd, near the Chinese border. He was killed in 1948 during clashes with Chinese troops. You can probably get more of an idea about Givaan when the museum in Ulaangom reopens. ■

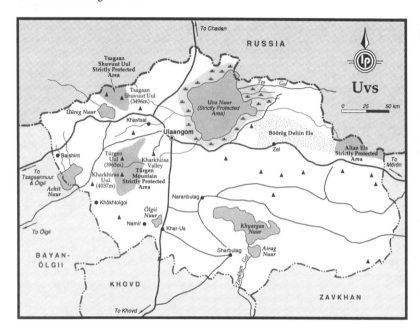

## Information

The staff at the bank, south of the cinema, were all aflutter when we asked about changing US dollars. The initial rate offered was about 20% less than in Ulaan Baatar; then, the manager decided it was all too hard. You may have better luck. Otherwise, there are usually a few moneychangers at the market.

## Dechinravjaalin Khiid
Дэчинравжаалин Хийд

The original monastery was founded in 1757 by Lamaav, whose name means 'monk father'. At the height of its glory, the monastery contained seven small temples, and 2000 monks were in residence. In 1937 this monastery suffered the same fate as most others in Mongolia – it was razed to the ground by Choibalsan's storm troopers, and the monks were either killed or sent on a 'Siberian holiday'.

Although the monastery, which is still being rebuilt, isn't a masterpiece, it is worth a visit, and the monks are friendly. It is in the middle of a park (full of concrete argali sheep and other local animals), only 150m west of the square.

## Museum

At the time of research, the museum was closed for renovations. When (or if) it reopens, the museum will doubtless contain the usual array of stuffed animals, and some memorabilia about the local heroes, Givaan and Tsedenbal. The museum is on the main street opposite the park.

## Places to Stay

**Camping** The only nearby place to camp is along Gumbukh Gol, which you cross as you come from Ölgii. Walk about 300m northwest of the town square, and find a spot. If you have your own vehicle, camping is far better along the Kharkhiraa Gol or anywhere south of the city on the road to Khovd.

**Hotels** The best place to stay is the *Tailor Hotel* – it had no name, so we called it this because it's at the back of a tailor's shop. A bed in a clean four room dorm costs T1200 per person. The owners are helpful and friendly. The shop/hotel is behind the post office; look for the telltale needle and thread sign above the door, or the noise of sewing machines.

The *Kharkhiraa Hotel* (Хархираа Зочид) is the big place on the main street. It has a good shop, a restaurant and cosy bar. Foreigners can expect to pay about T1980 per person for a simple room, and from T3300 to T4000 per person for a comfortable deluxe with bathroom, fridge and TV (though electricity is erratic), and even a chessboard.

### Places to Eat

The guanz at the *Tailor Hotel* can usually make some excellent steamed mutton dumplings, or buuz (if you can stand another 10 or more), and the *Kharkhiraa Hotel* offers the usual mutton goulash. Like the other western aimags, a few train wagons around the market serve as cheap guanzes. The comparative array of fresh bread and vegetables at the market is a very good reason to self-cater.

The best place for a meal is the *Khankhokhii Restaurant* (Ханхохий Рэсторан), just opposite (and upstairs) from the Kharkhiraa Hotel. A surprisingly edible plate of mutton, rice and vegetables costs T300, and they may have some tasty yoghurt or other surprises if you ask. If you fancy a warm beer, a nip of vodka or a rowdy conversation with a local, head to the unnamed bar next to the Khankhokhii.

### Things to Buy

Ulaangom gets our vote as the best market in western Mongolia, if not in all of the Mongolian countryside. You can buy delicious fresh bread and doughnut-type snacks, fizzy drinks and loads of vegetables – carrots, cabbage and potatoes, among others. After a few weeks living on mutton and fat in the countryside, this market is a godsend. The shops along the main street also have a fair selection of pickled vegetables, chocolate and rice. Stock up in Ulaangom before heading out into the countryside.

At the market, you can pick up a few unwashed wolfskins, more appealing Kazak carpets and a few clothes and household items from Russia – the border is close by.

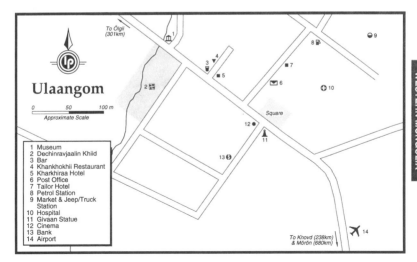

Ulaangom

0    50    100 m
Approximate Scale

To Ölgii (301km)

To Khovd (238km) & Mörön (680km)

Square

1 Museum
2 Dechinravjaalin Khiid
3 Bar
4 Khankhokhii Restaurant
5 Kharkhiraa Hotel
6 Post Office
7 Tailor Hotel
8 Petrol Station
9 Market & Jeep/Truck Station
10 Hospital
11 Givaan Statue
12 Cinema
13 Bank
14 Airport

## Getting There & Away

**Air** MIAT flies between Ulaan Baatar and Ulaangom, with a refuelling stop (often at Mörön), on Monday, Wednesday and Friday. Tickets costs US$120. The airport is a dirt field just 1km from the town centre.

**Jeep** Ulaangom is not overrun by jeeps, but a few do hang around the market. These can be hired for trips around Uvs and western Mongolia for around T150 per km. A few public shared jeeps leave for Ölgii and Khovd city when there is enough people to squeeze in.

The reasonable road between Ölgii and Ulaangom (301km), via Tsagaannuur, goes past the delightful Üüreg Nuur and through one of the most dramatic valleys in Mongolia. An alternative road bypasses Tsagaannuur by going south of Achit Nuur.

The Khovd city-Ulaangom road (238km) sees very little traffic, as most vehicles head east from these cities towards Ulaan Baatar. This road sometimes suffers from flooded rivers and collapsed bridges after heavy rain. (We had to take a 60km detour around the Kharkhiraa Gol.) The road to Mörön (680km) is the usual, roughish, unpaved Mongolian 'highway'.

**Hitching** It shouldn't be difficult to get a lift between Ulaangom and Mörön, but it's not as easy along the road from Ulaangom to Ölgii, via Tsagaannuur. From Ulaangom to Khovd, and to the Kharkhiraa Valley, hitching is a lot harder because there are so few vehicles. In Ulaangom, ask around the modern and busy petrol station near the market, and at the market itself.

## KHARKHIRAA VALLEY
ХАРХИРАА ТАЛ

Kharkhiraa is the name of a 4037m mountain, a river flowing into Uvs Nuur, and a delightful valley, 32km (as the crow flies) south-west of Ulaangom. The valley is surrounded by dense pine forests, has a crystal-clear river (from which it's safe to drink) and is often carpeted with flowers. It is a perfect place to stay a while and relax, or to go hiking –

except that foreigners are a 'star attraction', so the locals may want to talk to, and/or watch you, a fair bit.

## Places to Stay & Eat

The only place to stay is the *Kharkhiraa Resort*, a collection of quaint log cabins and huts hidden among the pine forests. We were able to pay Mongolian prices, but even if you have to pay three times more as a foreigner, it is still worth it. The Mongolian price for a rustic, semi-detached chalet, with two or three beds, a wood stove and a separate sitting room, is T980 per person – or T560 per person for dorm-style beds. Some of the pit toilets have great views (ie they have no doors).

According to the manager, it costs T420 extra per day for 'about' three meals. No prizes for guessing the main ingredient of the meals served here, so it's a good idea to bring some food from Ulaangom.

## Getting There & Away

If you don't have your own vehicle, you could easily charter a jeep from Ulaangom and arrange for the driver to pick you up later. The cheapest, but more exhausting, way is to get a lift to the turn-off at the power station, 11km west on the main road from Ulaangom. From the power station, a gentle, easy-to-follow, 25km trail leads to the gate of the resort. Hitching is not an option; almost no vehicles make it up here.

## KHARKHIRAA UUL & TÜRGEN UUL
ХАРХИРАА УУЛ & ТҮРГЭН УУЛ

The twin peaks of Kharkhiraa Uul (4037m) and Türgen Uul (3965m), which dominate the western part of the aimag, are curiously almost equidistant between Achit, Üüreg and Uvs lakes. As vital sources of the Uvs Nuur, the mountains are part of the Uvs Lake Strictly Protected Area.

They are among the more accessible peaks in Uvs, but not the easiest to climb. To get there, you will have to charter a jeep from Ulaangom or Ölgii, and be prepared for a rough, but scenic, trip. There are remains of some Uighur statues in the region, but you'll need a guide to find them.

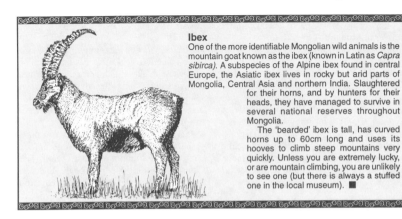

**Ibex**
One of the more identifiable Mongolian wild animals is the mountain goat known as the ibex (known in Latin as *Capra sibirca*). A subspecies of the Alpine ibex found in central Europe, the Asiatic ibex lives in rocky but arid parts of Mongolia, Central Asia and northern India. Slaughtered for their horns, and by hunters for their heads, they have managed to survive in several national reserves throughout Mongolia.

The 'bearded' ibex is tall, has curved horns up to 60cm long and uses its hooves to climb steep mountains very quickly. Unless you are extremely lucky, or are mountain climbing, you are unlikely to see one (but there is always a stuffed one in the local museum). ∎

## UVS NUUR
УВС НУУР

Uvs Nuur is a gigantic inland sea in the middle of the desert. The lake's surface occupies 3423 sq km, making it Mongolia's largest lake, though it's very shallow at an average depth of 12m. (Many locals believe it is bottomless.) Many textbooks – and most Mongolians – claim that Khövsgöl Nuur is the largest lake in the country, but that only applies to water volume, not surface area. Uvs Nuur is large enough for you to stand on one shore and not see the other side, creating the impression that you have indeed reached the sea.

Uvs Nuur is five times (about 12%) saltier than the ocean, and totally devoid of fish, but this doesn't mean the lake is dead. The lake's surface is at an altitude of 759m, making it the lowest point in western Mongolia. It has no outlet, so a lot of the shoreline is swampy, making it difficult to reach.

Except for the mountain tops, this is the coldest part of the country: in 1974 a temperature of minus 57°C was recorded. (Summer temperatures typically climb to over 40°C.) Despite the high salt content, the lake's surface freezes during winter. Trucks, often carrying students, take a shortcut (saving only 100km from the trip) across the lake to Russia. The trucks sometimes fall through the ice and the passengers face a certain,

quick, and horrifying death in this huge, freezing and isolated lake.

Despite the superlatives, compared with other lakes in western Mongolia, Uvs Nuur is disappointing: it is extremely large, difficult to reach and contains high levels of saltwater. It is also not great for swimming or camping. If you have a jeep, lots of time and a good guide, you will enjoy the scenery and birdlife, otherwise it is best to head for the prettier, smaller and more accessible Üüreg and Achit freshwater lakes.

### National Parks
Uvs Nuur, and parts of the area surrounding it, are in the 772,000 hectare Uvs Lake Strictly Protected Area, which also includes the Altan Els sand dunes and Tsagaan Shuvuut Uul. The park was established in 1994 to preserve the unique and varied ecology around the lake; to protect endangered snow leopards, foxes, wolves, deer and ibexes, among others; and to conserve the two mountains as vital sources for Uvs Nuur and other lakes in the region.

### Birdwatching
Ornithologists have documented over 200 species of birds around Uvs Nuur, including cranes, spoonbills, geese and eagles, as well as gulls which fly thousands of km from the

southern coast of China to spend a brief summer in Mongolia.

Birdwatchers, however, could be disappointed: the birdlife is there and *is* impressive, but it is extremely difficult to find. The lake is also huge; public transport around the lake is nonexistent; trails often turn into marsh and sand; locals know very little, if anything, about the birdlife; and you may not be there at the right time anyway. The best place to start looking for birdlife is where the rivers enter the lake, and on the island in the middle of the lake (but there is no boat for hire for thousands of km).

### Places to Stay

The nearest hotel is in Ulaangom, from where you could come on a day trip if you have your own vehicle. Otherwise, you can camp anywhere around the lake, but be careful where you pitch your tent. Many places near the lake are swampy – a haven for swarms of mosquitoes. Find a dry, open and breezy spot one or 2km from the lake.

### Getting There & Away

Approaching from the west, the lake (at 759m) is an awesome sight from the 2533m Ulaan Davaa pass. You could hitch a ride *to* the lake, and get off along the relatively busy Ulaangom-Mörön road nearby, but you will still need a jeep to get *around* the lake, unless you plan to do a helluva lot of hiking.

As the crow (or the Tawny Pipit) flies, Uvs Nuur is only 28km from Ulaangom. In reality, the trails along the southern and eastern sides skirt around the lake and very few actually lead *to* the lake because of sand dunes, creeks and swamps. The first trail we found which reached the lake was 56km from Ulaangom. The lake is more accessible if you park the jeep or pitch your tent on a trail, and walk about 2 or 3km to the lake.

The Russians built a 50km paved road along the western side of the lake, towards the Russian border, but this still doesn't make it easier to reach the lake; the edges of the lake are sandy and swampy in most places.

### ALTAN ELS
### АЛТАН ЭЛС

The road between Ulaangom and Mörön passes the Böörög Deliin Els sand dunes, which stretch about 70km east of Uvs Nuur. The sand dunes lead to the Altan Els (Golden Sands), part of the Uvs Lake Strictly Protected Area. Altan Els is another wonderful area for wildlife, if you can find any. You'll need a good jeep and driver, and you must be self-sufficient in everything before exploring this remote and hot region. The Altan Els are on the border of the Uvs and Zavkhan aimags, and are an easy detour from the Ulaangom-Mörön road.

### KHYARGAS NUUR
### ХЯРГАС НУУР

Khyargas Nuur receives a lot less attention than Uvs Nuur, being 'only' half the size and 'only' twice as salty as the ocean. The lake does provide an attractive summer home for birds, but it is not as scenic or accessible as other lakes in the region. It is still worth a stopover if you are travelling between Uvs Nuur and Khar Us Nuur in Khovd aimag, or driving or hitching towards Tosontsengel in Zavkhan through the mid-eastern part of Uvs aimag.

On the north-western side of Khyargas Nuur, there are some fantastic **hot springs**. Head for the abandoned village where the road leaves the lake, or ask directions at Naranbulag (Наранбулаг).

### AIRAG NUUR
### АЙРАГ НУУР

To the south of Khyargas Nuur, the freshwater Airag Nuur is at the end of the mighty Zavkhan Gol. Despite the name, the lake is not full of the famous fermented horse's milk, but is very popular for about 20 pairs of migratory pelicans. There were about 400 pelicans in the 1960s, but the numbers are tragically decreasing because poachers kill them for their beaks, which are used to make a traditional implement for cleaning horses, called a *khusuur*, or currycomb.

## ÖLGII NUUR
## ӨЛГИЙ НУУР

To confuse things a little, another freshwater lake in the region is called Khar Us Nuur, but it is sometimes referred to as Ölgii Nuur. The 20km-long lake is accessible, but is not quite as scenic as Üüreg and Achit lakes. You can swim and fish in Ölgii Nuur, but the camping is not as good – the winds can be horrendous, so pitch your tent securely.

The lake is a welcome place to stop between Ulaangom and Khovd city if you have your own vehicle. Traffic between Ulaangom and Khovd is generally sparse, but you could hitch to and from the lake if you are self-sufficient, have a tent and don't mind waiting.

## ÜÜREG NUUR
## YYРЭГ НУУР

The large and beautiful Üüreg lake (1425m above sea level) is surrounded by stunning 3000m peaks, including Tsagaan Shuvuut Uul (3496m), part of the Uvs Lake national park. The freshwater lake has some unidentified minerals and is designated as 'saltwater' on some maps. It's best to boil or purify all water from the lake anyway.

The lake is great for swimming (albeit a little chilly) and locals say there are plenty of fish. The surrounding mountains are just begging to be explored. One added attraction is that we were not attacked by swarms of bloodsucking midges – or perhaps we were just lucky.

### Places to Stay

Camping is naturally the only option. The ground is a bit rocky and there is no shade, but you do have access to squillions of gallons of drinking water. There are only a few gers in the area, so you feel like you have the lake to yourself.

### Getting There & Away

The definite attraction of the lake is its accessibility: it is just off the main road between Ulaangom and Tsagaannuur. You could hire a jeep from Ulaangom, and maybe arrange

for it to pick you up later (you hope), or hitch a ride there fairly easily – though some vehicles travelling between Ölgii and Ulaangom go via Achit Nuur these days.

The 90km road between Üüreg Nuur and Ulaangom passes through a valley which we have decided is the most dramatic in Mongolia (a land full of dramatic valleys). The 75km road between Üüreg Nuur and Achit Nuur is abysmal, but the landscape is extraordinarily varied: one minute you could swear you are in the Australian outback, and five minutes later, you seem to be in the Scottish Highlands. Along this road, you can see the permanently snowcapped twin peaks of Kharkhiraa Uul and Türgen Uul.

## ACHIT NUUR
## АЧИТ НУУР

The largest freshwater lake in Uvs, Achit Nuur is on the border of Uvs and Bayan-Ölgii aimags, and an easy detour between Ulaangom and Ölgii. It offers stunning sunsets and sunrises and plenty of fish. If you don't have your own fishing gear, you can probably buy some from the Russian and Tuvan fishermen who work there in the summer.

The lake is home to flocks of geese, eagles and other birdlife. One definite drawback is the absolute plethora of mosquitoes during the summer; they pour into every orifice, and we could hear them buzzing around the tent in the morning just waiting to suck out the rest of our blood. Some camping spots are better than others for mossies, so look around. Locals claim they are almost bearable by October.

### Getting There & Away

A new bridge just south of the lake has greatly increased the amount of traffic going past the lake between Ulaangom and Ölgii. You can hitch a ride to the lake from either city without too much trouble, or charter a jeep from Ölgii or Ulaangom. The trail from Ölgii is reasonably good and pretty, but the trails from Achit Nuur to Ulaangom and Üüreg Nuur are often tough, but also dramatic.

# The Gobi

Along the southern border of Mongolia, five provinces contain sections of the Gobi Desert: Bayankhongor, Dornogov, Dundgov, Gov-Altai and Ömnögov. The Gobi region is sparsely populated with little transport and roads, but it was, and still is, alive with wildlife. You will see thousands of wild and domesticated camels, cranes, hawks and gazelles (which seem to have taken a wrong turn from the pastures of eastern Mongolia), and there is no shortage of evidence that dinosaurs once roamed the region.

There are several things to keep in mind when travelling in this unique region. The nights will always be cold, so take a sleeping bag if you are not staying in a ger camp. Rabid dogs are not uncommon, so take extra caution around the towns or when approaching a ger. Most years, the plague rears its ugly

head in the western parts from about August to October. It is extremely unlikely that you will catch anything nasty, but quarantine restrictions could affect your travel in the region. Refer to the Health section in the Facts for the Visitor chapter for details.

Very few vehicles travel anywhere but on the main roads. This makes hitching difficult and dangerous. If chartering a jeep, make sure it is reliable. If travelling by public bus, jeep or, especially, if hitching, carry a sleeping bag, tent and sufficient water and food for emergencies. In some parts of the Gobi, we were lucky to see *two* functioning vehicles a day; every day, we saw about a dozen broken down, abandoned or out of petrol.

Take more water than you normally need. Except for aimag capitals and ger camps, water supplies are scarce and unreliable.

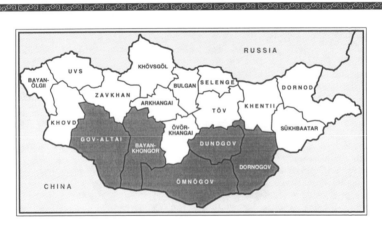

## Highlights
- Baga Gazarin Chuluu: remote region for camping, hiking and exploring caves
- Gurvansaikhan National Park: home to a valley of ice, huge, extraordinary sand dunes, dinosaur fossil sites; several ger camps to choose from
- Sangiin Dalai Nuur: lovely, tiny lake with remarkable birdlife; ruins of palace and temple in the middle
- Shargaljuut: hundreds of hot and cold water springs; excellent camping or stay at ger camp

---

**The Gobi Desert**

Some foreigners regard the Gobi as a remote, exotic and mystical place, perhaps like the Andes and the Amazon. Stretching from southern Khovd aimag to the Dariganga region in southern Sükhbaatar, and including parts of northern China, the Gobi is mainly grass, shrubs and rocks. Oases, which provide some shelter and water for nomads and animals, and sand cover only about 3% of the Gobi.

The Gobi is a land of extremes: decent rain falls only every two or three years; it can be well over 40°C during the summer, and below -40°C in winter; and storms of dust and sand are fearsome in spring. The very few lakes, such as Orog Nuur and Böön Tsagaan Nuur, are starting to permanently dry up, but underground springs provide the vital water.

The Gobi is understandably very sparsely populated, but the desolate landscape is home to the gazelle, *khulan* wild ass, Bactrian (two-humped) camel, *takhi* horse, rare Saiga antelope and the world's only desert bear – the Gobi bear. The appropriately named Desert Warbler and the Saxaul Sparrow hide in the saxaul shrub, the only species of shrub which can flourish in the Gobi. ■

---

A concrete or wooden structure in the middle of nowhere, with a few gers nearby, is a sure sign of a spring or well (though it may be dry). The water is usually delicious, but you don't know who, or what, has pissed in it, so boil or purify it. If the spring or well has a trough, fill it with water; by late evening, some parched gazelles and camels seemingly come out of nowhere to drink.

# Bayankhongor
## Баянхонгор

**Population:** 89,500
**Area:** 116,000 sq km
**Capital:** Bayankhongor
**No of Sums:** 19
**Elevation of Capital City:** 1859m
**Main Livestock & Crops:** camel, goat
**Ethnic Groups:** Khalkh

This strangely shaped aimag is dominated by the mighty Khangai Nuruu range to the north. Its southern part passes through the Gobi to the Chinese border and includes part of the Mongol Altai Nuruu range. Although somewhat higher than the Khangai Nuruu, the Mongol Altai is a bleak desert range where life is hard even for the durable argali sheep and ibex.

By contrast, the Khangai is lush, providing sufficient snowmelt to make livestock raising and human existence a viable proposition. Bayankhongor, which means 'rich tan' (named after the colour of the horses –

or your skin after a couple of hours in the sun) is home to wild camels and donkeys and the extremely rare Gobi bear.

Most travellers bypass the aimag while travelling along the major southern Ulaan Baatar-Khovd road, but Bayankhongor does have two interesting, albeit remote, attractions: the Shargaljuut hot and cold water springs, and the eastern section of the 4.4 million hectare Southern Altai Gobi Strictly Protected Area, also known as 'Gobi A'.

A Bactrian camel and rider is a common sight in the Gobi Desert.

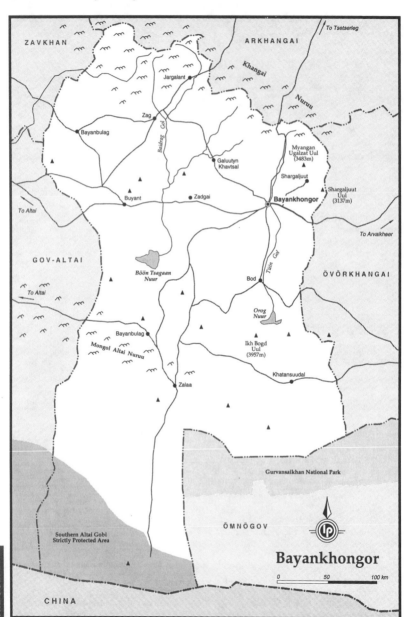

## BAYANKHONGOR
БАЯНХОНГОР

This sprawling capital of 23,000 people was established in 1942. Located close to the border with Övörkhangai and Arkhangai aimags, Bayankhongor city is where the Khangai Nuruu, with several peaks of 3000m or more, meets the northern Gobi. One of the nicer aimag capitals in the Gobi, Bayankhongor has reasonable facilities. It's a good place to stop during the long haul to or from the west, to start explorations to more remote regions to the south, or to go on a day trip to the Shargaljuut springs nearby.

### Information

Staff at the bank, next to the post office, initially said they would change money – US dollars only – but changed their minds a minute later. You could try if you are desperate, but don't count on it. Alternatively, change money at the market or try the hotels.

### Lamyn Gegeenii Dedlen Khiid
Ламын Гэгээний Дэдлэн Хийд

There was no ancient monastery on this particular site, but 20km to the east of Bayankhongor city there was a monastery with the same name. This complex once housed up to 10,000 monks, making it one of the largest monasteries in the country. As elsewhere in Mongolia, the communist police descended on the place in 1937 and carted off the monks, who were never seen again. The temple was levelled and today nothing remains. Sadly, the present-day monks seem to have little knowledge of the old temple's history.

The current monastery, built in 1991, is home to only 40 monks. The main temple is built in the shape of a ger, though it's actually made out of brick. It's on the main street, 200m north of the square.

The skyline of Bayankhongor city is dominated by a **stupa** on a hill to the west of the square. If you are staying for a while, take a walk up there for views of the town and nearby countryside.

### Museum

Bayankhongor's small museum is really only different from other aimag museums because it is inside a stadium in the park. Otherwise, it provides the usual displays and explanations of local flora and (stuffed) fauna, if you understand Mongolian and the museum happens to be open. It is officially open from 9 am to 5 pm on weekdays and costs T350 to enter.

### Places to Stay

**Camping** Bayankhongor city is not one of the better aimag capitals for camping. As

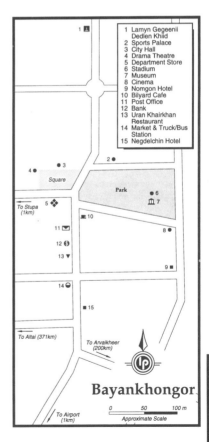

1 Lamyn Gegeenii Dedlen Khiid
2 Sports Palace
3 City Hall
4 Drama Theatre
5 Department Store
6 Stadium
7 Museum
8 Cinema
9 Nomgon Hotel
10 Bilyard Cafe
11 Post Office
12 Bank
13 Uran Khairkhan Restaurant
14 Market & Truck/Bus Station
15 Negdelchin Hotel

Square

Park

To Stupa (1km)

To Altai (371km)

To Arvaikheer (200km)

Bayankhongor

0    50    100 m
Approximate Scale

To Airport (1km)

elsewhere, the best place is the river. The Tüin Gol is a few hundred metres east of the city.

**Hotels** The *Nomgon Hotel* (Номгон Зочид) is an amazing place. Staff will probably offer you a huge, often luxurious, deluxe room for a reasonable, and negotiable, T5550 per person – but you may be able to get a cheaper simple room for around T1500 per person. If you arrive late (after 9 pm), you practically have to break the front door down to get in, as the staff lock up and go to bed early. The hotel is about 50m south of the park but is a little hard to find among the apartment blocks – you may need to ask for directions.

The alternative, the *Negdelchin Hotel* (Нэгдэлчин Зочид), at the southern end of the main street, offers rooms with attached toilet, but no shower, for around the same price as the Nomgon, but it isn't as good.

**Places to Eat**
The Nomgon and Negdelchin will serve the usual stuff for guests, but they are less enthusiastic about serving the general public. The huge, well-signed (in Mongolian) *Uran Khairkhan Restaurant* (Уран Хаирхан Рэсторан), just south of the post office, has some better-than-average mutton dishes. For a game of billiards and a drink, you could try the *Bilyard Cafe* (Билярд Кафэ), on the south-west corner of the park.

**Getting There & Away**
**Air** On Monday and Thursday, MIAT flies between Ulaan Baatar and Bayankhongor for US$70. The airport is a dirt field about 1km south of the city.

**Bus** As a central point in southern Mongolia, Bayankhongor is well connected by bus to Ulaan Baatar, making the bus an interesting and cheap, if somewhat uncomfortable, way to reach the western Gobi. Buses leave Ulaan Baatar every day but Sunday (T4477), and go via Arvaikheer. They stop at the market in Bayankhongor, about 100m south of the square.

**Jeep** It is safe to assume that you will not be able to charter a jeep in Bayankhongor city (or aimag); the city is poor and not developed for tourism – or for anything else, for that matter.

For some reason (certainly nothing to do with the amount of traffic), an excellent paved road starts about 20km east of Bayankhongor city, part of an ambitious plan to complete a decent Ulaan Baatar-Khovd road. The road between Arvaikheer and Bayankhongor (200km) is often rough. The 371km road to Altai is OK; just a little boring in parts.

**Hitching** Bayankhongor is on the main southern road between Ulaan Baatar and Khovd. A lot of vehicles going in either direction stop here, so getting a ride to Altai or Arvaikheer shouldn't be hard. South of Bayankhongor or to Shargaljuut you will have far less success. Ask around at the market (on the main street), which doubles as a bus and truck station.

**SHARGALJUUT**
ШАРГАЛЖУУТ
The major attraction in Bayankhongor aimag is the 300 or so hot and cold water springs at Shargaljuut. Only about 16km north-east of Bayankhongor city, the springs are one of the few natural attractions in the Gobi region which are easily accessible from an aimag capital.

The hot water, which can reach 50°C, is supposed to cure a vast range of aches, pains and diseases. The area was also popular with dinosaurs several millennia ago: there are fossils in the region, but you will need lots of archaeological equipment to find anything.

The springs are in the village of Shargaljuut, between the peaks of Myangan Ugalzat Uul (3483m) and Shargaljuut Uul (3137m), in the Erdenetsogt (Эрдэнэцогт) *sum*. The *Shargalzhuut Resort* (☎ 342 093; fax 53 627) at the springs primarily caters for organised tours. You can camp anywhere, or come on a day trip from Bayankhongor city if you have your own vehicle. The Terelj-Juulchin travel agency (see the Ulaan Baatar chapter for details) organises tours to the springs.

## BAIDRAG GOL
### БАИДРАГ ГОЛ

The long and wide Baidrag Gol flows south from the Khangai Nuruu range through the most magnificent network of canyons in Mongolia. There are numerous side canyons, one of the best known being Galuutyn Havtsal (Duck Canyon) in Galuut (Галуут) *sum*. The river finally terminates at Böön Tsagaan Nuur.

Although it's not raging white water, Baidrag Gol looks like it has some of the best potential for rafting in Mongolia. Upstream at Jargalant (Жаргалант), you could put in a raft, and then take it out again at the bridge where the Bayankhongor-Altai road crosses the river. No travel agency organises any rafting trips here, however; Tuul Gol, near Ulaan Baatar, is more accessible.

At the impressive bridge crossing the Baidrag Gol on the Bayankhongor-Altai road, there are several *guanzes*. This is a good place to break up a journey if you are travelling in your own vehicle, or hitching, between Bayankhongor and Altai. The river was almost pure mud when we passed by because of recent heavy rains, but normally the water is OK to drink if you boil or purify it first. About 10km further west of the bridge, in a real desolate part of the country, a special *ovoo* marks the dramatic change in scenery.

## BÖÖN TSAGAAN NUUR
### БӨӨН ЦАГААН НУУР

This large saltwater lake, at the end of Baidrag Gol, is popular with birdlife, especially the Relic Gull, Whooper Swan and geese. The region also boasts extraordinary **volcanic formations**, canyons of cascading streams and ancient **cave paintings**.

Juulchin and Nomads travel agencies (see the Ulaan Baatar chapter for details) include trips to this lake as part of their tours in the region. The lake is about 90km south-west of Bayankhongor city, in the *sum* of Baatsagaan (Баацагаан).

## OROG NUUR
### ОГОР НУУР

The saltwater Orog Nuur is at the end of the Tüin Gol, which passes through Bayankhongor city. Also referred to as Shar Burd Nuur (Шар Бурд Нууp), the lake is a good place to watch some birdlife. It is nestled in the foothills of Ikh Bogd Uul (3957m) in the *sum* of Bogd (Богд), about 110km south of Bayankhongor city.

The **rock inscriptions** in the nearby Bugiin Nuruu have intrigued locals and experts for centuries – they don't appear to have anything to do with Mongolia, so some believe they were created by aliens. You will need a guide to find these inscriptions, the nearby **dinosaur fossil sites** and **Tsagaan Agui** cave, where some relics of ancient civilisations have been discovered.

Nearby, the *Mongol Gobi Resort*, run by Juulchin, is the usual type of ger camp with the standard price of about US$40 per person, including meals. This camp caters for organised tours and may not always be open, so if travelling independently, book ahead with Juulchin.

# Dornogov Дорноговъ

**Population:** 48,200
**Area:** 111,000 sq km
**Capital:** Sainshand
**No of Sums:** 17
**Elevation of Capital City:** 938m
**Main Livestock & Crops:** camel, sheep
**Ethnic Groups:** Khalkh

Dornogov (East Gobi) is classic Gobi country – flat, arid and with a sparse population. In a good year, the aimag sprouts short grass which sustains a limited number of sheep, goats and camels. In a bad year, the wells go dry, the grass turns brown and the animals die. Unless there is a sudden demand for sand, Dornogov's economic future will continue to be based on the international rail line to China – though recent US interest in local oil reserves may improve things.

If travelling on the train to or from Beijing

THE GOBI

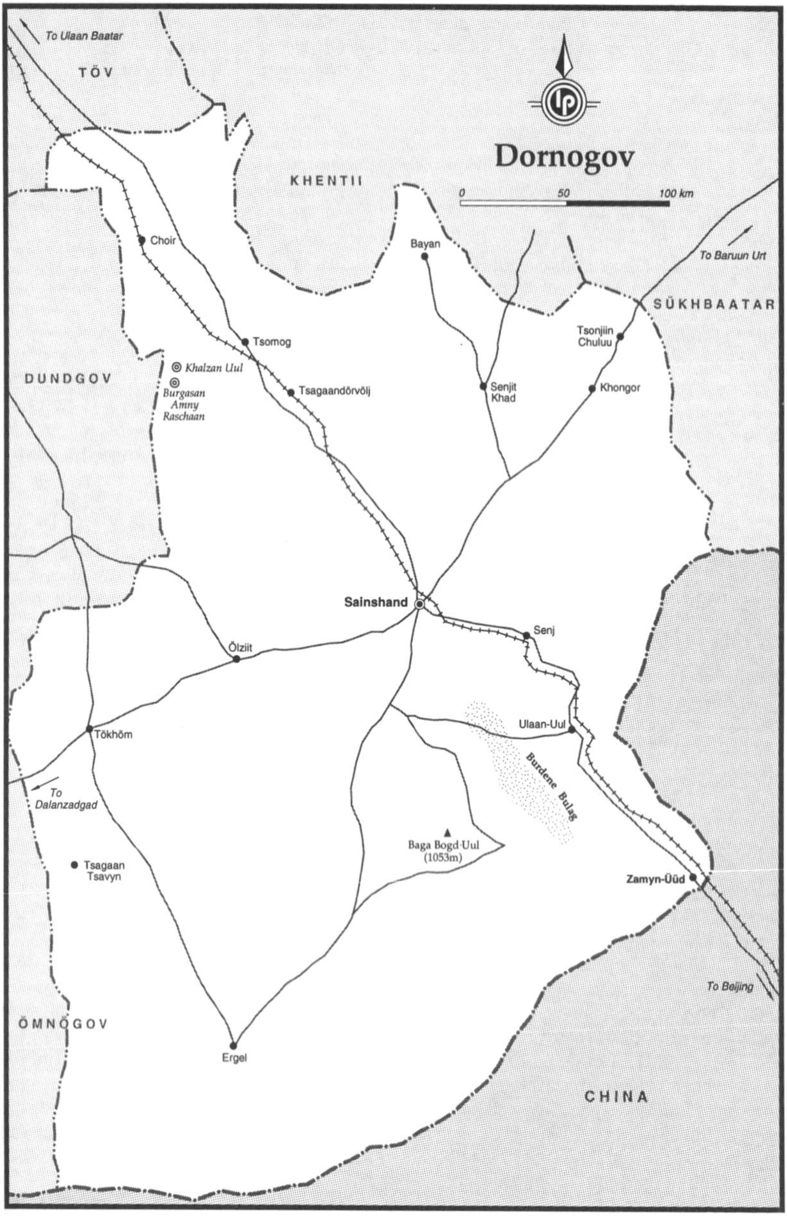

To Ulaan Baatar

TÖV

KHENTII

Dornogov

0      50      100 km

Choir

Bayan

To Baruun Urt

SÜKHBAATAR

Tsomog

Tsonjiin
Chuluu

◎ Khalzan Uul

DUNDGOV

◎ Burgasan
Amny
Raschaan

Tsagaandörvölj

Senjit
Khad

Khongor

Sainshand

Senj

Ölziit

Ulaan-Uul

Tökhöm

Burdene Bulag

To
Dalanzadgad

Baga Bogd-Uul
(1053m) ▲

Tsagaan
Tsavyn

Zamyn-Üüd

ÖMNÖGOV

To Beijing

Ergel

CHINA

THE GOBI

or Hohhot, you will see a lot of the desolate landscape from the window. If travelling around the Gobi independently, there is little need to come to Dornogov: there are very few interesting attractions, the roads are bad or nonexistent, water is scarce and the facilities are poor.

## SAINSHAND
### САИНШАНД

One of Mongolia's most dusty and dry aimag capitals, Sainshand (Good Pond) is important primarily because of its location. This city of 18,000 is on the main rail line to China, and not far from the Chinese border. The Soviets built a large military base here (now abandoned), and locals dream of converting it into a bustling industrial area.

If you are travelling around by jeep, Sainshand makes a useful place to refuel and stock up with supplies before heading out into the Gobi. However, you will find it difficult to rent a jeep here for trips to the desert – best to try in Dalanzadgad in Ömnögov aimag. Sainshand is also handy because it is the only aimag capital in the Gobi to be linked by train to Ulaan Baatar.

In 1995 some travellers reported hassles with the police in Sainshand because they didn't have a permit. Now that permits for the countryside are no longer required, we haven't heard of anyone having problems since.

Sainshand is inconveniently divided into two districts: one is the centre (where everything you will need is located), and the other is near the train station, 2km to the north.

### City Museum

This is a fairly standard aimag capital museum. There are plenty of stuffed Gobi animals, a collection of seashells and marine fossils (Dornogov was once beneath the sea) and some dinosaur fossils. The history section includes some eulogies to Manzav, the local *baatar* (hero) who distinguished himself fighting for Mongolian independence during the 1921 revolution. There is also a section devoted to the 'everlasting friendship' between Mongolia and the now extinct Soviet Union.

The entrance fee is T100, and the opening times are at the whim of the staff. The museum is in the centre of town, next to the Altangov Hotel.

### Museum of Danzan Rabjai

Danzan Rabjai (1820-76), a well-known Mongolian writer, composer and painter, was born about 100km south-west of Sainshand. Since he lived during the time when Mongolia was controlled by the Chinese Manchu dynasty, he often travelled to China and was a big hit with the emperor. Some gifts presented to Danzan by the Chinese are on exhibit in the museum. Danzan was also very interested in Chinese medicine, so the museum has a collection of his herbs. His paintings are also on display, including some erotic hermaphroditic art.

You may be asked to make an offering to the Buddha statue inside the museum instead of paying an entrance fee. The museum,

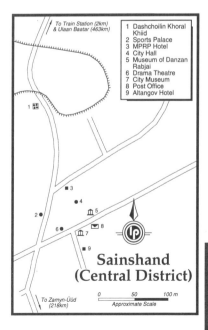

To Train Station (2km) & Ulaan Baatar (463km)

1 Dashchoilin Khoral Khiid
2 Sports Palace
3 MPRP Hotel
4 City Hall
5 Museum of Danzan Rabjai
6 Drama Theatre
7 City Museum
8 Post Office
9 Altangov Hotel

## Sainshand (Central District)

To Zamyn-Üüd (218km)

0        50        100 m
Approximate Scale

open from about 9 am to 5 pm on weekdays, is opposite the post office and worth a visit.

### Dashchoilon Khoral Khiid
Дашчоилон Хорал Хийд
This monastery, opened in 1991, is in a large walled compound at the northern end of the central district. There is an active temple, and though visitors are welcome, photographs are not allowed inside. The monks are very friendly and may offer you some food and drink.

### Places to Stay
**Camping** Sainshand, like most aimag capitals in the Gobi, does not offer anywhere decent to pitch a tent. The city is not built near a river, and it's spread out, so getting away from the ger suburbs will involve some walking. The best place to head for is the cliffs north of the monastery.

**Hotels** The *Altangov Hotel* (Алтанг ов Зочид) is where most travellers stay. Sainshand's popularity as a transit point for the Chinese border means that this place is sometimes packed out. (There may be a scramble for hotel rooms after the train arrives.) Basic, unexciting simple rooms currently cost a negotiable T5500 per person. It is next to the museum, in the central district.

The other hotel has no name, but is still referred to as the *MPRP Hotel* because it was owned and operated by the (communist) Mongolian People's Revolutionary Party. For foreigners, simple rooms with bath and toilet start at T2400 per person. You may be able to convince them to offer you a dorm-style bed for about T1500 per person. The hotel is just north of the city hall.

### Places to Eat
The two hotels have standard restaurants serving standard Mongolian food. During the day, try the restaurant in the city hall building. Otherwise, bring your own food.

### Getting There & Away
Because at least one train links Sainshand with Ulaan Baatar every day, there are no flights or scheduled bus services to or from Sainshand.

**Train** The local train from Ulaan Baatar, which goes through Choir and continues on to Zamyn-Üüd, leaves every day at 12.10 pm and arrives in Sainshand at the inconvenient time of about 10.30 pm – not a great time to find a hotel. Tickets from Ulaan Baatar cost T1799 for a hard seat and T4359 for a soft seat. The train returns from Zamyn-Üüd to Ulaan Baatar, stopping at Sainshand at 10.45 am. This service is not as busy as the northern line (which goes to the large cities of Darkhan and Erdenet), so travelling in hard-seat class to/from Sainshand is often not unbearable.

The Trans-Mongolian Railway and the trains between Ulaan Baatar and Hohhot (in Inner Mongolia) and Ereen (just over the Chinese border) stop at Sainshand, but you cannot use these services just to get to Sainshand. You must take the local daily train.

If you want to get off or on at Sainshand while travelling on the Trans-Mongolian Railway from Ulaan Baatar, you will have to pay the full price for the Ulaan Baatar-Beijing/Hohhot ticket (or vice-versa). Getting *on* the Trans-Mongolian at Sainshand is fraught with complications unless you have bought your Ulaan Baatar-Beijing/Hohhot ticket beforehand in Ulaan Baatar, and have arranged for someone to tell the train steward at the Ulaan Baatar station not to sell your seat. In Beijing, you cannot buy a Beijing-Sainshand ticket, but you can get off at Sainshand.

**Jeep** Jeeps are very hard to find in Sainshand. There is almost no demand for private or public jeeps because locals only travel to places connected by train, and almost no tourists come here. If you want to charter a jeep, look in Mandalgov (in Dundgov aimag) or, better, Dalanzadgad (Ömnögov).

Sainshand is 463km south-east of Ulaan Baatar, and 218km north-west of Zamyn-Üüd. The jeep road, which virtually parallels the train line from Ulaan Baatar to the border, is flat, dusty and dull, but not excessively rough by Mongolian standards.

**Hitching** For the same reasons that jeeps are scarce, hitching is also hard. You will get a lift to Zamyn-Üüd (but no further, because foreigners cannot cross the border by road), or to Ulaan Baatar, but the train is quicker, more comfortable and not expensive.

## SENJIT KHAD
СЭНЖИТ ХАД
Probably the best sight in Dornogov, Senjit Khad is a natural rock formation in the shape of an arch. It is about 95km north-east of Sainshand in Altanshiree (Алтанширээ) *sum*.

## TSONJIIN CHULUU
ЦОНЖИЙН ЧУЛУУ
This volcanic rock formation looks rather like a set of hexagonal organ pipes. It's in the extreme north-east corner of Dornogov, in the Delgerekh (Дэлгэрэх) *sum*, about 160km along the north-east road from Sainshand.

## BURDENE BULAG
БУРДЭНЭ БУЛАГ
These are some of the largest sand dunes in the Gobi, and among the most accessible. There are also cold water springs in the area, but you will need a guide to find them. The dunes and springs are in the Erdene (Эрдэнэ) *sum*, about 30km south-west of the *sum* capital, Ulaan-Uul (Улаан-Уул) – which is about halfway along the main road between Sainshand and Zamyn-Üüd.

## ERGEL
ЭРГЭЛ
Ergel, capital of the Khatanbulag (Хатанбулаг) *sum*, is a region noted for its cliffs, ancient archaeological artefacts and rare Gobi animals, such as ibex. The *sum* is 240km south-west of Sainshand and linked by a trail which only an experienced driver could find.

## TSAGAAN TSAVYN
ЦАГААН ЦАВЫН
This is an area with numerous petrified trees, some on the desert surface and many more buried beneath the sands. Tsagaan Tsavyn is in the remote *sum* of Mandakh (Мандах), about 200km south-west of Sainshand, and not far from the main road between Sainshand and Dalanzadgad.

## CHOIR
ЧОЙР
Choir is a town with big pretensions, about halfway between Sainshand and Ulaan Baatar. Just to the north of the town was the site of the largest Soviet air base in Mongolia. The Russians departed in 1992, leaving behind an eerie ghost town of concrete buildings and statues of MiG fighters. Some of the flats, which formerly housed military personnel, are now occupied by Mongolian families, but many sit empty, the windows broken, the plumbing ripped out and the walls scrawled with graffiti. The Russians left behind something else: the best paved runway in Mongolia.

To promote rapid economic growth, Choir formally seceded from Dornogov – it is now an autonomous municipality called Gov-Sumber (Говъ-Сумбэр) – and was declared a Free Trade Zone. Nothing much was done to promote the area; development was postponed after the change of government in 1996 and is unlikely to take place in the near future.

The only reason to visit Choir is to explore the nearby springs, or to refuel between Ulaan Baatar and Sainshand. You will have to camp; or ask around for a flat to stay in because the hotels are as developed as the Free Trade Zone.

To Choir, direct trains leave Ulaan Baatar at 5.30 pm every Monday and Thursday, and cost T1151/3020 for a hard/soft seat. The train returns to Ulaan Baatar on Tuesday and Friday at 6 am. The daily Ulaan Baatar-Sainshand-Zamyn-Üüd train and the Trans-Mongolian Railway also briefly stop at Choir.

## KHALZAN UUL
ХАЛЗАН УУЛ
Khalzan mountain is an area of natural springs about 50km south of Choir. Locals are crazy about this mineral water, claiming it can cure everything from hangovers to AIDS. Local entrepreneurs plan to bottle the water and sell it.

## BURGASAN AMNY RASCHAAN
БУРГАСАН АМНЫ РАСЧААН
This mineral spring is just a few km to the

south of Khalzan Uul. There are similar dreams of bottling the water and competing with Perrier.

## ZAMYN-ÜÜD
ЗАМЫН-УУД
This town has only two claims to fame: it's right on Mongolia's southern border and it is the hottest place in the country. The only reasons to come here are to save money by travelling from Ulaan Baatar to China on local trains, rather than on the dearer, international Trans-Mongolian Railway; or if you are planning to visit obscure villages by train in Inner Mongolia (China). There are one or two very basic hotels in town, but they are nothing to get excited about.

The daily train to Zamyn-Üüd, via Choir and Sainshand, leaves Ulaan Baatar every day at 12.10 pm. Tickets cost T2237 for hard seat, T5562 for soft seat. The train returns to Ulaan Baatar in the wee hours of the morning. From Zamyn-Üüd to Ereen (the Chinese town on the other side of the border) and beyond, check the current timetable at the station in Zamyn-Üüd.

If you are on the Trans-Mongolian train, or the service between Ulaan Baatar and Hohhot or Ereen, you will stop at Zamyn-Üüd for an hour or two while Mongolian customs and immigration officials do their stuff – usually in the middle of the night. Refer to the Trans-Mongolian Railway section in the Getting Around chapter for details.

# Dundgov Дундговъ

**Population:** 52,700
**Area:** 78,000 sq km
**Capital:** Mandalgov
**No of Sums:** 15
**Elevation of Capital City:** 1393m
**Main Livestock & Crops:** camel, goat
**Ethnic Groups:** Khalkh

Dundgov (Middle Gobi) is flat, dry plains, occasional deserts, rock formations and little else. The northern part of Dundgov is rela-

tively green, but the southern and eastern areas are mostly bone-dry.

Dotted around Dundgov (and Arkhangai aimag) are hundreds of ancient graves of revered Mongolian warriors. Little is known about these graves, but they probably predate Chinggis Khaan. The graves are about 3m deep, and often contain gold and bronze, but are left untouched because they are sacred. They are identifiable by an unnatural collection of large rocks on a small hump. In an area where there are almost no trees or bushes, don't be tempted to use these rocks for squatting and doing your 'business'.

The advantages of travelling around Dundgov are its proximity to Ulaan Baatar, the good network of jeep trails, and the flat ground which makes it easy to get around. Most visitors, however, ignore Dundgov and fly, or drive straight through, to the more developed, and tourist-oriented, Ömnögov aimag. If you are travelling overland to Ömnögov, it is worth taking the road via Sangiin Dalai, rather than directly to Dundgov's capital, Mandalgov.

### Organised Tours
A few travel companies use the Dundgobi Resort, near Sangiin Dalai, as a base for visiting the sights in the area, but on these tours you won't actually see much of the Gobi as such. If you are interested, contact Juulchin, Shuren Travel or Terelj-Juulchin (see the Ulaan Baatar chapter for contact details).

### MANDALGOV
МАНДАЛГОВЪ
Mandalgov came into existence in 1942, when the town consisted of just 40 gers. Today, it's a sleepy (and hot in summer) town of 11,000 (down from 19,000 five years ago). It offers the usual amenities for an aimag capital – an airport, hotel, monastery, museum and a couple of poorly stocked shops. There is more to see around Sangiin Dalai, but Mandalgov is a useful stop-off on the way to Dalanzadgad in Ömnögov. Most of the facilities circle the park, which is dotted with intriguing concrete animals.

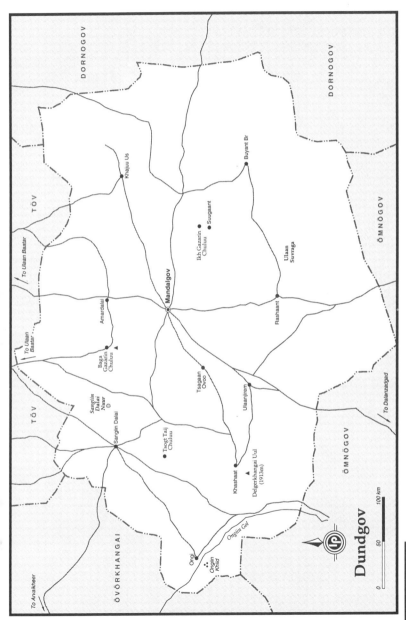

**Dundgov**

THE GOBI

## Museum

The museum is divided into two main sections: a natural history section and a more interesting culture and history section. Among the displays is a bronze Buddha sculpture made by Zanabazar, the great Mongolian artist and Buddhist. Also, there's a collection of priceless thangka scrolls, old flintlock rifles, bronze arrowheads, silver snuffboxes, pipes and chess sets carved out of ivory.

The museum (T250) is open during normal working hours, but you may have to find the caretaker anyway to unlock the doors. It is north of the park, next to Mandalgov Hotel.

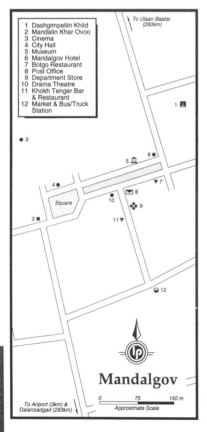

1 Dashgimpeliin Khiid
2 Mandalin Khar Ovoo
3 Cinema
4 City Hall
5 Museum
6 Mandalgov Hotel
7 Botgo Restaurant
8 Post Office
9 Department Store
10 Drama Theatre
11 Khokh Tenger Bar
& Restaurant
12 Market & Bus/Truck
Station

To Ulaan Baatar (260km)

Square

Mandalgov

To Airport (3km) & Dalanzadgad (293km)

0        75        150 m
Approximate Scale

## Dashgimpeliin Khiid

Дашгимпэлийн Хипд

In 1936 there were 53 temples in Dundgov. A year later, they were reduced to ashes and rubble by the Mongolian KGB. In 1991 Dashgimpeliin Khiid was opened to serve the people of Mandalgov.

The monastery's temple is small, consisting only of a concrete ger, but it's very active inside. Visitors are welcome, but should show the usual respect. Remember that photographs are not permitted inside without special permission. The monastery is only 100m north-east of the park.

## Mandalin Khar Ovoo

Мандалин Хар Овоо

On top of Mandalin Khar Ovoo, about 150m north-west of the park, is a viewing pavilion. It is worth the short climb for a panorama of all that Mandalgov has to offer (which isn't much). A forlorn monument dedicated to the 'everlasting friendship' between Mongolia and the Soviet Union stands nearby.

## Places to Stay

**Camping** Like other Gobi aimag capitals, Mandalgov has no great camping spots; the city has no river, and it's flat and dusty. If you want to pitch a tent, your best bet is to walk north of town and find somewhere past the Mandalin Khar Ovoo or monastery.

**Hotels** The pleasant *Mandalgov Hotel* (Мандалговъ Зочид) was the only place in town which was open at the time of research. No-frills simple rooms, which have attached bathrooms, cost a negotiable T5500 per person for foreigners. The hotel is on a corner, north of the park.

## Places to Eat

The surroundings may not be salubrious, but the food at the *Mandalgov Hotel* is not too bad. Locals seem to prefer the more upmarket *Khokh Tenger Bar & Restaurant* (Хох Тэнгэр Бар & Рэсторан), on the road to the market, though the bar is probably the bigger attraction. The only other place, the *Botgo Restaurant* (Ботго Рэсторан), on the southern side of the park, was closed at the time of research, but the staff promised that it will reopen 'later'.

### Getting There & Away
**Air** MIAT flies between Mandalgov and Ulaan Baatar on Tuesday and Friday. Tickets are comparatively cheap (US$35), but the planes are small and the flights are unreliable because so few people travel here, and it is relatively easy to get there by road from Ulaan Baatar. The airport at Mandalgov is 3km south of the city.

**Bus** Crowded buses (T1970) leave Ulaan Baatar for Mandalgov on Monday (and then go on to Dalanzadgad), and go directly to Mandalgov on Thursday. In Mandalgov, buses arrive and depart from the market, at the end of the main street heading south of the park.

**Jeep** Mandalgov is a poor aimag capital and not a tourist town, so finding a jeep to charter will create a real headache – Dalanzadgad is a far better place to look. When there is enough demand (which isn't often), public shared jeeps do travel to Ulaan Baatar – but very rarely south to Dalanzadgad. Most locals wait for the bus or hitch a ride on a truck.

Mandalgov is 260km south of Ulaan Baatar and 293km north of Dalanzadgad.

**Hitching** As the main road from Ulaan Baatar to Dalanzadgad goes through Mandalgov, hitching is the major form of transport to either place. Getting to Ulaan Baatar or Dalanzadgad on a truck, or another type of vehicle, won't take too long if you are prepared to ask around at the market and wait a while.

### DELGERKHANGAI UUL
### ДЭЛГЭРХАНГАЙ УУЛ
The highest peak in Dundgov, Delgerkhangai Uul (a relatively modest 1913m) towers above the arid plains in the south-west corner of the aimag. The peak is in the remote Delgerkhangai *sum*, within walking distance of the

capital, Khashaat (Хашаат). A reasonable jeep trail goes to Khashaat from Mandalgov.

### ULAAN SUVRAGA
### УЛААН СУРВАГА
In the southernmost *sum* of Ölziit (Өлзийт), near the *sum* capital of Rashaant (Рашаант), is Ulaan Suvraga, an area which might be described as 'badlands' or a 'painted desert'. The eerie, eroded landscape was at one time beneath the sea and is rich in marine fossils and clamshells. There are also numerous ancient **rock paintings** in the region.

The museum in Mandalgov has a photograph of Ulaan Suvraga, which you might want to look at to decide if it's worth the effort of getting there. Ulaan Suvraga is a rough 115km south-east of Mandalgov.

### ONGIIN KHIID
### ОНГИЙН ХИЙД
This is a small mountainous area along the Ongiin Gol, in the western *sum* of Saikhan-Ovoo (Саихан-Овоо). The ruins of one of the many monasteries destroyed in the aimag during the 1930s can be seen if you have a guide.

### YARAKH UUL
### ЯРАХ УУЛ
Yarakh mountain is near the village of Buyant Br (Буянт Бр), on the border of the two sums of Gurvansaikhan (Гурвансаихан) and Öndörshil (Өндөршил). It is an important archaeological site where a 300,000-year-old human skeleton was once found. The skeleton is now on display in Ulaan Baatar's Museum of Natural History.

### SANGIIN DALAI
### САНГИЙН ДАЛАЙ
In the *sum* of Erdendalai (Эрдэндалай), 114km north-west of Mandalgov, Sangiin Dalai is a camel-herding community in the middle of nowhere. It is a good base for visiting nearby attractions, however, if you have your own vehicle, and is a useful halfway stop between Arvaikheer (in Övörkhangai aimag) and Mandalgov, or as

THE GOBI

an alternative stop to Mandalgov between Ulaan Baatar and Dalanzadgad.

## Gimpil Darjaalan Khiid
Гимпил Даржаалан Хийд
This monastery, with its **Damba Darjalan Süm** temple, is a very pleasant surprise after travelling around the dusty and dull country-side. Built in the late 18th century and dedi-cated to the Dalai Lama during the first visit to Mongolia by a Dalai Lama, the monastery was once used by about 500 monks, and was the only one of nine in the immediate vicinity to survive the Stalinist purges by becoming a warehouse and shop.

The monastery was reopened in 1990, and now has a small contingent of 10 monks. If you ask someone in the village, the head monk will scurry across the streets and open it up for you. The inside of the temple is depressingly bare because just about all of the thangkas, statues and other religious items were destroyed in the 1930s. Photos inside the temple are not permitted.

### Places to Stay
Sangiin Dalai is dusty and very small. Walk about 100m in any direction from the mon-astery and pitch your tent. A few inquisitive locals, or a camel or two, may visit.

### Camels
Throughout Mongolia, you will see the two-humped Bactrian camel. They were domesticated thou-sands of years ago and are closely related to the rare wild camel known as the *khavtgai*. Of the 367,000 camels in the country, two-thirds can be found in the five provinces which stretch across the Gobi – 93,000 in Ömnögov aimag alone.

One of the five domesticated animals revered by nomads, camels are perfect for long-distance travel in the Gobi, but are slow (they average about 5km per hour); they are easy to manage (a camel can last for over a week without drink and a month without food); they are adaptable (a camel can survive the harshest winter); they can carry a lot of gear (up to 250kg); and they provide wool (an average of 5kg per year), milk (up to 500 litres a year) and meat.

Normally relaxed and seemingly snooty, male camels go crazy during the mating season in January-February – a time to avoid approaching one. If the humps are drooping, the camels are in poor health or need some food or water.

The number of camels is considerably lower than it was in the past years (476,000 in 1992 and 859,000 in 1960). They are being killed for their meat and many nomads are leaving the harsh Gobi and breeding other livestock. However, several national parks in the Gobi have been established to protect the 300 or so wild khavtgai camels. ■

Like most *sum* capitals, Sangiin Dalai has a nameless *hotel* for about T1000 per person. There is certainly no style or comfort, but you will probably have the place to yourself. Look for the decrepit building with yellow paint and blue windows.

The Juulchin-run *Dundgobi Resort* (☎ & fax 320 246), about 30km south of Sangiin Dalai and 45km north of Tsogt Taij, is the least impressive ger camp in the Gobi region. It is rarely used, so the facilities and food are poor, and it's in the middle of a dusty and hot plain.

### Getting There & Away

Every Wednesday, a bus leaves Ulaan Baatar (T2080) for Sangiin Dalai, bypassing Mandalgov. Otherwise to/from Sangiin Dalai, you will have to hitch a ride. Although the village is small, it is on a major jeep trail, so a few vehicles come through here every day.

### SANGIIN DALAI NUUR
### САНГИЙН ДАЛАЙ НУУР

Although far smaller than other lakes such as Uvs Nuur (in Uvs aimag) and Khar Us Nuur (in Khovd aimag), you can see some remarkable birdlife at Sangiin Dalai Nuur. Mongolian Larks and various species of eagles, geese and swans come to this spring-fed lake in summer and autumn. The Juulchin travel company runs birdwatching trips here and to other nearby lakes.

The **Khukh Burd Süm** temple, which sits on an island in the middle of the tiny lake, was built in the 10th century. Remarkably, the temple was built from rocks which can only be found over 300km away. It was abandoned and ruined a few centuries later.

Three hundred years ago, a palace was built here, and 150 years later, a writer built a stage for a play on top of the ruins. Enough of the temple and palace remain to give you some idea of what a magnificent place it must have been.

At the time of research, locals were building some huts on the side of the lake which they said could be used for accommodation. Otherwise, there is no shortage of camping

spots, or you could come on a day trip from the Dundgobi Resort, Mandalgov or Sangiin Dalai village if you have a vehicle

The lake is over halfway between Baga Gazarin Chuluu and Sangiin Dalai village. You will need an experienced driver to find it. There is no hope of getting here on public transport or by hitching.

### TSOGT TAIJ CHULUU
### ЦОГТ ТАИЖ ЧУЛУУ

About 75km south of Sangiin Dalai village, there are some inscriptions on rocks written by Mongolian scholars and nationalists, including the last-known descendant of Chinggis Khaan, Tsogt Taij. Written in 1621, in an ancient Mongolian script which is hard for locals to understand, the inscriptions are mildly interesting (if a little *too* well preserved, and hard to believe), but hardly worth a special visit.

### IKH GAZARIN CHULUU
### ИХ ГАЗАРИН ЧУЛУУ

This strange area of rock pinnacles is about 70km south-east of Mandalgov in the Gurvansaikhan (Гурваисаихан) *sum*, about 10km north of Suugaant (Суугаант).

### BAGA GAZARIN CHULUU
### БАГА ГАЗАРИН ЧУЛУУ

This is another granite rock formation in the middle of the dusty plains. In the 19th century, two revered monks lived here in gers – remnants of their **rock drawings** can be found in the area. The rocks are worshipped by locals who sometimes make pilgrimages here. Naturally, there is a 'legend' that Chinggis Khaan stayed at the rocks.

Five km away, the highest peak (1768m) in the area, **Baga Gazarin Uul**, will take about five hours to climb. The mountain also contains a cave with an **underground lake**. The **mineral water springs** and trees in the region make it a great spot to camp, and there are plenty of rocky hills, topped by **ovoos**, to explore.

Baga Gazarin Chuluu is in a very remote area, about 60km to the north-west of Mandalgov, and about 80km west of Sangiin Dalai village.

# Gov-Altai Говъ-Алтай

**Population:** 74,100
**Area:** 142,000 sq km
**Capital:** Altai
**No of Sums:** 18
**Elevation of Capital City:** 2181m
**Main Livestock & Crops:** camel, goat; wheat
**Ethnic Groups:** Khalkh

Mongolia's second-largest aimag is named after the Gobi Desert and the Mongol Altai Nuruu range, which virtually bisects the aimag to create a stark, rocky landscape.

There is a certain beauty in this combination, but there is considerable heartbreak too. Gov-Altai is one of the least suitable areas for raising livestock, and therefore one of the most hostile to human habitation.

Somehow a few Gobi bears, wild camels, ibexes and even snow leopards survive, often protected in the several national parks in the aimag. Most of the population live in the north-east corner, where melting snow from the Khangai Nuruu feeds small rivers, creating vital water supplies.

Gov-Altai is famous for its oases, and contains some remote sections of several

**Snow Leopards**
In the mountain regions of Gov-Altai, the snow leopard manages to survive the harsh environment and avoid poachers and hunters. Up to 50kg in weight and about 1m long (the tail is an extra 70cm), a snow leopard can easily kill an ibex three times its size. You shouldn't be disappointed about not seeing one, but unfortunately you will probably see many pelts and stuffed animals in the museums.

An estimated 7500 snow leopards live in an area of 1.5 million sq km across China, Pakistan, Afghanistan, India, Nepal and Mongolia (where 1000 to 1500 live). In these countries, education of the local populace and the establishment of several national parks will help protect these creatures from poaching and hunting (farmers shoot snow leopards because they kill livestock while their normal prey, such as marmots, are made scarce from hunting) and from urbanisation.

If you would like more information about the protection of the snow leopard, contact the International Snow Leopard Trust (☎ (206) 632 2421; fax 632 3967), 4649 Sunnyside Ave N, Seattle, Washington 98103, USA. ■

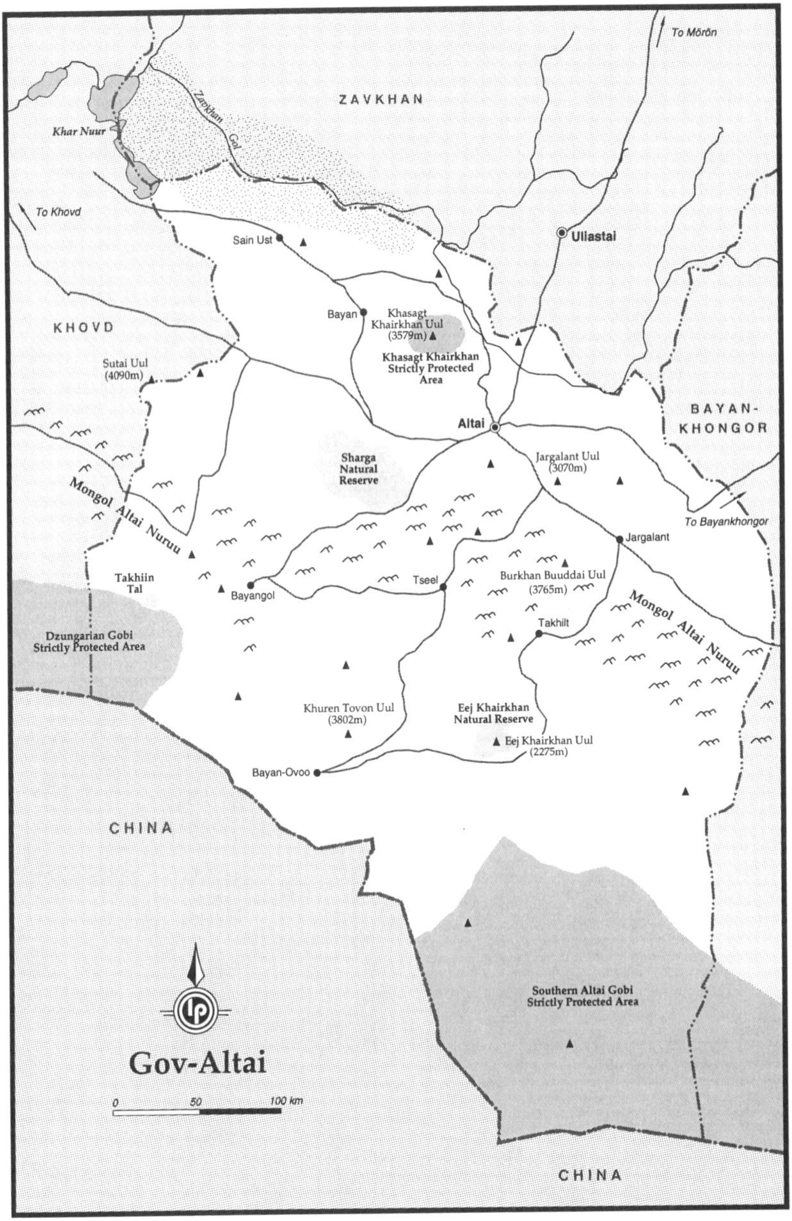

Gov-Altai

To Mörön

ZAVKHAN

Khar Nuur

Zavkhan Gol

To Khovd

Sain Ust

Uliastai

KHOVD

Bayan

Khasagt Khairkhan Uul (3579m)

Khasagt Khairkhan Strictly Protected Area

Sutai Uul (4090m)

Altai

BAYAN-KHONGOR

Mongol Altai Nuruu

Sharga Natural Reserve

Jargalant Uul (3070m)

To Bayankhongor

Jargalant

Takhiin Tal

Bayangol

Tseel

Burkhan Buuddai Uul (3765m)

Mongol Altai Nuruu

Dzungarian Gobi Strictly Protected Area

Takhilt

Khuren Tovon Uul (3802m)

Eej Khairkhan Natural Reserve

Eej Khairkhan Uul (2275m)

Bayan-Ovoo

CHINA

Southern Altai Gobi Strictly Protected Area

0   50   100 km

CHINA

THE GOBI

national parks, but there are no other reasons to spend much time in the aimag. Most travellers head further west to the more beautiful and interesting aimags in western Mongolia.

## National Parks

Gov-Altai's diverse and sparsely populated mountain and desert environment has encouraged conservationists to allocate a large portion of the aimag as national parks.

In lieu of any local park ranger, you should have a permit from the relevant ministry in Ulaan Baatar to visit the areas listed below. See National Parks in the Facts about the Country chapter for more information about these permits.

Dzungarian Strictly Protected Area, also known as 'Gobi B', is partially in the south-west of Gov-Altai; mostly in Khovd. The park was established to protect *khulan* wild ass and jerboa, among other endangered animals.

Eej Khairkhan Natural Reserve, a 22,000 hectare park, about 150km directly south of Altai, was created to protect the general environment.

Khasagt Khairkhan Strictly Protected Area is a 27,000 hectare park which protects endangered argali sheep, as well as the local environment.

Sharga Natural Reserve, like the Mankhan Natural Reserve in Khovd aimag, helps to preserve highly endangered species of antelopes.

Southern Altai Gobi Strictly Protected Area, also known as 'Gobi A', dominates the southern part of the aimag.

Takhiin Tal is on the border of the northern section of Dzungarian national park. Eight *takhi* wild horses were re-introduced into the wild here in 1996. Experts hope they will survive, and flourish, in this remote area of the Gobi.

## Organised Tours

Two Mongolian companies organise trips around Gov-Altai (refer to the Travel Agencies section in the Ulaan Baatar chapter for contact details): Mongolian Adventure Tours runs jeep and trekking trips in the aimag, but staff couldn't provide any details of exactly where they go; and Nomads explores sand dunes, gorges, lakes and the national parks by jeep, trekking and camel, as part of its trips to western Mongolia.

## ALTAI
АЛТАЙ

Nestled between the mountains of Khasagt Khairkhan Uul (3579m) and Jargalant Uul (3070m), the aimag capital of 17,500 is a dullish, dusty place, dominated by the huge Russian-Mongolian Friendship Monument. There are some trees along the streets, and the people are friendly – if you can find anyone. Altai is a classic example of somewhere to stop on the way to somewhere else – either to or from Khovd, or the national parks.

## Information

The bank, opposite the Altai Hotel, will change US dollars. It is open on weekdays from 9 am to 5 pm – with a lunch break from 1 to 2 pm.

## Dashpeljeelen Khiid
Дашпэлжээлэн Хийд

This small, attractive monastery was built in 1990 and is home to 30 monks. Unlike most others, there was no previous structure on this site. On most days from 10 am, you can witness a ceremony. The monastery is a short walk north-west of the town square.

## Museum

Every aimag capital has a museum, and Altai is no exception. It contains some feeble dinosaur fossils, a furnished ger, a stuffed khulan and a display devoted to famous people (not stuffed), including P Jasrai, a former (communist) prime minister of Mongolia who came from the aimag.

We had to find the caretaker of the museum, which is on the main street and opposite the park. He was drunk after spending the morning in the local bar, but still gave us an enthusiastic guided tour in Mongolian and charged us the precise, current tögrög equivalent of US$1 as an entrance fee.

## Places to Stay

**Camping** The road from Altai to Khovd goes through a surprisingly lush valley for about 10km. So, if you have a tent and, especially, if you have your own vehicle, head out there.

A great patch of ground, which you will have to share with a few cows, is only a 20 minute walk north-west of town.

**Hotels** Except for the basic plumbing, the *Altai Hotel* (Алтай Зочид) on the main street is quite luxurious. As a nice touch, many of the rooms even have telephones – though these seldom work. Foreigners are usually charged about T4500 per person for a simple room, but they may let you stay in a bed in a dormitory for around T1000 per person. Prices are negotiable: the owner cogitates about how desperate and/or rich you look, and then offers a number between 1000 and 10,000.

(When we asked if many foreigners stayed at the Altai Hotel, the waitress at the bar thought for a while, then brightly responded: 'We had one once. He didn't stay long. They are rare'. The previous foreigner was possibly the author of the first edition of this book – which only goes to show how many foreigners stay in Altai.)

The *Ödöö Hotel* (Өдөө Зочид) – so called because it is more of an agricultural business than a hotel – costs T975 per person. It has no running water, and the pit toilets are...um...a little basic, but the rooms are OK. The hotel is just north of the park. You'll need to ask directions – there is no sign on the building.

**Places to Eat**
The *Altai Hotel* manages to feed guests with a decent selection of mutton dishes. The bar in the hotel is a quasi-disco, complete with mirror-balls and a counter selling vodka, cola, tea and cigarettes.

The other, unexciting alternatives are the *Sutai Restaurant* (Сутай Рэсторан), south of the main square, and the *Bayanbulag Cafe* (Баянбулаг Кафэ), opposite the Department Store

**Getting There & Away**
**Air** MIAT flies from Ulaan Baatar to Altai and back on Tuesday, Thursday and Saturday for US$100. The airport is 2km north-west of the centre.

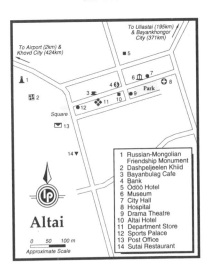

Altai

1  Russian-Mongolian Friendship Monument
2  Dashpeljeelen Khiid
3  Bayanbulag Cafe
4  Bank
5  Ödöö Hotel
6  Museum
7  City Hall
8  Hospital
9  Drama Theatre
10  Altai Hotel
11  Department Store
12  Sports Palace
13  Post Office
14  Sutai Restaurant

0    50    100 m
Approximate Scale

**Bus** Altai is as far as buses from Ulaan Baatar go – any further west, you will have to rely on hitching or take your own jeep. Buses to Altai leave from Ulaan Baatar on Monday and Thursday (T6500), and go through the other aimag capitals, Arvaikheer and Bayankhongor city.

**Jeep** Altai is not somewhere you should expect to find any reliable jeeps for hire. You are more likely to have success in Uliastai and Khovd city. Shared jeeps are just as uncommon; most people hitch on trucks or anything else that is going their way.

The road from Altai to Khovd city (424km) starts off through a lush valley, then becomes flat and boring. Later, the road disintegrates badly – you won't be able to average more than 25km per hour along this stretch. Altai is also 371km west of Bayankhongor city and 195km south of Uliastai.

**Hitching** There is some traffic along the main road towards Khovd and Bayankhongor, but you may have to wait a few hours for something suitable. Very few vehicles travel between Altai and Uliastai; you will probably have to wait for something to

THE GOBI

arrive from Uliastai first. Almost no vehicles venture into the south of Gov-Altai.

Altai has no market as such, but the town is small and friendly, so if you ask around and let it be known that you want a lift, something will come along.

## SUTAI UUL
СУТАЙ УУЛ

At 4090m, this is the highest peak in Gov-Altai, though part of it is in Khovd aimag. Permanently snowcapped, Sutai is an awesome sight when travelling along the Altai-Khovd road. Most climbers approach from the Khovd side. For more information, contact the Mongol Altai Club in Ulaan Baatar (see Activities in the Facts for the Visitor chapter).

## KHUREN TOVON UUL
ХУРЭН ТОВОН УУЛ

This peak in Altai *sum*, in the remote south-west of the aimag, reaches an altitude of 3802m, making it Gov-Altai's second-highest mountain. A jeep trail of sorts goes to the nearby *sum* capital of Bayan-Ovoo (Баян-Овоо).

## BURKHAN BUUDDAI UUL
БАРХАН БУУДДАЙ УУЛ

If you haven't had enough challenges by now, you could try climbing the relatively accessible peak of Burkhan Buuddai Uul (3765m) in Biger (Бигэр) *sum*. Make inquiries in the *sum* capital, Jargalant (Жаргалант) about the route, and don't be surprised if the locals think you're an idiot.

## SOUTHERN ALTAI GOBI STRICTLY PROTECTED AREA

The majority of the 4.4 million hectare national park, also known as 'Gobi A', lies in the south-east corner of Gov-Altai. Established over 20 years ago, the area has also been nominated as an International Biosphere Reserve by the United Nations.

The park is remote and very difficult to reach, which is bad news for visitors but excellent news for the fragile flora and fauna. Almost completely uninhabited by humans,

the park helps to protect about 50 Gobi bears and some wild camels, as well as the general environment and scarce water sources for the animals.

There are a few mountains over 1200m, and several springs and oases which only an experienced guide will find. To explore the park, start at Jargalant (Жаргалант), turn south-west on the trail to Takhilt (Тахилт), and head south on any jeep trail you can find. You will need a reliable vehicle and an experienced driver, and you must be completely self-sufficient with food, water and camping gear.

## EEJ KHAIRKHAN UUL
ЭЭЖ ХАЙРХАН УУЛ

Near the base of the Eej Khairkhan Uul (2275m), just north of 'Gobi A' national park, you could camp at some delightful **rock pools** and explore the nearby **caves**. You will need a guide to show you around. Almost no suitable drinking water is available, so take your own into the area. An A-frame hut is sometimes available for rent near the pools, but you should always have your own camping and cooking equipment.

About 30 minutes walk west of the hut are some spectacular, ancient **rock paintings** of ibexes, horsemen and archers – but you will need a guide to find them.

The mountain is about 150km south of Altai, and is part of the 22,000 hectare Eej Khairkhan Natural Reserve, which was established to protect the fragile environment.

# Ömnögov Өмнөговъ

Population: 44,800
Area: 165,000 sq km
Capital: Dalanzadgad
No of Sums: 14
Elevation of Capital City: 1465m
Main Livestock & Crops: camel, goat
Ethnic Groups: Khalkh

Ömnögov (South Gobi) is the largest but least populated aimag in Mongolia. It's not hard to see why humans prefer to live elsewhere.

THE GOBI

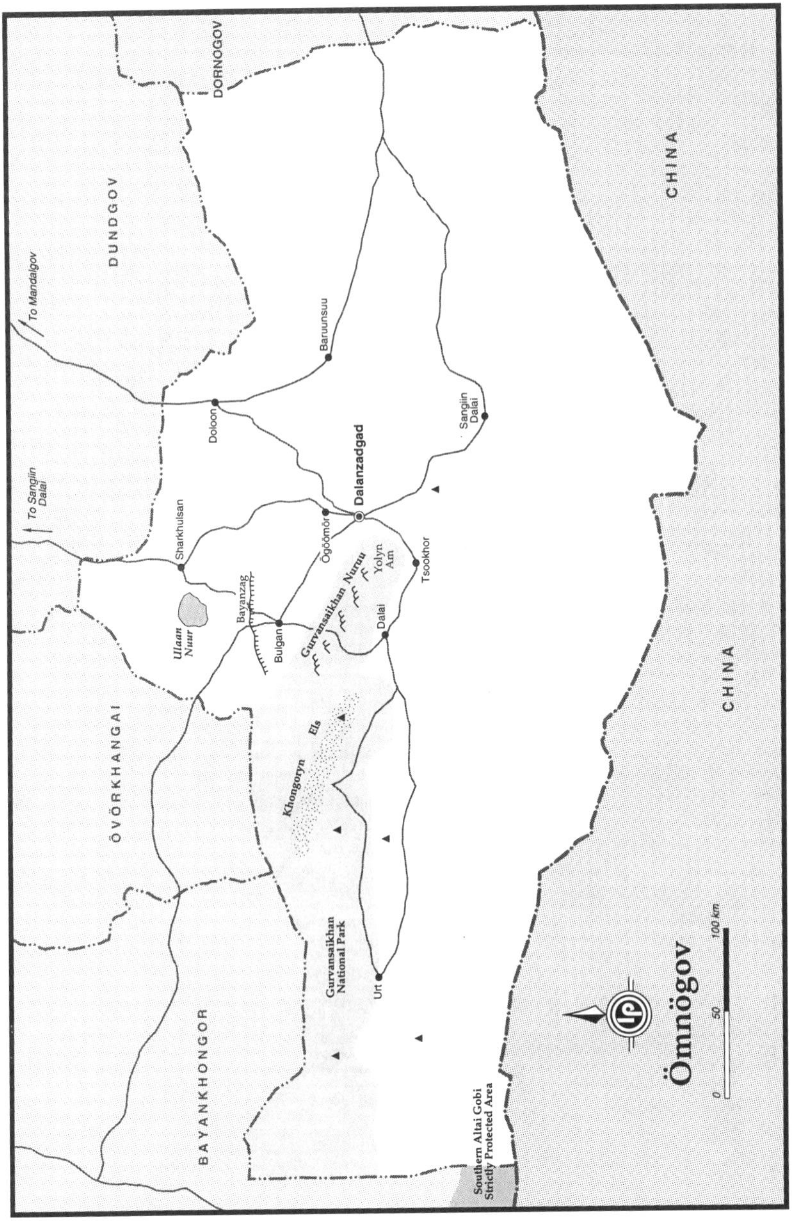

DORNOGOV

CHINA

DUNDGOV

To Mandalgov

Baruunsuu

To Sanglin Dalai

Dolood

Sanglin Dalai

Dalanzadgad

Shankhulsan

Ögöömör

Yolyn Am.

Bayanzag

Gurvansaikhan Nuruu

Tsookhor

Ulaan Nuur

Bulgan

Dalai

ÖVÖRKHANGAI

Els

CHINA

Khongoryn

BAYANKHONGOR

Gurvansaikhan National Park

Urt

Ömnögov

0   50   100 km

Southern Altai Gobi Strictly Protected Area

THE GOBI

With an average annual precipitation of only 130mm a year, and summer temperatures reaching an average of up to 38°C, this is the driest and hottest region in the country.

The Gurvansaikhan Nuruu range in the centre provides the only topographic relief in this pancake-flat region. These mountains reach an altitude of 2825m and support a diverse range of wildlife, including the extremely rare snow leopard. The mountains also make human habitation marginally possible by capturing snow in winter, which melts and feeds springs on the plains below, providing water for some limited livestock.

Ömnögov somehow supports thousands of Black-tailed gazelle, which you may see darting across the open plains. The aimag is also home to one-quarter (93,000) of Mongolia's domesticated camels. The two-million-hectare Gurvansaikhan National Park protects a lot of wildlife and is home to dinosaur fossils, sand dunes and rock formations. Environmentalists hope to also make the south-eastern section of the aimag a national park to protect the khulan.

Although the climate repels Mongolians, it doesn't seem to scare away tourists. Most visitors are surprised – and, often, a little disappointed – to find that the Gobi is not really a barren moonscape, or endless rolling sand dunes. True, some parts of the Gobi fit the desert stereotype of a wasteland of sand, rock, salt pans and scorpions, but most of this region is stubby grassland. Ironically, it's the aridness of the Gobi that protects its natural habitat: the land is too dry to support the hundreds of thousands of sheep and cattle that descend like locusts on Mongolia's greener pastures.

## Organised Tours

All Mongolian and foreign travel companies organise trips to this part of the Gobi because of its relative proximity to (and regular flights, in summer, from) Ulaan Baatar, and the accessibility of the various attractions. Virtually all trips include the Yolyn Am valley, sand dunes and the Bayanzag dinosaur site, with accommodation in one of the ger camps, but a few agencies do arrange something a little different and more interesting. (See Travel Agencies in the Ulaan Baatar chapter and Organised Tours in the Getting There & Away chapter.)

Juulchin organises the usual sort of trips, though some do include travel by camel and horse. Photography and birdlife enthusiasts can go on specialist tours.

Mongolian Adventure Tours goes further than other agencies in their search for dinosaur relics (which you can't take home).

Mongol Tour OK organises trips which include camel riding and visits to other interesting, and different, attractions in the area.

Nomads runs excellent tours around the Gobi, combined with Karakorum and other nearby attractions.

## DALANZADGAD
ДАЛАНЗАДГАД

The capital of Ömnögov aimag, Dalanzadgad is a soulless and windy town full of concrete buildings. Sitting in the shadow of the Gurvansaikhan Nuruu range, the town does have reasonable facilities and regular transport, so it's a good base for explorations into the desert. Besides the museum – which is not as good as the one at Yolyn Am – there is nothing to see or do. Most of what you will need is along the main street, which runs parallel to, and north of, the central park.

### Dinosaurs

In the early 1920s, one of the first discoveries of dinosaur eggs and bones was made by Roy Chapman Andrews, in the southern Gobi Desert. This, and subsequent expeditions, proved that *protoceratops*, *tarbosaurus* and *tyrannosaurus rex* dinosaurs roamed the area 70 million years ago.

With a bit of digging, you may be able to find some dinosaur fossils in the southern Gobi – but please be aware that these fossils are very precious and far more useful to palaeontologists. You will also get into serious trouble if you are caught exporting them.

The best place in Mongolia to see the remains of the dinosaurs is at the Museum of Natural History in Ulaan Baatar. ■

## South Gobi Museum

Surprisingly, this museum has very little on dinosaurs – just a few bones and eggs. (All of the best exhibits are in Ulaan Baatar, or in any of a number of museums around the world.) There are a few nice paintings, a huge stuffed vulture, and a display of thangkas and other Buddhist items, which presumably makes up for the fact that this is the only aimag capital without a functioning monastery or temple.

The museum is on the main street, on the other side of the park from the bright-pink Drama Theatre. It is open from 9 am to 3 pm and the entrance fee is T250 – but it costs more if you want to take photographs.

## Places to Stay

**Camping** Like other Gobi capitals, there is no river or any decent place to camp in Dalanzadgad. You will just have to walk one or 2km in any direction from town, and pitch your tent somewhere secluded.

**Hotels** The two hotels are considerably cheaper than the ger camps in the national park. They have signs outside in English and are opposite each other, so you can check out both of them, and negotiate.

The older *Govorvangsaikhan Hotel* (Говорванг саихан Зочид) charges T5500 per person for a basic but pleasant simple room without a bathroom. The deluxe room, with a sitting room and B&W TV, is luxurious but costs a ridiculous T13,750 per person.

Opposite, the *Devshil Hotel* (Дэвшил Зочид) is a little better, cheaper and easier to pronounce. It has simple rooms for the same price as the Govorvangsaikhan – T5500 per person – but its deluxe rooms for T8250 per person are worth a splurge if you have been camping in the dusty desert for a while.

## Places to Eat

If you are staying at the *Govorvangsaikhan Hotel*, they can provide three meals per day (mutton, mutton and...mutton) for a reasonable extra T2750 per day. You can also eat there if you aren't a guest. The restaurant belonging to the *Devshil Hotel* (it's next door

to it) is the best place to have a meal. It even has cans (sometimes cold) of Chinese beer and soft drinks.

The shops and market south of the park are reasonably well stocked.

## Getting There & Away

**Air** Dalanzadgad is normally connected to Ulaan Baatar by MIAT on Tuesday and Friday for US$70. During the peak season – ie 7 July to 1 September – MIAT also schedules extra daily flights between Ulaan Baatar and Dalanzadgad (and, sometimes, on to the tourist camps in the national park) for the same price.

This summer schedule is the only MIAT service with more than three departures a week, which shows how popular these flights can be. Book ahead, confirm again and again, and be prepared for the Mongolian Scramble when checking in and boarding the plane. The airport is a dirt field a few hundred metres north of the town.

**Bus** Because of Dalanzadgad's small population and as most tourists fly there, road transport is poor. One bus leaves Ulaan Baatar (T2343) on Monday for Dalanzadgad and stops at Mandalgov on the way.

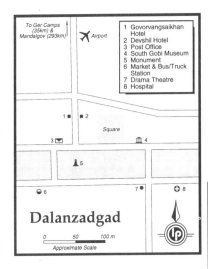

To Ger Camps (35km) & Mandalgov (293km)

Airport

1 Govorvangsaikhan Hotel
2 Devshil Hotel
3 Post Office
4 South Gobi Museum
5 Monument
6 Market & Bus/Truck Station
7 Drama Theatre
8 Hospital

Square

**Dalanzadgad**

0    50    100 m
Approximate Scale

**Jeep** Dalanzadgad is the natural starting point for trips into this part of the Gobi, and there are a few (but not many) jeeps for hire. Just ask any jeep driver you can find. They normally hang around the main street and are not scared of charging high tourist prices. Public shared jeeps are almost impossible to find; most people fly or hitch on a truck.

If travelling independently and staying at a ger camp in the national park, the camps listed below rent jeeps for T220 per km, including a driver-cum-guide. This is higher than normal, but in a remote and touristed area this is not too expensive, especially if you are sharing costs. The Havtgait ger camp will even rent out a bus, which carries more people but is not as mobile, for T330 per km, including driver-cum-guide.

Dalanzadgad is 293km south of Mandal-gov and 553km south-west of Ulaan Baatar.

**Hitching** Hitching around the Gobi Desert, including to the attractions in the national park, is totally impractical and dangerous, and should never be attempted. Hitching between Dalanzadgad and the major *sum* capitals in Ömnögov (for connections to Ulaan Baatar) and to Sainshand is possible but not easy. Make sure you carry plenty of water, and a tent and sleeping bag for the inevitable breakdowns.

The cheapest way to see the attractions in the national park is to take a bus or hitch to Dalanzadgad, where you can hang around for a few days and ask other independent travellers to share a jeep.

## SHARKHULSAN
ШАРХУЛСАН

The village of Sharkhulsan, in the *sum* of Mandal-Ovoo (Мандал-Овоо), is renowned for the number (about 14,000), and quality, of its camels. Just before the start of the Tsagaan Sar (lunar new year), which takes places in January or February, Sharkhulsan hosts the annual Holiday of the Ten Thousand Camels.

The highlight of this festive, family occasion is the 18km camel race across a nearby region called the Ongiin-Tal steppes. In 1996

nearly 200 camels took part, and the winner took just 45 minutes. And the prize? Another camel!

Nearby is **Ulaan Nuur** (Red Lake), the largest, and just about the only, lake in Ömnögov. It may not be there when you visit because it often dries out; and it won't quench your thirst either – it is very salty.

## GURVANSAIKHAN NATIONAL PARK

Stretching from the border with Bayan-khongor almost to Dalanzadgad, the two-million-hectare Gurvansaikhan National Park is the highlight of the aimag, and the overwhelming reason why any tourist comes here. Unlike other national parks in the Gobi, the Gurvansaikhan does contain a few attractions, and the facilities – ger camps and roads – are reasonably good.

Gurvansaikhan, which means the 'three beauties' and refers to its three ridges (though there are four), contains mountains, dinosaur fossils, sand dunes, rock formations and a valley which, incredibly, has ice for most of the year.

The park also contains over 200 species of birds, including the Mongolian Desert Finch, Cinerous Vulture, Desert Warbler and Houbara Bustard; and maybe 600 or more types of vegetation and plants, a lot of which only blooms after very infrequent heavy rain. The sparse vegetation does manage to support numerous types of animals, such as the Black-tailed gazelle, Kozlov's pygmy jerboa and khulan, and endangered species of wild camel, snow leopard, ibex and argali sheep.

If on an organised tour, your permit – which is little more than an entrance fee of T1500 per day – to the national park should be included in your tour. If travelling independently, you pay at the gate to the Yolyn Am valley, next to the museum.

### Yolyn Am
Ьолыын Ам

Yolyn Am (Vulture's Mouth) was originally established to conserve the birdlife in the region, but it's now more famous for its dramatic and very unusual scenery – it is a valley, stuck in the middle of the Gobi Desert, with metres-thick ice almost all year around.

The small **museum** at the gate on the main road to Yolyn Am has a collection of dinosaur eggs and bones, and stuffed birds and a snow leopard. The museum sells some of the best examples of the bright landscape paintings anywhere in the countryside. The two shops next door sell some reasonable souvenirs and (warm) drinks, and, amazingly, one shop has one of the best collections of Mongolian stamps in the country. Entrance to the museum and park is T1500, but should cost nothing if you are part of a tour.

From the museum, the road continues for another 13km to a car park. From there, a pleasant (though often *very* cold) 25 minute walk, following the stream, leads to a gorge full of ice. In winter, the ice is up to 10m high, and continues down the gorge for another 10km. It remains frozen for most of the year, except for about a month starting in late August. You can walk on the ice – but be careful, especially in late summer.

Guides claim that argali sheep walk along the steep valley ridges at about 5 am in summer. The extremely rare Gobi bear (only about 100 are in existence in Mongolia) also live in the area.

Yolyn Am is about 40km west from Dalanzadgad, and a little less from the ger camps.

## Bayanzag
Баянзаг

Bayanzag, which means 'rich in saxauls', is more commonly known as the 'flaming cliffs'. First excavated in 1922, the area is renowned worldwide for the number of dinosaur bones and eggs found there, which you can see in the Museum of Natural History in Ulaan Baatar or, mostly, in other museums around the world.

Even if you are not a 'dinophile', the eerie beauty of the landscape is a good reason to visit. It's a classic desert of rock, red sands, scrub, sun and awesome emptiness.

Locals will probably approach you at Bayanzag, the ger camps and even Dalanzadgad to buy some dinosaur bones and eggs. Please remember that these fossils are extremely rare, and it is also *highly* illegal to export anything remotely antique, including fossils, from Mongolia. If you get caught, you'll be in serious trouble.

Bayanzag is 65km north-west of Dalanzadgad.

## Khongoryn Els
Хонгорйн Элс

The Khongoryn Els are some of the largest and most spectacular sand dunes in Mongolia. Also known as the 'singing dunes', they are up to 800m high, 20km wide and about 100km long. You can climb to the top of the dunes with a lot of effort – three steps forward, one slide back. The views of the desert from the top are indescribable. With a good, local guide and reliable jeep, you can also explore the oases, saxaul forests and other dinosaur fossil sites nearby.

Unfortunately, the dunes are about 180km from Dalanzadgad and the ger camps, along

**Roy Chapman Andrews**
An American palaeontologist from New York, Roy Chapman Andrews (1884-1960) explored the Gobi in the 1920s and found the first dinosaur eggs, jaws and skulls in Central Asia. Andrews' first expedition was based at Bayanzag, which he renamed the 'flaming cliffs'. For political reasons, he abandoned his incomplete expeditions after about five years.

According to his books and biographies, he was a real-life adventurer who took the ambushes, raids and rebellions during the expeditions in his stride. He worked for US intelligence during WWI and also explored Alaska, Borneo, Burma and China. He wrote such Boys' Own classics as *Whale Hunting with Gun and Camera* (1916), *Across Mongolian Plains* (1921) and *On the Trail of Ancient Man*. Not surprisingly, Andrews is widely regarded as the model on which the screen character Indiana Jones was based. ■

shocking roads. There is no way to get there unless you charter a jeep or are part of an organised tour. To properly explore the area, you will need to stay the night out in the desert before returning to Dalanzadgad or the ger camps. Otherwise, you can stay at the *Duut Mankham* ger camp, which costs about US$35 per person, including meals.

### Places to Stay

**Camping** You can camp wherever you want as long as you stay a fair distance from the ger camps and have your own food and water.

**Ger Camps** About 35km west of Dalanzadgad, three ger camps cater primarily for organised tours. The *Tuvshin Resort* (☎ 326 419; fax 57 028) has good (hot) showers and toilets, and a decent restaurant and bar, but the location is uninteresting and the build-ings are ugly. The resort is used by any tour run in conjunction with Juulchin, and costs US$40 per person including meals, or US$25 if in a group of five or more. You can also rent jeeps, and go on organised tours of the nearby attractions.

Closer to Yolyn Am, the *Havtgait Resort* (☎ 31 1521; fax 384 097) has the nicest setting, and the facilities are less overrun by groups of tourists. The large dining room serves good food, and the activities are as diverse as karaoke singing in the evening and camel riding during the day. The price of US$40 per person with meals is more negotiable than at the Tuvshin Resort.

The *Juulchin-Gobi Camp* (☎ 312 769; fax 311 744) is near the airstrip. It is large and popular with organised tours, costs US$35 per person including meals, and is about the same standard as the others, but the location isn't as good.

# Glossary

**agui** – a cave
**aimag** – a province or state within Mongolia
**airag** – fermented horse's milk
**arkhi** – the common word to describe home-made vodka

**buuz** – steamed meat dumplings

**chuluu** – rock; rock formation

**davaa** – a mountain pass
**del** – the all-purpose, traditional coat or dress worn by men and women
**delgüür** – a shop
**dov** – a hill

**els** – sand; sand dunes

**gegeen** – a saint; saintlike person
**ger** – a traditional, circular felt tent, often used by Mongolians
**gol** – a river
**guanz** – a canteen or cheap restaurant
**gudamj** – a street

**hard seat** – the common word to describe the standard of the 2nd-class train carriage

**Inner Mongolia** – a separate province within China

**Kazak** – an ethnic group of people from Central Asia, mostly living in western Mongolia; people from Kazakstan
**khaan** – a king or chief
**Khalkh** – the major ethnic group living in Mongolia
**khiid** – a Buddhist monastery
**khot** – a city
**khulan** – a wild ass
**khüree** – another word for monastery
**khürkhree** – a waterfall
**khuurshuur** – a fried, flat meat pancake

**kino** – a cinema
**koumiss** – the Russian word for *airag*

**lama** – a Tibetan Buddhist monk or priest
**Lamaism** – commonly known as Tibetan Buddhism
**Living Buddha** – a common term for reincarnations of buddhas; Buddhist spiritual leader in Mongolia

**mörön** – another word for river

**Naadam** – a game; the Naadam Festival
**nuruu** – a mountain range
**nuur** – a lake

**ordon** – a palace
**örgön chölöö** – an avenue
**Outer Mongolia** – northern Mongolia during Manchurian rule (the term is not currently used to describe Mongolia)
**ovoo** – a shamanistic pile of stones, wood or other offerings to the gods, usually placed in high places

**soft seat** – the common word to describe the standard of the 1st-class train carriage
**sum** – the administrative unit below an *aimag*; a district
**süm** – a Buddhist temple
**stupa** – a Buddhist religious monument composed of a solid hemisphere topped by a spire, containing relics of the Buddha; also known as a pagoda

**takhi** – the Mongolian wild horse; also known as Przewalski's horse
**tal** – a valley; a steppe
**thangka** – a rectangular Tibetan Buddhist painting on cloth, often seen in monasteries
**tögrög** – the unit of currency in Mongolia
**Tsagaan Sar** – 'white moon' or 'white month'; a festival to celebrate the start of the lunar year

**tsam** – lama dances, performed by monks wearing masks during religious ceremonies

**uul** – a mountain
**uurga** – a traditional wooden lasso used by nomads

**urtyn-duu** – traditional singing style

**yurt** – the Russian word for *ger*

**zakh** – a market

# Index

# Phrasebooks

**L** onely Planet phrasebooks are packed with essential words and phrases to help travellers communicate with the locals. With colour tabs for quick reference, an extensive vocabulary and use of script, these handy pocket-sized language guides cover day-to-day travel situations.

- handy pocket-sized books
- easy to understand Pronunciation chapter
- clear & comprehensive Grammar chapter
- romanisation alongside script to allow ease of pronunciation
- script throughout so users can point to phrases for every situation
- full of cultural information and tips for the traveller

'... vital for a real DIY spirit and attitude in language learning'
*– Backpacker*

'the phrasebooks have good cultural backgrounders and offer solid advice for challenging situations in remote locations'
*– San Francisco Examiner*

Arabic (Egyptian) • Arabic (Moroccan) • Australian *(Australian English, Aboriginal and Torres Strait languages)* • Baltic States *(Estonian, Latvian, Lithuanian)* • Bengali • Brazilian • British • Burmese • Cantonese • Central Asia (Uyghur, Uzbek, Kyrghiz, Kazak, Pashto, Tadjik • Central Europe *(Czech, French, German, Hungarian, Italian, Slovak)* • Eastern Europe *(Bulgarian, Czech, Hungarian, Polish, Romanian, Slovak)* • Ethiopian (Amharic) • Fijian • French • German • Greek • Hebrew • Hill Tribes • Hindi & Urdu • Indonesian • Italian • Japanese • Korean • Lao • Latin American Spanish • Malay • Mandarin • Mediterranean Europe *(Albanian, Croatian, Greek, Italian, Macedonian, Maltese, Serbian, Slovene)* • Mongolian • Nepali • Pidgin • Pilipino (Tagalog) • Portugese • Quechua • Russian • Scandinavian Europe *(Danish, Finnish, Icelandic, Norwegian, Swedish)* • South-East Asia *(Burmese, Indonesian, Khmer, Lao, Malay, Tagalog Pilipino, Thai, Vietnamese)* • South Pacific Languages • Spanish (Castilian) *(also includes Catalan, Galician and Basque)* • Sri Lanka • Swahili • Thai • Tibetan • Turkish • Ukrainian • USA *(US English, Vernacular, Native American languages, Hawaiian)* • Vietnamese • Western Europe *(Basque, Catalan, Dutch, French, German, Greek, Irish, Italian, Portuguese, Scottish Gaelic, Spanish (Castilian), Welsh)*

## Lonely Planet Travel Atlases

**L** onely Planet has long been famous for the number and quality of its guidebook maps. Now we've gone one step further and produced a handy companion series: Lonely Planet travel atlases – maps of a country produced in book form.

Unlike other maps, which look good but lead travellers astray, our travel atlases have been researched on the road by Lonely Planet's experienced team of writers. All details are carefully checked to ensure the atlas corresponds with the equivalent Lonely Planet guidebook.

- full-colour throughout
- maps researched and checked by Lonely Planet authors
- place names correspond with Lonely Planet guidebooks
- no confusing spelling differences
- legend and travelling information in English, French, German, Japanese and Spanish
- size: 230 x 160 mm

**Available now:** Chile & Easter Island ● Egypt ● India & Bangladesh ● Israel & the Palestinian Territories ● Jordan, Syria & Lebanon ● Kenya ● Laos ● Portugal ● South Africa, Lesotho & Swaziland ● Thailand ● Turkey ● Vietnam ● Zimbabwe, Botswana & Namibia

---

## Lonely Planet TV Series & Videos

**L** onely Planet travel guides have been brought to life on television screens around the world. Like our guides, the programs are based on the joy of independent travel, and look honestly at some of the most exciting, picturesque and frustrating places in the world. Each show is presented by one of three travellers from Australia, England or the USA and combines an innovative mixture of video, Super-8 film, atmospheric soundscapes and original music.

Videos of each episode – containing additional footage not shown on television – are available from good book and video shops, but the availability of individual videos varies with regional screening schedules.

**Video destinations include:** Alaska ● American Rockies ● Australia – The South-East ● Baja California & the Copper Canyon ● Brazil ● Central Asia ● Chile & Easter Island ● Corsica, Sicily & Sardinia – The Mediterranean Islands ● East Africa (Tanzania & Zanzibar) ● Ecuador & the Galapagos Islands ● Greenland & Iceland ● Indonesia ● Israel & the Sinai Desert ● Jamaica ● Japan ● La Ruta Maya ● Morocco ● New York ● North India ● Pacific Islands (Fiji, Solomon Islands & Vanuatu) ● South India ● South West China ● Turkey ● Vietnam ● West Africa ● Zimbabwe, Botswana & Namibia

**The Lonely Planet TV series is produced by:** Pilot Productions
The Old Studio
18 Middle Row
London W10 5AT, UK

# FREE Lonely Planet Newsletters

**W**e love hearing from you and think you'd like to hear from us.

## Planet Talk

Our FREE quarterly printed newsletter is full of tips from travellers and anecdotes from Lonely Planet guidebook authors. Every issue is packed with up-to-date travel news and advice, and includes:

- a postcard from Lonely Planet co-founder Tony Wheeler
- a swag of mail from travellers
- a look at life on the road through the eyes of a Lonely Planet author
- topical health advice
- prizes for the best travel yarn
- news about forthcoming Lonely Planet events
- a complete list of Lonely Planet books and other titles

**To join our mailing list, residents of the UK, Europe and Africa can email us at go@lonelyplanet.co.uk; residents of North and South America can email us at info@lonelyplanet.com; the rest of the world can email us at talk2us@lonelyplanet.com.au, or contact any Lonely Planet office.**

## Comet

**O**ur FREE monthly email newsletter brings you all the latest travel news, features, interviews, competitions, destination ideas, travellers' tips & tales, Q&As, raging debates and related links. Find out what's new on the Lonely Planet Web site and which books are about to hit the shelves.

Subscribe from your desktop: www.lonelyplanet.com/comet

# LONELY PLANET

## Guides by Region

**L**onely Planet is known worldwide for publishing practical, reliable and no-nonsense travel information in our guides and on our Web site. The Lonely Planet list covers just about every accessible part of the world. Currently there are thirteen series: travel guides, shoestring guides, walking guides, city guides, phrasebooks, audio packs, city maps, travel atlases, diving & snorkeling guides, restaurant guides, first-time travel guides, healthy travel and travel literature.

**AFRICA** Africa on a shoestring • Africa – the South • Arabic (Egyptian) phrasebook • Arabic (Moroccan) phrasebook • Cairo • Cape Town • Cape Town city map • Central Africa • East Africa • Egypt • Egypt travel atlas • Ethiopian (Amharic) phrasebook • The Gambia & Senegal • Healthy Travel Africa • Kenya • Kenya travel atlas • Malawi, Mozambique & Zambia • Morocco • North Africa • Read This First Africa • South Africa, Lesotho & Swaziland • South Africa, Lesotho & Swaziland travel atlas • Swahili phrasebook • Tanzania, Zanzibar & Pemba • Trekking in East Africa • Tunisia • West Africa • Zimbabwe, Botswana & Namibia • Zimbabwe, Botswana & Nambia Travel Atlas • World Food Morocco

**Travel Literature:** The Rainbird: A Central African Journey • Songs to an African Sunset: A Zimbabwean Story • Mali Blues: Traveling to an African Beat

**AUSTRALIA & THE PACIFIC** Auckland • Australia • Australian phrasebook • Bushwalking in Australia • Bushwalking in Papua New Guinea • Fiji • Fijian phrasebook • Healthy Travel Australia, NZ and the Pacific • Islands of Australia's Great Barrier Reef • Melbourne • Melbourne city map • Micronesia • New Caledonia • New South Wales & the ACT • New Zealand • Northern Territory • Outback Australia • Out To Eat – Melbourne • Out to Eat – Sydney • Papua New Guinea • Pidgin phrasebook • Queensland • Rarotonga & the Cook Islands • Samoa • Solomon Islands • South Australia • South Pacific • South Pacific Languages phrasebook • Sydney • Sydney city map • Sydney Condensed • Tahiti & French Polynesia • Tasmania • Tonga • Tramping in New Zealand • Vanuatu • Victoria • Western Australia

**Travel Literature:** Islands in the Clouds • Kiwi Tracks: A New Zealand Journey • Sean & David's Long Drive

**CENTRAL AMERICA & THE CARIBBEAN** Bahamas, Turks & Caicos • Bermuda • Central America on a shoestring • Costa Rica • Cuba • Dominican Republic & Haiti • Eastern Caribbean • Guatemala, Belize & Yucatán: La Ruta Maya • Jamaica • Mexico • Mexico City • Panama • Puerto Rico • Read This First Central & South America • World Food Mexico

**Travel Literature:** Green Dreams: Travels in Central America

**EUROPE** Amsterdam • Amsterdam city map • Andalucía • Austria • Baltic States phrasebook • Barcelona • Berlin • Berlin city map • Britain • British phrasebook • Brussels, Bruges & Antwerp • Budapest city map • Canary Islands • Central Europe • Central Europe phrasebook • Corfu & Ionians • Corsica • Crete • Crete Condensed • Croatia • Cyprus • Czech & Slovak Republics • Denmark • Dublin • Eastern Europe • Eastern Europe phrasebook • Edinburgh • Estonia, Latvia & Lithuania • Europe on a shoestring • Finland • Florence • France • French phrasebook • Germany • German phrasebook • Greece • Greek Islands • Greek phrasebook • Hungary • Iceland, Greenland & the Faroe Islands • Istanbul City Map • Ireland • Italian phrasebook • Italy • Krakow •Lisbon • London • London city map • London Condensed • Mediterranean Europe • Mediterranean Europe phrasebook • Munich • Norway • Paris • Paris city map • Paris Condensed • Poland • Portugal • Portuguese phrasebook • Portugal travel atlas • Prague • Prague city map • Provence & the Côte d'Azur • Romania & Moldova • Rome • Russia, Ukraine & Belarus • Russian phrasebook • Scandinavian & Baltic Europe • Scandinavian Europe phrasebook • Scotland • Slovenia • Spain • Spanish phrasebook • St Petersburg • Switzerland • Trekking in Spain • Ukrainian phrasebook • Venice • Vienna • Walking in Britain • Walking in Ireland • Walking in Italy • Walking in Spain • Walking in Switzerland • Western Europe • Western Europe phrasebook • World Food Italy • World Food Spain

**Travel Literature:** The Olive Grove: Travels in Greece

**INDIAN SUBCONTINENT** Bangladesh • Bengali phrasebook • Bhutan • Delhi • Goa • Hindi & Urdu phrasebook • India • India & Bangladesh travel atlas • Indian Himalaya • Karakoram Highway • Kerala • Mumbai (Bombay) • Nepal • Nepali phrasebook • Pakistan • Rajasthan • Read This First: Asia & India • South India • Sri Lanka • Sri Lanka phrasebook • Trekking in the Indian Himalaya • Trekking in the Karakoram & Hindukush • Trekking in the Nepal Himalaya

**Travel Literature:** In Rajasthan • Shopping for Buddhas • The Age Of Kali

# LONELY PLANET

## Mail Order

Lonely Planet products are distributed worldwide. They are also available by mail order from Lonely Planet, so if you have difficulty finding a title please write to us. North and South American residents should write to 150 Linden St, Oakland, CA 94607, USA; European and African residents should write to 10a Spring Place, London NW5 3BH, UK; and residents of other countries to PO Box 617, Hawthorn, Victoria 3122, Australia.

**ISLANDS OF THE INDIAN OCEAN** Madagascar & Comoros • Maldives • Mauritius, Réunion & Seychelles

**MIDDLE EAST & CENTRAL ASIA** Arab Gulf States • Central Asia • Central Asia phrasebook • Dubai • Hebrew phrasebook • Iran • Israel & the Palestinian Territories • Israel & the Palestinian Territories travel atlas • Istanbul • Istanbul to Cairo • Jerusalem • Jerusalem City Map • Jordan & Syria • Jordan, Syria & Lebanon travel atlas • Lebanon • Middle East on a shoestring • Syria • Turkey • Turkey travel atlas • Turkish phrasebook • Yemen
**Travel Literature:** The Gates of Damascus • Kingdom of the Film Stars: Journey into Jordan • Black on Black: Iran Revisited

**NORTH AMERICA** Alaska • Backpacking in Alaska • Baja California • California & Nevada • California Condensed • Canada • Chicago • Chicago city map • Deep South • Florida • Hawaii • Honolulu • Las Vegas • Los Angeles • Miami • New England • New Orleans • New York City • New York city map • New York Condensed • New York, New Jersey & Pennsylvania • Oahu • Pacific Northwest USA • Puerto Rico • Rocky Mountain • San Francisco • San Francisco city map • Seattle • Southwest USA • Texas • USA • USA phrasebook • Vancouver • Washington, DC & the Capital Region • Washington DC city map
**Travel Literature**: Drive Thru America

**NORTH-EAST ASIA** Beijing • Cantonese phrasebook • China • Hong Kong • Hong Kong city map • Hong Kong, Macau & Guangzhou • Japan • Japanese phrasebook • Japanese audio pack • Korea • Korean phrasebook • Kyoto • Mandarin phrasebook • Mongolia • Mongolian phrasebook • North-East Asia on a shoestring • Seoul • South-West China • Taiwan • Tibet • Tibetan phrasebook • Tokyo
**Travel Literature:** Lost Japan • In Xanadu

**SOUTH AMERICA** Argentina, Uruguay & Paraguay • Bolivia • Brazil • Brazilian phrasebook • Buenos Aires • Chile & Easter Island • Chile & Easter Island travel atlas • Colombia • Ecuador & the Galapagos Islands • Healthy Travel Central & South America • Latin American Spanish phrasebook • Peru •Quechua phrasebook • Rio de Janeiro • Rio de Janeiro city map • South America on a shoestring • Trekking in the Patagonian Andes • Venezuela
**Travel Literature:** Full Circle: A South American Journey

**SOUTH-EAST ASIA** Bali & Lombok • Bangkok • Bangkok city map • Burmese phrasebook • Cambodia • Hanoi • Healthy Travel Asia & India • Hill Tribes phrasebook • Ho Chi Minh City • Indonesia • Indonesia's Eastern Islands • Indonesian phrasebook • Indonesian audio pack • Jakarta • Java • Laos • Lao phrasebook • Laos travel atlas • Malay phrasebook • Malaysia, Singapore & Brunei • Myanmar (Burma) • Philippines • Pilipino (Tagalog) phrasebook • Read This First Asia & India • Singapore • South-East Asia on a shoestring • South-East Asia phrasebook • Thailand • Thailand's Islands & Beaches • Thailand travel atlas • Thai phrasebook • Thai audio pack • Vietnam • Vietnamese phrasebook • Vietnam travel atlas • World Food Thailand • World Food Vietnam

**ALSO AVAILABLE:** Antarctica • The Arctic • Brief Encounters: Stories of Love, Sex & Travel • Chasing Rickshaws • Lonely Planet Unpacked • Not the Only Planet: Travel Stories from Science Fiction • Sacred India • Travel with Children • Traveller's Tales

# The Lonely Planet Story

**L** onely Planet published its first book in 1973 in response to the numerous 'How did you do it?' questions Maureen and Tony Wheeler were asked after driving, bussing, hitching, sailing and railing their way from England to Australia.

Written at a kitchen table and hand collated, trimmed and stapled, *Across Asia on the Cheap* became an instant local bestseller, inspiring thoughts of another book.

Eighteen months in South-East Asia resulted in their second guide, *South-East Asia on a shoestring*, which they put together in a backstreet Chinese hotel in Singapore in 1975. The 'yellow bible', as it quickly became known to backpackers around the world, soon became *the* guide to the region. It has sold well over half a million copies and is now in its 9th edition, still retaining its familiar yellow cover.

Today there are over 350 titles, including travel guides, walking guides, language kits & phrasebooks, travel atlases, diving guides and travel literature. The company is the largest independent travel publisher in the world. Although Lonely Planet initially specialised in guides to Asia, today there are few corners of the globe that have not been covered.

The emphasis continues to be on travel for independent travellers. Tony and Maureen still travel for several months of each year and play an active part in the writing, updating and quality control of Lonely Planet's guides.

They have been joined by over 120 authors and 280 staff at our offices in Melbourne (Australia), Oakland (USA), London (UK) and Paris (France). Travellers themselves also make a valuable contribution to the guides through the feedback we receive in thousands of letters each year and on our web site.

The people at Lonely Planet strongly believe that travellers can make a positive contribution to the countries they visit, both through their appreciation of the countries' culture, wildlife and natural features, and through the money they spend. In addition, the company makes a direct contribution to the countries and regions it covers. Since 1986 a percentage of the income from each book has been donated to ventures such as famine relief in Africa; aid projects in India; agricultural projects in Central America; Greenpeace's efforts to halt French nuclear testing in the Pacific; and Amnesty International.

## LONELY PLANET OFFICES

**Australia**
PO Box 617, Hawthorn, Victoria 3122
☎ 03 9819 1877  fax 03 9819 6459
email: talk2us@lonelyplanet.com.au

**UK**
10a Spring Place, London NW5 3BH
☎ 020 7428 4800  fax 020 7428 4828
email: go@lonelyplanet.co.uk

**USA**
150 Linden St, Oakland, CA 94607
☎ 510 893 8555  TOLL FREE: 800 275 8555
fax 510 893 8572
email: info@lonelyplanet.com

**France**
1 rue du Dahomey, 75011 Paris
☎ 01 55 25 33 00  fax 01 55 25 33 01
email: bip@lonelyplanet.fr
www.lonelyplanet.fr

**World Wide Web: www.lonelyplanet.com *or* AOL keyword: lp**
**Lonely Planet Images: lpi@lonelyplanet.com.au**